CULTURAL SUTURES

Cultural Sutures

Medicine and

Media

EDITED BY LESTER D. FRIEDMAN

Duke University Press

Durham and London

2004

© 2004 Duke University Press

All rights reserved

Printed in the United States of America on

acid-free paper ∞

Designed by C. H. Westmoreland

Typeset in Sabon with Franklin Gothic

display by Keystone Typesetting, Inc.

Library of Congress Cataloging-in-

Publication Data appear on the last printed

page of this book

The opening epigraph from "The Boy in

the Bubble," © Paul Simon, is used by

permission of the publisher, Paul Simon

Music.

For Rae-Ellen Kavey,

the heart doctor with the

soul of a poet

Medicine is magical and magical is art

The Boy in the Bubble

And the baby with the baboon heart

These are the days of miracle and wonder

This is the long distance call

The way the camera follows us in slo-mo

The way we look to us all

— PAUL SIMON AND FORERE MOTLOBELOA,

"The Boy in the Bubble," *Graceland*

Contents

Acknowledgments

Every anthology represents the combined efforts of a dedicated group of contributors. To those who gave their time and energy to write essays for this book, I offer my grateful appreciation. It was a distinct pleasure to work with all of you. At Northwestern University, I have benefited from gracious colleagues and generous administrators on two campuses. At the Feinberg School of Medicine, my thanks go to Ray Curry (Office of Medical Education), Kathryn Montgomery, Tod Chambers, and Ellen LeVee (Program in Medical Humanities and Bioethics). In the School of Communication, I am grateful for the assistance of Mimi White (Department of Radio/TV/Film). I also enjoyed working with the impressive professionals at Duke University Press, particularly Ken Wissoker, Christine Dahlin, and Pam Morrison. As always, my parents, Eva and Eugene Friedman, my children, Marc and Rachel Friedman, and my step-daughter, Allison Kavey, provided sustained encouragement, laughter, and hope for the future. My wife, Rae-Ellen Kavey, read my work with a keen eye and patient sensitivity. To her I owe more than words can express.

Introduction: Through the Looking Glass

Medical Culture and the Media

LESTER D. FRIEDMAN

The worlds of media and medicine exist in a unique symbiosis. Newspaper and magazine articles simultaneously report medical discoveries and dispense health tips, the same alluring blend of scientific information and comforting advice seen daily on local and network television: every newscast and morning show has designated health care special reports, in-house doctors, and medical advice segments. While radio physicians dispense advice in two-minute sound capsules, glossy magazines and sober journals feature stories about the latest cure for cancer, the wonders of Viagra, the morality of stem cell research, and the efficacy of alternative medical practices. Capitalizing on this public obsession with health care issues, drug companies pour billions of dollars into advertisements that promise better living through pharmacology, bypassing doctors and speaking directly to potential customers. The Internet — with its dizzying array of sites devoted to ethical dilemmas, medical advice, health care news, and prescription purchases — has become the newest, and most interactive, media source for medical information, sales, and discussion.

This national fixation with medicine has not been lost on those who create and package television, movies, and books for popular consumption. For the last few years, *ER* has topped the ratings chart, the most prominent among numerous blood-spattered medical dramas beamed directly into our living rooms. In fact, entire cable networks devote themselves almost exclusively to health care programming: rerunning medical shows from previous eras, providing health-oriented cooking classes, and creating reality-based productions. Similarly, movies spotlighting medical narratives and characters form a virtual genre stretching from flickering one reelers to contemporary blockbusters. Most major Hollywood performers have appeared in at least one — and most often several — films with medical themes and characters. Finally, a seemingly endless array of novels, self-help books, diet schemes, and medical memoirs pack bookstore shelves from New York City to Los Angeles — and everywhere in between. Medicine, it seems, has replaced baseball as our national pastime.

From our current vantage point, the melding of medicine and media seems inevitable. Over the past few decades, cataclysmic upheavals have radically transformed the physical, financial, and moral topography of America's health care culture. As a result, a new medical landscape is emerging. Contoured by the demands of managed care, the challenges of ethical dilemmas, and the promises of technological interventions, the medical terrain no longer shifts with glacial slowness. Changes and challenges now erupt with unparalleled frequency: contemporary controversies swirling around cloning, universal health coverage, stem cell research, and collaborative reproduction, just to name an obvious few, provide ample evidence of how medical events saturate our individual and communal lives. With such sweeping and dramatic transformations occurring so rapidly, it seems entirely understandable that the various media outlets would focus on the world of medicine.

The intricate web spun jointly by medicine and the media results from a collaborative process that resembles a mating ritual as much as a professional relationship. The media do not simply cannibalize the medical world for news stories and fictional plotlines. Health care institutions, medical researchers, and academic physicians all endeavor to manipulate the media spotlight for their own agendas, to accentuate their bright spots and deflect its harsh glare from less savory specters crouching in the shadows. For example, two of the nation's premier medical periodicals, the *New England Journal of Medicine* and the *Journal of the American Medical Association*, preview their most important articles for reporters before releasing them to the general public, garnering publicity and directing the dialogue between press and researchers. In this way, millions of people who would never read these journals or possess the sophisticated knowledge necessary to understand their studies watch researchers discuss their work in prepublication interviews with national news outlets. Statistics support their strategy. In a nationwide poll that the National Health Council conducted in 1998, 75 percent of those surveyed said they paid either a moderate (50 percent) or great (25 percent) deal of attention to medical information reported in the media, citing their primary sources of health care information as television (40 percent), doctors (36 percent), magazines and journals (35 percent), newspapers (16 percent), and the Internet (2 percent). Other figures are equally illuminating. Almost 60 percent changed their behavior or took action because of a media report, 42 percent sought further information, and 53 percent mentioned something from a news story to their doctor (Johnson 1998, 88; also see Chen and Siu 2001).

And why not. The same *New England Journal of Medicine* that hosts prepublication press conferences published an article (17 October 1991) which demonstrates that even researchers consistently cite papers publicized in the popular press, as distinct from those lacking such attention. Phillips, Kanter, Bednarczyk, and Tastad showed how references to articles published in the *New England Journal of Medicine* and subsequently covered in the *New York Times* received 72.8 percent more scientific citations (in the Science Citation Index) after they first appeared, followed by a "disproportionate number of scientific citations in each of the following 10 years." They concluded that "coverage of medical research in the popular press amplifies the transmission of medical information from the scientific literature to the research community." In other words, the *New York Times* is as much a conduit of information to the specialized world of medical research as to the lay public. Perhaps a larger-than-average number from this group reads "all the news that's fit to print," or more cynically, the mere fact of being reported in the *Times* deems a research study important.

An illustrative example of this interactive dance between medicine and the media appears in the 19 November 2001 issue of the *Chronicle of Higher Education*. It details how Marc Hendrick, an associate professor of pediatrics and surgery at UCLA, got his "big break" after a news release written by the public relations department at his own medical school dramatized an article about stem cells and fat he co-wrote in *Tissue Engineering*, not normally fertile soil for dramatic headlines. The result was a firestorm of media attention from the *New York Times*, National Public Radio, and a host of national news organizations. Such moments of national publicity, according to Chris Woolston, the article's author, can "brighten" an academic's entire career: "Media coverage can raise the profile of scientists, boost their grant support, and even speed the pace of scientific discovery. . . . In fact, a television spot or newspaper story can help build scientific partnerships. . . . [and] also help you rack up citations" (Woolston 2001, 1–3). He then quotes tips from Dennis Meredith, public relations officer at Duke University and author of *Communicating Science News*, to help scientists prepare for their time in the spotlight: polishing their presentations, preparing press releases, staying lively when working with TV crews, practicing with local interviewers, speaking clearly and slowly, and attending campus interview media-training programs. "Every scientist understands that funding is a political process," says Meredith; "if you want your research funded, you have to talk about it" (2). That last comment, whatever level of truth it may contain, transforms the medicine/media connection from the unavoidable into the indispensable.

Given this perspective, one can understand why virtually every hospital in the United States has a public/media relations department whose ostensible purpose is to translate highly specialized medical information into understandable form and disseminate that material as widely as possible. Yet equally important, if not so overtly declared, these departments also strive to place positive, basically upbeat stories in various media outlets, as well as respond quickly to negative publicity. Each has a stable of faculty experts who reply rapidly to media requests for pithy quotations and sound bites on any given topic, an available gaggle of pundits for print and television journalists to interview and quote. Because the modern, highly competitive medical environment demands that hospitals sell themselves to consumers, these institutions use roughly the same advertising tactics employed by companies to market their products (health care) and build brand-name loyalty (doctors on staff). Hospitals that survive and prosper in this aggressive climate will be those that keep their particular brand of health care delivery constantly before the eyes and in the ears of potential customers. To do so, they must first gain and then direct the attention of the media.

The delicate balance between using the media as an outlet for legitimate stories and exploiting it for a particular agenda raises a host of ethical issues. In the past, for example, the press often hid the health problems of prominent figures, most dramatically presidents in office, from the general public (see Bloom 1996). Now, however, presidential checkups that report nothing amiss garner national coverage, and questions about a candidate's health assume equal importance to his or her voting record. Such public intrusions would normally draw the ire of ethicists who routinely shroud private citizens under the protection of patient confidentiality. Yet here the public's right to know clearly trumps personal privacy. Dr. Timothy Johnson, himself a medical television journalist for almost all of his thirty years in broadcasting, raises many other troubling problems: the difficulties of identifying, processing, and reporting legitimate medical news to the general public; the competitive pressures on medical establishments to gain market share and increase funding for research; the spiraling commercialization of medical research by business interests; the blatant attempts to manipulate the media; the scientific meetings that have become "exercises in public relations organized for the benefit of the media"; the controversial role of medical journals; and the differences between reporting general news and medical news (Johnson 1998, 87–92). One could certainly add to Johnson's list issues such as the morality of cameras in the hospital, the broadcasting of medical procedures, the distinctions between informed consent for medical procedures and release forms for appearing in films and on television, the buying of editorials (Brennan 1994), the coverage by news media (Moynihan et al. 2000; Nelkin 1996; Shuchman and Wilkes 1997; Radford 1996), the lack of adequate checks and balances on the Internet, the problems with how medical research is disseminated (Wilkes 1997), and a host of concerns revolving around all the cardinal principles of bioethics.

In addition, fictional depictions of doctors and medical procedures in the media clearly have an impact on both the delivery of health care and patient expectations of their physicians. A *New England Journal of Medicine* study of 13 June 1996, for instance, explored how three popular television programs *(ER, Rescue 911,* and *Chicago Hope)* shape the public's beliefs about medicine, illness, and death. In particular, the authors demonstrate how misrepresentations of cardiopulmonary resuscitation (CPR) on such shows (67 percent of patients on the programs survived in the long term, whereas in the medical literature only about 2 to 15 percent survive) "undermined trust in data and fosters a trust in miracles that . . . can lead to decisions that harm patients" (7). Diem, Lantos, and Tulsky conclude that "given the media's extraordinary influence . . . physicians need to recognize and acknowledge the images the media presents . . . [as well as] address the images of CPR on television and present quantitative data about possible outcomes for your patients" (8). Left unsaid was the possibility that doctors may perform CPR, even when they realize the futility of such treatments, because families expect the procedure from watching medical television shows. This study represents simply one example of how the media affect daily health care.

All of this, of course, entails some risks as well as benefits. Take the case of Dr. George D. Lundberg, who served for seventeen years as the editor of the prestigious *Journal of the American Medical Association (JAMA).* Widely perceived as one of the most influential leaders in the biomedical publishing field, Dr. Lundberg was summarily fired from his position on 15 January 1999, just before the controversial article that caused his demise was published. Ratcliffe Anderson Jr., AMA executive vice president, spoke for the organization when it accused Dr. Lundberg of threatening "the historic tradition and integrity of the *Journal of the American Medical Association* by inappropriately and inexcusably interjecting *JAMA* into a major political debate that has nothing to do with science or medicine" (Goldsmith 1999, 403). Lundberg's transgression had been to publish a survey of college students regarding their perceptions of whether certain sexual practices constituted having "had sex." The survey, conducted by nationally prominent researchers affiliated with the Kinsey Institute, concluded, not surprisingly, that "individual attitudes varied regarding behaviors defined as having 'had sex' . . . [and] supported the view that Americans hold widely divergent opinions about what behaviors do or do not constitute having 'had sex' " (Sanders and Reinisch 1999). Yet appearing at a time when President Clinton was questioning "what is, is" and denying that he "had sex" with Monica Lewinsky because they never had intercourse, the fundamentally conservative board of the AMA saw Lundberg's willingness to publish what they labeled as "pseudoscience" as part of a liberal Left agenda to politicize the profession and bolster the White House's defense of the president's dubious distinctions.

Although *JAMA* received more than five hundred e-mails and some two hundred letters about the incident, the vast majority opposing the decision to fire Lundberg, the furor spilled well beyond the pages of usually stolid medical periodicals. Lundberg was widely perceived as a sympathetic figure, and ironically, Ratcliffe and the AMA board were castigated for threatening the journal's history and integrity, precisely the charges they had leveled against Lundberg. Media commentators, in particular, saw the dismissal as a direct challenge to editorial freedom and journalistic independence, the foundations on which any publication of merit must be built. Most critics found it reprehensible that the AMA had influenced editorial content and undermined academic freedom. They wondered aloud if the organization had become as partisan as the NRA. Although Lundberg was questioned about "rushing" the article into print, defenders pointed out that the piece had undergone *JAMA*'s rigorous peer review process and argued that work of particular interest to the public should not be silenced until controversial issues were resolved. Clearly, Lundberg's case, which itself became a story, raises many prickly issues about the connections between the media and medicine: the potential conflicts between sponsoring organizations and the periodicals they underwrite, the influence of politics on supposedly neutral realms of inquiry and discourse and the definition(s) of legitimate medical research — just to name the most obvious.

Although health care has always been a highly valued commodity, today, due in large measure to their ubiquitous presence in the media, medical issues occupy a central role in our national consciousness. Not surprisingly, therefore, scholars from diverse disciplines have attempted to analyze the various components that collectively constitute the institution of medicine. As medical practitioners study human bodies, so these academic investigators probe the anatomy of primary codes and philosophical assumptions that collectively constitute the theories, practices, and meanings of medicine. Their relentless, often hostile, dissection of the health care system, as well as the culture that both constructs and sustains it, has created a far broader and significantly deeper understanding of how profoundly this institution permeates our personal, professional, and communal lives. So, for example, academic writers have scrutinized the concepts of illness and wellness, the medicalization of morality, the socialization of physicians, and a host of other topics far too numerous to mention here. Perhaps ironically, their critical assessments have encouraged health care practitioners to tell their own stories, sometimes to explain themselves and other times to justify their actions. The resulting deluge of memoirs by doctors, nurses, and others in the field allows readers to experience the joy and despair of life within the medical world. Yet even with this blizzard of medical information from every imaginable medium, few scholars focus on the mediations that occur within that process.

This anthology of original essays scrutinizes a broad range of subtle and overt interconnections between medicine and the media. As such, these demanding and speculative investigations offer readers an expansive, interdisciplinary series of vantage points from which to contemplate, explore, understand, and (perhaps) challenge the abundance of ways different types of media present and affect the American health care system. Equally significant, the collection clearly demonstrates how pervasively the world of medicine engages and permeates the media that surround us. To accomplish these broad tasks, the book brings together an eclectic group of scholars and practitioners from diverse disciplines, including bioethics, cinema studies, medicine, communication studies, health care history, medical humanities, sociology, biology, African American studies, law, cultural studies, history, women's studies, English, American studies, philosophy, and health care education. By incorporating these methodologies and perspectives into a single volume, I hope to provide multiple points of access to, and comprehension of, this extensive topic.

The book is structured around six common types of popular communications media: print, advertisements, fiction films, television, documentaries, and computers. On a formal level, each of these presents its message via an interplay between verbal texts and visual images. In each, the balance between the verbal and the visual may be fairly conventional. Fiction films, to cite an obvious example, are primarily a visual medium, though words — in the form of dialogue, song lyrics, or even written expressions — form part of the overall impressions that viewers receive while watching a movie. The same holds basically true for television programs and documentaries. Conversely, newspaper stories are mainly verbal texts, though pictures catch the reader's attention, add drama to the article, and often illustrate actions. Advertisements, while often depending on the visual for their allure and appeal, incorporate text in conjunction — and sometimes in counterpoint — with the images to sell a particular product or idea. Computers, at least potentially, bring the most balanced mix of verbal texts and visual images to the discussion, depending on what functions users employ. E-mail, for example, is primarily a verbal exchange, though attachments can easily dispatch still pictures and digital movies from one site to another. Yet visual images of all sorts abound, and surfing often becomes a mixed verbal/visual adventure. Each part in the book takes into account this consistent interplay between visual images and verbal texts.

Print Media. Jonathan Metzl begins part I with a historical analysis of how print advertisements for psychotropic medications have consistently relied on Freud's concept of scopophilia as both a drive and methodology of persuasion. Spotlighting clearly defined differences in spectator positions within these visual/verbal constructs, Metzl demonstrates their capacity to open space for rethinking established notions of the psychiatric gaze and to destabilize the traditional identity of the psychiatrist. Arthur Caplan and Joseph Turow focus on the popular press's treatment of Dr. Jack Kevorkian, the country's most prominent proponent of physician-assisted suicide, following a *60 Minutes* segment that showed Kevorkian directly causing the death of a person who had requested his help. They conclude that by concentrating more on Kevorkian's character than on the ethical dilemmas inherent in euthanasia, the press failed to capture a unique opportunity to disseminate information about a complex social issue. Like Caplan and Turow, Otto Wahl also examines the effects of press coverage, but of a particular condition rather than a specific person. Typical newspaper stories about mental illness, he contends, dramatically influence all segments of society and diminish, rather than increase, the public's understanding of people diagnosed with these disorders. As such, these widely read accounts perpetuate public fears that inevitably lead to rejection, devaluation, and ultimately discrimination.

Advertisements. Part 2 opens with Joy Fuqua's essay about the installation of television sets in hospitals across the United States. This event, though rarely studied by scholars and historians, has been central to the transformation of the American hospital system and the rise of health consumerism. Her essay addresses the role of actual space in television history, the discourses that facilitated the "box's" arrival, and the conditions that accounted for its reception within health care institutions. Looking back at what was actually shown on television, Kelly Cole's essay concentrates on the 1950s, a time when the broadcasting industry, the advertising profession, and the medical community consciously aligned themselves to prevent a loss in their cultural power. The resulting "men-in-white ban" reflects the convergence of these three influential powers and remains a symbol for how they vanquished what they considered dangerous and deemed illegitimate. Finally, Norbert Goldfield uses a series of personally observed and photographed billboard advertisements as a reflection of the evolving relationship between physicians, patients, and managed health care organizations. Such signs reflect corporate efforts to appeal to consumers, depicting American icons in both humorous and traditional ways. While hopeful that health care will soon enter a revolutionary phase, he bemoans the current "tragic era" documented by these billboards.

Fiction Films. Stephanie Brown Clark's essay, which investigates the coupling of medicine and monstrosity via movie monsters, leads off part 3. Such depictions have a long history of both fascinating and disturbing viewers, but they also represent the limitations and contingencies of the cinematic and medical gazes. Focusing on one particularly popular Hollywood depiction, *The Doctor*, Lucy Fischer shows how that film enacts crucial issues in current debates on empathy and medicine, invokes gender issues, teaches compassion, questions postfeminist logic, and celebrates passion in health care practice. As such, the film functions as a prototype of the medical drama that offers ethical lessons as well as humanistic perspectives. Marilyn Chandler McEntyre also examines mainstream films that raise important questions about accessibility, accountability, and professionalism: *Awakenings*, *Lorenzo's Oil*, and *Wit*. All these films challenge an institutional conservatism that precludes creative approaches to complex medical problems, raising questions about what conditions protect those involved and reward calculated risk taking.

Television. Marc Cohen and Audrey Shafer open part 4 with a historical overview of visual imagery, moving from nineteenth- and twentieth-century painters and photographers to contemporary medical programs. Such popular images remain vital cultural reflections of historical and contemporary attitudes toward health care, often celebrating medical achievements and portraying its practitioners as fundamentally noble and essentially selfless. Beginning where Cohen and Shafer conclude, Gregg VandeKieft probes television's pervasive impact on the medical world, reviewing the evolution of the television physician and placing him or her within the broader context of the cultural paradigms that shaped these images. Shifting from television physicians to detectives, Sander Gilman studies obesity in social contexts, demonstrating how this condition initiates a wide range of interlocking questions about the cultural construction of disability. For him, fat detectives provide complex images for studies in disability and social reading in modern culture. Concentrating on two of the most popular doctor shows on television, *ER* and *Chicago Hope*, during the 1996–1997 season, Gregory Makoul and Limor Peer systematically analyze the shows' depictions of medical treatments, doctors, and patients. In particular, their study reveals how issues of professionalism, business and administration, and ethics emerge most frequently in these programs, along with depictions of humanistic doctors and troubled patients.

Documentaries. Martin Norden launches part 5 with his examination of activist Margaret Sanger's lost film *Birth Control* (1917). Seeing it as a dramatic example of revisionist history and cinema censorship, he unearths previously unknown information about this film as a vivid reminder of public passions that can be aroused when controversial bioethical concerns interact with media events. Christie Milliken's essay investigates World War II training films about disease and hygiene. Such sex education movies bring the complex interplay of ideologies into high relief, highlighting the tensions both within and between political traditions. Kirsten Ostherr also focuses on public health films, though using more global examples, and emphasizes the connections between post–World War II medical, scientific, and popular cultures. Her analysis shows how the "cinema of world health" invests the filmed image with an authoritative form of realism through scientific surveillance, mastery of the public sphere, and control of the private body. In this part's last essay, Therese Jones scrutinizes the two documentaries made about the Dax Cowart story: *Please Let Me Die* and *Dax's Story*. Basing her analysis on the theoretical concepts of Michel Foucault, Jones illustrates the extent to which these documentary texts are initially constructed—and then overtly reconstructed—by both discursive participants and interpretive communities.

Computers. Part 6 begins with Joel Howell's historical overview of how new tools, therapies, and techniques for the treatment of disease and prolongation of life dramatically alter medical practice. Starting with the x ray and concluding with the Internet, he observes how these dramatic technological advances reframe communications between physicians and patients within a new interactive system. Tim Lenoir's essay on surgery continues Howell's perspective, spotlighting a field newly saturated with information technologies. Calling attention to the forms of digital technology now redefining the medical body, he shows how media inscribe our contemporary situation. Faith McLellan's essay explores the Internet's effect on doctor/patient relationships. By providing unparalleled access to information, this "electronic intersection" reconfigures traditional notions about professional knowledge in at least four particular ways: (1) as a data resource, (2) as a creator of communities, (3) as a communication tool, and (4) as a basis for new technologies. In the book's final essay, Tod Chambers discusses illness narratives in cyberspace, a realm that grants one the ability to deceive without supernatural assistance and has the potential to challenge the persuasive power of the personal narrative in moral deliberations.

1 Print Media

The Pharmaceutical Gaze

Psychiatry, Scopophilia, and Psychotropic

Medication Advertising, 1964–1985

JONATHAN M. METZL

Scopophilia, literally the pleasure in looking, describes the ways in which post-Oedipal male subjects look. As defined in Freud's "Three Essays on Sexuality," scopophilia arises from the male child's preoccupation with sexual difference, and his desire to "complete a sexual object by revealing its hidden parts" (Freud 1905, 69, 181). In Freud's well-worn theory, the child scopophiliac becomes anxiously aware of "the private and forbidden," in the form of other people's private and forbidden genitals. The male child looks at these parts as if a voyeur, at the same time observing and completing his notion of himself in the process of observation. Thus do children learn — and then adults perfect — the technique of looking at another person as an object while coming to know themselves as subjects. In the process of observant apperception, men come to realize both the power of the gaze and the ways this power is gendered at the expense of something else. In the division of active and passive, men look and become empowered (active), while women are looked at (passive) (figure 1).

The assumptions embedded in a system in which men look and women lack have formed the basis of many social critiques of dominant modes of seeing. In the discourse of the politics of looking that has emerged in the twenty-five years since Laura Mulvey, Mary Ann Doane, and other critics began to apply psychoanalysis to the study of the cinematic signifier, the argument has been quite convincingly made that scopophilia has larger political implications for a culture where male viewers enjoy the socially sanctioned position of the gaze. Visual images substitute for early life experiences, and responses are often seen as collective assertions of power, themselves structured like the

In managing tense, anxious patients here's one combination that makes sense: your understanding counsel and **Serax**®
oxazepam, Wyeth

To help you relieve anxiety and tension
Serax®
oxazepam
Wyeth Laboratories   Philadelphia, Pa.

1. Passive female patienthood. Serax advertisement, *Archives of General Psychiatry* 31, no. 5 (1974).

unconscious. Dominant spectatorship is thus considered an act of filling in the gaps: men enjoy the privilege, to paraphrase Mulvey, of identifying with "more ideal, more complete" images of themselves, such as male movie stars, and of voyeuristically holding images of women in front of their own absences as if they were fig leaves in a gesture of *pudeur* (Mulvey 1989, 24). Patriarchal power is both destabilized by, and recuperated through, images of women (Mulvey 1989, 17; Pollock 1991, 22).[1] Meanwhile, resistance to this order has until recently come through a retheorizing of spectator positions in the name of co-opting, or refusing, the dominant mode of seeing (Bal 1991, 14; Pollock 1999, 220–29).

The supposition that print advertisements for psychotropic medications have historically relied on a scopophiliac's gendered connection between active and passive—in the form of coherent men actively looking as subjects, and subsequently feeling empowered to think of women as objects—also lies at the heart of many critiques levied by scholars in the humanities and social sciences against the marketing of pharmaceuticals to doctors. Here scopophilia is assumed to function not only as a drive, but as a methodology of persuasion as well. Numerous studies of these advertisements over the past quarter century argue that pharmaceutical advertisements coerce their viewers to gaze at depictions of women in various forms of passive patienthood in ways that expand existing epidemiological gender imbalances between women and men for mental illness. For example, Janet Walker's analysis of pharmaceutical advertisements in *Couching Resistance: Women, Film, and Psychoanalytic Psychiatry* (1993) describes a visual regime in which images are "almost always positioned to demonstrate the superior vantage point of the male psychiatrist," whose power allows him to look down on the women in his purview (32).[2] Similarly, Hawkins and Aber's "The Content of Advertisements in Medical Journals: Distorting the Image of Woman" (1988) decries the portrayal of women in medical advertisements, while speculating that "physicians and others who read medical journals might be influenced by overt and covert messages" of heterosexual conquest, which might cause them to "over-prescribe medications to women" (47). And Courtney and Whipple (1983) write that "such advertising reinforces a doctor's prejudice against women and causes them to prescribe mood altering drugs, rather than dealing with the cause of women's problems" (14). These studies, and many others, contain the implicit assumption of a coherent medical gaze that regulates the clinical interaction (Alpers 2000, 801; Glazer 1992, 56; Levy 1994, 327; Petroshius 1995, 41; Wolfe 1996, 4).

Such critiques have limitations. I have no doubt that pharmaceutical advertisements have historically benefited from bolstering the subjectivity of the male gaze while reifying the objectivity of its object: "mother and child" ads for Zoloft, Luvox, and Effexor are but a few contemporary examples of promotions that assume looking like a man is a requisite component of professional competency, even though many psychiatrists are women. Yet because the aforementioned studies set as their frame of vision the same heteronormative order insisted on by pharmaceutical advertisements, they risk reproducing the gender assumptions of scopophilia itself—and specifically the Oedipally derived, active/passive binary described in *Three Essays on Sexuality*. Focusing exclusively on the ways men look at representations of women then effaces the other types of identification—and indeed the other forms of anxiety—elicited by the advertisements. Although cited in Mulvey, subsequent critiques often overlook the fact that Freud later complicated the notion of scopophilia in "Instincts and Their Vicissitudes" (1915), among other works, to describe the ways in which the remnants of identification with the same-sex parent—the "negative Oedipus complex"—become manifest when the power of the gaze is transferred onto others, allowing the subject to feel the pleasure of being looked at (Freud 1915, 126–30). In my reading, this oversight becomes a metaphor for the ways many critiques of drug ads privilege the active/passive divide while ignoring the ways the advertisements also based their promotions on a man's concerns about his employment, his professional standing, and his feelings about looking at another man.

My brief visual analysis explores these anxieties by focusing on a shift in the representation of psychiatrists, and the pointedly psychotropic treatments they administered, in long-running, front and back cover advertisements in the *American Journal of Psychiatry* and *Archives of General Psychiatry*, arguably the two most influential psychiatric journals of the past half century, between the mid-1960s and the early 1980s. These time periods correspond roughly with the parameters of what is called the "biological revolution in psychiatry," in which prescriptive medication cures replaced psychoanalytic talking cures (Ayd 1991, 72; Shorter 1997, 324). Broadly speaking, psychoanalytic terms and concepts dominated the ways psychiatrists conceptualized and treated many mental illnesses through the 1960s (Brown 1976, 13). Images from this era assume the unquestioned power of the embodied male psychotherapist, while advertisements make the case, to an often doubtful audience, that medications are valid participants in the previously exclusive interaction between psychotherapist and patient. By the mid-1970s, however, psychotherapeutic techniques fell out of favor in key sectors of the profession as it moved from being "psychotherapy focused to drug-management focused" (Wallerstein 1991, 421; Pulver 1978, 615). Many psychiatrists and historians of psychiatry argue that these changes altered how psychiatrists saw their patients, specifically by replacing a diagnostic system that embodied gender biases with a system that treated everyone in the same fashion (Klerman 1984, 539). However, the ads suggest a concomitant shift in the ways psychiatrists saw themselves: once shown prominently, psychiatrists grow ever smaller in advertisements between 1965 and 1985 and are ultimately replaced by representations of both patients and larger-than-life medications. This trend continues to the present day: psychiatrists almost never appear in either direct-to-the-physician (DTP) or direct-to-the-consumer (DTC) advertisements, while patients and medications figure prominently.

This representational shift reveals much more than an evolution of advertising techniques or cultural aesthetics, although these were obviously major causes of the phenomenon I describe. Rather, the disappearance of the psychiatrist's corporeal form suggests an alteration in the construction of the psychiatric spectator position — and its inherent connection to power and privilege — during the era in which pharmaceuticals and pharmaceutical companies rose to enormous clinical and financial influence in the field of psychiatry (Luhrman 2000, 203). Subtle manipulations of perspective, point of view, and other variables allow me to theorize that as prescription-writing skills replaced talking skills, a visual power once embodied in the human form was transferred onto the ever-growing symbol of medications. This transference yields two readings of the psychiatric gaze: the emergence of psychotropic medication may have enhanced a psychiatrist's power by offering new forms of disciplinary regulation; or, in light of the emergence of HMOs, conglomerated pharmaceutical companies, and encroachment from other medical specialties, medication may have forced psychiatrists to consider the tenuous nature of their own professional identities.

The 1960s

If mainstream film worked through a narcissistic pleasure by allowing male viewers to identify with their ego ideal, then print advertisements for psychotropic medications in 1964 worked even harder. Here men did not have to imagine an identification with a more powerful, more complete representation of themselves. In a visual system in which doctors were still doctors, patients were patients, and medications were hardly ever pictured, a doctor's identification was enacted effortlessly on the page. Such relations were enforced through the conventions of visual representation in the year an advertising campaign for the sedative Deprol ran in the pages of the *American Journal of Psychiatry* and *Archives of General Psychiatry* (figure 2).

The advertisement presents a dilemma common to many representations of clinical scenes in the 1960s: How can a visual image convey an entirely verbal interaction, a talking cure? And how can this image then introduce its product into the narrative, when the privileged interaction takes place only in the company of men? The image does so by using subtle visual cues to enact a visual hierarchy in which psychotherapy is marked as the site of power, while medications are relegated to the role of humble adjuncts. Psychotherapy, in this instance, involves an interaction between men who appear to have much in common in terms of the visual markers of race, gender, and class. Both

2. Helps the patient work with you. Deprol advertisement,
American Journal of Psychiatry 120, no. 6 (1964).

doctor and patient appear to be white, clean shaven, short haired, well groomed, and both dress in the white-collar clothes of suits and ties. As a result of these similarities, the advertisement reveals in an image what can only be partially described in words: a strong bond exists between the two men, who work together in the creation of "Rapport!"

But rather than equality between the two figures, the image highlights the authority of the physician by well-marked differences. One of the men appears significantly older than the other; he is also bespectacled and shown in profile, thus obstructing much of his face, while the younger man is seen in frontal view, his mouth slightly ajar. These markings work to identify the older man as the listener (a point highlighted by the prominence of his right ear in the image), and the younger man as the speaker (highlighted by the now superfluous quotes below). However, perspective and position are the most important differences separating the two men. The bespectacled older man, who appears in the foreground, is thus phantasmagorically larger than the younger man. Moreover, his placement to the side of the image, and in near direct opposition to the younger man, situates him in the position of privilege and power — if following the discourse on the gaze, privilege and power mean the right to look without being looked at. His off-center position allows the older man to gaze at the younger man while not opening himself up to the scrutiny of the socially and psychically produced look, the "non-innocent look of culture" (Olin 1996, 208–19). Meanwhile, the younger man is placed in the position of object not only as the result of appearing smaller than the older man but because his frontal, centered position (and his lack of eyeglasses) casts him as the focus of the older man's gaze. These points of contrast serve to illustrate differences in status between the two men. And the power that allows for this distinction, ironically in a scene illustrating a verbal interaction, is visual. The gaze sanctions and identifies the bespectacled older man as the "psychiatrist." Suddenly interpolated, the younger man is therefore marked as "the patient" by his position in this symbolic order.[3]

Identification between a viewer—either a viewer of a movie or a reader of a medical journal—and a visual image is a rather tangled web, and certainly much more complicated than a simple binary of doctor and patient. As theorist Jacqueline Rose rightly argues, "the relationship between viewer and scene is always one of fracture, partial identification, pleasure, and distrust" (Rose 1986, 89). In other words, viewers are as likely to identify with the subservience of a patient as with the dominance of a doctor, and often with both at the same time. Similarly, overt constructions of power are often built on acknowledgments of power's unsteady ground. I thus make no claim that an audience of physicians, an oversimplified and visually stereotyped category by design, looked at this or any image in a quantifiable or predictable way. What can be claimed, however, is that a Deprol image showing two men provides insight into the ways in which visual power and authority were constructed in many pharmaceutical advertisements in the 1960s. By foregrounding the viewer at the expense of the viewed, the ad's construction almost forces viewers of the advertisement to look from the position of privilege, to look through the doctor—literally through his glasses—and down at the patient. This configuration allowed the physician-viewers to enter into a visual identification with the doctor and against the patient. The image subtly coerces these viewers into helping the doctor gaze at the patient, while the patient is therefore defined in opposition to these two medical gazes.[4]

In contrast to cinema and painting, advertisements deploy the assumptions of the dominant culture from which they emanate to promote specific products. However, no medications are pictured in the image. Rather, the advertisement asks viewers to assume that unseen medications are already inside the patient, and that the interaction takes place after medication treatment has begun. Moreover, while the text claims that medications "help the patient work with you," the visual message implies that by helping the patient act like a patient, they help the doctor much more. Secretly working in the service of the doctor, the medications yield to the constructed power dynamic in which the doctor looks on, and in looking controls the interaction. A psychiatrist who saw the ad, the image seems to say, should feel helped and supported by Deprol in his work, but not threatened by the notion, however subtly implied, that Deprol might in fact be doing his work for him.

Constructing medications as unseen helpers in the scopic interactions of psychiatrists and patients is a convention common to many psychotropic advertisements through the mid- to late 1960s. Medications hardly ever appear in these images and are often described as "adjuncts" or "helpers" in the work of psychotherapy, but never primary treatments. Ads for Miltown between 1960 and 1967, for example, describe the minor tranquilizer as "an effective adjunct to psychotherapy," a point often illustrated by clinician's eyeglasses. Similarly, in a two-scene advertisement for the phenothiazine Taractan from September 1966, the psychiatrist is marked in the initial image by his foregrounded, enlarged position, and by his thick-framed spectacles (figure 3). In the subsequent image (not shown), the patient is markedly calmer, while the physician is able to remove his glasses when the medications begin to "work." In these and other instances, medications are constructed as giving way to the much more important, man's work of psychotherapy. And the power depicted is not the power to listen to patients but the power to look at them as if looking at an advertisement.

Set up for easy access and a seemingly unidirectional flow of identification, these images thus suggest a visual transference without the murkiness of countertransference. Psychiatrists were asked to observe more powerful, more complete images of themselves, and to employ their diagnostic acuity and powers of observation to gaze as men while locating mental illness — itself deliberately ill defined to maximize the use value of the product — entirely on the patient. Medications, though unpictured, facilitated and focused this interaction as if a pair of glasses. Thus did the images suggest a visual hierarchy in which psychotherapists dominated many clinical interactions, and medications were on the upward slope of acceptance and success.

A particularly useful therapy for the anxious patient with coexisting depression

3. Bespectacled authority. Taractan advertisement, *American Journal of Psychiatry* 123, no. 2 (1966).

(below) 4. Embodied, "elavated," and suddenly larger than the psychiatrist. Elavil advertisement, *Archives of General Psychiatry* 35, no. 1 (1978).

Psychiatrists such as Martin Fleischman argue that the success of psychotropic medications over the last quarter of the twentieth century — the so-called third revolution in psychiatry — created new interactions between psychiatrists and patients (Fleischman 1968, 1260).[5] Yet advertisements from the 1970s and 1980s suggest that the success of psychopharmaceuticals brought about more than new clinical relationships — it brought about new visual relationships as well. Once depicted by hermetic verbal exchanges between men, clinical interactions increasingly involved the appearance of third participants: medications. Their appearance in the images of advertisements indicated that the process of alleviating and ablating symptoms took place outside the office altogether. To be sure, the clinical encounter between doctor and patient was acknowledged as a necessary step in diagnosis and treatment, but the images suggested that the real treatment occurred in alliance between patient and medication, long after the verbal interaction ended.

It is tempting to argue that scenes of clinical encounters exposed the psychiatrist without his glasses at precisely the same moment medications appeared in these images. This would seem to be borne out by an advertisement for the antidepressant Elavil that appeared monthly in the *American Journal of Psychiatry* and *Archives of General Psychiatry* from January 1978 through March 1979 (figure 4). The advertisement appears in many ways similar to the Deprol image: two men sit in a room, engaged in what appears at first glance to be a dialogue; the doctor, identified by his foregrounded position, listens while the patient, placed at the center of the image, speaks.

However, the Elavil image clearly subverts the conventions of visual pleasure assumed only a decade earlier. The notably unbespectacled psychotherapist is no longer able to gaze effortlessly on a complaisant object, for the doctor (and, of course, the viewer) is through a subtle shift of perspective lowered to the point where he appears to be looked down on by the patient. The psychiatrist is also rotated slightly away from the viewer, creating the impression of a direct conflict between doctor and viewer on one side, and patient on the other. Meanwhile the patient, while still placed at the focal point of the image, appears to be embodied, "elevated," and suddenly larger than both the psychiatrist and the viewer. The patient's edge-of-the-seat posture and intense expression, combined with his threatening, opened hand, raise the possibility of an interpersonal dynamic based on a different kind of rapport.

Were one to miss this inversion of perspective, a three-scene epilogue appears on the second page of the advertisement. Here the patient, having arisen from his chair, dwarfs the smaller doctor as he walks out the door of the office. Beneath the men, the no longer obscene medications complete the narrative, as read from left to right and top to bottom. The text of the advertisement explains, "He's getting better . . . and elavil® is helping." However, the doctor's lack of glasses and the inverted size relationship between patient and doctor raise the possibility that "helping" changed from the 1960s to the 1970s. In this time span, the medications may have helped too much, hypertrophying the patient at the expense of the doctor while visually and chemically destabilizing the relationship between the two men.

In truth, however, it was more common for the medication to efface the relationship altogether. Depictions of psychiatrists in any form become rare throughout this era. In a trend beginning in the early 1970s and continuing to the present day, the corporeal representation of psychotherapists and psychiatrists literally disappeared from psychotropic advertisements. In their stead appeared representations of patients and, ever more frequently, representations of medications. A front-cover Thorazine advertisement from the *American Journal of Psychiatry* in April 1971 conveys this replacement by telling a visual joke: the analyst's couch is inhabited by a large capsule of Thorazine, baring his chemical soul and understanding his problems better (figure 5).[6] Where id was, the image reveals, there lay ego. At first glance, the image suggests that the punch line of the joke is the replacement of the patient by the medication, whereby the medication occupies the rightful place of the patient in the familiar, binaried rapport of speaker and listener. As such, the enlarged capsule implies that medicated patients are better patients, and that medications shore up the structure of the psychotherapeutic — and the psychoanalytic — dialogue.

Yet quite obviously the doctor is missing, as well. The Deprol scene, to recall, privileged the interpersonal interaction between a foregrounded psychotherapist and an upstaged patient and asked the viewer to assume that the unpictured psychotropic medication "enhanced" their connection. In the Thorazine advertisement, however, the medication is foregrounded and enlarged, requiring immediate recognition, as it occupies the slightly off-center position of scopic authority. The now empty chair of the psychoanalyst, only recently vacated, judging by the

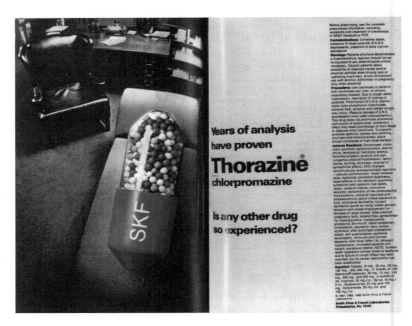

5. Where id was, there lay ego. Thorazine advertisement,
American Journal of Psychiatry 126, no. 10 (1970).

indentations in the seat, is relegated to the position once constructed
for the patient. In this sense, the position of visual power — the signifier
if not the name previously connected with the psychiatrist — is specifically the position occupied by the oversize medication. The medication
not only assumes the rightful place of the patient; rather, and more
important, the medication can also be seen to inhabit the place of the
psychiatrist. This point is reiterated by the accompanying text, which
mocks the "years of analysis" and a notion of "experience" rendered
superfluous by Thorazine's immediate, visual efficacy.

The advertisements thus suggest an almost direct inversion, by visual
palindrome, of the power relations presented in earlier images: if in the
1960s medications were presented as adjuncts or helpers to men, in the
1970s and 1980s the medications *became* the men. Image after image
over the coming years would replicate this theme. A 1979 advertisement for the tranquilizer Navane presents a centrally placed, jittery
bottle of pills against a dark background (figure 6). The text above the
bottle — "Does his tranquilizer need a 'tranquilizer'?" — implies that the
medication stands in for the patient, thus asking the physician to ob-

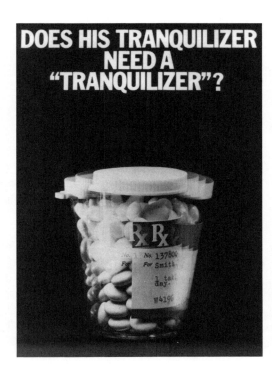

DOES HIS TRANQUILIZER NEED A "TRANQUILIZER"?

6. Does his tranquilizer need a "tranquilizer"? Navane advertisement, *Archives of General Psychiatry* 36, no. 3 (1979).

serve, and then treat, the symptoms of the bottle as if those of a person. Once again, however, the visual authority of the bottle, combined with the unseen name of the doctor on the label, reveals that the medication occupies the space once held by the doctor as well. Meanwhile images that in effect functioned as lenses in the 1960s, inviting entry and even providing glasses to assist with visual penetration, became mirrors two decades later — a point documented by long-running Loxitane ads in which enlarged capsules command immediate respect (figure 7). Similarly, Pamelor ads from the late 1970s leave little doubt that interactions between "patients and clinicians" are mediated through visually imposing medications that replace human forms and that "provide," "begin," and "allow" treatment.[7] In each case, medications assume an agency once considered the sovereign domain of men. Capable of action, diction, and reflection, medications occupy spaces previously inhabited by human forms, while reinforcing the notion that, in the space of two decades, medications develop scopic authority within these images. If, as Sylvan Barnet claims, visual perspective is often relayed in painting through the construction of a hierarchical scale in which "a

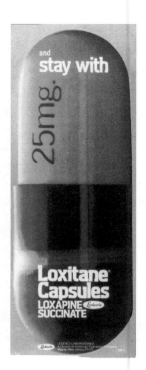

7. Capsules that
command respect.
Loxitane advertisement,
*Archives of General
Psychiatry* 37, no. 7 (1980).

king, for instance, is depicted bigger than a slave, not because he is
nearer, but because he is more important," then we might well believe
that medications had very quickly ascended to royalty, while their human predecessors had met with rapid demotion (Barnet 1997, 37).

It goes without saying that this shift was largely the result of stylistic
and cultural factors that had little to do with psychiatry. Advertisements had generally become more direct in their product placement
since the 1960s, the result of a movement in product promotion that,
according to Susan Josephson's *From Idolatry to Advertising: Visual
Art and Contemporary Culture* (1996), encouraged viewers to "look
directly at the subject matter without an awareness of technique"
(157). Moreover, American culture was surely more familiar with the
sight of drugs than it had been at the time of the Deprol advertisement.
However, these trends merit special consideration in the context of
advertisements directed at psychiatrists, and to assume that size or
stylistics were the only things that mattered is to miss part of the point
of this particular shift in representation. What also changed was the
constructed framework from which an image addressed a psychiatrist
as viewer, or the position from which the psychiatric spectator was

asked to recognize visual pleasure, defined by Mulvey and accepted by subsequent theorists as a man's right to an "undiluted appreciation of the image" (22).

Reading Disappearance

Contemporary work in the history of psychiatry, and the implicit system of valuation in contemporary psychiatry itself, suggests that the shift from an image of an enlarged physician to a depiction of a larger-than-life medication represents the progressive enhancement of a physician's power as a result of the emergence of medications. Frank Ayd (1991) claims that the "amazing success" of the benzodiazepines and other medications led to a system in which psychiatrists could prescribe "ever more precise" forms of treatment (71), and Mitchel Wilson (1993) argues that the events of the 1970s and 1980s created a "narrowing of the psychiatric gaze in contemporary psychiatry" (408). And in *Of Two Minds: The Growing Disorder in American Psychiatry* (2000), T. M. Luhrman's critique of biological psychiatry and psychopharmacology similarly assumes that "when new psychopharmacological treatments and theories emerged and successfully treated what psychoanalysis could not, the new psychiatric science claimed to win the ideological battle and to supplant its former rival" (203).

When extended to a consideration of visual identification, such arguments suggest that psychiatrists looking at pharmaceutical advertisements between the 1960s and the 1980s were empowered by the sight of medications, and that the flow of images thus traces the embellishment of the power, professional standing, and likely the personal wealth of those embracing the non-talking cure. Whereas the images of advertisements once provided viewers with more powerful depictions of themselves, the images of the 1970s and 1980s came to show viewers the larger, if somewhat commodified, wholes they could become. Here the growth of the symbol signifies the metonymic enhancement of a doctor's human judgment and precision, and the paradigmatic replacement of outdated modes of thinking. Psychotherapy, thought by many in the biological faction of the profession to be a blunt and decidedly untechnological treatment, was replaced by the brand-name luster of a new treatment modality. Implicit in this reading is the assumption of an ever more coherent male spectator position: as medications grew larger, so grew the precision of the therapeutic interventions psychiatrists were able to provide for their patients.

The possibility that psychiatrists were empowered by scopic visual images, even though they illustrated their own vanishing, also finds resonance in recent work at the intersection of medical and visual cultures through the use of the Foucauldian notion of the coherent gaze of power. In this scholarship, much like in the flow of images, the disappearance of a corporeal form of control leads to new, unseen forms of regulation. For example, Kay Cook (1996) contends that the process of "medical authoring" extends from the "physician's gaze to the medical gaze," from the empathic look of the physician to the institutionalized eye of the CT scan (63).[8] When extended to psycho-pharmacology, this scholarship allows the consideration that the progress of medications came to symbolize a discipline of the mind.[9] As extensions of the medical establishment, pills brought a form of obedient control that, as Jacqueline Zita (1998) argues, yielded "a form of disciplinary expectation that goes beyond Michel Foucault's now rather quaint notions of body disciplines. . . . Pharmaceutical discipline is an expectation that calls for a psychical rearrangement of body's most intimate matter" (70). In this formulation, disappearance assumes coherence. Doctors spend less time with patients, but medications perform the doctor's work, a cost effectiveness that paves the way for the ultimate form of managed care. Prescribed, ingested, signified, and metabolized, psychotropic medications allow psychiatrists to regulate and normalize their subject from within, long after the interpersonal interaction between doctor and patient has ended.

However, to conflate the ostensible power relations between old and new forms of treatment, or between disappearance and hegemony, is to overlook the other side of this particular narrative of progress: prosthetic symbols are often constructed to disguise a lack of potency rather than to enhance it. The very need for a product that helped the doctor help the patient "go deeper" carried with it the a priori assumption that the patient had not been able to go deep enough before. From this perspective, the images also undermine the power structure they seem to laud, or to efface the medical gaze that these images claim to bolster. Psychiatrists, the images imply, could not look deep enough on their own. Rather, for the propagation of their careers and their profession, they required medication to help them see, and to help them see patients. Without such assistance, the skills on which many of these viewers depended for their very livelihoods would become obsolete. As such, it can be argued that the flow of images speaks not only to a physician's enhancement but to his professional insecurity as well.

That the success of psychotropic medications was a source of professional disquietude is a point well documented in the pages of the same psychiatric journals in which the advertisements appeared. Ongoing debates in the *American Journal of Psychiatry*, *Archives of General Psychiatry*, and many other journals in the 1970s and 1980s attest to the ways in which practitioners were forced to come to terms with the implications of a new praxis, accompanied by a new system of valuation and remuneration. Psychotropic medications generally, and the "third revolution" specifically, were widely greeted with what Fleischman politely described as "sophisticated pessimism" (1261).[10] And the 1976 Survey of Psychoanalytic Practice cited the "looming financial crisis" for psychoanalytic practice due to "the proliferation of other forms of treatment," most notably "the increasing use of psychotropic drugs in the management of patients who previously would have been referred for psychotherapy and psychoanalysis" (Pulver 1978, 613–31).

The images suggest ways in which this uncertainty translated into a successful marketing strategy, based on the destabilization of the traditional identity of a psychiatrist as a man whose embodied knowledge was enhanced only by his glasses and whose detached observations allowed him to provide a therapeutically neutral (if increasingly prescriptive) form of evenly hovering attention. To think this way means instead reading the change in ads through synecdoche, a part cut off from, and standing in for, a whole. This difference in spectator position—between a coherent and an apprehensive mode of seeing, or between a part of a whole and its replacement—then opens a space for rethinking established notions of the psychiatric gaze. Far from disappearing from view in the name of empowerment, this psychiatrist might also have been in the process of becoming objectified in a symbolic visual language that threatened to render him expendable.

If so, then psychoanalytic notions of identification are indeed useful in understanding this form of promotion, although for different reasons than the ads' manifest active/passive plots might lead us to believe (figure 8). This is because the flow of images suggests a narrative in which the power vested in pharmaceuticals—ironically in a profession by its own admission becoming more "biological" and "objectifiable"—became more abstract than actual. This might best be understood by analogy: as Freud gave way to Lacan, and as scopophilia became the gaze, so did the power located in the body of man evolve into a power inherent in the metaphor, the signifier, the abstract suggestion. In the ads at least, this shift from a talking cure to a capsule, or from the language of psychotherapy to the order of psychopharmacology, be-

New
MOBAN
molindone HCl
Concentrate
20 mg/ml

Easily administered
in fruit juice...has
a subtle cherry flavor
when taken alone

8. Raising
questions about
the marketing of
potency. Moban
advertisement,
*Archives of
General Psychiatry*
37, no. 7 (1980).

came condensed into the symbol of medication. Medication represented, exaggerated, and lauded a potency attributed to the doctor, but one that the doctor himself could not deliver.

The construction of a product as potent is, of course, not surprising in any advertisement, and especially in an advertisement for a product where potency is itself a viable commodity (Pies 1998, 14). Within the images, however, this conquest is complicated because the potency of medications is clearly the same force once located in the psychiatrist. The images subtly suggest the increasing purview of medications and at the same time trace the demise of the spectator positions of men. Medications grew ever larger and ego idealized, while the human form was relegated to invisibility, thus casting the viewing physicians as bearers, rather than the makers, of meaning. Relegated to the role of passive observers, these viewers were then asked to recognize a relation to power that would increasingly not be theirs in the decades to come. In this sense, the same psychiatrists who could open a journal and identify with the more powerful, more complete representation of themselves in 1964 were asked in the coming years to identify with the image of the selves they had once been.

This progression then complicates the assumption of a coherent medical gaze as signifying a division between active/male and passive/female, at the expense of other readings.[11] "The phallus," psychoanalytic critic Rosalind Minsky (1996) writes, "is a sign of power in patriarchal societies that symbolizes a division between the sexes . . . and that those who 'have' rather than 'lack' it are privileged" (150). These advertisements illustrate the contextual, contingent, and ever-changing nature of this binary. Doctors who have the phallus one day may be in a position of looking anxiously at it the next, while the prescription writing often assumed to be an extension of power and privilege can also be seen to represent an acceptance of the impossibility of return. In the context of the threat of a demise in professional status, this rapid demotion in spectator position suggests a masochistic inversion of the assumedly sadistic hierarchy of visual identification: in journals where viewers were assumed to be male psychiatrists, and in images consciously constructed for the visual pleasure of men, these particular men were asked to look — or to be looked at — as women.[12]

There is no chance, however, of leaving this reexamination of the medical gaze on the stable ground of an inverted heterosexual binary. Quite clearly the awareness of the possibility of lack opens a space between nostalgia and narcissism — a spectrum that Freud realized in revising the notion of scopophilia to account for the ways in which the remnants of identification with the same-sex parent become manifest when the power of the gaze is transferred onto others. In the former, nostalgic position, the subject realizes the power of pure loss, fueled by the evanescent if illusory memory of unity. (Here Zoloft ads depicting mothers and children below the inscription "Power That Speaks Softly: Proven Efficacy in Major Depression" speak to the power of the memory for the nuclear family once imagined and then rendered conceptually impossible by the ever-shifting flow of competencies.) In the latter narcissistic position, meanwhile, one may have never lost at all. Between the 1960s and the 1980s, psychiatry objectified its explanations of identification, arguing that identity itself was the result of biological absolutes rather than contextual contingencies. Yet when traced over this same time period, the seemingly fixed position of doctor presents a startling shift in the ways identification was promoted: doctors were asked not to be the phallus but to want it.

At stake in recognizing the possibility of both accepting and rejecting symbolic castration, or of projection and ingestion, is a further critique of the marketing of pharmaceuticals during the very era in which psychiatry quite famously institutionalized the notion that cathexis to similarity was a disease (Alexander and Selesnick 1966, 356). To be sure, critics are right to assert that these ads promoted the recognition of lack, in which women both mirrored and created a man's anxiety, while problematically providing a system in which prescription writing offered a predictable means of recuperation. At the same time, the images also suggest a means of stepping outside of the compulsory heterosexuality insisted on by the ads and their critiques while remaining within the system. As Freud and pharmaceutical advertisements both seem to agree, the desire repressed in the formation of the unconscious involves a connection with both parents. In this sense, drugs that would become known as "mother's little helpers" represent the remnants of fathers as well. The images thus hint at the ways resolution was not merely contained by, or recuperated through, the stability of the scopophilic sense of loss insisted on by pharmaceutical advertisements. Rather, playing on the instability between positive and negative, diagnosis and prescription, losing and never having given up, or acceptance and sophisticated pessimism, the advertisements found a space in which to treat many forms of visual pleasure. In the process, the assumptions at play in a system where men are doctors, women are patients, and medications help them both play the part begin to break down. Psychotropic advertisements then suggest new possibilities of identification, and new markets of desire.

Notes

1   In "Degas/Images/Women; Women/Degas/Images: What Difference Does Feminism Make to Art History," Griselda Pollock (1991) describes a series of "normative tropes of art history ... an ideological 'order of things': men make art by looking at women. Man is the subject, woman the object, and art the production of that hierarchical exchange" (23).

2   Walker discusses Sandril advertisements in which "a beam of light projects from behind the white-haired doctor, onto the anxious woman," a "bright light" that isolates her "fundamental details or supposed essence as it isolates her figure, presenting her for psychotherapy and the rehabilitation with which it is coupled" (32).

3   For an interesting discussion of the division of visual power between two figures as mediated through ocular prostheses, see Tamar Garb's (1993,

219–29) discussion of the role of binoculars in Renoir's painting of an opera balcony, *La loge* (1874).

4 Of course an image allowing easy access for a man to look through a man at another man contests Mulvey's notion of a "straight, socially established interpretation of sexual difference" (33–49). I argue, however, that the obvious homoerotic implications of this image ironically work to reinforce the point I am making about the seeming stability of the role of the psychotherapist in these early advertisements. In later advertisements, the rigid separation between men discloses an anxiety about maintaining the privilege that the Deprol advertisement seems to take for granted. Man as an object of display would become so forbidden as to be ruled out entirely. The way the Deprol advertisement so easily looks at a man, and the likely possibility that such an act of looking had little shock value in the conservative pages of the *American Journal of Psychiatry*, further illustrates the unquestioned power of this particular gaze at this particular point in time.

5 The first revolution was brought about by Pinel during the "humanitarian reforms" of the French Revolution; the second by Freud and psychoanalysis.

6 A medication generally used in inpatient wards, the Thorazine advertisement highlighted the medication's usefulness in outpatient psychotherapy with mentally ill patients.

7 See Pamelor advertisement, *Archives of General Psychiatry* 35, no. 1 (1978).

8 See also Lisa Cartwright's analysis of early medical films, *Screening the Body: Tracing Medicine's Visual Culture* (1992).

9 See also Thomas Szasz's "The Case against Psychiatric Power" (2000).

10 "Despite our sophisticated pessimism, these new medications seemed to work" (Fleischman 1968, 1261).

11 This point is made by Kaja Silverman, among other critics. See Kaja Silverman, *The Acoustic Mirror: The Female Voice in Psychoanalysis and Cinema* (1988, 15).

12 See also the case study of the Wolf Man, whose visual pleasure lay in attaining a "narcissistic" sense of "passivity" (Freud 1918, 100–112); and the case study of the Rat Man, whose neurotic crisis was set off by a misplaced pair of eyeglasses (Freud 1909, 158).

Taken to Extremes

Newspapers and Kevorkian's Televised

Euthanasia Incident

ARTHUR L. CAPLAN AND JOSEPH TUROW

Jack Kevorkian, who is currently serving a prison sentence in Michigan, played a crucial role in putting the issue of physician-assisted suicide center stage in the arena of American politics. Beginning in 1990, his actions to help various persons to die set off storms of controversy in the popular media and in academic medical and bioethical circles (W. Smith 1997; Snyder and Caplan 2000). Yet despite his influence, Kevorkian was often described, even by admirers, as a zealot.

The American Heritage Dictionary defines a zealot as "a fanatically committed person, . . . a person possessed by excessive zeal for and uncritical attachment to a cause or position." It goes on to characterize zealotry as an incident that reflects a person's "excessive and uncritical commitment" to an idea or ideal.

Clearly, whether a person or act is zealous is in the eye of the beholder. Press historians and sociologists have confronted the social meaning of extreme zeal through explorations of the ways in which the mainstream press has constructed individuals and groups as zealots, marginalizing them and their actions in the process. With the exception of the abortion controversy, when researchers have focused on contemporary coverage of zealots and zealotry by American media, their work has centered on "terrorist" activities (e.g., Weimann and Winn 1994; Schnuck 1992). Their analyses have spoken to the media's reflection of U.S. government foreign policy as well as to the relative lack of interest in international news by the American press (Picard and Alexander 1991; Martin and Hiebert 1990).

Missing from these discussions, however, is an understanding of the extent to which zealous actions function as critical incidents that encourage a broadening of press discussions of social issues underlying the events. Does a startling or shocking domestic incident that the American press labels as zealotry catalyze the nation's news outlets to explore a wide range of views about the issues involved and their public relevance? The question reflects on a gamut of bizarre events that individuals and groups carry out at least partly to rivet public attention to their political cause, from the so-called Unabomber's booby-trapped packages to the exploits of the Ku Klux Klan to cyber-sabotage. More generally, the question addresses an enduring issue about press coverage itself. Does the journalistic reliance on storytelling narrow or expand public discourse about contentious domestic sociopolitical issues?

To understand the way in which the press treated the "zealotry" of Jack Kevorkian, we examined print media coverage of a videotaped euthanasia that was broadcast by the popular CBS news magazine program *60 Minutes*. Kevorkian planned the death with an eye toward having it broadcast on national television, carried out the killing on a patient with ALS disease, taped the killing with the patient's permission, and subsequently offered it to the CBS show. The tape was aired as part of a segment hosted by Mike Wallace on 22 November 1998.

Kevorkian said he did this to force the public and politicians to accept the legitimacy of euthanasia and assisted suicide. Did he succeed? How did press discussions of euthanasia and assisted suicide change as a result of the broadcast? Using those terms as keywords, we conducted a content analysis on a large random sample of U.S. newspapers during the months before, during, and after the broadcast.

The results were startling. The broadcast killing sparked a large rise in articles that mentioned euthanasia or physician-assisted suicide. The increase in articles did not, however, lead to a broadened discussion of bioethical or legal issues surrounding euthanasia, end-of-life care, and the pros and cons of physician-assisted suicide. Instead, the articles overwhelmingly framed Kevorkian's activities as a crime-and-personality story. The comments of prosecutors and defense attorneys dominated the media coverage accorded the incident. Their statements far, far outnumbered other sources such as physicians, nurses, ethicists, patients, and advocacy group representatives who could shed light on the substantive ethical, social, and clinical issues surrounding end-of-life-care and assisted suicide. The crime-and-personality coverage of Kevorkian's act muted the slight coverage in the media of philosophical, social, and political issues surrounding euthanasia and assisted suicide already present in media accounts in the weeks and months before the broadcast of Kevorkian's killing. Diminished attention to these topics remained weeks after the videotape aired on national television. Kevorkian's act brought discussion of the ethics of assisted suicide and euthanasia to a grinding halt as the media concentrated on whether he was crazy, whether he ought be punished, and, if so, how.

Past Coverage of Social Activism

Many writers have noted that the ideology of mainstream news in the United States is inherently conservative: it depicts historically normative institutional practices as preferable to challenges to those practices. It should come as no surprise, then, that throughout the nation's history, mainstream press outlets tend to dub as "fanatics" individuals and groups that have been fiercely committed to rapid or unusual forms of political or social change. Nerone (1994) and Solomon (1991) underscore this dynamic in descriptions of the ways major American newspapers treated abolitionists, labor unions, and suffragists during their formative periods. Nerone notes, for example, that "mainstream [press] forces cherished an image of abolitionists as wild subversives" (87) who exploited taxpayer-funded services such as the post office for demonic, propagandistic ends. Writing about the growing labor movement of the early twentieth century, Nerone describes how the *Los Angeles Times* "appealed constantly to the image of the sober industrious worker and demonized unionists as the opposite: vicious, lazy, jealous" (173). Solomon reveals a similar dynamic with respect to newspaper coverage of turn-of-the-century suffragettes.

Explorations of mainstream press conflicts with social movements during the 1970s provide evidence that the pattern of marginalization continued to the modern era. Gitlin (1980) captures this process nicely in his description of the way reporters framed Students for a Democratic Society as a dangerous organization and, in the process, delegitimized its radical ideological platform against the Vietnam War. Tuchman (1978) suggests that the *New York Times* treated the "women's liberation" movement in a similarly marginalized way. She shows how female workers within the *Times* were able to expand and normalize coverage of political aspects of women's lives, if not of the actual women's lib groups themselves.

These studies are important for detailing the way in which mainstream journalism has often reflected the interests of society's establishment when dealing with people whose worldviews appear to pose a threat to middle-of-the-road values and politics (Gans 1979). At the same time, the studies do not address a key related question: Having dubbed persons or groups as fanatic and their action as dangerous, do mainstream press outlets go beyond that? That is, do they use events that the fanatics stage to explore the social issues that underlie them and present a range of (presumably more socially acceptable) solutions?

Broader scholarly literature on journalism does not offer clear-cut answers to these questions. Barnhurst and Mutz (1997) state that "there is a growing consensus that contemporary reporting has altered [the definition of news] to deemphasize events in favor of news analysis" (27). They concede, however, that most conclusions about increased analysis in news have centered on political reporting. In their own research, they found increased analytical coverage of crime, accidents, and employment in three major newspapers throughout the twentieth century. The categories in that research, though, did not allow the authors to explore the extent, nature, or depth of the social interpretation.

The extent, nature, and depth of social interpretation that follows in the wake of a zealous or fanatical act is a crucial component of journalism's construction of zealotry. Incendiary incidents that journalists define as fanatical uniquely merge "sensational" or "criminal" deeds with the perpetrators' own presentation of political reasons for their behavior. Moreover, from 1960s bra burners to the Unabomber to those manipulating huge street puppets to protest the World Trade Organization or genetically modified foods, many people who perform socially provocative acts have said that they carry them out at least in part to garner press coverage of the underlying conditions and issues that merit public attention.

How mainstream press outlets cover this convergence of the explicitly sensational and the explicitly ideological have contemporary political and social implications. A pattern of press discussion of the problems that ignited such acts might mean that ideologically committed plane hijackers, hunger strikers, bombers, and other extremists have a good chance for success in their publicity aims despite being personally branded as zealots. But even if mainstream press outlets avoid becoming direct mouthpieces for the zealots' interests, they might still find in their actions an opportunity to explore many facets of a social problem in front of a large, interested audience. The question recalls Walter Lippmann's 1922 metaphor about the press only intermittently shining its light on various aspects of society. When it comes to extremist incidents that rivet societal and press attention, is the press's basic impulse to broaden or narrow the sociopolitical beam?

The Case of Kevorkian

The controversy surrounding Jack Kevorkian presents a good opportunity to investigate this topic. He first entered into the debate about physician-assisted suicide in the late 1980s when he wrote a series of articles which argued that as part of their duty to relieve pain and suffering, physicians should assist those requesting suicide. In 1990 he helped Janet Atkins, an Oregon woman who had been diagnosed as suffering from early stage Alzheimer's disease, to commit suicide. Kevorkian decided to help Atkins carry out her suicide in Pontiac, Michigan, because the state had no explicit law banning assisted suicide. He was brought to trial for his role in the Atkins death but was released when the judge found insufficient evidence to prosecute him for murder (Robertson 1999; Betzold 1998).

During the 1990s Kevorkian remained active as a proponent of assisted suicide and as an individual who assisted those, both terminally ill and not, in committing suicide. He publicly admitted involvement in fifty deaths and stated that he had assisted persons in dying in at least another fifty instances. His license as a physician was removed as a result of his involvement with assisted suicide.

On the *60 Minutes* broadcast of 22 November 1998, Kevorkian stated that he had become frustrated at the failure of his campaign to achieve a right to suicide assistance for any person who requested it. "The issue," he said, "has got to be raised to the level where it is finally decided" (*60 Minutes* transcript, 1998). Consequently, he said, he decided to take a sensational next step. He would directly cause the death of a person who had requested help in dying and offer the opportunity to a national news organization to tape the act. He contacted *60 Minutes* producers, and they agreed to broadcast a tape in which Kevorkian administers a lethal preparation to ALS sufferer Thomas Youk with Youk's agreement. The 22 November program aired the tape to an audience of millions. Because he had not only assisted the death but undertaken the key action that caused it, Oakland County, Michigan, district attorneys charged Kevorkian with murder. Several months later, he was convicted of second-degree murder and sentenced to prison.

Subsequent to the broadcast, *60 Minutes* was subjected to heated criticism from viewers about the decision to put Kevorkian's tape on the air. No significant response was aired concerning these criticisms. But after a symposium on the whole affair at the University of Michigan on 22 February 1999, at which Mike Wallace was a participant, *60 Minutes* decided to revisit the topic of assisted suicide and did so in a broadcast that aired in May 1999.

Kevorkian's public activities had important consequences. As a result of a voter referendum, the state of Oregon enacted legislation that was passed in November 1998. Proponents of the legalization said many times that the most difficult problem they faced was separating their proposal from the activities of Jack Kevorkian (Caplan, Snyder, and Faber-Langendoen 2000). Kevorkian was seen by these Oregonians as a zealot whose actions were so out of the mainstream that they put the entire political movement in Oregon at risk to achieve the end that Kevorkian claimed he sought.

The Study

We investigated whether and how Jack Kevorkian's 22 November 1998 appearance on *60 Minutes* affected mainstream U.S. newspapers' discussion of euthanasia and assisted suicide. We examined newspaper coverage of these topics from 15 October 1998 through 14 January 1999. To take into account any disclosure of the tape's contents to the press before 22 November, we considered that the month of broadcast began on 15 November. (As it turned out, there was no such prior disclosure.) For article sampling purposes, we divided our time span into three months: 15 October to 14 November, 15 November to 14 December, and 15 December to 14 January.

Using the Lexis-Nexis full-text database of large- and medium-circulation U.S. newspapers, we retrieved all articles that mentioned *euthanasia* or *assisted suicide* in the headline or body during that period; the number totaled 1,756 in 129 papers. Because we noted that most of the articles clustered around the period of the broadcast, we were concerned that choosing a random sample directly from the population of 1,756 pieces would not yield enough articles from the four weeks before and after that time. Consequently, we decided to choose randomly the same number of articles — 200 — from each of the four weeks. In total, our sample comprised 586 randomly selected articles.

We designed our analytical instrument to assess whether these articles mentioned issues that lie at the center of contemporary discussions of euthanasia and assisted suicide among health policy professionals (e.g., Caplan 1995, 1998; Uhlman 1998; Snyder and Caplan 2000). These professionals include bioethicists, health care analysts, legislators, judges, physicians, patients, and patient advocates. The broad issues were media ethics (whether 60 *Minutes* was correct in airing the segment); crime/murder; humane alternatives to euthanasia and assisted suicide; legislative activities; public opinion or polling; critiques of euthanasia and assisted suicide; the personalities of those involved; and economics.

We also noted the presence of specific key topics connected to the larger ones. When it came to the legislative models, coders noted whether the assisted-suicide laws of the Netherlands or the state of Oregon were discussed. They also noted whether the paragraph mentioned safeguards or competency tests of those seeking death. The keywords *humane alternatives* included a range of activities, from withholding treatment to pain control to spiritual or religious support to hospice care. Mention of critiques of euthanasia or assisted suicide related to five major points that are emphasized in the bioethical literature (Caplan 1995, 1998; Nuland 1994; Uhlman 1998). They included moral and religious prohibitions to euthanasia or assisted suicide, concern that allowing euthanasia by physicians undermines public trust in them, concern that it violates long-standing precepts of medical ethics, concern that it encourages killing people who cannot afford to pay costs associated with long illnesses, and the "slippery slope" argument that opening the door to physician-assisted killing of the dying will lead to killing of the disabled and other vulnerable persons (Caplan 1998).

In the final section of the instrument, coders noted paragraph by paragraph what kinds of people reporters quoted or cited in their discussions about euthanasia and assisted suicide. Were they ethicists, AMA spokespeople, M.D.'s, nurses, end-of-life patients, their relatives, police, judges, prosecutors, legislators, 60 *Minutes* producers, Kevorkian himself, Thomas Youk (the man Kevorkian killed), members of the pro-euthanasia Hemlock Society, religious spokespeople, science scholars, or humanities scholars?

The eight coders who worked on the project were graduate students in the University of Pennsylvania's bioethics program. We told them that we were studying press coverage of euthanasia around the time of the Kevorkian euthanasia episode, which had happened only weeks earlier. Before coding the articles in earnest, they went through three weeks of intensive training with the investigators and had decision rules clarified for reliable coding. By the end of the training period, the intercoder reliability average was 0.89.

Findings

Press Coverage as a Whole

As noted earlier, an exploration of the Lexis-Nexis database found 1,756 articles in 129 U.S. newspapers that appeared from 15 October 1998 through 14 January 1999 and mentioned euthanasia or assisted suicide in the headline or body. The way in which the articles concentrated during the three four-week periods reflects the clamor that occurred around the *60 Minutes* broadcast. The period starting seven days before the broadcast—from 15 November to 14 December—saw by far the largest number of pieces, 947, or 54 percent of the entire sample. By contrast, the time between 15 October and 14 November saw 468 articles, 26 percent of the total. The four weeks between 15 December and 14 January saw an even smaller number—343 articles, or 20 percent of the total.

Because we chose our entire sample of 586 articles evenly across the three periods, we did not expect it to reflect directly the skew in coverage caused by the program. Nevertheless, in examining the sample as a whole, we could already note that the broadcast stood out as a major incident among an otherwise slight and superficial coverage of euthanasia and assisted suicide during the three periods. Headlines, which indicate attention paid to a topic, provide an example.

Among the 586 articles, our analysis found 159 headlines that specifically mentioned individual topics relevant to euthanasia, assisted suicide, or the broadcast incident. Figure 1 shows the distribution of these topics across the headlines. (Because coders could note more than one topic in a headline, the percentage totals to more than 100.) *Crime* and *personality* related to euthanasia and assisted suicide stood out among the particular topics, appearing in 45 percent and 38 percent of the headlines, respectively. *Crime* invariably referred to Kevorkian's killing of Thomas Youk. When personality references appeared in a headline, they typically centered on reporters' characterizations of Kevorkian variously as zealous, fanatical, and, most commonly, "Doctor Death." Ethical issues were raised, but they were nearly all related to the propriety of *60 Minutes'* broadcast of Kevorkian killing Youk. They appeared in 8 percent of the headlines.

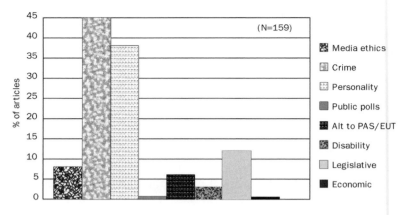

1. Headline topics related to euthanasia and assisted suicide ($N = 159$).

Coverage of policy and ethical issues paled in comparison to crime and personality in the headlines. Legislative issues appeared in 12 percent of the headlines. Alternatives to euthanasia and assisted suicide, concerns surrounding suicide and the disabled, public opinion polls, and economic issues constituted fewer than 10 percent of the topics.

The relatively frequent mention of crime and personality also showed up in the body of the articles, as table 1 indicates. Legislative issues related to euthanasia or assisted suicide made a relatively strong appearance; they showed up in 27 percent of the pieces. Other key end-of-life policy topics, however, rarely received mention. These include key areas such as physicians' ability to control the pain of dying patients so they will not want to commit suicide (noted in 13 percent of the articles); the experiences of Oregon and the Netherlands with assisted-suicide laws (12 percent); concerns surrounding suicide and the disabled (11 percent); the presence of realistic alternatives to euthanasia and assisted suicide (10 percent); and a number of other issues (far fewer than 10 percent). When these topics were raised, they received little attention. They appeared in more than one paragraph only 5 percent of the time.

Crime and personality, by contrast, had high profiles in the body of the articles. Fully 43 percent of the 586 pieces mentioned crime, with 27 percent of these mentioning it in more than one paragraph. As for personality — meaning questions about the mental status and zealotry of Kevorkian — 26 percent of the articles addressed themselves to this theme. Although the number was virtually the same as those that mentioned legislative issues, personality received more attention in the sto-

Table 1. Mention of Topics Related to Euthanasia or
Assisted Suicide in Body of Articles, 15 October 1998–
14 January 1999 (percentage)

	$(N = 586)$
Crime	42
Legislative activities	27
Personality	26
Pain control/good medical care	13
Experience in Oregon/the Netherlands	12
Disability issues related to death and dying	11
Alternatives to euthanasia or assisted suicide	10
Safeguards	6
Hospice care	6
Withholding treatment	4
Withdrawing treatment	4
Helping patient not feel abandoned	4
Spiritual/religious support	3
Additional treatments	3
Competency tests	2
Allowing for patients change of mind	2
Minimizing financial burden	1

ries. Twenty-three percent of the articles that discussed personality, but only 5 percent of the articles that mentioned legislative issues, did so in more than one paragraph.

Missing from all but a tiny percentage of articles were the five critiques of euthanasia and assisted suicide that health and bioethical experts consider crucial to evaluating public policies with respect to these topics. Table 2 shows that only two of these critiques showed up in more than 4 percent of the articles, and that even those were rare. Moral prohibitions to euthanasia or assisted suicide appeared in 14 percent of the articles. The slippery slope argument came up in 10 percent of the articles. Virtually unmentioned across the three months was the argument that if euthanasia or assisted suicide was legal, the high medical costs of certain patients would encourage their relatives, hospitals, or insurance companies to terminate care. Health experts have noted that public debate for and against this proposition is crucial if future corporate, legislative, and judicial decisions are to be influenced by an aware citizenry (W. Smith 1997; Byock 1996; Quill 1993; Caplan, Snyder, and Faber-Langendoen 2000).

Table 2. Mention of Critiques of Euthanasia or Assisted Suicide in Body of Articles, 15 October 1998–14 January 1999 (percentage)

	(N = 586)
Moral prohibitions	14
Slippery slope	10
Costs and other factors will increase pressure to carry it out	4
Violates medical ethics	3
Undermines trust of doctors and caregivers	2

Kevorkian's Role in the Press Discourse

The vast majority — 77 percent — of all the references to Jack Kevorkian during the twelve weeks that we studied occurred during the four weeks around the *60 Minutes* incident. Kevorkian was also highly associated with the mention of crime and personality. Fully 69 percent of the 272 articles that mentioned him discussed crime in relation to euthanasia or assisted suicide. In the 314 articles in which he did not appear, only 21 percent mentioned crime in relation to euthanasia or assisted suicide. Personality came up in only 14 percent of the 314 pieces without Kevorkian. When Kevorkian was mentioned, however, 41 percent of the articles referred to issues about *his* personality.

We wondered if Kevorkian's presence was also associated with policy issues. We speculated that articles mentioning him in just a few paragraphs would emphasize the alleged crime and his supposed unusual personality, while those mentioning him in several paragraphs would devote space to policy issues, with or without crime and personality. To test this speculation, we divided the appearance of Kevorkian in the body of the article into three categories — no mentions, mentioned in one to five paragraphs, and mentioned in six or more paragraphs.

Table 3 shows that our speculation was partly correct. Compared to articles that did not feature Kevorkian, those that did saw a jump in the appearance of half the twenty-two key policy issues regarding euthanasia and assisted suicide. Of the ten that increased, however, only four — disability issues, Oregon/the Netherlands, pain control, and legislation — rose to a substantial presence. Of these, mention of legislation in various states to outlaw or support end-of-life activities climbed dramatically with the increase in paragraphs mentioning Kevorkian. Table 3 also indicates, however, that crime and personality

Table 3. Association of Topics and Critiques Related to Euthanasia or Assisted Suicide with Mention of Kevorkian, 15 October 1998–14 January 1999 (percentage)

	K0* (N = 314)	K1* (N = 193)	K2* (N = 79)
Alternatives to euthanasia/assisted suicide[a]	9	15	3
Disability[a]	8	14	19
Legislative[a]	24	26	43
Polls[a]	5	9	13
Economic concerns[a]	2	8	14
Oregon/the Netherlands[a]	5	21	17
Safeguards[a]	3	4	19
Competency tests[a]	1	4	5
Allowing change of mind	1	3	4
Withholding treatment	3	5	3
Withdrawing treatment	4	5	4
Pain control[a]	8	20	19
Religious/spiritual support	2	5	1
Minimizing the financial burden	1	1	—
Helping patient not feel abandoned[a]	3	8	1
Hospice care[a]	5	10	1
Additional treatments	2	6	1
Slippery slope[a]	4	11	24
Coercion because of costs	3	5	4
Violates medical ethics[a]	1	5	8
Undermines trust in physicians	1	3	4
Moral/religious prohibitions	14	14	14
Crime[a]	21	58	96
Personality[a]	14	30	67

*K0 = no mention of Kevorkian in article; K1 = mention of Kevorkian 1–5 times; K2 = mention of Kevorkian 6 or more times.
[a]Differences between time periods (absence/presence of variable) significant at the .05 level or better using the chi square statistic.

remained by far the most common topics when Kevorkian was mentioned in both fewer than five and more than five paragraphs.

We wanted to know if the mild association we detected between the increased appearance of Kevorkian and the appearance of certain policy topics was linked merely to the *mention* of individual issues or to the actual discussion of several issues in some detail. To find out, we created an "index of discussion" by adding the number of paragraphs in which the twenty-two topics were mentioned in each article. The higher the index number, the fuller the discussion of topics related to euthanasia and assisted suicide. We ran a correlation between the number of mentions of Kevorkian in an article and the index. We found a mild .15 relationship using Pearson's R. In only a relatively small percentage of articles, then, did Kevorkian's increased presence associate with intensive discussion of policy issues.

60 Minutes and the Press Discourse

Not surprisingly, all 210 articles that appeared in our sample during the month around the 60 Minutes broadcast mentioned Jack Kevorkian at least once. Because those articles represented 77 percent of all pieces that noted Kevorkian, we might expect that the tendencies noted in the previous section would show up when we compared the four weeks previous to the 60 Minutes broadcast to the four weeks around the broadcast. We expected a dramatic increase in crime and personality and a moderate rise in the mention of ethical and social issues. We were wrong.

Crime and personality did rise substantially in the articles between 15 November and 14 December compared to the four earlier weeks. The modest rise in issues that we saw with the mention of Kevorkian did not happen, however. The association we noted earlier between Kevorkian and a few ethical and policy issues was scattered unevenly across the three time periods and not concentrated in the month around the broadcast. The result was that the appearance of only one of the topics rose slightly from the first to the second period. The rest either did not change or actually declined from their mention a month earlier.

Table 4 presents findings about the three time spans. It shows that during the broadcast month the number of articles that focused on euthanasia or assisted suicide (rather than just mentioning one or the other term) *was* substantially higher than the month before or after the broadcast month. This increased "focus" reflected the large number of stories centering on Kevorkian's 60 Minutes tape.

The rise in focus was not accompanied by an increased attention to policy issues. Legislative topics, mentioned in a strong 43 percent of the articles in the month before the broadcast, actually declined by 17 percent during the broadcast month. The topics of polls and the experiences of Oregon and the Netherlands, with previously small mentions to begin with, also declined. Thirteen other key topics, rarely men-

Table 4. Association of Topics and Critiques Related to Euthanasia or Assisted Suicide with Three Time Periods (percentage)

	15 Oct.–14 Nov. (N = 176)	15 Nov.–14 Dec. (N = 210)	15 Dec.–14 Jan. (N = 200)
Alternatives to euthanasia/assisted suicide[a]	9	10	11
Disability	11	13	11
Legislative[a]	43	26	15
Polls[a]	13	7	4
Economic concerns	5	3	5
Oregon/the Netherlands[a]	16	13	8
Safeguards[a]	6	10	0.5
Competency tests	43	4	0.5
Allowing change of mind	2	4	0.5
Withholding treatment	2	5	4
Withdrawing treatment	5	6	2
Pain control	14	17	10
Religious/spiritual support	3	3	3
Minimizing financial burden	1	—	1
Helping patient not feel abandoned	5	4	5
Hospice care	7	5	7
Additional treatments	2	4	5
Slippery slope[a]	8	14	5
Coercion because of costs	5	3	4
Violates medical ethics	2	5	2
Undermines trust in doctors	2	3	—
Moral/religious prohibitions	10	16	15
Crime[a]	26	68	33
Personality[a]	17	41	19
Media ethics[a]	2	21	7
Article focus is euthanasia[a]	30	71	30

[a]Differences between time periods (presence/absence of the topics) are significant at the .05 level or better using the chi square statistic.

tioned in the first period, remained at their low levels. Only "safe-guards" and "slippery slope" saw statistically significant increases, albeit small ones. An additional point, not shown in the table, is that only 6 percent of topics were mentioned in more than one paragraph per article when they did show up. Discussions of policy topics during the month that the Youk killing was broadcast were superficial as well as rarer than they were in the month before the TV program.

Instead of noting issues, the articles during the second period concerned themselves with details of Kevorkian's alleged crime and bizarre personality. These subjects were not new with the 60 Minutes spot. Kevorkian's previous indictments and trials relating to assisted suicides had already primed reporters to brand him as an end-of-life fanatic, a crazed zealot, and a criminal. The appearance of crime and personality topics in the month before the broadcast reflects Kevorkian's prior reputation, to some extent. With the airing of the Youk tape, though, mention of crime in connection with euthanasia or assisted suicide soared from 26 percent to 68 percent of the articles. Personality rose from 17 percent to 41 percent. Questions of media ethics — whether 60 Minutes was correct to air the alleged crime — showed up in 21 percent of the pieces.

The small extent of differences between the coverage of these topics in editorial and straight or "hard" news pieces ought to be mentioned here. Across the three periods, opinion matter such as editorials, op-ed columns, and letters to the editor made up 38 percent of the articles mentioning euthanasia or assisted suicide. During the weeks around the 60 Minutes broadcast, however, these opinion articles shot up to 56 percent of the total. Although the other two periods revealed no substantial differences in topics between the hard and opinion stories, the editorials from the period of the broadcast did highlight two topics substantially more than the hard news did. They were pain control, which appeared in 24 percent of the opinion pieces and only 10 percent of the straight ones, and the ethics of 60 Minutes' decision to broadcast the Youk tape, which appeared in only 14 percent of the straight news but in 51 percent of the opinion pieces. Apart from these exceptions, the opinion and straight news articles closely paralleled each other with respect to the scant appearance of topics related to euthanasia and assisted suicide and the high percentages of crime and personality.

A close reading of all these articles for the overall press response to the 60 Minutes incident emphasized what the data presented so far in this section imply: reporters and editorialists overwhelmingly framed Kevorkian's euthanasia as a crime-and-personality story. Doctor Death

Table 5. Association of Sources Quoted or Cited in the Articles with the Three Time Periods (percentage)

	15 Oct.–14 Nov. (N = 176)	15 Nov.–14 Dec. (N = 210)	15 Dec.–14 Jan. (N = 200)
Ethicist	3	3	2
AMA	1	5	1
M.D.	3	3	1
Nurse	—	0.5	—
Other health worker	2	0.5	—
Prosecutor[a]	2	23	0.5
Defense attorney[a]	6	18	0.5
Judge	1	7	2
Legislator	3	5	4
Police	1	1	1
Mike Wallace	—	6	—
60 Minutes executives	—	—	1
Kevorkian	5	33	2
Thomas Youk	—	1	0.5
Youk's family	—	4	0.5
Hemlock spokesperson	2	3	1
Religious spokesperson	10	4	10
Humanities scholar	1	2	2
Science scholar	—	1	1

[a]Differences between time periods (absence/presence of source) significant at the .05 level or better using the chi square statistic. All other differences between time periods not significant.

had gone further than ever to pursue his fanaticism, killing someone on national TV. Several editorials took up the appropriateness of *60 Minutes'* decision to play the tape. Much more of the writing in hard news and editorial matter, though, turned on the mechanics of the criminal process and Kevorkian's responses. Would a jury convict Kevorkian of murder, as prosecutors insisted? Would he really defend himself without a lawyer, as his former attorneys seemed to suggest? What would the future of this septuagenarian be if he was sentenced to prison?

The flavor of the crime-and-personality discussion is reflected in the sources whom reporters quoted or cited during the month around the broadcast. As table 5 shows, Kevorkian's comments were cited or quoted most; these tended to be comments that reflected on his personality or chances of going to jail. Apart from Kevorkian himself, prosecutors and defense attorneys were clearly the most popular sources. Reporters hardly ever turned to people who would be able to elucidate the medical, legal, and bioethical issues surrounding Thomas Youk's death. The articles hardly ever presented legislators, ethicists, physicians, or representatives of any professional organization of doctors, nurses, or social workers. Spokespeople from the Hemlock society, religious organizations, and academia were also virtually absent.

Table 5 indicates that the appearance of these end-of-life experts had not been high during the first period studied — the weeks before broadcast. The *60 Minutes* incident could have served as an opportunity for reporters to seek alternative voices to Kevorkian in order to clarify the topic of euthanasia for their readers. That they did not do so then or from December 15 to January 14 — the third period studied — emphasizes how little Kevorkian's videotaped euthanasia contributed to discussion of end-of-life issues in the press.

As the crime-and-personality frame carried into the third period, it ironically further suppressed the policy topics that had already diminished in appearance during the month around the broadcast. Table 4 shows that most of the other policy issues remained at the same very low level where they had been during the previous eight weeks. Compared to the previous two-month period, however, mention of legislation fell further, from 26 percent to 15 percent of the pieces. Mention of polls and Oregon and the Netherlands also declined, and "safeguards" diminished to less than 1 percent.

What Did Kevorkian Do with the Press, and What Did the Press Do with Kevorkian?

Far from encouraging more discussion of substantive issues surrounding end-of-life decisions, Kevorkian's actions ironically reduced it. None of the 129 newspapers in our sample used the televised euthanasia as a way to open up public discussion of controversial end-of-life issues. They did not turn to experts who could have shed light on implications of the incident for the larger society. The press preferred, instead, to focus on the crime and personality — Kevorkian himself was the story.

From the standpoint of people interested in social policy regarding the end of life, this finding is deeply disturbing. Decisions about when and how to die are very frequent in an aging and technologically dependent society such as the United States. Requests for assistance in dying are not uncommon, and many health care providers choose to act on those requests (Quill 1993; Snyder and Caplan 2000). Americans confront these issues and the laws governing them not as citizens concerned with social policy but as patients and relatives at their most vulnerable moments of pain and suffering. At the same time, spirited policy decisions about these activities are negotiated in legislative and judicial arenas by insurance firms, lobbying organizations, health maintenance organizations, and health professionals. Those policy decisions take place outside the public limelight even though their outcomes profoundly affect what patients and their families do and can do, when and how.

The Kevorkian incident riveted the attention of the nation on euthanasia and assisted suicide. Whatever else it was, it was a great opportunity to make the broad public aware of the key issues. It did not. The press failed to capture the opportunity that Kevorkian presented. Character won out over substance.

Stepping back to the broader topic of the press's coverage of domestic zealotry, this study provides a validation of the essentially conservative and sensationalist impulses of the American press. The "if it bleeds it leads" motto that sets much of the front-page news agenda certainly predicted the attention to Kevorkian's euthanasia on *60 Minutes*. At least in the case of Kevorkian, zealotry was not covered heavily beyond the "bleeding." The claim by Barnhurst and Mutz (1997) that news analysis of "social problems, interpretations and themes" is triumphing over event-centered reporting certainly does not apply here. Recalling Walter Lippmann's searchlight metaphor, the press's basic impulse when confronting people and groups it dubs fanatics may well be to narrow, rather than broaden, the beam of social discourse. This may well harden the public against zealous acts. In the long term, however, the failure to move beyond the issue of how to respond to zealotry and what makes individuals become zealots does little to shed light on the deeper issues that underlie zealotry.

Journalists may approach domestic zealotry as a news form unto itself, with scripts and tropes that distinguish it much as "media events" have developed a particular rhetoric (Dayan and Katz 1992). What distinguishes domestic zealotry from other sorts of domestic news is that its perpetrators merge the sensational and the explicitly ideological — two characteristics that do not normally collide in everyday reportage. As such, the phenomenon provides an interesting setting for asking questions about the link between ideology, the construction of legitimacy, and the relationships between journalists and their sources.

Our preliminary discussions with journalists and Kevorkian's associates, for example, suggest that the construction of Kevorkian's image was very much a two-way street. Kevorkian learned how to manipulate the press and pursue his agenda quite skillfully. His courtroom appearances, complete with him wearing stocks to show that he was being persecuted by a Puritanical society, were carefully calculated to capture media attention — and they did.

It may be that Jack Kevorkian got exactly the kind of attention he wanted in the media. Seeing himself as a martyr to his cause, Kevorkian's main goal was not to keep out of jail. Rather, it was to play down the idea that there are many alternatives to euthanasia. His intention was to portray himself as helping Thomas Youk choose between two stark choices — years of unbearable suffering or an easy, painless death. From that standpoint, the patterns that we found during the weeks of the broadcast may well have been the result of a complex series of long-standing interactions between Kevorkian, reporters, and editors.

Zealotry is increasingly in evidence in American political discourse. In some ways, the press justifies its attention to rash acts and crazy behavior, be it on daytime talk shows or on the evening news, by arguing that in the end the rapt attention to the actions of those pushing the edge helps all of us better understand the core issues and challenges that present themselves to us as citizens and voters. That may be, but there is nothing in the press response to Jack Kevorkian's decision to televise an incident of euthanasia that would support this view.

[An earlier version of this essay appeared in Journalism 1, no. 2 (2000). The authors would like to thank John Bracken, now a Ford Foundation fellow, for his important help on this project. The research was funded through a grant from the Robert Wood Johnson Foundation.]

Stop the Presses

Journalistic Treatment of Mental Illness

OTTO F. WAHL

Mental illness is a topic about which most laypersons know a little but few know a lot. What knowledge they have comes from a variety of sources. Some people learn about mental illnesses through high school and college courses. Some read on their own about these conditions. Others pick up brochures and handouts at health fairs or physicians' offices. Those seeking specific information often consult the Internet. Still others learn about psychiatric conditions through their own personal experiences, either as a sufferer or relative or close friend of a person with a mental illness. However, the primary source of public knowledge about mental illness, according to a 1990 Robert Wood Johnson Foundation survey, is mass media, news media in particular (DYG 1990). When asked the sources of their information about mental health, fewer than one in three of the approximately 1,300 Americans surveyed reported that they had received information from mental health professionals. About half the sample cited family, friends, and books as sources of information. Far more, 87 percent, indicated television news and programs as their source of information about mental illnesses. Newspapers were cited by 76 percent, magazines by 74 percent, and radio by 73 percent. Such results make clear that news sources make significant contributions to what people know about mental illnesses.

In addition, there have been dramatic instances where news reports not only provided information about mental illness but also led to actions and policy changes. The 1975 undercover exposé of the abysmal and abusive treatment provided to individuals with mental retardation at Willowbrook State School in New York led to official investigations, class action lawsuits, institutional changes, and new laws and regulations, as well as propelling reporter Geraldo Rivera to national prominence. The revelation of appalling conditions of neglect and abuse of psychiatric patients at Milledgeville State Hospital in Georgia by *Atlanta Constitution* reporter Jack Nelson earned him a 1960 Pulitzer Prize and contributed to substantial improvements in standards and treatment of people in psychiatric hospitals. On the less clearly positive side, press revelations that vice presidential candidate Thomas Eagleton had undergone ECT treatment for depression resulted in his resignation from the ticket, despite his distinguished record of service both before and after the 1972 election.

News coverage of mental illness can have effects in less dramatic ways, however. Overall and continuing patterns of news coverage may have accumulating effects on the impressions and resultant behaviors of the general public regarding mental illnesses. Mental health advocates, moreover, have expressed concern that some of these patterns reflect biases and misconceptions that contribute to continued misunderstanding of mental illnesses and perpetuate attitudes, behavior, and policies toward people with psychiatric disorders that make recovery more difficult. In this essay, I will explore some aspects of newspaper coverage of mental illnesses that may diminish, rather than increase, the public's understanding of people diagnosed with these disorders.

One important issue in news coverage is selectivity. No news organization can cover all the events that occur in our society and around the world. Editors, publishers, and reporters must select the events to cover and the stories to be presented to the public. If their selections are somehow skewed or unrepresentative, the public will receive an inaccurate view of the world. Evidence from a variety of sources suggests that news coverage of mental illness may be selective and misleading.

First of all, newspapers tend to select and present stories that link mental illnesses with crime and violence. In a study of 201 United Press International (UPI) stories related to mental illness appearing in 1983, for example, Russell Shain and Julie Phillips reported that 86 percent of the UPI stories dealing with former psychiatric patients focused on violent crimes committed by the ex-patients. Researchers from the Glasgow Media Group, studying tabloids in the United Kingdom, found that the commission of a violent act was the most common kind of news item involving a mental illness, leading them to conclude that "this is a media world populated by 'psychopaths,' 'maniacs,' and 'frenzied knife men'" (Philo, McLaughlin, and Henderson 1997, 50). A report from another research group in England also found violence to be the most common element in "mental health" stories, with almost half of all coverage linking mental illness with violence (G. Ward

1. Crime and violence are the most common newspaper stories involving mental illness. Headlines from the *Washington Post*, 7 and 16 July 1999; *St. Louis Post-Dispatch*, 23 September 1999; *Denver Post*, 18 February 1999; *New York Times*, 30 April 1999; and *New York Daily News*, 19 November 1999.

1997). My own laboratory recently completed an analysis of U.S. newspaper articles appearing in 1999 and found a similar, although less pronounced, trend (Wahl, Wood, and Richards 2000). We identified articles through a computer search using the keywords "mental illness." We then randomly selected fifty of these articles from each of six U.S. newspapers—the *New York Times*, the *Washington Post*, the *Los Angeles Times*, the *St. Louis Post-Dispatch*, the *Boston Globe*, and the *St. Petersburg Times*—and rated the content of the articles with respect to a variety of elements, including the major themes and messages of the articles. The most common theme of the articles was that people who have mental illnesses may be dangerous, occurring in 77 (23 percent) of the 300 articles reviewed. Apparently, the public reads or hears about mental illness most commonly within a context of crime and violence (figure 1).

Newspaper stories of mental illness and violence, furthermore, often effectively claim the attention of readers by their location and styles of presentation. Several journalists have told me that the dictum "If it bleeds, it leads" is one that indeed influences their work. This selection rule may be particularly true for stories involving both mental illness and violence. David Day and Stewart Page (1986), examining 103 articles about mental health from Canadian newspapers, found that stories about homicides committed by people who have mental illnesses were more likely to receive front-page or lead-story coverage than were other kinds of (more frequent) homicides. Pamela Kalb-fleisch (1979), examining newspaper homicide stories in the United States, found that insanity was one of the three basic ingredients for a "top story" (the other two being unpredictability and victims similar to oneself).

Day and Page also found that crimes committed by persons with mental illnesses were more likely than other crimes to be the subject of multiple stories. Our own recent analysis of 1999 newspapers revealed a similar trend. Take, for example, the 3 January 1999 slaying of Kendra Webdale, who was pushed in front of a New York City subway train by a young man who had tried unsuccessfully to get help for his long-standing mental problems. This tragic incident generated more than forty newspaper stories in the *New York Times* over the course of the year. Stories of equally heinous crimes not involving a suspect with mental illness got far less coverage. On 8 January 1999 — only five days after the subway slaying — a twenty-three-year-old woman confessed to killing a cab driver when she tried to rob him and found only a quarter in his pocket. This cold act of murder was reported in only a single story. When a Queens man fired into a crowd and killed two innocent people in retaliation for a fight a day earlier at a nightclub, it earned a single story on the back pages of the Metro section. When two men beat an East Village community activist to death, the event, again, was reported in a single story, as was the murder of a popular rap performer in Queens.

The obvious consequences of such skewed coverage are incorrect public beliefs about the association of mental illnesses with violence and exaggerated fears of those with mental disorders. Research has consistently shown that the vast majority of those with psychiatric disorders are neither violent nor criminal and that those with mental illnesses account for a small percentage of the criminal violence in the United States. Equally consistent evidence, however, shows that the general population fears people with psychiatric disorders and expects violence from them. More than half the respondents in a 1993 *Parade Magazine* survey, for example, agreed with the statement "Those with mental disorders are more likely to commit acts of violence" (Clements 1993). Similarly, in another study, 38 percent of five hundred interviewees agreed that "people with mental illnesses are more dangerous than the rest of society" (M. Fraser 1994). One of most recent studies of public attitudes toward mental illness duplicated a survey conducted in 1950 and found that the association of violence with mental illnesses has actually increased since that time (Phelan et al. 1999).

The connection between news reports of violent crimes committed by people with histories of psychiatric disorder and increased fear has also been demonstrated through experimental research. In a study completed in our laboratory (Thornton and Wahl 1996), we asked individuals to read a newspaper article concerning a psychiatric patient who killed a young girl at an outdoor fair in Connecticut. The article was introduced with a bold headline, "Girl, 9, Stabbed to Death at Fair; Mental Patient Charged," and contained the "top story" elements described by Kalbfleisch — a psychiatric patient behaving unpredictably toward an innocent victim. Following the reading of this article, research participants filled out a survey concerning attitudes toward mental illness. Compared with a comparable group who read a neutral article, those who read the target article expressed stronger beliefs that people with mental illnesses were dangerous, in need of supervision and restriction, and a source of fear and anxiety. If one article can have such an effect, it is likely that the steady stream of such stories contributes even more to continuing public fears of people with psychiatric disorders.

Fear of those with psychiatric disorders, in turn, contributes to rejection, avoidance, and discrimination. In a recent nationwide study of mental health consumers (people who have received mental illness diagnoses and/or treatment), the majority of consumer respondents reported being avoided and rejected by neighbors, coworkers, and even friends and family after they developed a mental illness (Wahl 1999). Neighbors no longer let their children play at the consumer's home. Coworkers no longer invited consumers to join them for lunch. Moreover, fear clearly was an important element in creating these situations. As one consumer observed: "If you say you are going to see a psychiatrist, people get kind of panicky. They think maybe you need to be locked up or that you're going to attack them" (46). Similarly, many consumers were denied jobs because of employer fears that they would be putting other employees at risk by hiring someone with a psychiatric treatment history. Indeed, when the Equal Employment Opportunity Commission (EEOC) published guidelines in May 1997 related to the Americans with Disabilities Act (ADA) that prohibit employment discrimination against people with mental disabilities, the *Richmond Times Dispatch* ran an editorial cartoon implying that this law would require employers to hire dangerous madmen (figure 2). The cartoon

2. A job applicant with mental illness is depicted as a potential ax murderer. From the *Richmond Times-Dispatch*, 1 May 1997.

showed three men. One is sitting at a desk with a sign saying "Supervisor." One is holding a briefcase labeled "EEOC" and explaining, "No, you may *not* ask a job applicant about a history of mental disabilities . . . that's discrimination." The third man, the apparent job applicant, is wearing a hockey mask and holding a raised ax. The newspaper followed that cartoon with a column suggesting that a reasonable accommodation for a person with schizophrenia would be "to lock all other employees in a reinforced steel cage to guarantee their safety" (MacKenzie 1997, A12). The exaggerated association of mental illness with crime and violence in the news media, then, helps ensure that people with mental illnesses, who may be especially in need of support, understanding, and opportunity, are met instead with fear, rejection, isolation, and discrimination.

Repeated stories of violent acts committed by people with mental illnesses may also result in strengthening arguments for forced treatment. In a recent national survey, investigators from the Indiana Consortium for Mental Health Services Research found that people who viewed those with mental illnesses as dangerous were more likely than others to also endorse coercive treatment — that is, to agree that persons described as having psychiatric symptoms should be forced by law to take prescription medication or be admitted to a hospital (Pescosolido et al. 1999). To the extent, then, that news coverage contributes to public views of people with mental illnesses as violence prone, it may also lead to increased public demands to use whatever means necessary to get "dangerously disturbed" people off the streets. Sometimes, in fact, the press itself calls for such action in response to events it covers. When a young woman in Manhattan was struck in the head with a brick in November 1999 and no motive could be identified for the attack, the *New York Daily News* covered its front page with the headline "Get the Violent Crazies off Our Streets." It also published a lengthy editorial urging people to "hospitalize the deranged."

When Andrew Goldstein (dubbed by the tabloids as "the subway psycho") took the life of Kendra Webdale in New York City, the extensive coverage of the murder did, in fact, lead to easing of barriers to involuntary treatment. New York State—and other states as well—responded to the flurry of news stories, editorials, and public outrage by passing what has become known as "Kendra's law." This law permits communities to require individuals with serious mental illnesses to participate in designated outpatient treatment whether or not they wish it. That Goldstein had himself wanted, sought, and been denied treatment shortly before the tragic incident did not stop frightened citizens from supporting this controversial outpatient commitment statute.

News coverage that strengthens the public's association of violence with mental illness may also mislead people about the causes and solutions for violence in our society. The high visibility of people with mental illnesses committing violent acts, along with presentation of those illnesses as the implied explanation for such criminal behavior, allows others to conclude wrongly that mainly those with psychiatric disorders commit violent acts. The public, then, may be distracted from considering—and attempting to correct—other factors that may play a far larger role in societal violence than does mental illness (e.g., poverty, availability of weapons, pervasive models of violence). The problem of violence becomes perceived as a psychiatric rather than a societal one—or, as some have suggested is even more appropriate (Osborn 1998), a public health issue—and meaningful steps beyond incarceration of people with mental disorders are not pursued. The end result is that people with mental illnesses are punished with loss of liberties, while crime remains virtually untouched.

Not only do news media focus selectively on violence with respect to mental illness, but their coverage also tends to select the most dysfunctional and disabled individuals to present—that is, those whose lives and behaviors simultaneously appear more dramatic and conform more closely to the stereotypes of classical madness that audiences are likely to recognize. It is no surprise that the composite portrait of a person with mental illness, which Day and Page extracted from the newspaper articles they examined, involved "personality characteristics implying dangerousness, unpredictability, dependency, anxiety, unsociability, unhappiness, unproductiveness, and transience" (815). Even stories alerting the public to conditions of need tend to show people with mental illnesses in a poor light — as helpless, overwhelmed by their dramatic symptoms, and relatively unresponsive to treatment. Rarely do newspaper articles show individuals with mental illnesses as attractive, likable, or competent people; rarely do they show them as having successes beyond simply coping with their illnesses or making positive contributions to their communities. In our recent examination of 1999 newspapers, we looked specifically for stories that showed people with mental illnesses in some kind of positive role. We found such stories were relatively rare (occurring in only 17 percent of the 300 articles reviewed); stories that focused exclusively on negative characteristics were more than twice as likely (38 percent).

It is important to note that the negative characteristics of people with mental illnesses dominate news stories because of story selection, not because those with mental illnesses have no accomplishments or positive traits. Many people with mental illnesses have accomplished great things — becoming effective mental health advocates, establishing computer networks, creating powerful works of art, becoming national and world leaders, and winning coveted awards (including the Academy Award, the Pulitzer Prize, and even the Nobel Prize). However, the news media seldom present the positive accomplishments of mental health consumers but tend to focus instead on dysfunction and disability. Take, for example, the series of stories published by the Vancouver (Canada) *Province* in November 1995. This paper apparently intended to alert the community to the possible harm resulting from impending reductions in mental health services. To accomplish this worthy goal, the paper elected to present the consequence of reduced services as an increase in pitiful and/or threatening mental patients wandering the community, beginning the series with front-page pictures of grim, despairing faces and the headline "Madness on Our Streets."

One person to be interviewed for this series was a man with bipolar disorder who had been working with a local mental health consumer group to develop programs that might help compensate for the reduction of funded professional services. The man brought materials on his group's activities. He was eager to show these to the reporter and to talk about his accomplishments. When asked, he did discuss his own psychiatric history and told the reporter that he had once believed he would be rescued from his troubled existence by aliens from outer space. He noted, however, that he had not had a manic episode or hospitalization in at least ten years and was proud that he was now functioning as an effective mental health advocate. After the interview, the man was asked if he would agree to be photographed for the story. He was then asked to put up the collar on his jacket and fold his arms across his chest as if huddled against a chill wind. The man, to his credit, declined to adopt this misleading pose and was instead instructed just to stand comfortably, with his head slightly raised. As he lifted his head, the photographer went to his knees and took the photo angled upward. The resulting story in the newspaper, which showed the man apparently looking to the skies, was headlined "Ruled by Outer Space" and focused on the man's symptoms of ten years ago rather than his current situation.

If people were to form judgments about those with mental illnesses from what they read in most news reports, as research suggests they do, they would likely conclude that those with psychiatric disorders are worthy of pity but not respect. Impressions that individuals with mental illnesses are not people with whom one would want to associate or work or study are reinforced. Rejection and avoidance are encouraged, along with further devaluation and continued public perception of people with mental illnesses as distinctly different "others" with whom it would be difficult to identify or empathize.

Stories of failure and helplessness also reinforce views of those with mental illnesses as incompetent and of treatment as relatively ineffective. In doing so, those stories may also undermine the community's motivation to expend limited resources on the amelioration of mental illnesses; psychiatric patients, the larger community may believe, are neither worthy of such generosity nor likely to use it well. The absence of stories of accomplishment leads the public to believe, incorrectly, that people with mental illnesses can seldom achieve meaningful accomplishments. Those negative expectations, in turn, lead to lowered goals toward those with mental illnesses. They lead public and professionals alike to be satisfied with programs that teach college graduates how to be janitors and to suggest to people leaving psychiatric hospitals that remission of symptoms and assisted living arrangements are the highest goals they can attain. About one in every three of the consumers in our national study told us that they had often or very often been treated as less competent because of their mental illness and/or told to lower their expectations in life (Wahl 1999).

Multiple perspectives, competing theories, and varied interventions characterize the mental health field. Newspaper coverage of mental illness does not always communicate this variety, however. Balanced news reporting of mental illness is sometimes compromised, for instance, by restriction of the sources from which reporters receive their information. One finding in our survey of 1999 newspaper stories was that nonmedical experts were seldom quoted in articles about mental illness. Medical experts (psychiatrists, neurologists, medical researchers) were cited in about 10 percent of the 300 articles; nonmedical experts (psychologists, social workers, university professors) were cited in only 2 percent. Moreover, this skew was even more pronounced in 1999 than in a comparable sample of 1989 papers. Inclusion of mental health experts other than physicians appears increasingly rare in newspapers, leading to almost exclusive reliance on medical authorities for information about mental illnesses and their treatments.

Such reliance on medical experts may seem, at first glance, not much of a problem. Psychiatry is the field that deals with mental illnesses, and psychiatrists would seem to be reasonable people to consult for expert information. However, other professionals also deal with mental illnesses, and they often have different perspectives on the causes of disorder and the treatments appropriate for psychiatric disorders. Ask medical doctors about mental illnesses, and they will likely stress biological bases, genetic influences, and pharmacological treatments; this is what their training and experience have stressed. Nonmedical experts may place greater emphasis on social, psychological, and environmental influences on behavior and the importance of social and community support, as well as personal therapy or counseling. When the main experts consulted are medical ones, a strongly medical/biological conception of mental illness emerges, and the public remains largely unaware of other legitimate views. Indeed, this is what we found in our analyses of newspapers. The most frequently mentioned treatment was medication, despite the fact that behavioral and other therapies have proven effective for many of the disorders mentioned. Similarly, despite growing recognition in the mental health field of the importance of community support programs to full recovery of people with serious mental disorder, such interventions were rarely mentioned in the newspaper articles we examined. Hospitalization, on the other hand, was commonly described.

Other perspectives tend to be neglected as well in most news reporting. In particular, those whose lives are most affected by mental illnesses — those who have experienced psychiatric illnesses and the ministrations of the mental health system — are the least likely to be consulted by reporters. As the executive director of the Disability Media Project has pointed out, "Reporters often talk with service providers or national organizations run by people who don't have disabilities, but seldom consult the real experts — people with disabilities and the organizations run by them" (Levine 1999, 2). These latter sources of comment have important perspectives to add to the issues of mental health care and planning, and their perspectives may differ substantially from those of professional caregivers and public officials. Those who find their sexual desires, sleep, and digestive cycles impaired by psychiatric medications, for instance, may have a different view of the problem of "noncompliance" than do practitioners or health care delivery officials. Those who have experienced abuse within the mental health system may not agree with Department of Mental Health representatives about the adequacy of available care or the need for involuntary treatment. Nevertheless, the perspectives of mental health consumers have been persistently absent from stories about mental illness.

Again, the absence of broad input may lead the public to incorrect conclusions about the state of mental health and treatment, to false impressions about the clarity and universality of policy and treatment decisions, and to continued ignorance about the capabilities of those with mental disorders. When the perspectives of mental health consumers are routinely omitted, it is easier to conclude that the value of psychotropic medications is incontrovertible and that anyone with a serious mental illness who resists taking them does so as a consequence of his or her diseased mind. When no one talks to homeless persons with mental illnesses about how and why they are on the street, it is easier for the public to conclude that mental confusion and not economic hardship is the explanation or that these people are insanely "choosing" squalor rather than avoiding "treatment" options that they may consider even more unpleasant and dehumanizing. In addition, as Suzanne Levine observed in her 1999 Internet piece "Reporting on Disability," one would not even know, from reading available newspaper stories, that there is an active disability rights movement and might well infer from the absence of reported perspectives of people with disabilities that such individuals are incapable of speaking for themselves.

Even the language used by the press to talk about mental illness may influence public perceptions and policies. References to people as their disorders (as schizophrenics, manic-depressives, borderlines, etc.) are both dehumanizing and disrespectful. Such references imply that the most important, indeed defining, characteristic of the individual is his or her disability. They discourage others from looking beyond the symptoms and disease label to the person and the common human characteristics — caring, desire, loyalty, aspiration — possessed by that individual. Advocates, then, have urged the use of "people-first language" that recognizes and communicates that sufferers of mental illness are people first, people for whom illness is only one of many aspects of their identity (Blaska 1993). Strongly recommended is use of terms such as "people with schizophrenia," "a person with panic disorder," and "an individual diagnosed with manic-depression." Our study of newspaper stories about mental illness, however, found limited and inconsistent use of people-first language and widespread reference to people as their disorders.

Even more troubling is use of slang expressions for mental illness within the context of newspaper stories. It is unlikely one would read articles referring to people with other forms of disability as "gimps" or "cripples" or "spastics." Most newspapers recognize that such references convey and encourage disrespect and have editorial policies prohibiting such references. However, it is not uncommon to find newspaper stories referring to "crazies" (as did the *New York Daily News* article mentioned previously) or "lunatics" or "maniacs" or "psychos." Often these slang terms, or any number of a vast array of other disparaging designations for psychiatric disorder, are contained in headlines, particularly in tabloid headlines, to draw reader attention to the story (Wahl 1995; Philo, McLaughlin, and Henderson 1997). By using slang such as they would not apply to other serious disabilities, the press sends a message to the public that mental illness does not deserve the same sensitivity displayed toward other problems. Once again, this may undermine public motivation to commit resources to such an "undeserving" group. Use of slang in newspaper stories also provides a model for public speech and perpetuates the public's tendency toward openly using disparaging references to mental illness. Indeed, more than 75 percent of the mental health consumers in our national survey said that they had witnessed people referring to mental illness in disparaging and offensive ways.

Press representations of mental illness such as those noted earlier also have direct effects on the attitudes, emotions, and behaviors of mental health consumers themselves. The disrespectful references to themselves that consumers encounter repeatedly in their daily papers make it difficult for them not to feel misunderstood, unappreciated, discouraged, and even angry. They increase the sense of alienation and isolation that many people with mental illnesses already experience. The predominantly negative newspaper images of mental illness also likely prevent many people with mental health problems from seeking help. Individuals will not want to identify themselves with the dangerous, unproductive, pitiable people they read about in their newspapers. They will be reluctant to undertake treatment that may mark them with a stigmatizing label (mental illness) and engender fear and rejection from others. The U.S. surgeon general has estimated that fewer than one-third of the 44 million people in the United States with diagnosable mental disorders seek mental health treatment, and he has further identified fear of stigmatization as a major factor discouraging people from seeking treatment (U.S. Department of Health and Human Services 1999, 8).

Unattractive images of mental illnesses in the news media also contribute to damaged self-esteem and internalized stigma, through which people with mental illnesses come to accept the negative images of themselves that they find displayed all around them. As one consumer in our study put it: "There's no way you can totally not internalize some of what you get from outside if it's repeatedly the same feedback" (Wahl 1999, 138). Indeed, one person was led to observe that all the negative images of mental illness she encountered "made me feel like I must be some kind of freak, that I was nothing, that I had no opportunity to ever hope that there would be any kind of way that I would come back to be somewhere you could call normal" (139).

It may be obvious by now that the issues of newspaper coverage of mental illnesses are similar to those raised with respect to representations of minorities. Social scientists have recognized that when members of minority racial and ethnic groups appear in newspapers mainly as welfare recipients, substance abusers, and perpetrators of crimes, public fears and continued discrimination are facilitated. When members of minority groups are seldom featured in stories of success and accomplishment and when their opinions are rarely deemed worthy of inclusion, it is harder for the public to value these individuals. When people who belong to these groups encounter predominantly negative images of themselves, it is hard for them to feel pride or hope for a better future. These are the same concerns that have been raised for mental illnesses. Indeed, some have suggested that treatment of those with psychiatric disorders—both journalistic and societal—may be better viewed as a civil rights, rather than a mental health, issue.

The skewed patterns of newspaper coverage of mental illness and their potential effects have certainly not gone unnoticed in the mental health community, and numerous efforts are under way to try to improve the situation. Increasingly, mental health advocacy organizations such as the National Stigma Clearinghouse have developed "stigma watch" programs to monitor and respond to media depictions of mental illness (Arnold 1994). Participants in these programs write, call, fax, and e-mail reporters and editors to express their concerns or praise about news coverage of mental health issues and urge journalists to become more knowledgeable about mental illnesses and more sensitive in the ways they present them. These efforts have succeeded in having replies printed and in gaining pledges from newspaper reporters and editors to improve their coverage of mental health matters.

More and more, mental health advocates are inviting journalists to their conferences to join in the examination of issues related to press depictions of mental illness. Reciprocal invitations for mental health professionals to discuss these issues at journalism conferences have also increased. Mental health consumer groups have established speakers bureaus of consumers willing and available to talk to the press so that their voices may be better included in news coverage of mental health issues. The *Columbia Journalism Review* has published a resource guide for journalists covering mental health issues (Voss 1998), and the Disability Media Project is developing a curriculum for journalism students. Finally, the Carter Center Mental Health Task Force, continuing its long-standing commitment to combating stigma and improving public understanding of mental illness, established the Rosalynn Carter Fellowships in Mental Health Journalism in 1996. Each year, six working journalists are selected and provided stipends to complete a proposed project related to mental health. Fellows are matched with, and mentored by, mental health experts as they complete their projects, which have included radio programs, newspaper articles, television news segments, and even a book. So successful has the program been that the work of two of the first-year fellows were nominated for Pulitzer Prizes.

Several patterns in newspaper coverage of mental illness have been identified that likely affect public understanding of mental illness. These include selective presentation of violence and dysfunction, absence of nonmedical and consumer perspectives, and use of disrespectful language in reference to mental illness. These patterns may perpetuate public fears of people with psychiatric disorders and lead to rejection, devaluation, and discrimination, as well as to damage to the self-esteem and motivation of mental health consumers exposed to them. Fortunately, there is also substantial activity within the fields of both mental health and journalism to improve news coverage of mental illness. It is hoped that these activities will be successful and that as news coverage of mental illness becomes more sensitive, accurate, and balanced, so will the knowledge and attitudes of those large numbers of people who look to the news to inform them.

2 Advertisements

The Nurse-Saver and the TV Hostess

Advertising Hospital Television, 1950–1970

JOY V. FUQUA

Drawing both from scholarly studies of television's installation in U.S. homes and from examinations of television as a form of "public amusement" in places outside the home, this essay explores various ways television has been incorporated into the institutional structure of U.S. hospitals. Far from being tangential, television has been central to the development and transformation of the U.S. hospital and the rise of health consumerism. As characters in their own right, hospitals remain one of the most common dramatic contexts for American television programming. Yet the specificity of television *in* hospitals remains virtually unexamined, even though from 1950 until the present, television was an omnipresent component of hospital life. My essay addresses this space in television history through an examination of the discourses that facilitated television's arrival and the conditions for its reception in the institutional context of the modern U.S. hospital.

This lack of scholarly focus on television in a decidedly nonhomelike setting and in a context that, for the most part, is neither pleasurable nor relaxing is understandable. Other than works by Lynn Spigel (1992), Anna McCarthy (2001), and Karen Riggs (1998), few academic examinations of television have, to date, addressed its role in places like waiting rooms, airports, bars, Laundromats, elder care facilities, prisons, churches, operating rooms, hotel rooms, schools, department stores, shopping malls, automobiles, or any of the other places where television (however defined) is watched, regarded, attended to, or viewed.

Television's development and installation in American homes parallels the expansion of many other economic institutions, including the growth of the postwar consumer health care system. According to television scholar Lynn Spigel (1992), mass media representations during the 1950s portrayed television as a threat "to the very foundations of domesticity upon which American broadcasting was built" (9). In particular, she notes how television threatened to disrupt "gender-based ideals of domestic labor" (9). However, just as television posed a threat to these foundations of domestic or home work, it also undermined "gender-based divisions" of hospital work. Undertaking a form of labor designated as women's work, the nurse's main goal is to care for the patient. With the introduction of television into the hospital, the "women in white" began, according to the following advertisements and magazine articles, nursing the TV sets as much as the patients. If, as Spigel has shown, television in the home was believed to disrupt "women's lives and the gender-based ideals of domestic labor," in the hospital television disrupted women's work by fitting too smoothly into the "gender-based ideals" of nondomestic labor (9). Not only were women, as wives and mothers in the home, expected to ensure the family's pleasurable television viewing, but they were also expected, as nurses, to facilitate the patient's television-viewing experience. Indeed, as televiewing produced more work for women in the home, it also produced more work for nurses (most of whom were women) in the hospital. Sensing administrators' potential opposition to television, manufacturers responded with a variety of attendant technologies such as elaborate remote control and automatic devices, as well as integrative nurse-call systems such as that offered by the aptly titled Nurse-Saver.

While there are and always have been male as well as female nurses, all of the images of nursing in *Modern Hospital* are of white women. As a publication widely read by a variety of hospital professionals and personnel, *Modern Hospital* provides a way of historicizing the gender- and race-specific aspects of nursing. For instance, as historical texts, the advertisements feature white female nurses administering to white female patients in, most often, private rooms. Moreover, these advertisements and their supporting feature articles show an increasing emphasis on integration and connection in relation to the capacity of hospital communication systems. Ironically enough, while at a technological level, emphasis was placed on the integrative aspect of communication technology and sophisticated patient monitoring devices, at an administrative level personnel were challenged by integration of another sort. In the wake of the 1964 Civil Rights Act, all institutions receiving federal funds were bound by law to take steps to end segregation based on race. Thus the installation of television in hospitals needs to be situated as part of larger cultural contexts that include the rise of the "semiprivate room" and the "all-private room" hospital and the decline of the Nightingale open ward system. The history of the installation of "private" patient entertainment coincides with an increase in what, on the surface, appears to be a democratization in public accommodation. Read another way, this increase in available privatization of patient accommodation can be understood as an institutional response to Title 6 of the Civil Rights Act. In other words, at the height of the popularity of *Julia*, Norman Lear's "color-blind" situation comedy that featured an African American nurse as its lead character, the nation's hospitals began to implement changes in hiring and patient care practices (Bodroghkozy 1992, 143). So while white viewers may have welcomed Diahann Carroll into their living rooms via their television sets, the extent to which those same white viewers would find it acceptable to share a semiprivate room with a total stranger, much less one who just happened to be African American, remains debatable.

Administering Television

Mapping television's installation in hospitals involves sifting through several different layers of archival materials, including advertisements, architectural plans and illustrations, and editorials in commercial or trade and professional publications such as *Modern Hospital* (published by McGraw-Hill), *Hospital Progress* (published by the Catholic Hospital Association), and *Hospitals* (published by the American Hospital Association). As pieces of historical evidence in their own right, they show how television came to be an accepted piece of equipment in U.S. hospitals. Although popular magazines offered "pictorial displays of television sets in domestic settings," advertisements in *Modern Hospital* told hospital administrators (mostly men) and other hospital workers (including nurses and dietitians, mostly women) about ways to integrate television into this institutional space (Spigel 1992, 5).

Professional or trade hospital magazines such as *Modern Hospital* from the 1950s tell a rich story about television's circulation and reception in spaces outside the home. Asked to manage their hospitals in the manner that housewives manage modern homes, hospital administrators turned to *Modern Hospital* for advice on a variety of issues and topics. Divided into generic categories based on the hospital's division of labor, each issue of the magazine highlighted a "Hospital of the Month." Presented as ideals, these "model hospitals" guided administrators and other decision-making personnel in constructing new hospitals or in renovating existing ones. These texts told managers and administrators how to incorporate television into patient rooms and other hospital areas. Replete with architectural plans for hospital renovation, sample recipes for hospital kitchens, and advice about matters such as noise reduction for clamorous hallways, *Modern Hospital* served as a professional version of popular home design magazines. Its status as a limited-circulation professional or trade magazine distinguished it from mass-circulation magazines such as *Ladies' Home Journal* or *American Home*. *Modern Hospital* framed its representation of the institution through the lens of domesticity (with explicitly gendered labor categories). In a way, it professionalized consumerism. The magazine's advertisements and feature articles address a market, however, defined by institutional, rather than individual, buying power.

Modern Hospital, *Hospital Management*, and *Hospital Progress* provided companion discourses about health care and television to those found in popular consumer magazines. The conversation about the possibilities of television in the modern hospital was informed by wider cultural assumptions about television's purpose in the home. Considering that the same manufacturers, Sylvania, Zenith, and RCA, for example, made sets for both industrial and home use, television was defined in apparently contradictory ways as both a complicated piece of modern machinery necessary for the smooth functioning of the hospital and, for patients, a familiar and even healing presence. According to manufacturers, the level of familiarity or complexity of the device was tied to, among other things, purpose and place. Indeed, an entire parallel industrial network of television-watching equipment emerged to construct and then meet the specificities and requirements of a variety of in-hospital audiences (including patients, medical staff, and students).

There were several ways for hospitals to collect televiewing fees. In the pre-cable era, patients rented sets by the day. The sets were usually wheeled into patient rooms or were suspended from ceilings or walls. However, just because a patient had the money to pay for this service was no reason to assume that he or she could actually watch television. Frequently, television reception quality was poor. Elaborate antenna systems were installed to address such problems. Also, television manufacturers advertised unique reception features for institutional viewing. Only with the advent of cablecasting could "quality" transmission be guaranteed. One institutional television provider, the Telerent Leasing Corporation, founded in 1957, continues to provide industrially designed televisions, carts, wall-mounting brackets, and many different personal remote control and listening devices for many different types of health care facilities. Now called TeleHealth Services, the company remains the largest provider of health care television products in the United States.

More than merely selling a product, however, television advertisements in medical trade journals offered idealized visions of the modern hospital brimming with the latest and greatest health technologies. However, ideas about the ideal patient went hand in hand with images of the powerful modern hospital. To the exclusion of other types of patients in other hospital settings, advertisements for hospital television represented white female patients in private rooms. The images portrayed female patients reclining in beds surrounded by flowers and color-coordinated furniture ensembles. Clad in beautiful lingerie, the female patients are shown enjoying the convenience of modern remote control devices and uninterrupted televiewing. This mise-en-scène suggests that thanks to television, hospitalization is and should be a pleasurable experience for female patients. Moreover, images from 1950 through the 1960s represented television as a luxurious novelty or as a way to pamper patients who could pay for the pleasure of watching. These images were inflected with class, race, and the socioeconomic positions and expectations of their ideal audiences.

These images of female patients enjoying their televiewing experiences stand in stark contrast to the domestic scenes analyzed by Spigel in *Make Room for TV* (1992). Whereas advertisements in popular-press periodicals rarely — if ever — showed women at rest or engaging in "guilt-free" home televiewing, these advertisements for hospital television represent women as doing nothing other than watching TV. With little else, apparently, to distract them, female patients in the hospital are allowed to watch television in uninterrupted pleasure. In a time when hospitals were competing with each other for patients who could pay, these luxurious amenities helped to increase admissions at hospitals that could promise such visions of health and hotel-like pampering. Moreover, the advertisements avoid all indications of displeasure, illness, or pain. The female patients are shown free of any outward indication of illness — visions of beauty and wellness.

However, while it may have been good, according to the advertisements, to distract female patients from their pain by watching television, it may not have been such a great thing for nurses. As human remote controls, nurses adjusted television sets as frequently as they tended to patients. Television was initially a disruptive force for women's work in the hospital as well as in the home. The advertisements suggest as much through direct references to nurses' labor and television set reliability. Manufacturers and television rental and lease companies responded to this situation by guaranteeing the reliability of the sets and the automatic control of patients over their own televiewing experience.

The advertisements throughout the 1950s and 1960s show an increasingly context-specific sense of the requirements of televiewing, as television manufacturers, starting in the late 1950s, responded to a series of practical concerns regarding the use of their products in the hospital. Making certain assumptions about how televiewing in hospitals was different from televiewing at home, manufacturers offered a series of guidelines directed to hospital administrators, not only outlining how patients should watch television but also identifying the ideal hospital televiewer. With their unwieldy remote control and nurse-call electronic devices, patients had to be taught how to watch television away from home. The industry responded to hospital standards and official procedures by designing televisions specifically for in-hospital use. In the advertisements for these sets, manufacturers promised these professional consumers an ease of cleaning and sanitization, along with increasingly privatized listening and viewing systems. With names like the Roommate (RCA) and the Bedside 19 (Magnavox), manufacturers tried to convey a sense of intimacy, compatibility, and privacy. Most importantly, by installing these televisions, the modern mega-hospital could, according to manufacturers, make these spaces a little more like home.

Manufacturers also emphasized the extent to which their sets could easily be integrated into the daily requirements of patient care. Nurses' labor was addressed at the level of communication technology with the development and marketing of, among other devices, the Nurse-Saver by the Standard Electric Time Company of Springfield, Massachusetts (1960). Nurses were in charge of administering and managing television along with other technical medical equipment. The introduction of television into hospitals coincided with a more general increase in the level of technical devices that nurses were responsible for controlling. *Modern Hospital* and other trade and professional magazines provided officially sanctioned forums for debates regarding such labor issues.

Both television manufacturers and hospital administrators assumed that in addition to monitoring the patient, the nurse would take care of the television. Nurses, in this context, became unremunerated television repairpersons summoned to a patient's bedside not to perform a

1. Body parts or color contrast. What's a nurse to do, attend to the patient or the TV?

lifesaving intervention but to correct the vertical or horizontal hold (figure 1). As the 1968 Philco advertisement makes clear, nurses were responsible for attending to their patients' bodies as well as their television sets. The female patient may have lost her appendix, but the more urgent situation involves the loss of her color contrast. Philco responds to administrators' fears about nurses' labor by saying, "A temperamental color TV can take up a lot of valuable nursing time. And, naturally enough, many hospital administrators have written off color TV as a headache they can do without." Philco, however, offers a nontemperamental television — one that "soothes away many of the aches of offering color TV" to patients. Moreover, the advertisement constructs the women as the ideal consumer/viewer. Philco promises to send a "small ladies' make-up kit" with the receipt of the attached coupon. The free makeup kit is supposed to demonstrate how, "apart from Philco color TV, it's the only way we know to get the flesh tones right."

In addition to "self-adjusting" sets, manufacturers also marketed gadgets such as corded and wireless remote controls, integrated nurse-call communication systems, privatized television and radio image/sound controls. Patient care included taking care of the patient's television. Before television could become fully operational in hospitals, manufacturers had to sell the idea to administrators. This professional audience had to be convinced that television would be cost-effective.

Moreover, television had to be integrated into the smooth operation of hospitals. Taking its place alongside monitoring systems, IV stands, chairs, and beds, television had to be unobtrusive. On the one hand, television was understood from an administrative perspective as a costly enterprise, so installation had to generate revenue for the hospital. On the other, television had to be offered to patients in such a way that it did not interrupt the work of nurses, physicians, and staff. Television manufacturers had to ensure that the patient could see and hear the television while it remained out of everyone else's way. Television's entrance into the hospital was, under these circumstances, a highly conditional one: specific requirements regarding design and reception had to be met before television could be admitted into private and semiprivate patients' rooms. While postwar middle-class consumers were busy installing their sets in suburban ranch houses and other home sites, television was becoming an ordinary part of the modern hospital. Indeed, as a means of declaring its status as a public monument to all that was technologically cutting-edge, and of injecting elements of comfort and familiarity into an increasingly intimidating and incomprehensible medical context, television was the perfect prescription for modern hospitals. Since television began to be used for patient entertainment, it has been an important feature in what architecture historians Stephen Verderber and David J. Fine (2000) have called the deinstitutionalization of the general hospital. Whether as houses of tomorrow or hospitals of the future, television's presence signaled the extent to which they were to be understood as, respectively, "machines for living in" and "machines for healing" (20).

In terms of aiding both the fiscal state of hospitals and the physical condition of patients, television manufacturers encouraged hospital administrators to make television more than a mere amenity. Advertisers gave administrators various ways to use television in hospitals. Through promotional examples, manufacturers explained how television, through closed-circuit educational programs, patient surveillance, and patient entertainment, could indeed go hand in hand with the self-described mission of the modern megahospital. Hospital administrators, in turn, responded to advertisers' suggestions and patients' demands for incorporating television into the overall mission of mid-century hospitals. Part of that mission included the construction of carefully crafted and managed public images that, as hospital historian Rosemary Stevens (1999) has noted, represented modern hospitals as "having something valuable to sell: surgery, glamour, expertise, healthy babies" (10). In a competitive medical marketplace, hospitals used television, at least initially, to attract middle-class and other patients who had the ability to pay for private rooms and medical procedures.

Stretching Nurses, Hostessing TV

Two decades before they could watch *Captain Video* or *The Goldbergs* in their private or semiprivate hospital rooms, patients and convalescents were entertained by traveling performers, books and magazines, radio, and motion pictures. Yet television, more than any other medium, posed unique problems for hospital routines. In terms of both noise and nurses' labor, television threatened to disrupt patient care and women's work. Just as some cultural critics saw television as distracting housewives from their daily work, so some hospital administrators feared that television in patients' rooms would disrupt nurses' labor. Female nurses or other women workers are never represented as the consumers of the entertainment technologies; they are represented as the ones who administer technologies, and some medical treatments and procedures, to the patients. Nurses may be affected by the presence of the technologies, control them and monitor them, but the women workers are never positioned as ideal users. Yet their presence is acknowledged at the level of product design and in the written text of the advertisements for equipment such as the 1953 Vokalcall audiovisual nurses' call system by Auth Electric Co., Inc. Thanks to the "new Vokalcall," "one nurse can do the work of two." Later advertisements emphasized the integration of the nurse-call button with remote controls for radio and television. However, as Ruth Schwartz Cowan (1983) and Susan Strasser (1982) show in their studies of the relationship between domestic appliances and women's labor in the home, technological innovation does not necessarily produce actual "labor-saving" devices. Instead, through "time-saving" devices such as electric washing machines and, in the case of nursing, electric patient beds, technology makes it possible for women to do more in the same amount of time. Hence, this would account for the advertisements' emphasis on the so-called labor-saving aspects of hospital television and nurse-call patient communication systems.

Articles and editorials discuss the installation of television in patient rooms as early as 1950, but the first official marketing of "hospital TV" began during the mid-1950s. By 1960, each issue of *Modern Hospital* contained at least one advertisement for specific television models or rental and leasing services. Typical of the advertisements for closed-circuit television systems is one from General Precision Laboratory Incorporated for patient surveillance purposes. Designed specifically for hospital patient surveillance, the "GPL *ii*-TV" seeks to persuade administrators that it is the ideal system because "by just flicking a switch, a nurse can keep an eye on all patients — in private rooms and in wards." As a "revolutionary, visual communications tool," the television monitoring system acts as an extension of the nurse's vision. When it comes to patient surveillance, the nurse is the ideal user or viewer; watching the patients on television is part of her job. Although the advertisements feature female patients and nurses, the subject of address is usually a hospital manager or administrator (assumed to be male). Even in the case of closed-circuit surveillance television, women are consistently featured as the ideal viewers and users of the technology. The advertisements for hospital television emphasize the extent to which patients may vicariously "visit" their family and friends by watching the same programs in different places, face-to-face communication mediated through the television and telephone systems.

One such use of closed-circuit television in hospitals involved the construction of a specially designed "father's room" at Southwest Texas Methodist Hospital in 1964. As a result of the medical staff's policy that "fathers should be kept out of the maternity suite," the hospital installed two television monitors, "one for watching the routine television programs and the other on a closed-circuit whose camera is trained on the newborn baby" (Letourneau and Hamrick 1964, 52). This example illustrates the ways that, as Anna McCarthy (2001) has argued, "the audiovisual and material forms of TV blend with the social conventions and power structures of its locale" (2). Indeed, this particular viewing locale was given shape through the space of the "father's room" and by the function of the specificities of the closed-circuit system. This example shows how both broadcast and closed-circuit television worked hand in hand in some institutional contexts. Although the father is denied vision of the actual birth, he sees the baby "on the monitor immediately after birth" (Letourneau and Hamrick 1964, 52). The hospital staff explained that this separation was designed to "reduce some of the hazards of bringing people into the maternity suite who might be suffering from some infection that could be transmitted to mother and baby" (53). At the same hospital, children are likewise prevented from visiting patients. So the closed-circuit system is used to simulate face-to-face communication. Described as being "almost like visiting in person," this television system allowed patients to see their children in a sanitized and hygienic setting (Bickford 1956, 51). For instance, in 1956, at Morristown Memorial Hospital in Morristown, New Jersey, Visit Vision made it possible for underage children to visit patients through a closed-circuit television system (Bickford 1956; Drumheller 1959).

A similar article from a 1958 issue of the American Medical Association's consumer magazine, *Today's Health*, promotes the "tele-visit" by emphasizing how the "push-button age" has "hit hospitals" (Earle 1958, 10). Through the "first completely integrated system to apply, by mechanical means, the 'self-help' concept of patient care," this closed-circuit system cuts hospital costs by reducing nursing labor and increasing patient autonomy (11). The writer lists eleven different things that the patient (a woman) can do without having to call a nurse. Some of these things include selecting television or radio programs, controlling volume and adjusting tuning, regulating heating and air-conditioning systems, raising or lowering the height of the bed, opening or closing windows and draperies, and operating a closed-circuit television system to visit with people who are not permitted in the patient's room. The writer closes by endorsing these new technological developments because they "lighten the nurse's burdens" and, not tangentially, reduce what "hospital authorities call 'hotel-type' services" (11). As in the case of radio, advertisements for hospital television represent female nurses as the ideal attendants and female patients as the ideal viewers. Through photographs and advertisement illustrations, nurses are shown adjusting television sets just as often as they are depicted administering to their patients.

DeLores J. Schemmel, R.N., (1953) described the passing of the "days when just one level of nurses with one type of preparation could perform all of the nursing functions for our patients" (59). She compares nurses' labor to assembly line labor:

> We could then use the assembly line technique for service something like the "wash-a-teria," sometimes called the "minute wash" — where the first man directs the car line; the second vacuums the seat and floor of the machine; the third soaps the chrome; the fourth washes the car body; the fifth dries the machine, while the last man does the polishing. Unfortunately, giving good nursing care isn't that simple because our product is a specialized personal service to people and not inanimate things. (61)

Indeed, while it is the nurses' duty to care for the patient, to what extent is it part of the job description to attend to machines? In this context, television becomes yet another machine that prevents, rather than facilitates, patient care.

Advertisements that focus on nurses' labor represent the "automatic" and "instant" aspects of time- and space-merging technologies. The 1963 advertisement for General Electric's nineteen-inch Designer TV (specially adapted for hospitals) is typical of the hospital-as-vacation and female viewer as oblivious to her domestic duties. In this cartoon-style advertisement, a man sits at a woman's bedside as she stares past him at the television set. The caption reads, "Gee, honey, I know our set at home doesn't have 'daylight blue,' but the baby's three weeks old already." Daylight blue refers to the "glare-free" screen (figure 2). The ad suggests that the female patient is enjoying her television experience so much that she does not want to leave the hospital. Oblivious to everyone and everything — even that she has a new baby to look after — she wants to stay put and watch TV. It suggests that television, even in the hospital, distracts female patients from their domestic responsibilities. The pernicious aspects of this advertisement are increased through the implication that she would rather be in the hospital than home caring for husband and child.

EvenView Corporation, makers of hospital communications, depicts the passive female patient lying in bed smiling up at a male visitor (figure 3). The text reads: ". . . and *after* visiting hours what will she do?" With the male visitor not by her side, what will the woman do with all that time on her hands? Watch television, of course. While EvenView acknowledges that television "is no substitute for loved ones, it does bring cheer and relaxation" to those bored female patients. As an additional bonus, television reduces "nurse attention." Thus, television helps the nursing staff to manage time and to be more efficient workers, according to these advertisements.

Wells Television, Inc., was one of the leading hospital television installation and rental companies (figure 4). This advertisement is typical in the way that it promises to put the viewer where the action is, to unite the patient with the exterior world. In "Meanwhile, back at home," the advertisement draws a direct parallel between the home and the hospital. The upper image shows a photograph of a man and two children watching a baseball game on television while the lower illustration depicts a female patient lying in bed — remote in hand — watching the same program. The written text claims that watching television "produces a sense of security" for the patient. Televiewing facilitates a "telepathic togetherness with the world he knows" and a feeling of familiarity, literally, a feeling of familial-ness. The "telepathic togetherness" is produced through televiewing.

A 1960 Wells Television advertisement continues to emphasize the

2. The lure of the visual. Distracting female patients from their domestic and maternal duties.

continuity between inside and outside. "Take them out to the Ball Game!" depicts a baseball player throwing a ball through the television screen. Such "realistic" qualities are attributed to televiewing by the inclusion of the corded remote control attached to the television. This advertisement directly addresses hospital administrators with "Give your patients a world of entertainment." It suggests that television allows lonely patients to "pass their hospital hours in happy content-ment, with their constant companion, the TV set." Although friends' and families' visiting hours are restricted, the television is always there. However, while the advertisement emphasizes television's ability to connect the patient to the outside world, he, ironically enough, "lives in a cheerful world of his own." The advertisement assumes that tele-viewing transports the viewer to another place, that the viewer be-comes completely "preoccupied with TV" and that this all-consuming kind of attention "results in fewer demands for services." In short, televiewing as preoccupation or distraction is a good thing, from an administrative point of view. From a patient's perspective, the implica-tions are less than positive. While televiewing patients may indeed make fewer needless calls to the nurses' station, the implication is that patients call nurses out of sheer boredom rather than actual need. Some patients may indeed be bored, and some patients may call nurses out of boredom. However, what is significant about the advertisement

The Nurse-Saver and the TV Hostess　85

3. The next best thing to "him." TV as constant companion for lonely female patients.

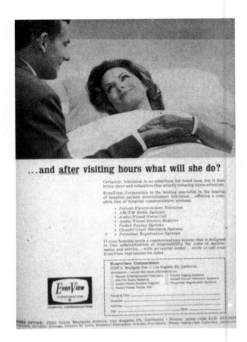

4. "Telepathic togetherness." A sense of security while the female patient is away from home.

is the way that the leasing service makes television seem like an attractive possibility from an administrative perspective. The advertisement reminds administrators that "pampering patients produces hospital income!" The implication is that televiewing patients require less work. Television, in this sense, helps the hospital manage not only their bottom lines but their patients as well.

Advertisements for hospital communication and patient entertainment systems explicitly acknowledge nurses' labor, using terms such as "automatically," "automatic," "efficiency," and "instant." From Du-Kane Corporation's Nurse-Call Equipment that enables "Nurse Jones" to "visit 12 critical patients every two minutes . . . *automatically*" to advertisements for items such as their "Pocket Paging Receiver" that emphasizes "how 4 ounces of extra efficiency could save a life," technology saves not only time, according to these texts, but labor. This labor-saving aspect of integrated communication systems is visually represented through the image of a female hand holding or pointing to a "push-button" remote control device. The woman's hand, replete with painted fingernails, displays the size and manageability of the device. As in the 1967 advertisement for the RCA Victor Remote Control Color TV, all it takes is a simple touch of the finger either to summon a nurse — instantaneously — to the patient's bedside or listen to the radio. More specifically, the "nurse" button is situated in such a way as to make it, effectively, another channel to choose from. The advertisement stresses, through the repetition of the word "instant," that at the simple touch of a button, a patient "receives an instant answer from the duty staff." The nurse becomes just another form of entertainment. This proximity between the nurse-call button and other controls for television and radio suggests that the nurses' response should be quick and immediate — just change the channel! The advertisements may stress the extent to which these new technologies decrease "needless calls" to nurses; however, they also emphasize how these devices actually increase certain expectations about what constitutes effective and efficient women's work.[1]

This emphasis on saving or even stretching nurses' labor is no more powerfully represented than in a 1966 advertisement for Standard Register's new Source Record Punch Machine (figure 5). The advertisement offers an illustration of a medieval limb stretcher, or rack, with the description "The nurse-stretching machine. (We've brought it up to date.)" The photograph below the illustration features a nurse in uniform operating the new "nurse-stretcher." The new machine claims that it "stretches nurses." In other words, if the administrator installs Source Record Punches at nursing stations, "nurses can spend more time nursing patients, not paperwork" or other machines.

However, this potential of the medium to distract the nurse was not lost on television manufacturers, who quickly incorporated this tension into various advertisements. Sylvania even went as far as to create the Sylvania Television Hostess so that those busy nurses would not be bothered by "nuisance calls" from frustrated televiewing patients. However, before the advent of the Sylvania Television Hostess in 1966, the administration of a patient's television experience was in the hands of the nurses. The Sylvania TV Hostess was one part of a more extensive hospital campaign for a "total television system" that "communicates, observes, teaches, trains, protects and does everything else in sight" orchestrated by the Commercial Electronics Division of Sylvania/GT&E (figure 6).

The Sylvania TV Hostess professionalizes the care of the patient's television and takes the "responsibility of operating a patient-TV service off the staff's shoulders." Dressed in an official uniform, the Sylvania TV Hostess can be seen as an acknowledgment of television's potential to disrupt nurses' routines. In one of the few advertisements to feature a male patient, this 1968 depiction of the TV Hostess explicitly genders the labor of television care. While it is the task of nurses and hospital administrators to take care of the patient, it is the job of the Sylvania TV Hostess to take care of "their TV." In the hospital, "seven days a week," the Sylvania TV Hostess controls all the patient's televiewing needs. From set activation, to remote control explanation, to fee collection, the Hostess is "trained in hospital etiquette" and will "make sure everything goes smoothly." Thanks to the Hostess, nurses are no longer compelled to make needless trips up and down long corridors simply to adjust the vertical hold. By 1972, the Sylvania TV Hostess had changed her name to the TV Attendant, no doubt as a response to the changing social and cultural context that surrounded hospitals brought about by, among other things, second-wave feminism.

With the beginning of the 1970s, advertisements in *Modern Hospital* represent nurses within towering "mission control" floor stations, presiding over huge computer and communication systems. One promotional advertisement for the pharmaceutical corporation A-H Robbins offers a salute to "today's hospital nurse." As a white woman, with short hair and glasses, reads a printout from a computer, the text describes how "the old image of the nurse as a handmaiden and drudge

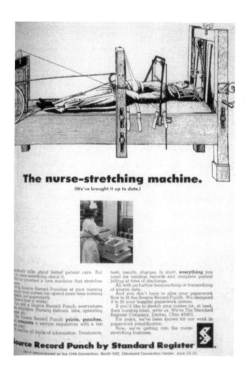

5. The modern rack. Nurses' bodies and their labor get "stretched" through modern communication and data collection devices.

6. The Sylvania TV Hostess. Letting nurses attend to patients, not televisions.

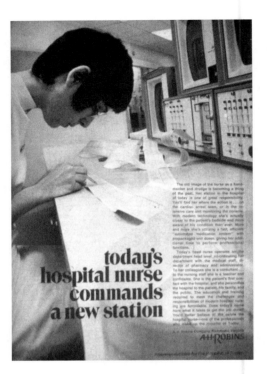

7. No longer "handmaidens" or "drudges." Today's nurses in command of their patients through modern technology.

is becoming a thing of the past. Her station in the hospital of today is one of great responsibility. You'll find her where the action is . . ." (figure 7). Incorporating the language and iconography of the women's liberation movement, the advertisement claims that through the use of "modern technology," the nurse is "actually closer to the patient's bedside and more aware of his condition" than ever. Technology, in this context, has the potential to erase the time and space that separates nurse from patient.

While television manufacturers and communication specialists promised to save the labor of nurses and increase the efficiency of patient care through elaborate and technologically sophisticated systems, the implementation of such devices frequently produced more work for already overworked staff. Employed by hospitals to "assist in the introduction of methods that facilitate service," new "efficiency experts" began to radically alter what most nurses considered their accepted roles. In 1965, one year before the nation's nurses participated in a massive labor strike, Eleanor C. Lambertsen, R.N., Ed.D., declared that these new technical systems were driving nurses away from patients' bedsides. Trained to "nurse people, not machines," Lambertsen emphasized the extent to which the "technical revolution" in U.S. hospitals "has added a new complication to the understanding of what the appropriate responsibilities of the registered nurse should be" (144). Lambertsen's concern is that whereas the "industrial revolution in hospitals has created a demand for technicians capable of supervising and generally caring for the increasing variety of technical devices," why should nurses be "singled out as the responsible person in these new areas?" Lambertsen's point is not that these newfangled devices are being used and that nurses are being asked to learn how to use them but that "new voices" seem to be redefining the entire concept of nursing and nurses' labor. She admonishes her readers not to "fall back on the old, old answer that has been with us since the dark ages of medicine: Let the nurse do it!" What Lambertsen is arguing for, in many ways, is indeed recognized by Sylvania through the introduction of the Television Hostess. However, Lambertsen's anxiety regarding the appropriate object of nurses' labor is underscored by a certain nostalgia for an unmediated encounter between nurse and patient, an encounter unmediated by machines. Lambertsen's fear is that nursing education is far too narrow and dependent on "some intricate system of machinery." She explains that the "benefits of automation" must be kept in "appropriate balance with the skills of professional workers."

In this labor environment, it is easy to see how Sylvania's Television Hostess seemed to respond to Lambertsen's criticisms of modern hospitals and nurses' labor. However, as patients literally become television through a wide variety of imaging and monitoring systems, the distinction between patient and machine is historical rather than actual. The problems that Lambertsen identified in 1965 have not disappeared because of new advances in technology. Television may or may not be part of the problem for today's nurses, but its initial entrance into hospitals foregrounded issues of patient care, labor, and technological innovation. In fact, a recent tour of a New Orleans hospital indicates that television is no longer understood as tangential to patient care. Like the in-flight television airplane programs that demonstrate passenger safety features, television in hospitals is understood as a necessary component of any patient-hospital experience. Today's hospital patients can choose television programs that detail a given hospital's institutional history or describe various surgical procedures. In the effort to save time and costs, hospitals rely on television and specially designed institutional programming not only to comfort but to care for their patients.

1   The problem of television as a potentially disruptive force for nurses' labor is explicitly addressed in the 1959 CBS dramatic anthology series *Playhouse 90* production "Diary of a Nurse."

Exorcising

"Men in White" on Television

An Exercise in Cultural Power

KELLY A. COLE

On 1 March 1952, the Television Board of the National Association of Radio and Television Broadcasters implemented the first version of the Television Code, which included among its many programming and advertising directives a provision titled "Dramatized Appeals and Advertising." Crafted in conjunction with representatives of the American Medical Association (AMA), it stated in part: "When dramatized advertising material involves statements by doctors, dentists, nurses or other professional people, the material should be presented by members of such profession reciting actual experience or it should be made apparent from the presentation itself that the portrayal is dramatized."

In 1957, under intense pressure from the AMA and government regulators, the board amended this clause, commonly referred to as the "men-in-white" ban, to state: "Advertising involving physicians, dentists or nurses must be presented by accredited members of such professions" or accompanied by the written words "A Dramatization" for at least ten seconds. A little over a year later, the ban was tightened to prohibit any portrayals of doctors by actors, any medical props or settings, and any reference to undocumented scientific research. The ban was publicly lauded as an example of broadcasters cooperating with the advertising industry and the organized medical community to further the public interest without government intervention. However, the events that precipitated the ban and the spirit in which it was enacted were anything but cooperative.

While a great deal of attention has been devoted to TV in the 1950s and 1960s, especially topics such as the quiz show scandals, the often antagonistic relationship between advertisers and broadcasters, and even the popularity of medical dramas, that these topics were ever linked has received little notice. For a brief moment in the late 1950s, however, all three groups — the television industry, the advertising profession, and the medical community — found themselves in danger of losing the cultural power they had accumulated in the first half of the twentieth century. Each in its own way was experiencing some sort of public relations crisis. At the juncture of these crises appeared the men-in-white ban, which reflects not only a convergence of three influential powers but a nexus in which each struggled for control over the American consumer of the 1950s and 1960s.

The image of the men in white served as a symbol in relation to which these three groups could elevate themselves; by banning white coats from commercials, broadcasters and the AMA vanquished what was dangerous and illegitimate. In turn they, along with the advertisers who complied with their rules, became trustworthy and valid. Spanning the years that the ban was debated and amended, the ever-present concept of the public interest acted as a shield for competing professional organizations to pursue their own ends. The debate over images of doctors in ads came to a head in 1957; however, this convergence of three different interests can only be understood by tracing the roots of their development and showing where they intertwine.

Advertising Legislation and the Medicine Man

Over the course of the men-in-white debates in the press and trade publications, commentators frequently referred to "patent medicine men," symbolically loaded cultural figures who date back to the colonial era in the United States. Technically a misnomer, as their salesmen rarely held patents, the term "patent medicine" came to refer to the universe of nostrums and elixirs that fell under the more accurate heading of proprietary drugs. So-called quacks who practiced on the margins of legitimate medicine marketed the drugs, often fraudulent, sometimes outright dangerous, directly to the public. By invoking this practice of quackery in relation to television advertising, critics deliberately tapped into patent medicine's long and checkered history.

An ongoing source of antagonism for the organized medical community, the snake oil salesman also taints the history of advertising and, by extension, television, the modern-day marketplace. One might say the medicine man is the undesirable cousin in everyone's family tree. In the late nineteenth century, he contributed to what Jackson Lears (1994) calls a "carnivalesque commercial vernacular" in the American consumer landscape (142). This notion of the carnivalesque is useful for understanding the patent medicine men both literally, as they often drew on theatrical practices in presenting their wares, and theoretically. The carnival can be read historically as a place that undermines authority and inverts traditional distinctions between high and low culture. At these carnivalesque moments, the interdependence of the high and low—each needed to define and structure the other—becomes most apparent (Stallybrass and White 1986, 26). The argument that high discourse is often structured in relation to low discourse can aptly be applied to the medical profession, which depends on the identification and exclusion of quacks or untrained practitioners as dangerous.

The establishment of a professional organization, be it the AMA or the American Association of Advertising Agencies, seems to activate "the symbolic extremities of the exalted and the base," and, as the argument goes, in certain historical contexts "each extremity structures the other" and even depends on the other for its very meaning (Stallybrass and White 1986, 3). Thus the patent medicine men, as descendants of the snake oil salesmen, were the "other"—they played the "low" culture to the AMA doctors' "high" culture. As a rebellious other, the patent medicine men's constant inversions of the hierarchy, their defiance of prohibitions, and the challenge they presented to the "prevailing truth" of the medical profession made them dangerous, but also useful; they served as a dramatic foil for the heroism of the AMA.

The utterance of the words "patent medicine man" also conjures up a history of legislative struggle in the realm of drug and (later) broadcast regulation. The Pure Food and Drugs Act of 1906 represents, among other things, one of the first attempts by Congress to rid American society of medical quackery. Signed into law by Theodore Roosevelt, it regulated the labels of patent medicines. According to historian James Harvey Young (1992), "the law did not strike a blow against self-medication, but sought to make it safer. It was based on a favorite Progressive assumption . . . that the average man was intelligent enough to plot his own course and would avoid risks if he was aware of them" (37). Significantly, the prevailing attitudes toward the average person's ability to medicate himself or herself would show a marked shift by the 1950s, when self-medication replaced outright dangerous medicine as the primary danger posed by the medicine men.

With the development and popularization of radio in the 1930s came an onslaught of advertising previously unimaginable to legislators; in the words of one historian, drug promotion was "exploding on radio throughout the land" (Barnouw 1978, 26). The new commercial medium presented a novel and in many ways ideal venue for promoting medical products and procedures. The direct address of radio, the addition of a persuasive voice being brought into the consumer's home to convey advertising text, made radio seem both more intimate and more effective than print advertising. From the point of view of the AMA, the newfound ability of medicine men to gain access to audiences through extended broadcasts was a threat, both to the public's health and to the AMA's reputation as health experts. The most successful of these radio salesmen — or the most egregious violators of the public trust, depending on who is writing the history — were actually forced off the air. Intense lobbying by the AMA prompted the Federal Radio Commission (the forerunner to the Federal Communications Commission) to revoke the broadcast licenses of these salesmen. Not easily deterred, they resurfaced across the Mexican border to resume their "medical practices" and pose further regulatory dilemmas. Colorful figures such as Dr. John R. Brinkley, famous for his goat gland operations, Hal and Carr Collins of "Crazy Water Crystals" fame, and Norman Baker, who (as legend had it) referred to the AMA as the "Amateur Meatcutters Association," were men who plagued the AMA and carried the tradition of the snake oil salesman well into the twentieth century (Fowler and Crawford 1987, 56).

In this convergence of advertising and technology, the struggle for control was not only a battle for the right to sell medicine to the public; it was also a struggle over who would police the airwaves. The proliferation of medical advertising on the radio ultimately helped precipitate a revision of the Food and Drug Act. The Wheeler-Lea Act and the Food, Drug, and Cosmetic Act were both passed in 1938 for ostensibly the same purpose. However, one was intended to strengthen the Federal Trade Commission's (FTC) policing powers over advertising, while the other gave power to the Food and Drug Administration (FDA) to regulate labeling; this resulted in an ongoing battle between the FDA and the FTC for control of advertising that lasted into the mid-1950s. A large part of the problem stemmed from the fact that, as Young (1992) points out, "The two 1938 laws posed different standards for labeling and advertising. . . . Whereas the FDA could attack labeling 'false or misleading in any particular,' the FTC could only combat advertising 'misleading in a material respect.' Thus a broad, gray border zone continued in which exaggerated advertising assertions retained legality" (301). Far from coordinating their efforts, the two regulatory bodies often worked at cross-purposes.

A decade and a half later, the problem of regulating advertising would erupt again over a new medium, television. This time, it was couched in terms not of harmful medicine but of deceptive claims; the public needed to be protected, not from quacks but from themselves and their gullibility. Corresponding to the new visual component that television introduced into the debate, the terrain of struggle shifted from words to images. In an effort to avoid government intervention, however, the concerned parties endeavored to deal with it on their own.

The AMA: Organized Medicine

The American Medical Association was formed in 1846 at a convention in New York City. Its nominal raison d'être was to supply the ever-growing population of medical practitioners with a sense of community and conformity. In addition to ensuring certain standards throughout the profession, the AMA served as an effective public relations machine. Initially the organization's ranks were small, but toward the turn of the century, as medicine became more reputable and closely linked to scientific advances, individual physicians began to see the advantages in organizing their profession. "Between 1900 and 1910, AMA membership grew from 8,400 to 70,000; by 1920, 60% of the country's physicians were members" (Malmsheimer 1988, 26). Much of this organizational zeal was brought about in opposition to patent medicines and a desire to legitimize, once and for all, a profession that had been rife with con men and quacks. Paul Starr (1982) discusses the relationship between the patent medicine business and the AMA as adversarial from the start, describing the relationship in almost carnivalesque terms: "The nostrum makers were the nemesis of the physicians. They mimicked, distorted, derided and undercut the authority of the profession" (127). But the medicine men did serve the purpose of offering a model against which "legitimate" doctors could define themselves.

By the 1950s, organized medicine had accumulated a great deal of power; having consolidated local medical organizations and established themselves as experts, the AMA held sway over federal and state legislators and helped shape the growth of medicine in the United States. However, this rise in status was not without its drawbacks. In the 1950s, doctors began to develop a reputation as distant and superior, which contributed to a general public criticism of the medical community. This problem was accentuated by the contrast between the idea of personalized care and the growing demands of an expanding health care system, inherent in which was a certain amount of bureaucracy. The introduction of Medicare in 1958 only contributed to the sense of loss of control. At the heart of these issues was a concern over the decline of individual doctor/patient relations, which generated a great deal of anxiety for the AMA and amounted to a public relations crisis on a profession-wide scale.

Understanding that their cultural power rested in their ability to maintain the public trust, the organized medical community took steps to combat negative perceptions of the profession. In 1955, they conducted a $30,000 nationwide survey of four thousand people, publishing the results a year later in *Newsweek* under the title "Like Your Doctor?" Although the results were far from damning — only 1 percent of those polled said they "do not like" their doctor — the community-wide fear persisted. The AMA also developed an "active interest in image making at the media level" (Turow 1989, 29) and became acutely sensitive to how doctors were being depicted on the most influential medium of the day, television. Much as they had been vocal in criticizing "unrealistic or harmful depictions" in Hollywood films of the 1930s (7), the association in the 1950s turned its attention to the fictitious representations of doctors on television — no matter how minor.

An article from a 1957 *Journal of the American Medical Association* entitled "How Authentic Is Medicine on Television?" lauds the producers of *Lassie* for having the good sense to approach the AMA for their "definitive professional attitude" about a hypothetical situation. Posing the rhetorical question "Why all this fuss about a brief scene in a half-hour dog story?" the article points out that, more than avoiding the "guffaws [and] comments of ridicule" of medical professionals, the producers wished to present an authentic portrayal of medical situations for the vast audience of impressionable citizens. Fully aware that they were at a turning point, the AMA was asserting itself as a "friendly" source of guidance. The overly cordial language belies a forceful message: "Until last year, many a network executive did not realize that professional assistance on a medical script was available." The attempts of the AMA to police the representations of doctors were thinly veiled in a spirit of cooperation. To meet the "growing demands" of producers of every medium, the article reported, the AMA had created a Physicians Advisory Committee on Television, Radio, and Motion Pictures, which was based in New York and Los Angeles.

Much like the medical community, the advertising profession passed through a historical transformation after the turn of the century, when the food and drug law put an end to what Lears calls "the golden age of patent medicine." Advertisers who had been involved in writing copy for patent medicines attempted to distance themselves from their unseemly past. They made a concentrated effort to align themselves instead with the more respected professional image of "Doctor," with their copy serving as advice. Idealized images of doctors frequently appeared in the illustrations of print ads, their credibility being used to sell products as diverse (and as far afield of the medical profession) as cars, cigarettes, and guns (figures 1 and 2). In the 1920s, the J. Walter Thompson agency went so far as to use real-life "authoritative physicians in white coats" for testimonial ads to boost a failing account. The AMA responded with outrage, prohibiting its members from participating in advertising and prompting the agency to turn to European doctors for its paid testimonials (Marchand 1985, 17). The struggle between the medicine man and doctors had always been over controlling the body of the patient and the public, and even as the advertisers shed their past image, they continued to compete with the AMA over who would control where and how patients got their information.

By the 1930s, advertisers were carving out a niche for themselves as experts, fulfilling what they perceived as the American need for guidance in a modern society that was changing and becoming increasingly complicated. And with the dawn of radio, agencies found themselves in control not only of the ads but also of the programming. The development of a single-sponsorship model on radio (which would last into the late 1950s on television) put the production of programs into the hands of advertisers rather than networks, thus placing agencies in a prominent position of cultural power. By the 1950s, the role of the advertiser, as seen from his (or her) point of view, was not unlike that of the family physician. Dispensing wisdom and offering "expert" advice, the advertiser helped to guide the sponsor through the perilous world of broadcasting and the anxious American consumer through a sea of perplexing product options. Viewing their audience as unintelligent and lethargic (and largely female), advertisers chose to portray themselves as members of a "helping profession" (Marchand 1985, 67).

This hard-won legitimacy, however, proved difficult to maintain. It was always vulnerable to threats of false advertising, which could bring

Exorcising "Men in White" on Television   99

1. Guns don't kill people . . .
Print advertisement, 1916.

2. Smoke two packs and call me in the morning.
Print advertisement, 1946.

on "public skepticism," tarnish the reputation of advertising as a business, and — worse still — invite government regulation (315). Despite the successes that some agencies enjoyed during this period, the legacy of the patent medicine men continued to linger in regulatory skirmishes over false advertising, which would erupt periodically throughout the 1950s until the quiz show scandals brought a resounding condemnation of the entire business. The intense public scrutiny and media hyperbole surrounding the scandals indicted not only the advertisers but the medium they had been instrumental in shaping: television.

Broadcasters and Their Code

From the earliest days of broadcasting, station owners had gone to great lengths to avoid government intervention. The National Association of Broadcasters (NAB), established in 1923, emerged in the radio and television era as the self-regulatory body of the industry. Their official government counterpart was the FCC, set up to make sure broadcasters fulfilled their duties to act "in the public interest." In the ongoing drama that was regulation in the mid-1950s, the FCC's primary role was to wait in the wings and threaten to make an entrance. Always hovering, potential government action was held at bay only by the efforts of the NAB, who would often step in with preemptive regulation. Such was the case with deceptive advertisements on television, the regulation of which came in the context of the Television Code.

The code was painstakingly crafted and officially adopted in 1951. Apparently, it was met with little enthusiasm from the press. Justin Miller, the president of what was then called the National Association of Radio and Television Broadcasters, reacted to the "jaundiced cynicism" of the newspapers in a memo dated 1 November 1951: "Some of these cynics take such a sour view of the whole world that they undoubtedly would have condemned Moses for promulgating the Ten Commandments, the American Colonists for promulgating the Declaration of Independence, and Jesus Christ for giving the Sermon on the Mount" (J. Miller 1951). Miller goes on to lambaste the "jealousy" of the newspaper people, who would like to "break down" broadcasting, and highlights their refusal to regulate themselves.

Like any tirade, Miller's words say more about his state of mind than the subject itself. The NAB was at a critical moment that would decide its ability to regulate television, and the internal office correspondence indicates that the organization's members needed morale boosting.

The code, much like the FCC, had its problems; paramount among them was its utter lack of efficacy. Despite the NAB's insistence that it was a "shining example of self-regulation," it was often unclear, generally ignored by broadcasters, and ultimately unenforceable (Barnouw 1978, 353). Regardless of the lack of respect that individual station managers might have had for the code, however, it was in the best interests of all concerned that it at least maintain the outward appearance of an effective tool. Similarly, it was in the best interests of the broadcasters that the FCC remain in good standing with the public, since its actions (or inaction) often benefited the broadcasting community. In the 1950s, neither of these things seemed to be the case.

The reputation of the FCC went steadily downhill in the 1950s, a time that one former chairman dubbed "the whorehouse era" (Baughman 1985, 13). It was, according to James Baughman, "a regulatory rat's nest, waiting to be exposed" (13). Although never substantiated, widespread reports of impropriety in issuing licenses were damaging to the FCC's image. In 1957, the Speaker of the House, Sam Rayburn, organized a special committee to investigate misconduct in the FCC. The matter snowballed and eventually involved an FBI investigation. This low point in the history of the FCC is the beginning of the period William Boddy (1990) aptly characterizes as TV's "public relations crisis" (98).

Unfortunately for broadcasters, the FCC was not the only focus of public scrutiny in the late 1950s. The popular press at the time reported growing concern about television programming, due in large part to the intimations of scandal on wildly popular quiz shows such as *The $64,000 Question* and *Twenty-One*. In 1957, just as the FCC story was breaking in magazines, both *Look* and *Time* were publishing articles about accusations that the shows were rigged. Though assuring readers that these were just rumors, the articles helped spread them (Boddy 1990, 102). The scandal would officially break a year later, striking a nerve with the public by exposing a national deception and challenging the way audiences viewed television and reality itself.

In 1957, these three industries — the medical community, advertising agencies, and broadcasters — were in crisis. Each of the groups had amassed tremendous cultural power, and each saw its power being threatened, even slipping away. Into this nexus came the men-in-white ban, which functioned as the ideal escape valve. Each group had prior history with the medicine man and had increased its legitimacy by defeating him. Here was the chance to drag him out of the attic in order to vanquish him all over again.

In October 1956, *Time* reported that the FTC would begin to monitor radio and television commercials for traces of "false and misleading" advertising ("The Great Medicine Show" 1956). Five months later, the Television Board of the NARTB approved an amendment to the Television Code, which read:

> Dramatized advertising involving statements or purported statements by physicians, dentists, or nurses must be presented by accredited members of such professions or it must be made apparent that the portrayal is dramatized by super-imposing the words "A Dramatization" in a *highly visible* manner during the initial 10 seconds of the scene. If the scene portraying such professional persons is less than 10 seconds, the words "A Dramatization" shall then be visible for the entire length of the subject scene. ("TV Board" 1957)

The NAB's primary concern, as stated here, is that television viewers can distinguish between commercial depictions of medical advice and advice from real doctors. These regulations were meant to protect the "gullible public," an easy prey for manipulative advertisers.

In May 1957, the FCC and the FTC, who had combined forces in an "ad probe," brought the first official complaint against television advertising, citing "visual deception" (Fingal 1957). The accused were the makers of Rolaids; their transgression was producing a commercial featuring a man in a white coat addressed as "doctor." Equally abhorrent to the commission as the fake doctor himself was the demonstration in which he burns a hole through a cloth napkin, with what he claims is stomach acid, to show the damage it can cause. The FTC considered this "visual deception" invidious on two levels: it exploited the nature of the television medium, and it contained a visual impersonation of a medical professional. The AMA was quick to jump into the fray, adopting "a resolution charging that 'misleading' advertising . . . by the purveyors of patent medicines . . . cause irreparable harm to the general population." Significantly, the AMA also called for "closer liaison" between themselves and the broadcasting industry ("AMA Hits TV Drug Ads" 1957).

Meanwhile, the networks were aware that the medical community was watching them closely. In an interdepartmental report to the continuity acceptance personnel of NBC, code authority director Stockton Helffrich (1957) described the following incident:

Exorcising "Men in White" on Television   103

Complying with expectations of dentists of the broadcast media, where it comes to counteracting exaggerated fears of and prejudiced sentiments towards dental therapy, our Hollywood colleague John Graves arranged for deletion from a shooting script for "Blondie" of a line carelessly included. "But this is like going to the dentist. I'd rather get it over with now." Totally gratuitous in the context involved and so easily changed.

This instance of voluntary censorship speaks to the desires of broadcasters to maintain an amiable relationship with the AMA and their colleagues. While it cannot be defined as "misleading" or even dangerous to depict a character as reluctant to go to the dentist, it clearly taps into what dentists consider their image problem. Such "gratuitous" references — the taking of their professions' names in vain, so to speak — were at the heart of the debate between the medical professionals and the broadcasters shaping the representations of doctors in particular ways.

Pressure to clean up false advertising was also coming from the public arena. In January 1958 Dr. Morton J. Rodman, a professor at Rutgers University, delivered a talk on WATV in Newark "blasting" television's medical ads. He mimicked the infamous Rolaids advertisement by pouring concentrated stomach acid on a cloth. Needless to say, this did not result in a hole in the cloth, thus proving that advertisers had indeed misled the public. Rodman's televised speech (which was ostensibly to be on the dangers of self-medication) concluded with a lambaste of medical commercials, which he considered "potentially as dangerous as a loaded gun" ("Professor Charges" 1958).

The public nature of his tirade shook up the advertising industry, but it was just the beginning of a negative publicity blitz that continued throughout the year. In May 1958, the New York State Medical Society called on the AMA to take further measures to stop fake doctors on TV commercials, specifically requesting federal regulation. The *New York Times* subsequently published an editorial ("Those TV 'Doctors,'" 16 May 1958) praising the Medical Society for its actions and lending the voice of the press to the criticism of medical ads. Calling the commercials "an insult to the intelligence of the listener and viewer, a slur on the medical profession and an outright danger to the gullible," the editor declares "the patent medicine show still goes on full blast" ("Those TV 'Doctors'"). Although the AMA had a valuable ally in the press, it was the organization's influence with Congress that made it truly formidable.

The threat of government regulation cast a heavy shadow over the broadcasting industry; the AMA had the ability to make the threat real. In June 1958 *Broadcasting* reported that on Capitol Hill a subcommittee of the House Government Operations Committee was "definitely interested" in the "white coat debate" and that the AMA and ADA "have indicated to the subcommittee they favor hearings on the subject" ("NAB Out to Unfrock 'Doctors'" 1958). In the same article, the magazine declares that the "white coat is now out of style in medical TV commercials." It was referring to the fact that that same week, the TV Code Review Board had "amplified" the men-in-white ban—which, as of January, would prohibit the appearance of physicians in advertisements, the use of props or settings to suggest a medical association, and reference to scientific studies that could not be fully documented. This further "interpretation" of the ban was couched in a "spirit of cooperation" with advertisers eager to comply ("'Men in White' Ad Ban Amplified" 1958). The AMA and the ADA praised the new restriction, calling it "definitely in the public interest."

Of this minor skirmish, *Printer's Ink* commented that although the AMA had asked to seek federal control of commercials, "The federal government didn't have time to get into the situation," because the TV Code Review Board, in "amplifying" the ban, beat them to it ("Fake TV Doctors Must Go" 1958). This preemptive capitulation to the indirect demands made by the AMA was rewarded by good publicity—something the NAB desperately needed to prove to the government that the association could function independently. All the while, the NAB could justify its self-preservation as being in the best interests of its audience.

Following this incident was a series of revisions in the wording of the men-in-white ban as advertisers worked to find loopholes in the newly specified language. For example, when the ban was expanded to prohibit statements by dentists and nurses as well as physicians, one advertiser came up with the idea to use lab technicians. Although they still wear white coats, he reasoned, they have only half-length sleeves ("Fake TV Doctors Must Go" 1958). Given the specificity of the code language (intended to clarify rules for eager-to-comply advertisers), it was nearly impossible to prohibit by name every permutation of medical representation.

Another—and more threatening—loophole exercised by ad agencies was to employ real doctors for testimonials. A 1958 issue of *Advertising Age* reports worry in the medical community over this possibility: "The [medical] society seems to fear that advertisers and agencies will decide the best way to circumvent the intent of the ban on 'white coat' commercials will be to hire real medicine men" ("Real Doctors May Be

Used" 1958). A similar mention of this form of circumvention appears in *Printer's Ink*, which relays the reported price offered to doctors for commercial appearances — or, as the New York Medical Society put it, the "price tag on medical integrity" — to be $6,000 a year. This sum, according to one medical journal, is nearly twice the salary of resident physicians in their local hospitals ("Query for Tyro Doctors" 1958).

The seduction of the real men in white had begun, and the issue of whether it was ethical and responsible for doctors to do testimonials became the problem of the AMA. As far as the NAB was concerned, the case was closed as of 1959. They report that "member stations, all three networks, advertising agencies and sponsors alike have cooperated to the fullest in removing actors dressed as doctors from the American television screen" ("No More 'Men-in-White'" 1959). As for the real doctors on TV, "Accredited physicians, dentists and nurses are appearing, and are acceptable under the code. It is now up to the professions to police their own people and we have told them so" ("White Coats Now on Pro's" 1959). After years of wielding their power over the broadcasters, the advertisers, and the government to protect their reputation, medical leaders faced a threat to their power coming from within their ranks, a challenge of professional solidarity.

Defining "Doctor"

In 1959 the quiz show scandals shook television, and the aftershocks were felt in every corner of the entertainment industry. The government, whose intervention had been successfully fended off for decades, finally had a good reason to get involved. *Business Week* reported that "scandals may bring federal licensing of networks, more scrutiny of program content, and a new drive against misleading commercials" ("Quiz Probe" 1959). Among those who had the most to lose were the advertising agencies, which would be forced to surrender control over television programming. As for the ads themselves, these were subjected to closer monitoring by the FTC, stronger regulation from the broadcasting industry, and further threats of government regulation; in the wake of such a staggering public deception, the ad agencies and networks were under increasing pressure to "keep misleading and exaggerated commercials off the air" ("TV Told" 1959). And still, skirmishes on the borders of the men-in-white ban continued with, among other things, the Medical Society of the County of New York's protest against the "usage of the title 'doctor,' when that person is not a physician" but rather the holder of a Ph.D. (ibid.).

Although Americans were seeing less of doctors on commercials, the white coats were still prevalent on television in the 1960s — in network programming. The phenomenal popularity of shows such as *Ben Casey* and *Doctor Kildare* brought depictions of doctors into American homes on a weekly basis. Part of the publicity surrounding these programs was a trend to identify the actors with the characters they played; Joseph Turow (1989) discusses how this conflation was not just a reaction of dedicated audiences but actively encouraged by the press (67). The AMA, by this time, was a vocal resource for the producers of television, with power to dissuade them from creating unrealistic or unflattering scenarios. However, their control did not extend to advertisers, who persisted in using medical representations in their advertisements — worse still, many of those representations were "real" doctors doing testimonials. This presented a serious dilemma for the medical community: the AMA expected TV viewers to accept the verisimilitude of fake doctors in television programs but wanted them to reject the credibility of real doctors in advertisements.

In January 1963, the NAB once again revisited the men-in-white ban, tightening it to prohibit not only actors but real doctors, nurses, and dentists from appearing in commercials. Subsequent discussion of the ban went as far as to keep third-person references, terms, and visual depictions that in any way implied a connection to the medical profession from the screen ("Television Board Tightens" 1963). The wording would continue to be tinkered with well into the 1970s.

Conclusion

As the architects of the 1957 men-in-white ban describe it, "The intent of the rule was reasonably to protect the consumer public in the area of health from encouragement toward excessive self-diagnosis and self-medication" ("'Men-in-White' Rule Clarified" 1965). The ban was ostensibly about getting actors dressed as doctors out of commercials; the purpose was to prevent the image of the doctor from being exploited and thereby to protect the public from being misled. However, the terms in which the debate was put discursively linked this practice of advertising to a history of patent medicine, rendering the ads not just deceptive but ultimately dangerous and depraved. In fact, the intense anxiety that these medical ads generated in all three groups belies their claims that they were merely cooperating in the public interest. Behind the debate about how best to protect the public lay the real issue: how to exert power and maintain authority over the public.

In the late 1950s, the medical community, the advertising profession, and the broadcasters were all linked over one struggle; each had its own agenda. Trying to work through their respective crises, they used representations as their battleground, attempting to repair or regain the credibility that was slipping away. In the debate over the men-in-white ban, one can see how the reincarnation of the medicine man and his subsequent expulsion from the television screen served the interests of all concerned, providing an — if not contrived, then certainly con-venient — "other" against which each group could redefine itself. In this respect, the men-in-white ban was more than a demonstration of "the effectiveness of voluntary self-regulation," as the chairman of the TV Code proclaimed; it was one small example of the manipulations of power at work ("No More 'Men-in-White'" 1959).

Drive-By Medicine

Managed Care Ads on Billboards

NORBERT GOLDFIELD

It is almost impossible to look at a newspaper and not find an article about challenges to today's health care system. Many of these stories focus on consumer complaints about their managed care organization (MCO), which gave rise to many congressional efforts to pass and have the president sign a Patient Bill of Rights. The relationship between physicians and their patients is similarly undergoing significant change. An exploration of advertisements represents one means of examining this new triangular relationship among doctors, patients, and MCOs. After providing historical background, this article will focus on one particular type of advertisement, billboards, which serve as a trenchant yet amusing metaphor for analyzing the evolving relationship between physicians, patients, and MCOs. Different types of billboards reflect MCO efforts to appeal to what they believe is important to consumers at a particular point in time. The article will conclude with observations on the most recent changes in billboard advertising of MCOs and their implications for our health care system.

The Promise and Decline of MCOs

How did we get to this point of unremitting hostility toward the concept of managed care when, as eventual and current patients, we would all appreciate receiving from a team of health professionals coordinated services that provide a judicious balance between cost and quality? It cannot just be media hype. Unfortunately, in its initially successful effort at controlling costs, managed care lost sight of the other side of the cost-quality balance and neglected quality of care. As the *Wall Street Journal* recently opined: "Not long ago, some optimistic policy makers predicted that managed care would be the nation's antidote to runaway health care costs. No more" (9 August 1999, 1). Yet it did not start out this way.

Managed care, as initially practiced by a small number of organizations, means the provision of coordinated services for a group of patients. In the health center where I work, we have the financial flexibility to hire, for example, nurse practitioners who provide home care for complex patients up to and including the delivery of intravenous medication. In other words, coordinated care should give the patient "peace of mind" (figure 1). Coordinated care is provided by a health care team consisting of physicians, nurses, and other health professionals needed for the well-being of the patient. Coordinated care, not the abuses highlighted in the current debate, is good managed care. Tragically, coordinated care is largely ignored in today's world of managed care. Not only consumers but physicians and other health care providers are dissatisfied with their MCO relationship.

Similar to the challenges in the relationship between MCOs and patients, the relationship between physicians and their patients is also undergoing significant change. Until recently, patients trusted their physicians to fulfill their Hippocratic obligation and prescribe the best course of treatment. This trust entailed a ceding of power to physicians and, to a lesser extent, other members of the health care team. However, over the past decade, consumers have witnessed a sea change in their traditional relationship with the health care community. In part, consumers have finally begun to appreciate the need to become more knowledgeable about their own health (Goldfield 1999). MCOs have tapped into the discomfort of consumers and physicians with the current state of managed care. MCOs are using advertising to try to influence the perceptions of consumers and physicians of managed care.

Advertising: From Poster to Billboard

Advertising is a quintessential part of American culture and has a time-honored place in American culture. Advertising for health services is as old as advertising itself. In the nineteenth century, producers of quack pharmaceuticals advertised their medicinals in both print and poster media (Lears 1994; J. Fraser 1991).

However, until recently, promotion for the delivery of health services did not constitute a significant portion of advertising expenditures in

1. Psychological security. Health care that gives you peace of mind.

the United States. Two interrelated events led to an expansion of advertising for health care services: the passage of Medicare in 1964 and a concomitant explosion of health care expenditures that began shortly after the passage of Medicare into law (Goldfield 2000). Managed care organizations developed in response to the explosion in health care costs. Today most Americans enroll in some form of managed care plan. In many communities, particularly large urban areas, intense competition occurs between MCOs for customers. MCOs appeal to these potential customers in a variety of print and visual media including billboards.

We see the billboard for only a fleeting second. What does the driver "see" when his eyes scan the following messages (which may or may not be accompanied by visual images)?

— "Our Plan Is to Keep You Healthy"
— "Our Plan Gives You Peace of Mind"
— "It Is between You and Your Doctor"

MCOs advertising their product are obviously trying to sell their product. Yet they are also trying to fulfill two other advertising maxims: provide information, and if possible, entertain the viewer. Unfortunately, Americans mistrust MCOs so much that it is hard for these

Drive-By Medicine 111

organizations to present information that is not immediately suspect, let alone entertain the viewer. With each of the headlines listed, the MCOs attempt to encourage the viewer to think of the header as an infomercial.

While a relatively new phenomenon, billboard advertisements have become a common feature on today's highway landscape. Particularly in urban centers, it is not uncommon for highway drivers to see frequent billboards highlighting the wonders of a particular MCO. This is true especially during the fall, the time when most health insurance programs or plans allow consumers to change their MCO. As a consequence, billboards represent an ideal form of communication between MCOs and an important constituency — middle-class working individuals. Many of these individuals have health insurance through work and thus must often choose between competing plans. Alternatively, the driver's place of work offers only one plan, and MCOs would like to encourage viewers to ask the benefits department to include the particular plan in the benefit package.

MCOs and Billboard Messages

One can view billboards for MCOs from two different perspectives. On the surface, the ads trumpet a particular MCO and attempt to attract consumer interest in that organization. This type of appeal to generic consumer interest is a manifestation of standard, well-established, and well-understood advertising practices (Freedberg 1989). Of greater interest, MCO ads illustrate in ironic and subtle ways the many changes occurring in today's health care delivery system. It is perfectly consistent with the American marketplace of ideas for MCOs to use advertising, in general, and billboards, in particular, to convince drivers that joining their health plan will address their particular areas of concern. So, for example, they use the most time honored advertising technique: wrapping the American flag around the product (figure 2).

MCOs have adopted other American icons in both humorous and traditional ways. "We've got the Blues" offers an ironic and telling commentary on an American cultural symbol (figure 3). The blues, as an American musical form, often express life in the midst of misery. Such music is not typically associated with healthy-looking, laughing, white, middle-class people lounging in bed and extolling the virtues of Blue Cross/Blue Shield.

2. Using cultural symbols. Wrapping the flag around health care.

3. Using cultural symbols. "We've got the Blues."

Other typical advertising themes that have seeped into MCO strategies include the following:

—Equivalence between MCO objectives and young middle-class Americans. Young middle-class individuals incur low insurance expenses and are therefore extremely attractive enrollees for MCOs. MCOs may appeal to values of a particular era (for example, of the 1950s, a time popularized as one of calmness and economic progress).

—Benefits of competition.

—Cultural emphasis on youth, success, and good health. These are characteristics that the MCO would like to associate itself with and, if possible, encourage the driver to think that enrollment in the MCO will result, like eating a particular brand of breakfast cereal, in better health.

—Efforts to establish a brand name for the MCO. Even the illustration for the brand evokes images of youth and health. The color blue is one associated with calmness. While the content may appear completely neutral, the billboard clearly intends to fulfill a key advertising maxim: at a minimum, do not switch from one brand of cigarette or MCO the viewer is currently enrolled in. This use of billboards is particularly important in an era of managed care in which 20 to 25 percent MCO disenrollment is not uncommon (Goldfield and Nash 2000).

—A focus on individualism, freedom, and the American West. While the relationship between health insurance and freedom is unclear, it is certain that the insurance company would like its enrollees to believe that participation in its MCO entails few hassles (figure 4).

—Public service. MCOs hope that highlighting services provided in a public spirit will humanize the organization.

—Sponsorship of public non-health-care event such as a walk.

—Sponsorship of public health-care-related event such as free health screening. Americans consider themselves extremely charitable, and there is a long tradition of company sponsorship of charitable events. Today many Americans will likely associate MCOs with other companies, such as tobacco companies, that are trying to deflect their poor reputation through sponsorship of charitable events.

MCO billboards go beyond these traditional advertising themes and tactics and explore many aspects of the new triangular relationship between doctors, patients, and MCOs. Figure 5 documents the perceived (on the part of both consumers and physicians) diminution in the power, authority, and role of physicians. While consumers increasingly understand the impact of financial incentives on physician behavior, they do not generally blame their physician. Rather, they

4. Health care without hassle. Blue means freedom.

5. Triangular relationships: Doctors, patients, and MCOs.

blame the MCOs for their avarice, resulting in MCO placement of inappropriate burdens on the doctor-patient relationship.

MCOs may present themselves as part of the family, much in the same way that family physicians traditionally presented themselves. Such a strategy would work if MCOs could convince consumers that the former provided truly coordinated care. In the current hostile environment, it is difficult for consumers to reshape an already negative opinion about MCOs.

While these billboards might appear in conflict with each other, they reflect the debate going on at that particular point in time between MCOs, doctors, and patients. Figure 5 depicts a time of less tension between these three groups, while the emphasis on physician-directed care comes at a time of legislative efforts to curb MCOs entry into the doctor patient relationship.

MCO billboards frequently focus on the cost and availability of services. For example, MCOs often promise, in their billboard advertising, to provide easy access to preventive care services. There are many reasons that MCOs focus their advertising on preventive services in contrast to services that sicker individuals need. Healthy individuals typically see little difference between MCOs. Providing preventive services can provide an inexpensive incentive (from the MCO's perspective) for healthy individuals to select a particular MCO. MCOs provide these services not because they believe that they prevent breast cancer if they provide free mammography screenings. Consumer disenrollment from MCOs is too high to be able to make an impact on a disease that takes years or decades to occur.

Even healthy individuals want to become more physically fit and attractive. A number of MCO billboards borrow from the original patent medicine billboard themes and imply that joining a particular MCO will result in greater strength and vitality. One billboard features a person at risk, a middle-aged white male, improving his health as a consequence of enrolling in an MCO. While an MCO depicting such an image may be putting itself at financial risk (older people incur more care than younger individuals), the MCO mitigates that possibility by promoting, in nearby locations, other billboards with exactly the same image containing young, healthy males or females. Typically, MCO billboards depict young, healthy-looking, middle-class families (with one child). Simply put, if an MCO is paid virtually the same if it enrolls a healthy versus a sick individual, it is clearly in the MCO's interest to attempt via its billboard advertising budget to selectively attract healthy, usually younger, individuals.

6. Health care after hours: The MCO hotline.

Increasing consumer mistrust in MCOs is also reflected in the types of services MCOs promise. Many contemporary consumers view MCOs as organizations putting up barriers to care instead of practicing optimal management of care. Yet some MCOs advertise services that, in essence, replace certain functions typically performed by physicians, particularly in the area of coordinated care (figure 6). The MCO in this billboard encourages the consumer to call the MCO's hot line, rather than the consumer's own physician, for emergency asthma services any time of day or night. Unfortunately, physicians are not available at all times for a quick consultation. Faced with urgent after-hours questions, consumers often turn to the emergency room for assistance. In providing this consultation hot line, the MCO is hoping both to build goodwill and to decrease expensive emergency room visits.

While a number of MCOs prohibit direct consumer access to specialist physicians, other MCOs highlight this access in attractive billboards. MCOs have largely implemented open access in anticipation of the passage of the "patient bill of rights."

Quality of Care and MCOs

There is continual debate between advocates and detractors about the impact of MCOs on quality. Can one define quality, or is it only in the

eye of the beholder? The Institute of Medicine provided an encompass-
ing definition of quality as it pertains to health services: "Quality of
care is the degree to which health services for individuals and populations increase the likelihood of desired health outcomes and are consistent with current professional knowledge" (Lohr 1990, 21). This definition focuses not just on individuals but on entire populations. In
addition, quality of care from this perspective does not focus exclusively on the outcome of care (mortality rate, health status) but also
focuses on processes (prescription of the appropriate medications; access to a nebulizer when appropriate) and structural (e.g., access to
care at convenient times for the consumer) measures of quality.

Billboards advertising MCOs highlight many aspects of quality discussed in this definition. MCOs often promise improved quality, either
as broad, unsupported assertions or with specific reference to a published survey. In addition, billboards highlight some of the following:

— Structural measures
  availability of many doctors
  availability of health care providers when you need them
  easy access to services at any time
— Process measures
  good listening skills
— Outcome measures
  increased satisfaction
  lower mortality

Content and Visual Analysis of Specific Billboards

The themes discussed in the previous sections will be linked to an
analysis of a small number of the billboards themselves. In this analysis, I combine an analysis of the advertisements from both a health
care trend and an advertising perspective. In particular, I borrow from
the perspectives of Roland Barthes in his seminal essay "The Rhetoric
of the Image" and Erwin Panofsky in his extensive work analyzing the
many ways of interpreting images (Barthes 1977; Panofsky 1995). As
Barthes states in his introduction: "In advertising the signification of
the image is undoubtedly intentional; the signifieds of the image are
formed a priori by certain attributes of the product and these signifieds
have to be transmitted as clearly as possible. If the image contains
signs, we can be sure that in advertising these signs are full, formed

with a view to the optimum reading: the advertising image is frank, or at least emphatic" (33).

Panofsky offers another, three-level model for the analysis of visuals such as billboards. "The first level is that of primary or natural subject matter consisting of lights, color, shape and movement and the elementary understanding of representation, whether of people, objects, gestures, poses or expressions, and the interrelations which comprise events. The second level is that of . . . conventional subject matter which relates to the wider culture. At this level, motifs . . . are linked to themes and concepts. At the third level we come to intrinsic meaning or content, which is discovered by ascertaining those underlying principles which reveal the basic attitudes of a nation, a period, a class, a religious or philosophic persuasion" (28).

All the billboards analyzed in this section reflect the signs that Barthes highlights in his essay. They all require a general cultural knowledge, that is, an awareness of the tensions currently in play in the managed care industry. When one strips away this cultural knowledge, there remain advertising themes that one finds in any billboard advertising. Using Panofsky's classification schema, one finds several levels of visual analysis.

One significant difference between billboards advertising MCOs and those that typically highlight a particular product (such as spaghetti sauce, for instance) is the significant presence of words in all billboards advertising MCOs. Very often the words in a billboard extolling an MCO are as prominent, if not more so, than the visuals, if any. While many of us can immediately recognize a particular spaghetti sauce, drivers need verbal cues to help recognize a particular MCO. Even with the words, it will often be the case that only a minority of drivers will recognize the MCO. An MCO billboard infomercial will not be of interest to the typical driver. Rather, it is trying to provide reinforcement to drivers who are faced with the decision of whether or not to stay with the MCO.

The billboards analyzed in this section share another characteristic that Barthes highlights in his essay. Each of the billboards "offers us three messages: a linguistic message, a coded iconic message, and a non-coded iconic message" (24). While Barthes points out that the viewer, the driver, receives the two iconic messages at the same time, it is important to distinguish between the two. The driver immediately recognizes the content of a particular image, such as a doctor and pediatric patient in the first billboard discussed hereafter. This is the noncoded iconic message. But the MCO would like the viewer to drive by and, ideally, also take away from his viewing experience a coded message that relates the interaction between the doctor and patient to the MCO highlighted in the billboard. There are both "literal" and "symbolic" messages in all the billboards discussed in this essay.

In one billboard for Well-Care, a health plan in Connecticut in the 1990s, the driver sees a white woman in a physician's white coat with a white child. The physician assumes an authoritative yet friendly parental posture over a child who is paying rapt attention—an appealing scenario to the women drivers passing by. This friendly, soothing scenario serves two functions: it is one that women drivers (certainly the intended audience) would like to see in their physician, a maternal individual in whom one can have confidence for one's own family. Becoming a member of this MCO (or not leaving this MCO) helps to reinforce confidence and provide pleasant feelings to the female driver that this MCO might help her with any family issues. At a minimum, the billboard attempts to compare favorably the MCO to the driver's own family, if it is a healthy one, and the "well-care" that this MCO promises.

The interplay between words and image reflects the general challenge facing MCOs, that is, the driver's relative lack of familiarity with specific MCOs. Most Americans paint all MCOs with the same negative brush. This billboard uses words to try to distinguish itself from other MCOs in several ways. In large white (the same color as the doctor's coat) letters, the MCO announces its name for the driver to remember. If nothing else, the MCO would like the viewer to drive by and remember the name "Well-Care" when the time comes to decide which, if any, MCO, to select. Unlike an established brand of spaghetti sauce, this billboard also highlights that it is a "new" health plan. Even if it is not chronologically new, Well-Care would like to convince viewers, if they can assimilate more than one word (Well-Care) as they drive by, that it is not a typical, old-style MCO that interferes with the doctor-patient relationship. The words announce the name together with the fact that it is new and pair this information with an image of a physician and a young consumer.

The MCO associates its own image with that of one of the most trusted images in American society, a photograph of a physician in an authoritative white coat striking a sympathetic pose with a young, healthy-looking patient. The MCO does this in two ways. First, the billboard uses the same white color to depict itself and the physician. Second, the name "Well-Care" is associated with the visual image of a healthy-looking physician and patient. Billboards advertising MCOs never show people who look like a "patient," the typical person who is not feeling well and seeks care from a physician. As Sander Gilman states in his book *Picturing Health and Illness*, ugly patients look sick (Gilman 1995). They may not even get better. Beautiful patients obey their physicians and don't get sick or implicitly get well as soon as they follow their physician's instructions.

In any type of advertisement, there exists a strong connection between image and text. Words on a billboard typically shape the viewer's momentary gaze at the image. Without the words, the driver looking at the woman in a white coat smiling at the young girl would have no association with an MCO. "The text directs the reader among the various signifieds of the image, causes him to avoid some and to accept others; through an often subtle dispatching, it teleguides him toward a meaning selected in advance" (Barthes 1977, 25).

Unlike established items and brands, the MCO has an uphill battle in achieving its objectives in this billboard advertisement. While most advertisers can easily combine a naive ("a simple enumeration of elements") with a "structural description" ("seeking to apprehend the relation of these elements"), most MCOs, and certainly this one in particular, would be pleased if the viewer drives by with a recollection of the naive elements, the name itself.

Although most physicians today are men, the MCO uses an image of a female physician. Placing a woman in the role of physician may reflect the increasing number of women physicians in the United States. Does having a child in the picture arouse sympathy for the plan? Is the billboard particularly appealing to female drivers? Does showing a child relate to the fact that a mother or woman often makes the decision regarding a health plan for the family? The female head of the family is largely responsible for arranging for the health care needs of the children. Mothers are typically responsible for "well-care" visits for her children. The MCO realizes this and encourages an equivalence between its name and the typical role of female drivers who have a family.

Well-Care also highlights the fact that it is a locally based MCO. Are local health plans really better for the consumer? What are local health plans? Does it relate to having local people on the board? Do local health plans encourage more local participation than national health plans? Are local health plans like your local doctor? These questions are never answered (there is no difference in measures of quality between locally operated and nationally owned MCOs). In fact, they are never asked. Being local simply equates to being good. The billboard tries to instill a sense of neighborhood friendliness, similar to the sense one has with having a local family physician. Consumers, of course, realize that MCOs are not their family physicians. Yet Well-Care is, via this billboard, trying to "drive" into the doctor-patient relationship and is trying to take on some of the intimate, "neighborly" features of the stereotypical doctor-patient relationship.

The colors blue and white in one Kaiser Permanente billboard are somewhat eye-catching. At the same time, the billboard designers intended the predominance of blue as a moment of serenity or calmness for the driver as he or she speeds by a constantly changing landscape. In fact, the colors in all the ads analyzed attempt to provide the driver with a second of calm and, as a consequence, attract the driver's attention. The use of a single color in the majority of the available space represents an abrupt change to what is occurring in the driver's visual field. In addition to this function for the blue in this ad, the white in the billboard for after hours care (figure 6) also represents a moment of serenity. The designers of the Well-Care billboard in figure 1 use yellow as the predominant color, not only to enhance calmness for the driver but also to provide a cheery, sunny companion to the happy-looking people in the visual image. The yellow builds on the overall effect that the MCO is trying to accomplish—a healthy-looking customer.

The totally verbal billboard (FIRST CHOICE in large letters occupying more than half of the billboard, followed in smaller size lettering by U.S. NEWS AND WORLD REPORT, NEWSWEEK) advertising Kaiser attempts to achieve several completely different objectives. Unfortunately, some of the objectives are impacted by the presence of an adult video store right next to the billboard. Billboards as part of a very broad visual landscape depend on the driver's field of vision.

Kaiser, one of the oldest MCOs in the United States, purposely restricted itself to words in its billboard to make the advertisement appear like a news story. This billboard is a form of camouflaged ad. It thus restricts itself to a newspaper-headline-like set of words that attempt to focus on a message it would like to communicate. Unfortunately, words alone, no matter how attractively colored and placed, form no substitute for an attractive interplay between an image and text.

This Kaiser billboard provides a reference that the driver could check up on, one clearly meant to validate the message. It is highly unlikely that a driver will ever take the time to examine the reference. In providing the citation, Kaiser adds to the "newsworthy" character of the headline. Of course, questions come up: First choice in what (quality or payment)? What aspect of quality? What do patients want in an MCO? Do people pay any attention to report cards? In fact, the literature does indicate that consumers are interested in report cards and are willing to act on the information provided (Goldfield 1999). Kaiser already had an established reputation in this particular community. People either liked or disliked this MCO in strong terms. Kaiser was not trying to convince consumers who were not members of the plan to join Kaiser. Rather, it was trying to reinforce already positive feelings among consumers who might have begun to think of switching but had basically pleasant associations with the MCO.

Placement of a billboard is extremely important. All MCO billboards I have seen are located in the downtown areas of major metropolitan areas, ensuring the maximum viewership of individuals often having to slow down for traffic. Ideally, a billboard should be placed on a site where drivers must slow down. The MCO advertising the Well-Care billboard, for example, located its billboard on a curve of a freeway running through a downtown metropolitan area.

The billboard for the M.D. Health Plan starts out with the driver as a potential patient (figure 5). The words are underlined in red, the color of blood, the signature of life. The color red is also eye-catching; it represents a highlighter and therefore draws the viewer's attention to the message expressed in the billboard. It is difficult for drivers to read messages as they fly by on an expressway. The color red serves to direct the driver's attention to the message. M.D. Health Plan would like the driver to associate the MCO with a healthy doctor-patient relationship. It purposefully does not include an image with this text. Red serves as the image in this words-only billboard. The striking color on a stark white background drives the viewer's attention to the essential message that M.D. Health Plan is trying to communicate.

If it's between you and your M.D., what is the role of the MCO? This billboard plays on the stereotypical negativity that consumers associate with MCOs, but it does not provide any positive images of what the MCO actually can do. An MCO that does not interfere with the doctor-patient relationship does not place any barriers between the two. This particular billboard is particularly interesting in that it clearly appeals to several different audiences. In particular, this billboard also appeals to physician-drivers. As is well known, physicians are as disenchanted as are consumers with MCOs. While many of the reasons are similar, such as the barriers to procedures the physician would like to perform, physicians also believe, correctly, that MCOs do not pay as generously as traditional health insurance. M.D. Health Plan, an MCO that physicians in this locale used to own until they sold it for a hefty financial gain to a large for-profit MCO, would like to convince local physicians that it still has their interests at heart.

Conclusion

Herman Melville's novel *The Confidence-Man* contains a character, the "Missouri bachelor," who asks the following question of an herb doctor: "Who is your master, pray, or are you owned by a company?" Americans are not ecstatic over the fact that today companies not only own doctors but in fact, like other sectors of the American economy, own the American health care system. MCOs are struggling with this sullied image and have understandably turned to advertising to clarify their role in the American health care system.

Billboards advertising MCOs, both visually and verbally, examine many themes using many styles in an effort to influence the viewer. While many billboards do not stray beyond a message advocating brand loyalty, MCOs use billboards for several other purposes. When the MCO highlights on a billboard a specific message, it is one that typically attempts to address consumer concern with perceived or real MCO policies. Promises by MCOs to provide unfettered access to specialists represent a topical response to consumer frustration with MCO interference with consumer choice of physician. Aside from access to care (such as specialists) and satisfaction, surely an important measure of quality, it is unusual for today's billboards touting MCOs to deal concretely with quality of care provided by these organizations. MCOs will inevitably begin to employ concrete messages pertaining to quality as they understand better how to market their adherence to guidelines or protocols of care and decreased mortality for a particular procedure such as a coronary bypass—without making the message too dry.

Whether the MCO billboard is trying to instill consumer loyalty or convince consumers that the care the MCO provides is high quality, billboards advertising MCOs provide the viewer with an amusing yet trenchant view of the rapidly changing relationship between patients (all consumers eventually become patients), their physicians, and the MCOs which pay and sometimes manage the care. Many viewers will see them and wish they could return to an era in which these billboards were not necessary.

However, the disappearance of billboards advertising MCOs from America's highways would certainly negate the increased consumer power that the messages within these billboards potentially reveal. Granted, this increased power has not yet reached a level at which consumers really do have a role in shaping significant aspects of MCO operations. This will occur only when MCOs have the economic incentive to truly assist physicians and consumers in managing the care of their enrollees. Today economic incentives encourage MCOs to identify and enroll healthy individuals — a phenomenon well illustrated in many MCO billboards. It is unlikely whether the rapidly changing health care system will enable MCOs to continue with this enrollment strategy. Drivers and passengers will place greater credibility on MCO billboards when salient information on quality of care is presented. Billboards touting increased satisfaction and brand loyalty are hopefully just the beginning phase of a revolution in health care which will lead to improved outcomes of care for consumers. In the meantime, the photographs in this article exemplify the tragic era in American medicine that both doctors and patients are living and dying through.

[I would like to thank Marshall Harmon for feedback and Angelo Merluccio for help with scanning the photographs.]

3 Fiction Films

Frankenflicks

Medical Monsters in Classic Horror Films

STEPHANIE BROWN CLARK

The cultural practice of exhibiting human curiosities, or "monsters," passed inevitably from the platform and the pit to the cinematic screen at the end of the nineteenth century beginning with Thomas Edison Manufacturing Company's version of *Frankenstein* (1910), one of its first moving pictures. Contemporaneously, the Selig Polyscope Company produced the first motion picture version of *Dr. Jekyll and Mr. Hyde*. By the 1930s, the nascent American motion picture industry's production of monster movies was epidemic and included James Whale's *Frankenstein* (1931), Rouben Mamoulian's *Dr. Jekyll and Mr. Hyde* (1931), and Erle Kenton's *Island of Lost Souls* (Dr. Moreau) (1933), among many others. Although the catalog of monster movies produced during the so-called Golden Age of Horror is extensive, it is the cluster of films about medical monsters, created out of the scientific manipulations and interventions of doctors such as Frankenstein, Jekyll, and Moreau, that invite an investigation of the odd coupling of medicine with monstrosity.

Science and Cinema

In 1895 Auguste and Louis Lumière invented the Cinématographe, an instrument for recording and projecting living motion; their invention borrowed some of its technology and inspiration from the work of other Europeans and Americans, notably Thomas Edison. In turn, Edison borrowed from French advances in film and sequencing cameras to develop his kinetoscope (1894) to record and reproduce objects in motion, which could then be viewed.

In 1903 the Edison Manufacturing Company produced a one-minute

1. Weird science. The creation of the monster was only possible because Frankenstein allowed his normal mind to be overcome by unnatural thoughts. *Frankenstein*, 1910, Thomas Edison Manufacturing Co. Courtesy of Jerry Ohlinger Movie Materials.

motion picture for public audiences, called *The Electrocution of an Elephant*, which recorded the execution of Topsy, one of the animal attractions at Coney Island's Luna Park, whose uncontrollable instincts caused her to kill three spectators. Several years later, the Edison Manufacturing Company announced the first motion picture version of *Frankenstein*, a "liberal adaptation of Mrs. Shelley's famous story." In this 1910 version, a monster is not electrified into life but boiled into being in the scientist's cauldron (figure 1).

At first glance, the execution of an uncontrollable animal, and the creation of a transgressive human monster, seem a strange and grotesque choice of subjects for the earliest of motion pictures. Yet the choice of subjects points to an implicit but often unnoticed interdependency between science and cinema as visual cultures. The interdependency is both historical and conceptual. Auguste Lumière, the so-called patriarch of cinema, was a scientist, primarily interested in medical research about tuberculosis and cancer. Although Lumière himself seems not to have considered the scientific applications for his Cinématographe, his contemporaries did and used it in their laboratories to observe the motions of the body. Many cinematic devices and techniques were developed and used by scientists researching optics and physiology.

Both scientific and popular cultures shared a particular fascination with *life* and "a frenzy for the visible" (Cartwright 1995; Comolli

1977; L. Williams 1989). At the turn of the twentieth century, cinema reflects and informs "the public fascination with scientific technology and its capacity to determine the course of life and death of living beings," from celebrity elephants to fictional monsters. These kinds of "physiological and technological spectacles of 'life'" represent a "transversal fascination across popular, public, and professional visual cultures" (Cartwright 13).

Michel Foucault locates the rise of biology in the late nineteenth century, when the conceptual model of man as a mechanical, nonevolving clock was reconfigured as a living, evolving organism subject to biological processes and interactions. At the beginning of the twentieth century, physiological and cinematic practices "focus upon the temporal and spatial decomposition and reconfiguration of bodies as dynamic fields of action in need of regulation and control" (Cartwright 1995, 47). Topsy's electrocution and Frankenstein's concoction of a monster satisfied the scientific and public desire to observe the flux and instability of biological bodies. The pleasures of observation in science and cinema are inherently visual.

The birth of cinema owes some of its creation to the scientific preoccupation with "seeing" in the early nineteenth century. In his book on medical perception, Foucault notices the emergence in medicine of what he calls an "epistemology of sight" in which what could be known was conditioned by what could be seen. Writing in French, Foucault suggests a linguistic and epistemological relationship between *voir, savoir,* and *pouvoir*—seeing, knowing, and power—in medical practices, which he calls "the medical gaze." The medical gaze of physicians in hospitals and newly emergent clinics at the beginning of the nineteenth century was directed at living bodies recategorized as unhealthy, abnormal, and disintegrated by disease processes against a taxonomy of health, equilibrium, and integrity. The voir of this medical gaze is inseparable from its savoir and pouvoir, so that the physician not only practices observation, or surveillance of the body in the hospital bed, but also authorizes interventions to control functions and processes within the body, which will determine the course of the life or death of the body under the medical gaze.

The preeminence of the visual in medical culture in the nineteenth century anticipates the birth of the cinema at the beginning of the twentieth century. As Cartwright has noticed, both the cinematic gaze and the medical gaze are directed at seeing bodies as spectacles of life, empowered by scientific technologies to intervene with the bodies and determine the course of the life and death of living beings. What has been less noticed is the strange kinship between the medical and the cinematic focus upon the explicitly and floridly abnormal or monstrous body. The fascination with life, and the frenzy for the visible in science and cinema, was also attended by a cultural and medical predilection for monsters.

If the cinematic gaze shares with the medical gaze the pleasures and the puzzles of the body, particularly the body rendered unhealthy, unregulated, and abnormal by unseen dysfunctions or pathologies, it is hardly coincidental that so many of the first cinematic productions were monstrous. When Universal Studios premiered James Whale's *Frankenstein* in November 1931, Paramount was in the midst of producing *Dr. Jekyll and Mr. Hyde*, and MGM was at work on *Freaks*. What followed was the unimagined success of the emerging genre of the sound horror film, and the beginnings of the Golden Age of Horror (Senn 1996, 21). The popularity of monster viewing at the movies is inseparable from the cultural frenzy for the visible, and the medical endorsement of the "epistemology of sight." Monstrous bodies are always in some way about seeing (Pender 1996, 144). And yet the public medical and cinematic gaze at monsters is a highly problematic practice.

Monstrosity and Multiplicity

In his memoirs published in 1923, Dr. Frederick Treves, physician at the London Hospital, recollected his first look at the so-called Elephant Man, "on exhibit" in a rented room off White Chapel Road in 1884. Treves remembered the banner that advertised the spectacle: "It was the figure of a man with the characteristics of an elephant. The transfiguration was not far advanced. There was still more of the man than of the beast. The fact — that it was still human — was the most repellent attribute of the creature . . . the loathsome insinuation of a man being changed into an animal" (Montagu 1979, 31).

The physician attributes Merrick's monstrosity to the visual ambiguity of its/his body; Merrick is not a human "being" but a human "becoming" an animal in a process of transformation that is "incomplete." Consequently Merrick is trans-formational, in between forms human and beastly. It/he is neither one thing nor the other. The in-betweenness or liminality (the Latin *limen* means threshold) of his body and identity as person/pachyderm confounds Treve's medical gaze. As such, Merrick was considered a monster. In David Lynch's *The Elephant Man*

(1974), an official announces that this particular exhibit is closed, explaining that "freaks are one thing, but this is monstrous."

Historically, "monster" has been a persistent and popular term for individuals who have visible physical bodily differences. Its etymology derives from *monstrere* (to show or demonstrate). However, it is also a medical term and has been used in scientific literature for centuries to describe congenital or acquired bodily defects, or dysmorphologies, commonly called "monstrosities." The scientific study of monsters, named teratology by French experimental embryologists Isidore and Etienne Geoffrey St. Hilaire in 1832, has its etymological origins in the Greek *teras* or Latin *terata* (monster).

Mark Dorrian (2000) has described the operative principle of monstrosity as "the coming together of what should be kept apart; the sense . . . that something is illegitimately *in* something else." Monstrosity merges; monstrosity morphs: "things that should be kept apart come together and live through one another" (313). The metaphysics underlying this principle is Platonic unity; monstrosity results from multiplicity within unity, "the many in the one," as two orders of deformity — disproportion and combination. Accordingly, beauty is a matter of geometry, integrity, and proportionality of form described by Vitruvius as *homo bene figuratus;* disfigurement, disintegration, disproportion of the body result in aesthetic and biological definitions of monstrosity. Biologically, dysmorphologies refer to bodily defects in which parts of the body are either absent or excessive (disproportion), or a part is doubled, wholly or partially, along one of its axes (combination).

Merrick's ambiguity is at once compelling, confounding, and intolerable. Elizabeth Grosz suggests that it is not gross deformities alone that make monsters so unsettling and fascinating to the viewer, but the blurring of identities between the viewer and the monster: "Monsters involve all kinds of doubling of the human form, a duplication of the body or some of its parts," provoking the viewer's fear "of the immersion or loss of identity with another." She suggests that "this fear, like the fear and horror of ghostly doubles or Doppleganger, is a horror at the possibility of our own imperfect duplication, a horror of submersion in an alien otherness, an incorporation in and by another" (Grosz 1996, 64–65). The result of this multiplicity in unity is a collapse of formal discriminations and the emergence of an impure form in which "an unnatural and filthy equivalency reigns." Monstrosity multiplies, merges, and mirrors, so that the monster's liminal body not only defines him as undefinable but engenders a further monstrosity out of the blurred identities between monster and viewer. The monster complicates and unsettles the pleasures of seeing abnormalities in their various forms and insists on provoking a look at the fundamental instability and liminality of personal identity.

Identity, however, is a matter of body. And soul. It is the psyche which has complicated the medical and the cinematic gaze at monsters. If the eye became the predominant and determining sense as the means to knowledge after the nineteenth century, the physical body, normal and abnormal, had the distinct advantage of its visibility. Given medicine's valuation of an "epistemology of sight" that depended on, and seemed limited to, the visible, it is understandable that medicine should have privileged the body. The body was privileged because its material surface could be observed. Legitimate science constrained medical practice to the level of the perceived; the embodied self, or psyche, was simply impossible to see. Beyond the boundaries of the medical gaze, the psyche remained difficult to know and control.

Although cinema emerged in part out of scientific technologies intended to visualize the physiological functions of the body, the invisible psychological dimensions of character represented a visual conundrum to doctors and directors. Perhaps the monster, as the subject of so many early cinematic productions, reflects the public and scientific desire to visualize not only the body but the soul.

Monsters and Movies

Edison's *Frankenstein* is less concerned with the biophysiology of the monster and his creation than with the psychological abnormalities of the doctor. The 1910 dramatic synopsis notes indicate that "the Edison Company has carefully tried to . . . concentrate its endeavors upon the mystic and psychological problems that are to be found in this weird tale. . . . Instead of creating a marvel of physical beauty and grace, there is unfolded before [Frankenstein's] eye and before the audience, an awful, ghastly abhorrent monster" (Weibel 20). The notes insist that "the story brings out the fact that the creation of the monster was only possible because Frankenstein had allowed his normal mind to be overcome by evil and unnatural thoughts." Frankenstein's "unnatural" and disintegrated psychological state engenders a physical monster. Frankenstein creates out of his own thoughts an embodiment of his unnatural psyche in the physical form of a separate and self-standing monster. The strange reciprocity between the doctor's mental state and the monster's physical status blurs their individual identities so that monster and maker both become "something unnatural *in* something else."

In the spectacular closing mirror scene described in the film notes, the equivalency between doctor and monster is made visually explicit; the restoration of the doctor's mental health through "the strength of [his] love for his bride and the effect of this on his mind" causes the monster to disintegrate visually:

> The monster broken down by his unsuccessful attempts to be with his creator enters the room, stands before a large mirror, holds out his arms entreatingly, but gradually the real monster fades away, leaving only the image in the mirror. A moment later Frankenstein himself enters. Standing directly before the mirror we see the remarkable sight of the monster's image reflected instead of the monster's own. Gradually, however, under the affect of love and his better nature, the monster's image fades and Frankenstein sees himself in his young manhood in the mirror. (Riley 1989, 19–20)

In this earliest of monster movies, a "filthy and unnatural equivalence" between doctor and creature represents a kind of monstrous merger of identities, body with soul. The visual ambiguities exploited cinematically in this ingenious mirror scene evoke horror at what Grosz has called "the submersion into an alien otherness and incorporation in and by another" (Grosz 1996, 65).

The psychological composition of the monster was apparently critical to James Whale (figure 2). In the opening scene, Frankenstein and his deformed assistant, Fritz, are scavenging for the final and crucial body part for the creature among the dead and the executed. Frankenstein announces "we must find [a] brain." Fritz breaks into the anatomical theater where Dr. Waldman has just described two brain specimens, one labeled "normal" and "the most perfect specimen that has ever come to my attention," and the other "the abnormal brain of the typical criminal." This brain, according to Waldman, exhibits "all of the degenerate characteristics that . . . check with the history of [its owner], whose life was one of brutality, violence, and murder." Waldman makes explicit his equivalence between brain and psyche. Fritz intends to retrieve the "perfect" brain but is startled by a loud noise, drops the specimen jar which breaks. Instead he takes the intact criminal brain. Once the creature is animated, and behaving badly, Waldman explains that the stolen brain belonged to a "brutal and vicious criminal" whose evil is "indelibly impressed" on the tissues. Franken-

2. "It's alive!" Dr. Frankenstein examines his creation. *Frankenstein*, 1931, dir. James Whale. Courtesy of Jerry Ohlinger Movie Materials.

stein "pales . . . looks defeated," but apparently dismisses this information; the brain is, "after all, just a piece of dead tissue." The monster is made of matter and therefore is "soulless, uniform and homogeneous" (Zakharieva 2000, 419–20).

And yet the physiological explanation for the creature's mental and moral abnormalities was troubling to the doctor, and the director. In the film's most notorious scene, Whale imagined the monster playing the "flower game" with a young girl, little Maria; the smiling monster, thinking Maria a flower, playfully tosses her into the water, and she drowns. Boris Karloff, who played the monster, wanted the script to be changed so that the child would not die or be hurt; "this was the nearest the Monster came to having a soul" (Riley 1989, 37). Whale insisted that "the death has to take place." Such a scene would jeopardize the integrity of the monster's character. His goodness would be inconsistent with the psychopathology of the brutal and vicious criminal mind, and inexplicable if the monster's psyche is only soulless cortical matter.

The significance of the brain is emphasized visually in the monster's peculiar flattop and scar. Jack Pierce, who made up the monster,

3. Skin deep. "Bits of thieves, bits of murderers . . . evil stitched to evil." *Mary Shelley's Frankenstein*, 1994, dir. Kenneth Branagh. Courtesy of David Del Valle Archives.

claimed that his anatomical research indicated that the most expedient way to remove or insert a brain was to "cut off the top of the skull straight across like a pot lid, hinge it, pop the brain in and then clamp it tight," which accounted for the monster's flat, square head "like a shoebox" with "that big scar across his forehead" (Riley 1989, 34). The skull shape of Whale's creature is visually emphasized. Whale's invention of the brain scene at the beginning of the film serves to reinforce the material nature of the monster's pieced-together body and to frame the problem of the monster's soul.

If Whale emphasized the skull, Kenneth Branagh emphasized skin. In his film *Mary Shelley's Frankenstein* (1996), Branagh opted for florid facial sutures to emphasize the composite form of the monster or "reanimant." When the monster finds a mirror, he reflects on his composition from "bits of thieves, bits of murderers, . . . evil stitched to evil stitched to evil" (figure 3). The stitched-togetherness of the monster, particularly his face, "this traditional mirror of the human soul that grounds the definition of a unified being" lacks the unity of composition that marks it as beautiful (Zakharieva 2000, 418, 423).

The visual juxtaposition of the monstrous body being made inside Frankenstein's laboratory and the image of Leonardo da Vinci's beautiful Vitruvian man, *homo bene figuratus*, posted on the outer cupboard emphasizes the disfigurement, disintegration, and disproportion of the reanimant's body. The monster's identity depends on a process of *re-membering* that is physical, psychological, and radically unfinished. The monster asks Frankenstein: "What of my soul? Do I have one? Or was that a part you left out? Who were these people of which I am composed? Good people? Bad people?" Frankenstein answers: "Materials. Nothing more." The monster resists the reduction of his being to the biological. He asks: "Do you know that I know how to play the flute? In which part of me did this knowledge reside? In these hands? In this mind? In this heart? And reading and speaking? Not things learned as much as things remembered. Who am I?" Frankenstein is unable to supply him with an identity and replies that he does not know. Articulate monsters in horror films invariably ask questions of identity; their makers can supply a biological explanation about the physical body as "dead tissue" or "materials," but the metaphysical components of identity, the "what" of the monster's soul, remain invisible to the clinical and cinematic gaze, beyond knowing and controlling.

Visualizing the psychological interior of doctor and monster is also critical in director Rouben Mamoulian's *Dr. Jekyll and Mr. Hyde* (1931). Mamoulian deployed an innovative perspective technique in the opening scene, which situates the viewer inside of the doctor's head, to experience the disembodied and subjective condition of being Dr. Jekyll. Mamoulian explained: "The camera begins by being Jekyll and Hyde. . . . I wanted to put the audience in to Jekyll's shoes and make them feel a little sharper the vertigo that Jekyll goes through" (Senn 1996, 38). If the viewer is inside Jekyll's head, it is impossible to see what he looks like physically, except through a mirror. In the initial shot, Jekyll is first seen looking at himself in a mirror (figure 4). While Mamoulian's point-of-view technique foregrounds Jekyll's subjectivity, and his *milieu interieur*, the mirror scene simultaneously points to the instability of his identity as merely a representation. Grosz reminds us that the shape of one's own externality is always inaccessible by direct means; one cannot visualize oneself except by looking at a mirror representation in which one's image is projected "outside" (Grosz 1996, 65).

Subjectivity is central to the film's director and to its doctor. In his lecture to the medical students, Dr. Jekyll asserts that he "will not talk about the secrets of the body, but the soul of man." The soul of man is not a singularity, but a multiplicity of souls, "chained together": the one "strives for the nobilities of life, we call his good self," and the other "seeks an expression of impulses that bind him to some dull animal relation with the earth; this we may call the bad." Jekyll pro-

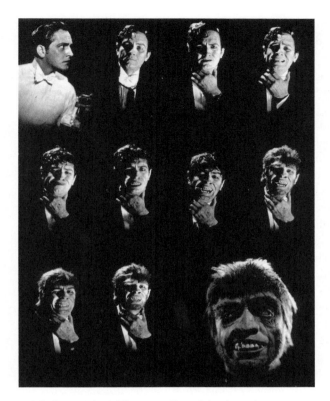

4. Jekyll unstitched. The unraveling of the doctor's
psyche into two souls. *Dr. Jekyll and Mr. Hyde*, 1931,
dir. Rouben Mamoulian. Courtesy of Jerry Ohlinger
Movie Materials.

poses to separate them. The scientific unchaining or unstitching of the
apparent seamless integrity of Jekyll's psyche into two souls creates a
monster. Monstrosity arises here out of the doubling not of body parts
but of psychic parts within one body to produce "many in the one." Dr.
Jekyll's homogeneous self is exposed as an unstable heterogeneity of
identities.

As Mamoulian understood Jekyll's hypothesis, the distinction between these psychic twins is "not between good and evil, but between
the sophisticated spiritual self in man and his animal, primeval instincts" (Senn 1996, 37). To represent this other soul visually, Mamoulian imagined a simian and bestial Mr. Hyde, who would be "an exact
replica of the Neanderthal Man" (35). In effect, this other soul is
turned inside out so that what was interior to Jekyll is now exterior and

visible. The monster's name, *Hyde*, puns on sight/site. *Hide* suggests that which is deliberately made to be invisible and secret by being covered over by something else; *hide* is also a synonym for skin. What is hyde-ing inside Dr. Jekyll is relocated and exposed at the epidermal surface. The model of a monster hiding behind a respectable or aesthetically pleasing front seems to produce a deep, structured subjectivity, but that hidden self "subverts the notion of an authentic self and makes subjectivity a surface effect" (Halberstam 1995, 64).

The transformation of Dr. Jekyll into Mr. Hyde replicates the opening scene, in which the initial metamorphosis is filmed through the eyes of Dr. Jekyll, who holds a vial of elixir in front of a mirror. As Jekyll's metamorphosis begins, the loss of a controlling presence is signaled by the erratic spinning of the camera; when Jekyll collapses, the camera also follows him to the floor. When the transformation is complete, the camera moves back to the mirror, and the audience looks into it to see the bestial and hairy Hyde looking back. Inverting the same mirror metamorphosis sequence in the Edison *Frankenstein*, the doctor degenerates to monster, as a body effect of the monstrous aspect of his psyche. Dr. Jekyll, like the Edison Dr. Frankenstein, "allowed his normal mind to be overcome by evil and unnatural thoughts" that effectively created the monster.

Even in Whale's film, which does not deploy the laboratory mirror as the site of this doctor/monster transformation, the film's creation scene visually juxtaposes the mental disintegration of the doctor and the creature's animation. The twitch of the monster's sutured hand is a physical sign of animation in "life." Simultaneously, Dr. Frankenstein staggers and places his own hands on the table on which his monster lies, shouting, "It's alive!" According to the screenplay notes, he was to "laugh crazily" and sway precariously to suggest that he is "bordering on collapse" that is both physical and psychological (Riley 1989, 31). Frankenstein's psychological collapse has been anticipated by his professor, Dr. Waldman, who earlier observed that "Herr Frankenstein is greatly changed"; Frankenstein's best friend, Victor, called him "insane," and his fiancée, Elizabeth, remarked that he is "ill."

In both *Frankenstein* films, and in *Dr. Jekyll and Mr. Hyde*, the unnormalizing of the doctor's mind is implicated in the birth of his monster. Although Jekyll's research program was intended to induce absolute mental hygiene (health), in which he would be "clean not only in [his] conduct but in [his] innermost thoughts and desires," he diagnoses himself as "ill in soul."

Jekyll is provoked to experiment with the separation of his soul after his fiancée's father, Brigadier General Carew, refuses to advance the couple's wedding date for respectability's sake; Carew argues that "there is such a thing as respectful observance." Jekyll's desire for a "proper" wedding and marriage with Muriel are repeatedly frustrated; his satisfaction is postponed. When he discovers that she has been taken away to Bath for a month, he actively begins his research. The unclean, unnatural, and animal instincts of Jekyll's other soul are configured sexually in Mamoulian's version. Jekyll's otherness is represented as sexual unhealthiness, or perversity. Mamoulian emphasizes the sadism of Hyde's relationship with Ivy Pierson, whom he forces to become his mistress: "I hurt you because I love you. I *want* you. And what I want, I get!" Sander Gilman has argued that "perversion is the basic quality ascribed to the sexuality of the Other" (Gilman 1985, 73).

Mamoulian's treatment of Jekyll and his other self in terms of sexual propriety and perversity had its antecedents in Adolph Zukor's 1920 version of *Dr. Jekyll and Mr. Hyde*. Zukor's film was based on the novel of Robert Louis Stevenson, published in 1886, and adapted for the stage the following year by theatrical entrepreneur Thomas Russell Sullivan, starring Richard Mansfield in the principal role. Zukor borrowed from both the novel and the play but also incorporated elements from Oscar Wilde's *The Picture of Dorian Gray*, which was published in 1891 (Glut 1978, 85). According to David Skal, "*Dorian Gray* was Wilde's *Frankenstein*." Dramatic adaptations and subsequent cinematic versions of the two narratives conjoined *Dorian Gray* and *Jekyll and Hyde* "in a lucrative hybrid formula, cemented in Rouben Mamoulian's 1931 film" (Skal 1998, 72).

Wilde's novel is unsettling in its implications about identity itself. While the most sinister of Dorian's perversions are inferred to be homosexual, his sexual inversion is superimposed on a second kind of inversion of soul and body. In the novel, Lord Henry Wotton remarks: "Soul and body, body and soul—how mysterious they were! Who could say where the fleshly impulse ceased or the psychical impulse began?" (Wilde [1891] 1981, 58). In fact, the separation of the soul from the body is exactly the aesthetic outcome of the portrait. The effect of this separation is a visual "inversion" of the normally hidden inner life of Dorian's soul, made visible in the portrait. It is his soul that is monstrous; his body retains its physical beauty. Monstrosity is turned inside out: "Frankenstein's monster terrified people because of his appearance; Jekyll and Dorian are monstrous because an exterior hides a corrupt self" (Halberstam 1995, 74). Subjectivity comes to the surface, where it can be seen. The portrait becomes a self-consuming artifact: "through some strange quickening of inner life the leprosies of sin were slowly eating the thing away" (Wilde [1891] 1981, 100). Dorian is consumed internally, just as Jekyll is eaten away from within by his Hyde.

In 1896 Wilde was arrested on charges of gross indecency. Wilde's identity merged with that of his monstrous creation; *Dorian Gray* was used as evidence against him. At this time, H. G. Wells had begun *The Island of Dr. Moreau*, which he claimed was written in reaction to Wilde's "scandalous trial" and "the graceless and pitiful downfall of a man of genius." Wells claimed that his novel was "the response of an imaginative mind to the reminder that humanity is but animal rough-hewn and in perpetual internal conflict between instinct and injunction" (Skal 1998, 76).

Although Wells persistently rejected attempts to adapt his novels to either stage or screen, he finally agreed to a production by Paramount in 1934, directed by Erle C. Kenton, starring Charles Laughton, and retitled *Island of Lost Souls* (figure 5). In this film, Dr. Moreau's scientific project is the creation of hybrids of all kinds through selective reproduction. He attempts to transform animals into humans by inter-species mating. Unfortunately, the metamorphosis is unstable. Moreau complains that his creatures' "beast flesh keeps creeping back." The existing beast folk are monstrous because of their hybridity; they are neither wholly animal nor wholly human. When the beast folk revolt against Moreau, the Sayer of the Law tells him: "You made us things, not men, not beasts. Things." It is impossible to know if the nature of their apparent monstrosity, the quality of hybridity as "something illegitimately in something else," belongs to the beast in the man, or to the human in the animal. The ambiguity of their being is framed as a case of mistaken identity. When shipwrecked Edward Parker is brought to the island, he observes the "strange looking natives" and assumes them to be human. When Parker discovers Moreau in his lab with a screaming subject, he believes he has witnessed the "vivisection of a man" in the House of Pain. Moreau corrects him and explains that the creature he saw "started as an animal"; his procedure was intended to excise the beast flesh, to "burn out all of the animal" and make the creature "completely human." The doctor's surgical procedure on his creatures' bodies is only temporarily and partially successful. Moreau, like Frankenstein, attempts to construct and control his monsters through the body, as if identity is inscribed on the flesh.

Flesh is sacred on Moreau's island. According to the law, the beast folk are "not to eat meat" or "to spill blood." In the climactic final scene, in which the beast folk rise up against Moreau, he is brought to the House of Pain, where his creatures eviscerate and dismember his body. Moreau's flesh is brutally transformed by the raging interventions of the beast folk whom he has created. The manimals spill Moreau's blood and presumably eat his flesh. The doctor is, in effect, consumed.

In director John Frankenheimer's postmodern remake of *The Island of Dr. Moreau* (1996), starring Marlon Brando, this scene is explicitly cannibalistic. The shipwreck survivor, renamed Edward Douglas, reminds the leader of the insurrection, the hybrid Hyena-Swine: "You all killed [Moreau] the Father, you all ate his flesh." Through murder, the beast people have literally in-corp-orated Moreau, but without the effect of becoming like Moreau. They remain neither wholly animal nor wholly man, but somewhere in between.

In the 1996 film, Dr. Moreau performs no surgeries to excise "beast flesh"; his project is not to change the physical composition of his experimental subjects but to create a perfect soul by excising the destructive elements in the psyche (figure 6). Moreau tells Douglas that he has seen "the devil under his microscope and metaphorically cut him to pieces. . . . The devil is that element in human nature that impels us to violence and debasement. For seventeen years I have been striving for some measure of refinement in the human species." Moreau overlooks the "monstrous deformities" of the natives, which appall Douglas: "These creatures represent a stage in the process in the eradication of destructive elements found *in the psyche*, and I have almost achieved perfection. If in my tinkering, I have fallen short of the human form by a snout, or claw or hoof, it really is of no great importance" (italics mine). Frankenheimer's film complicates monstrosity by making it an essentially interiorized condition, reframed against gene and genealogy instead of sexual reproduction and perversity. The device of the mirror as site of interface between doctor and monster is supplanted by the transparencies of glass, a confrontation with the monster *in vitro*—under the microscope and in the petri dish. The blurring of identities between doctor and monster in this film may be inferred to be cloning; Moreau's M'aja, who is dressed identically to Moreau, seems intended to be a disfigured and dwarfed copy of the doctor.

Frankenheimer's *Moreau* shares with other postmodern horror films of doctors and their monsters the relocation of monstrosity of the body to a condition of embodiment. Embodiment as a condition is equivocal about where the fleshly impulse ceases or the psychic impulse begins.

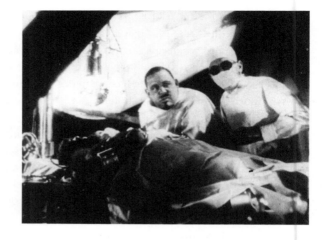

5. Moreau's hybrids. "The beast flesh keeps creeping back." *Island of Lost Souls*, 1933, dir. Erle C. Kenton. Courtesy of David Del Valle Archives.

6. Marlon's hybrids: "These creatures represent a stage in the eradication of destructive elements of the psyche." *The Island of Dr. Moreau*, 1996, dir. John Frankenheimer. Courtesy of David Del Valle Archives.

Frankenheimer's doctor postulates a code of humanness in the fragile double helix of our DNA which bridges soma and self. Unlike the 1933 Moreau, who alters living forms with "a slight change in a single unit of germ plasm" to destroy the "beast flesh," the modern Moreau manipulates suboptical genetic material to cut the devil of disease within the psyche to pieces. In so doing, his gene-splicing project problematizes the relationship of the body's material composition (genes) and mind.

In its most recent rendering, this question of embodiment is literalized in the classic horror films *The Silence of the Lambs* (1991) and its sequel, *Hannibal* (2001) (figures 7 and 8). The doctor is recast not as research scientist but as psychiatrist. Hannibal Lecter is a doctor of the psyche, who also cannibalizes his victims' bodies. His is a hybrid identity, constituted as both "Hannibal the Cannibal," and "Lecter the Intellecter." He conjoins a pathological predilection for the flesh and a professional appetite for the contents of the mind. The elaborate final scene of *Hannibal* presents the doctor's merged psychological and cannibalistic tastes. He gets inside the head of FBI agent Paul Krendler, whose skull he has expertly unhinged, and carefully picks his brains, figuratively and with a fork. He carefully feeds Krendler his own brain, which he swallows. Krendler is simultaneously dismembered and dissected, and also remade. Through his act of self-cannibalism, Krendler's body is simultaneously consumed and also reincorporated and digested to become part of his body again, as if brain and mind, body and soul, could be endlessly reconstituted.

Lecter's monster making is psychological. Hannibal does not make a monster by his own hand in a lab typical of Frankenstein, Jekyll, and Moreau; he "gets inside your head" and exposes the monstrosities of his victim's psyche at the skin's surface. Skin and psyche for Lecter are seamless. He gets "under one's skin, into one's thoughts and he makes little of the classic body-mind split as he eats bodies and sucks minds dry" (Halberstam 1995, 164). The monsters in *The Silence of the Lambs* and *Hannibal* are self-made. Buffalo Bill, Lecter's former patient, attempts to remake himself by constructing a "woman suit" from the flesh of his victims. In the sequel, Lecter induces Mason Verger to "try peeling off your face and feeding to the dogs." Verger performs his own procedure with a piece of broken glass, which leaves him monstrously disfigured.

In these most recent versions of the doctor/monster horror film, personal identity, constituted by body and soul, becomes a process and an effect of which subjectivity is a condition to be made, unmade, and

7. You are what you eat. Hannibal Lecter and Paul Krendler. *Hannibal*, 2001, dir. Ridley Scott. Courtesy of Jerry Ohlinger Movie Materials.

8. Self-made monsters. Buffalo Bill, Lecter's former patient, attempts to remake himself by stitching a "woman suit" from the flesh of his victims. *The Silence of the Lambs*, 1991, dir. Jonathan Demme. Courtesy of David Del Valle Archives.

remade endlessly: "Lecter illustrates to perfection the spooky and un-canny effect of confusing boundaries, inside and outside, consuming and being consumed, watching and being watched" (Halberstam 1995, 164).

Conclusion

The emergence of cinema first as a scientific, then as a cultural, tool to visualize the dynamic life processes, known as physiology, recon-figured the body at the beginning of the twentieth century. The phys-iological body could no longer be considered as a static, unified struc-ture, but now was seen as a dynamic and unstable phenomenon. In particular, the monstrous body became the site of cinematic and scien-tific attention because it is a representation of the body's liminality "in transformative motion; it is the body in the act of becoming" (Dorrian 2000, 312). It was the strange ambiguity of transformation, the in-betweenness of being human and something else, that confounded Dr. Treves when he first observed the Elephant Man, and continues to fascinate and frustrate the medical and the cinematic gaze at monsters in horror films.

Like the recent Lecter films, the older, classic horror films, like *Frankenstein, Dr. Jekyll and Mr. Hyde*, and *Island of Lost Souls/Dr. Moreau*, present abnormal, scientifically produced bodies and souls that disturb assumptions about beauty, normalcy, health, and selfhood. Monsters suggest "the epistemological menace of unstable identities" (Halberstam 1995, 64). Identity is a messy, even filthy, heterogeneity for everybody, including monsters. Anomalous human bodies "gesture towards other modes of being and confuse comforting distinctions between what is human and what is not" (Thomson 1996, 1). Medical monsters who subvert medical control of their doctors remind us that an essential and homogeneous self is not begotten, but made or "pro-duced." The made-up and composite nature of these various monsters is exquisitely fragile and contingent on the doctor in every case. The monstrous psyche and body are contingencies and constructions. They are both, as Moreau's assistant Dr. Montgomery observed, "unstable phenomena."

In these films, the directors must represent the inner psychology of the characters visually. The physical body stands as a visual sign of one's inner nature. The physical anomalies of the monster's form are inscribed with pathological significations about his/its psyche. Sharon

Snyder refers to this visual practice as an "ideology of the physical," which constructs "an imagined reciprocity between the physical surface of the body as a medium that exposes the more abstract and intangible landscapes of psychology, morality, and spirituality" (Mitchell and Snyder 1997, 13). The popular and cinematic gaze desires to see the monster's formal corruption as a material sign of an analogous disturbance or degeneration in the condition of his soul.

And yet such an ideology is destabilized by monsters. The visually different body fascinates and disturbs as it reminds us that *embodiment* is not reducible to the *body*. "Notwithstanding the objectifying and deracinating demand of the medical regime, embodiment remains an unstable nexus of discursive forces that explodes the distinction between mental and bodily realms" (Clark and Myser 1996, 352). Monsters point instead to the liminality of being, and to the limits and contingencies of the cinematic and the medical gaze.

Big Boys Do Cry

Empathy in *The Doctor*

LUCY FISCHER

> When physicians fall sick they learn the value of
> empathy . . . they discover how great a price they have
> paid for suppressing emotions. — Howard Spiro,
> *Empathy and the Practice of Medicine*

The Doctor (1991) is a work about the contemporary medical scene, adapted for the screen from the autobiography *A Taste of My Own Medicine*, by Dr. Edward E. Rosenbaum. At the beginning of the film, we are introduced to Dr. Jack McKee (William Hurt), a droll, impersonal, technologically oriented heart surgeon who likes to "cut and get out." During the course of the narrative, however, he falls ill with a cancerous, laryngeal tumor that forces him to view the medical institution from a new perspective — that of a sick individual. This regrettable rite of passage causes McKee to discern numerous problems in modern medical practice (many of which he has personally perpetrated). As he proceeds through treatment, he is transformed as a human being, a physician, and an educator of medical practitioners.

On the one hand, *The Doctor* presents itself as a simple parable of role reversal or of the tables turned. Alternately, it can be viewed as an ethical lesson concerning how we should do unto others as we wish to be treated ourselves. But beyond such melodramatic and moralizing impulses, the film highlights and enacts many crucial issues that arise in current debates on empathy and medicine, and the proper role of affect in a physician's work life.

Changes in medicine's theoretical orientation and the subsequent restructuring of health care institutions gradually reordered diagnostic and therapeutic priorities. The theoretical grounding of practice shifted from a personal knowledge of unique individuals to the universal and objective knowledge of physiological processes.
— Maureen A. Milligan and Ellen Singer More,
The Empathetic Practitioner

Most discussions of the role of empathy in medicine establish some kind of dichotomy between the poles of science and human emotion. The argument goes that prior to the nineteenth century, when medicine depended less on scientifically based models and measures of human physiology, medical practice was primarily based on interactions between doctors and patients. As Stanley Joel Reiser (1993) states: "The instruments of physical diagnosis [e.g., the stethoscope] redirected the physician's attention from a focus on the patient's experience to a focus on the body's structure" (126). Given such a radical change, physicians acquired scientific information about a patient's physiognomy rather than concentrating on the ill person's feelings. Clearly, since the methods of procuring data were highly scientific, the patient often had more contact with medical laboratories and technicians than with physicians. Further contributing to this transition in medical practice was the professional assumption that, as highly (and expensively) trained scientists, physicians made better use of their valuable time ordering and interpreting test results than focusing on personal interaction. In the light of "objective" measures of human bodily function, therefore, patient testimony began to be discredited. These factors contributed to a reduction in face-to-face encounters between physicians and patients, as well as to a loss of a doctor's communicative skills.

One of the crucial interpersonal skills in health care is that of empathy — which is defined as "the process . . . by which one perceives and understands the subjective experience of another person" (Lavasseur and Vance 1993, 79). It is the alleged loss of this quality in modern physician behavior that troubles many members of the medical community. As Milligan and More (1994) state, "the very idea of 'professionalism' has proved profoundly detrimental to many practitioners' sense of personal integration and responsibility. In its desire to shun the subjective and personal in favor of the objective and universal, scientific professionalism risks detaching personal responsibility from technical expertise" (5).

Aside from technological advances in medicine and the ascension of "pure" science, critics cite other reasons for the loss of empathic skills in medical practice. Some find the impersonality (and even brutality) of medical education part of the problem, with physicians replicating the kind of dispassionate handling they received from their teachers and mentors with their patients. As Shimon M. Glick (1993) states, "callous and inconsiderate treatment of students and residents during times of personal difficulties . . . may result in undesirable and impaired behavior toward patients" (93). Others see the growth of group or team medicine as leading to a diffusion of personal concern and responsibility in dealing with patients (Spiro 1993, 3). Additionally, some critics find the contemporary focus on medical "cases" versus individuals as contributing to empathy's decline. As Spiro notes: "In clinical medicine, we talk mostly about the 'case' and not about the person; reports are written in the passive voice to imply that truth is being uncovered by an ineluctable force" (10). Other commentators see lapses in empathy as arising, in part, through the growing fragmentation of medical practice, with patient care delegated to numerous physicians, each with a specialty regarding a particular body part (Glick 1993, 87). Finally, some question whether distance is advisable for all medical specialties. As Spiro asks: "Is it as helpful to the internist as to the surgeon?" (12).

Beyond such institutional modifications, personal reasons exist why physicians may avoid feeling empathy for their patients. Dealing with sick people, some of whom will die, can heavily drain a doctor's emotional life. To immerse oneself in the full tragedy of each patient's pain and trouble could be an impossible task for one who must also be a competent, reliable day-to-day practitioner. Surely physicians use certain degrees of separation to keep their affective side at bay. But when does such distanciation cease to function in a purely protective manner and begin to endanger the doctor/patient relationship?

Some writers think that the entire dichotomy between science and emotion is misconceived, in that it treats medical practice as a case of either/or. In truth, they argue, no instance of quality care exists without a combination of objectivity and involvement. As Glick observes: "A failure of compassion will inevitably lead to *poor science* in medicine because it ignores data critical to the patient's care" (91). For E. J. Cassel, such gaps frequently "cause suffering by applying . . . technical knowledge without regard for the personhood of [the] patient" (Lavasseur and Vance 1993, 81). Finally, Jodi Halpern (1993) asserts that emotions have their intellectual component as well. As she remarks, "Empathy involves using emotions for *cognitive purposes*. The notion that *experiencing* emotion is necessary to accurately *understand* someone challenges the ideal of 'detached concern' " (171; first italics mine). In addition to constituting good science, empathy has been seen as entering into medicine's moral dimension. As Milligan and More (1994) note: "We . . . believe that any *ethical* practice of medicine requires a certain amount of empathy" (4; italics mine).

Commentators also note that today's physicians have lost their "narrative/interpretive" skills through their disregard of patient testimony — formerly the major source of knowledge about the progress of an individual's disease. As Helle Mathiasen and Joseph A. Alpert (1993) observe: "Only with narrative competence can a physician deliver empathetic care. Without a robust narrative knowledge of the patient, the physician cannot . . . accompany the patient through the illness experience" (150). Similarly, Halpern (1993) finds that "empathy helps physicians understand patients and communicate better with them, which enhances diagnosis and treatment" (172).

> The ability to enter the patient's life, the essence
> of empathy, is practiced less often than the ability to
> enter the patient's body through medical technology.
> — Stanley Joel Reiser, "Science, Pedagogy, and the
> Transformation of Empathy in Medicine"

Clearly, *The Doctor* is a narrative of patient testimony, albeit a fictional one based on an autobiographical account. While on the screen Dr. McKee initially fails to sensitively read his clients' story lines, we, as viewers, like good doctors, must succeed in discerning *his*. Part of McKee's narrative entails his deficiency in empathic behavior. Numerous examples of this inadequacy propose themselves. At the beginning of the movie, Dr. McKee and assisting physicians perform heart surgery on a young man who has attempted suicide. The scene is set with the kind of music that McKee insists on listening to in his operating room. One of the first selections is "Big Girls Don't Cry" — an anthem to emotional stoicism. His "closing music" is (as always) "Why Don't We Get Drunk and Screw," a song whose lyrics, sung by Jimmy Buffet, mock not only love but, in the OR context, any reverence for holding a human life in one's hand. Furthermore, Jack jokes to his fellow surgeons about how the young man being saved should have taken a course on suicide so that he could have performed it successfully. McKee later suggests that if the young man had really wanted to submit to torture, he should have taken up golf. In a scene that follows, a colleague of McKee's, Dr. Eli Blumfield (Adam Arkin), an ear, nose, and throat surgeon, calls Jack in to look at a patient about to undergo surgery, but who is still semiconscious. McKee immediately jokes with the patient about how he should fire the anesthesiologist; Dr. Blumfield quickly explains that McKee is "only kidding."

In another vignette, McKee sees a female patient who is recovering from heart surgery with a large scar on her chest. With a look of sorrow and angst, she confesses that her husband asks whether the scar will always be so visible — a sign to her that she has lost her sexual allure. McKee fires back: "Tell him that you're a *Playboy* centerfold and have the staples to prove it." Not surprisingly, in the first scene on rounds with his residents, Jack lectures them about the "danger in feeling too strong about your patient, in becoming too involved." Rather, he asserts that surgery is about "judgment" which requires that one be "detached." This speech and the kind of gallows humor that McKee has perfected allow him to face the dire responsibilities of his job, but we sense that his defense has gone too far. His brand of flippant, glib behavior seems especially ironic since he is a surgeon of the heart — an organ that is, metaphorically, seen as the seat of human passion.

What is resonant about *The Doctor* is the fact that Jack McKee has allowed his professional alienation to factor into his family life — as though the loving and nurturing part of him has entirely atrophied. In the film's early scenes, his offhand and comical conversations with his wife, Anne (Christine Lahti), make it clear that he often forgets certain family obligations (like showing up for parents' night at his son's school). When he comes home unexpectedly one day, Anne shouts to their son that Daddy wants to speak to him; the boy automatically reaches for the telephone to talk. Anne, then, jokes that Daddy is making a special "personal appearance" — obviously a rare occurrence. To its credit, the film does not portray the relationship between Jack and Anne as entirely hostile. Rather, it has tinges of romance and flirtation but clearly lacks emotional depth. The same holds for Jack's kinship with his son: it is not gothic but, instead, simply empty. As a visual metaphor of the defect in the family's emotional core, their kitchen (the center of a house's hearth and home), is being gutted in preparation for its renovation (figure 1).

1. Dr. Jack (William Hurt) and Anne (Christine Lahti) McKee try to restore their relationship in the midst of a kitchen renovation following Jack's cancer surgery. The Museum of Modern Art Film Stills Archive.

2. Dr. Jack McKee (William Hurt) attempts to explain his illness to his rather distant son (Charlie Korsmo). The Museum of Modern Art Film Stills Archive.

After Jack becomes ill, he imposes the same distance between himself and Anne as he has between himself and his patients. When she says that "We'll" beat the cancer, he erupts in anger, yelling, "*We* don't have it. It's not a team game!" Subsequently, when he goes for a biopsy, he dismisses her from the hospital, telling her to go home. When she finally begins to tune him out, he chastises her for being "cold." Later in the drama he admits to a fellow patient (while holding his arm out at a distance): "I've kept [Anne] . . . over there for so long . . . [that] now I can't get my arm down." Jack's son has been made in his own image. When Jack finally tells him about his illness, the boy is in a rush and says he has to go. If medicine is not a team game for Jack and his patients, neither is it a team game for his family (figure 2).

The same holds true of his medical practice. On one occasion, after Jack momentarily hesitates in the operating room, a colleague, Dr. Murray Kaplan (Mandy Patinkin), informs him that members of their group have decided that Jack should not practice for a while. Jack shouts: "Can everyone wipe that caring look off his face, because it's a royal pain?" Interestingly, the physicians have not really been caring but are simply concerned with the possibility that Jack's illness will lower their positive group performance evaluation, either through appointment cancellations or potential lawsuits.

Finally, as an emblem of how Jack refuses to "share" his malady with others, when he is admitted to the hospital for surgery, he is outraged to find that there are no private rooms available, a perk he has expected for his physician status. Thus he will have to share a room with another sick individual, a fact that he finds abhorrent. Jack's emotional distance from his patients is mirrored in both familial and professional aspects of his life.

> We believe that the doctor-patient relationship
> often closely resembles the prototypical male-female
> relationship. — Janet L. Surrey and Stephen J. Bergman,
> "Gender Differences in Relational Development"

The Doctor also subtly invokes gender issues that ultimately circle back to the subject of empathy. Throughout the narrative, the medical world is portrayed, quite insistently, as sexist. In the opening OR scene, when McKee and his cohorts sing "Why Don't We Get Drunk and Screw," they tease Nancy, a middle-aged African American nurse, who never sings along—a sign that she has either a heightened sense of propriety about the surgical process or an elevated sense of what constitutes misogyny. Jack's treatment of the female heart patient with a scar on her chest is another instance of insensitivity to sexual difference. McKee jokes about the woman's bodily appearance without seeming to realize that, culturally and traditionally, this is the "centerpiece" (if not the "centerfold") of a woman's life. Later on, as Jack and Anne drive home together one night, his beeper goes off. When he answers the call, it is the wife of a heart surgery patient inquiring whether her husband can mow the lawn (as he insists on doing), an issue around which she expresses great consternation. Jack can barely contain his laughter at what he obviously views as her hysterical female anxiety. In yet another sequence (after Jack realizes that he must see a throat specialist), he asks his fellow doctors for their recommendations. They point to Dr. Leslie Abbott (Wendy Crewson), a female physician who is walking through the hospital corridors. One man says, "There's your ear, nose, and throat *man.*" They then proceed adolescently to ogle her from afar, claiming that she "does great throat." While at first glance these scenes suggest societal sexism that does not seem especially relevant or limited to the medical profession, the film ultimately ties this syndrome to the male medical establishment's capacity for empathy.

Social psychologists such as Nancy Chodorow recognize that female children in traditional families grow up with different relational skills than do male. Because of a girl's bond with her mother (her most obvious role model), she develops competence in tasks commonly associated with women, among them the ability to connect and communicate with people and to share their feelings. In the conventional home, where women are primarily mothers and homemakers, it falls to them to keep the family together on both emotional and functional levels. The ordinary male child, on the other hand, separates himself from his mother and her interpersonal skills, since he must give up a close identification with the female to become a "true man." Hence researchers claim that the genders have different stances on empathy. As Surrey and Bergman (1994) note: "Healthy growth takes place through and toward connection. Developmental differences between women and men, however, can have significant implications for male-female relationships. These may include differences in empathetic attunement, in emphasis on mutuality in relationship, and in orientation to the relational process" (113).

In this equation, women are found to have superior communicative skills to men. Since until quite recently medicine has been largely a male profession (and still is, when it comes to prestigious surgical specialties), this meant that doctors, in general, were found to be deficient in emotional attachment. On the other hand, within the sex typing of the medical profession, nurses (who were predominantly female) were seen to be the "heart" to the physician's "mind." As Lavasseur and Vance (1993) remark, "nursing as a profession has historically been concerned with empathy and its place in the patient-caregiver relationship" (76). Here we might reevaluate the reaction of Nurse Nancy to the singing of the profane country music song in the OR. Perhaps she does not like to join in because she has empathy for the patient, who might feel degraded by the lyric "Let's get drunk and screw" if he knew it were being played. On the other hand, when Dr. McKee undergoes surgery himself, his colleagues make sure that Nancy assists, given that he is so fond of her. On this one occasion, she sings the song to him (before he is given anesthesia), and he is pleased. Obviously her decision to sing or not to sing depends on her sense of the patient: in one case she finds it unseemly, but in another she sees it as a means of kindness and reassurance.

Certainly, medical culture has changed in recent years, especially with the rise of feminism and the rapid entry of women into the medical profession. While feminism has been successful in changing the number of female medical students, it may not have altered medical culture in more profound ways. Rather than male doctors becoming more like women, female doctors have become more like men — learning to underplay their emotive skills in favor of a more scientific approach. Similarly, with nurses (or nurse practitioners) now responsible for more surgical and technical interventions, it is possible that they will have less time for (or interest in) personal interaction with patients (Lavasseur and Vance 1993, 79).

Hence, while we might expect the narrative of *The Doctor* to be peppered with sensitive female physicians who contrast with Jack McKee, this is not the case, a fact that saves the film from suspect and banal oppositions. In the autobiography on which the drama is based, Dr. Rosenbaum actually is treated by *no* female physicians; all the specialists he consults are men. Hence it is a pointed decision on the part of the film's scenarist and director to foreground the issue of gender in medicine. There is one female resident in the film who is, in fact, compassionate and balks at Jack's rampage against "caring," as he intones "cu[t] straight and car[e] less." But the central female physician, Dr. Abbott, the ENT specialist whom Jack first consults, conforms (as she must for success) to the male medical model, despite the fact that other physicians treat her as a sexual object. When Jack first appears in her office to see whether his throat irritation is serious, he tries to shake her hand; she, however, is busy washing up and declines the gesture. As she gets ready to examine him, she immediately turns on a monitor on which his face is pictured — seeming to annihilate his physical presence. As required, she inserts a large probe into his mouth. While his colleagues had claimed that Dr. Abbott would "do good throat," it is Jack who now seems in the female sexual position. As Dr. Abbott attends to the probe, she watches the monitor screen instead of Jack, surveying his larynx. Later, as she curtly informs Jack that he has a tumor, the shot composition depicts him on the monitor behind her, and the editing refuses to cut back to Jack for his direct response. Hence it is a second-order image of Jack that we perceive, as though to emphasize Dr. Abbott's alienation from her patient (and his from her). Rather than couch her remarks with any tact or delicacy, she simply states that he has a "growth," leaving him shocked and stupefied as she exits the room.

In Jack's second encounter with Dr. Abbott (after she has performed a biopsy), she informs him that the growth is malignant and recommends radiation, which is handled by another physician. When, during his treatment, Jack's growth becomes larger, Dr. Abbott meets with him to alert him of the problem. Once more, she drops the news like a lead balloon, allowing him to suffer in silence rather than engaging in conversation with him. When she informs him that the last resort is surgery, she begins to call her secretary to schedule the procedure but pauses for a while to adjust her lipstick in the mirror. When she schedules the surgery for late afternoon, he protests, knowing well that physicians are "tired, ragged, and hungry" at that time and not at their best. She responds with indignation: "I am the doctor, and you are my patient. I am telling you when I'm available." While her adjusting her makeup seems the worst of female stereotypes, her handling of Jack's request for morning surgery seems the worst of male authoritarianism. If, as a woman, she has ever learned relational skills, the medical establishment has pummeled them out of her through its preferred model for achievement. Sensing this, Jack ultimately decides to fire Dr. Abbott, claiming that he "used to be" a physician like her.

Instead he turns to a warm (but less elite) male physician, Dr. Eli Blumfield, to perform the procedure (figure 3). As though to feminize him in relation to the WASP male medical model, the script marks him as a Jew whose colleagues call him "the rabbi." Although Blumfield's mortality rates are the lowest in the hospital, this has not led Jack to

3. Dr. Jack Mckee (William Hurt) consults his colleague Dr. Eli Blumfield (Adam Arkin), an ear, nose, and throat surgeon. The Museum of Modern Art Film Stills Archive.

choose him over the more respected Dr. Abbott. No one has considered whether Blumfield's interpersonal skills (versus fancy training) may contribute to his patients' positive prognoses. Interestingly, in his auto-biography, Dr. Rosenbaum makes much of his own Jewish back-ground, an issue displaced in the movie onto the figure of a minor character. In another race-related characterization, the only compas-sionate male resident in McKee's group is Asian — as though masculine "otherness" is, once again, associated with femininity. While a tall white resident refers to "the terminal" patient in room 1217, the small Asian knows that the man's name is Mr. Winter.

Speaking and listening are complementary . . . but speaking holds the more valued position in our method of communication. . . . Perhaps this is because listening, the receptive mode, appears to most observed as a void, a silence, an emptiness. — Julia E. Connelly, "Listening, Empathy, and Clinical Practice"

When Dr. Jack McKee falls ill, it is with a laryngeal tumor, a problem that affects his ability to speak. In the early stages of the disease, he is wracked with a persistent cough or tickle in his throat that interrupts the flow of his words. After surgery, he must remain silent for a period of time and is told that he may lose his voice entirely. At the outset, the particular disease that afflicts Jack seems entirely arbitrary. We think: he might as well have had diabetes or bone cancer. In fact, however, the specific syndrome he endures is highly relevant to issues of physician empathy.

As feminist scholarship has shown, speech, language, and voice have traditionally been associated with the male — since, for eons, education, law, art, history, and politics were controlled and authored by men, not women. Similarly, women have often been associated with silence or with blockages of linguistic performance (Silverman 1988; Kozloff 1988; Lawrence 1991; Rosaldo and Lamphere 1974). With command over vocalization and the word, men have acquired a great deal of semantic power that seems lacking in the female linguistic stance. Rather, women have been cast in the role of "good listeners," since they have had little, ostensibly, to contribute to the ongoing cultural discourse.

To some degree, this question of active male speech versus passive female silence has inflected the medical profession — with male physicians preferring to talk instead of listen to their patients. Yet as many have observed, empathetic skills depend on being able to absorb the thoughts of the sick individual. As Julia Connelly (1994) notes: "In medical encounters . . . both the patient and the physician should be *listeners as well as speakers*. Yet one individual, the physician, is so dominant" (174; italics mine). Had Jack McKee been truly listening to his female patient who expressed discomfort with her chest scar, he would never have made his heartless joke about her resemblance to a *Playboy* centerfold. Instead of being compassionate, he used his rapier verbal wit at the expense of assuaging her emotional discomfort. Beyond simply gleaning patient affect, listening skills are important to physicians in doing the more respected "detective work" of diagnosis (174).

Hence it seems some sort of poetic justice that Dr. McKee, who is so lacking in listening skills, should be faced by a disease that compromises his ability to speak and enhances his need to hear. From his first visit with Dr. Abbott, his vocal abilities are challenged and humiliated. When she informs him that he has a tumor, he is dazed and speechless. When she sticks a tongue depressor in his mouth, he can only utter a guttural, animalistic "Ahhhhh." By the end of the film, he is temporarily silent (following his operation) and must listen to his wife with his responses limited primarily to scribbling on a dry-erase board. Significantly, among the phrases he writes are "I need you" and "I'm sorry" — as though silence alone has put him in touch with his emotions. Fittingly, the first words he vocalizes to Anne are "I love you," which he follows by a silent, mimed, and melodramatic enactment of the sentiment. While Jack is recovering from surgery, he also uses a whistle to get Anne's attention. Rather than employ it sparingly, he blows it loudly and annoyingly, in the manner of a male drill sergeant or gym teacher. In fact, he wields it in a hostile manner that makes Anne angry and frustrated. Ironically, it is her breakdown from this situation that eventually leads to the couple's rapprochement, just as their new kitchen, clearly an "objective correlative," begins to take shape.

Physician, heal thyself. — Luke 4:23

In *The Doctor*, Jack McKee becomes an empathetic practitioner only because he becomes ill himself. Surely this is not a salutary or productive way to teach compassion to physicians. Although a sickness may make one more open to the problems of others, it can also have the opposite effect. As Mathiasen and Alpert (1993) note, "severe mental and physical agony can deaden the feelings. It may actually be [only] exceptional individuals who grow into empathy through their own pain" (136). Certainly, other ways must exist to encourage sensitivity in medical practice. At the end of *The Doctor*, McKee tries a rather improbable method: he checks his interns into the hospital as patients, assigning each of them a particular disease. They will be required to submit to all the tests that persons with such a malaise would undergo. Hence, by having the tables forcibly (and artificially) turned on them, the interns are urged to comprehend the position of their patients. Again, such a procedure is unworkable and probably illegal. So what other means exist for encouraging empathy in the health field?

It is here that the importance of the humanities for the medical community is featured. As Spiro (1993) observes, "empathy has two faces, *the esthetic* and the personal" (8; italics mine). Thus writers stress the impact on medical students and doctors of an immersion in the world of culture. Mathiasen and Alpert (1993) remark: "Instead of suffering . . . a physician may learn empathy through the enjoyment of literature and art" (136). In so doing, a doctor may hone his narrative and interpretive skills, helping to improve his reading of patient cases. Furthermore, since engagement with fiction requires a suspension of disbelief, physicians can gain an ability to transcend their own personal worldview and enter that of another. "Through their appeal to the imagination, literature and art enable the reader and viewer to experience the point of view and the sensations of another human being" (136).

Here it seems significant that when we perceive the story of *The Doctor*, we are doing so through the cinematic medium. In watching a physician who displays little narrative competence in processing the stories of his patients, we are simultaneously required to be narratively astute ourselves in watching his story on film. While the focus of the drama is on observing the empathetic lapses of our protagonist, we, as viewers, must consistently take his point of view (although he is often unable to adopt the perspective of others). So we must develop empathy for a rather unsympathetic figure.

In particular, as film theorists have made clear, the cinema foregrounds and insists on the suturing of the character's and spectator's points of view in a way that many other arts do not (Branigan 1984). In a movie, one not only learns abstractly about a character's thoughts and feelings (as one does through language in literature) but quite literally sees through his or her eyes, as editing connects spectator vision with that of the on-screen character. Thus cinema seems an especially interesting (and self-reflexive) narrative mode to foreground questions of empathy and to impart the notion to health professionals. One sequence of *The Doctor*, in particular, highlights the importance of the point-of-view shot and its ability to represent diverse perspectives to the viewer. Significantly, it is also an episode that appears in Rosenbaum's autobiography. When Jack is wheeled into surgery for a biopsy, he is taken from his room on a gurney lying flat on his back. A point-of-view shot is inserted here of the hospital ceiling, which the spectator views as though lying on the gurney with Jack. As Jack sees the world, quite literally, from a new vantage point (that of the patient), we see the world as he does. Here it is interesting to note that the book on which the film is based is written in the first person, from the perspective of Dr. Rosenbaum—clearly a traditional voice for the autobiographical genre.

Toward the closing of the film, it is apparent that McKee regards his patients in a new light. When a Hispanic man facing a heart transplant struggles with the notion that for him to live another must die, McKee listens to his testimony and takes it seriously rather than dismiss its sentimentality. When the man wants to embrace McKee before leaving his office, the doctor awkwardly allows such physical contact. When we finally see the man's heart surgery take place, McKee strokes the man's head and talks to him. Moreover, he shuns his own favorite OR music in order to play a Latin song. Now, even when his patients are unconscious, he seems concerned for their feelings and well-being.

In terms of *The Doctor*'s cinematic narrative, though written by a man (Ron Nyswaner), the film is directed by a woman, Randa Haines, who has also made films such as *Dance with Me* (1998), *Wrestling Ernest Hemingway* (1993), and *Children of a Lesser God* (1986). Given *The Doctor*'s focus on questions of empathy, and the drama's highly nuanced examination of a particular case study, the filmmaker's gender seems consequential. Throughout the film, it has often been women, such as Jack's wife Anne, who have led him back to his emotional side. Another female within the narrative also fulfills that function, a fellow patient, June (Elizabeth Perkins). McKee first encounters her when he sits in a waiting room before having radiation treatment. While he is vociferously upset about bureaucratic delays, she takes the perennial wait in stride. As he reencounters her at various appointments, he begins to learn patience from her and to divest himself of his doctorly sense of entitlement and rage. He becomes interested in the story of her illness, although at first he cannot respond to her testimony with honesty. When she describes how physicians repeatedly missed signs of her brain tumor, she asks Jack whether this might constitute malpractice. He hedges (though, we assume, he knows that it does). Furthermore, to make her feel better, he lies to her about her prognosis, claiming that his father had once treated a patient with the same condition who lived until old age. She initially takes comfort in his fairy tale but later realizes that it is untrue and angrily confronts him.

As time goes on, Jack leans on June for support and connection, since her situation (though more grave) parallels his. He does so, however, at the expense of becoming closer to Anne. One day, at Jack's suggestion, he and June drive into the desert to attend a concert she wishes to see (figure 4). Ultimately, they fail to attend it. Instead, motivated by June's sober joie de vivre, they dance in the beauty of a desert sunset. Although June eventually expires, her spirit and courage profoundly touch and transform McKee. At the end of the film, he stands on the hospital roof (where the two of them had previously talked), reading a letter she has left for him. It tells him a parable about a farmer who had always scared off the animals on his property and then, due to loneliness, tried to welcome them with his arms outstretched. The ani-

4. Dr. Jack McKee (William Hurt) and his friend and fellow patient June (Elizabeth Perkins) spend an afternoon together in the desert as an escape from the pain and pressure of their illnesses. The Museum of Modern Art Film Stills Archive.

mals, however, thought him a frightening scarecrow and stayed away. Given that Jack had earlier told June that he keeps people at "arm's length," we identify him with the farmer/scarecrow. As Jack stands on the hospital roof, laughing amidst the birds, it is clear that he comprehends the moral of the tale.

Significantly, in Rosenblum's autobiography, there is no direct equivalent for June. He does meet a woman with a brain tumor who, like June, wears a bandanna, and he admires her perseverance, but the two do not enjoy an extended relationship. Thus Haines and Nyswaner have expanded that "bit part" to create another strong but nurturing female role. In the book, it is actually Dr. Rosenbaum's case that deserves a malpractice suit, since numerous physicians have failed to diagnose his problem as cancer. He chooses not to bring it to court because, as part of the male physician "buddy system," his doctors are all his colleagues and friends.

As previously mentioned, in the opening of *The Doctor*, the tones of an old rock-and-roll classic, sung by men, blast through the operating room: "Big Girls Don't Cry." In the title of the song, there is an inverted reference to the more usual aphorism, "Boys don't cry." In beginning the drama in this manner, the film immediately highlights the question of emotional expression and its appropriateness for the adult, gendered world. The fact that the scene takes place in a hospital makes clear that the narrative is also referencing the question of affect and sexual difference in the medical profession. On one level, June is a "big girl" who does not cry but instead shows bravery and equanimity in the face of adversity. On the other hand, she remains fully open to her pain and sadness; she is not numb, only audacious.

Given the primacy of women within the narrative of *The Doctor*, it seems not extraneous that the movie comes to the screen via the directorial hand of Randa Haines — who, in foregrounding the question of empathy and medicine, takes a stereotypical "female" perspective. While, on the one hand, women physicians like Dr. Abbott buy into the male notion that "big girls don't cry" (or emote) if they wish to advance, Haines questions this postfeminist logic. Rather, she asserts the viability of passion in medical practice, for both sexes. In so doing, she succeeds in creating precisely the kind of humanistic work that Mathiasen and Alpert envision, one that proves valuable to the modern medical profession.

[Thanks to editor Lester Friedman for several important insights that are reflected in this paper.]

Institutional Impediments

Medical Bureaucracies in the Movies

MARILYN CHANDLER MCENTYRE

In his 1992 short story "Fidelity," Wendell Berry recounts the adventures of a young man who "kidnaps" his father from an ICU unit and takes him home to die. Although those who love him know it is his time to die, "the people of the hospital did not call it dying; they called it a coma. They spoke of curing him. They spoke of his recovery" (112). Uncle Burley's family "said little in reply, for what he knew was not what they knew, and his hope was not theirs" (112). But they are not docile. With tacit consent, relatives and neighbors support the son in his scheme to liberate Uncle Burley from the "hospital people." Since his action is illegal, Danny is pursued by the law, but family and friends enter into a heartfelt conspiracy to protect the kidnapper and affirm the rightness of Uncle Burley's return to his "place on earth" to die. The story, though gently comic, might also be read as an American tragedy. By accepting and normalizing death in the hospital, Berry suggests, we have abdicated one of the essential functions of human community, which is to gather in support and celebration around the definitive events of life: birth, coming-of-age, marriage, and, just as importantly, death. As caregiving is increasingly relegated to professionals and institutional settings, Americans suffer a significant loss not only of control but of opportunities for spiritual community and mutual nurturing.

Berry's strongly anti-institutional view lies close to one end of a spectrum of opinion about consigning the sick and dying to hospitals and professional care. Only since the end of the nineteenth century has the role of hospitals in the United States expanded to include much enlarged functions of medical research and education, and only in the twentieth century have hospitals become professionalized bureaucracies designed to serve a paying public rather than loosely organized institutions for social welfare that served mostly the indigent poor

(Starr 1982, 177–78). During that time, the quality of hospitals has come to be assessed largely in terms of what cutting-edge technologies they afford and employ in the service of cure. What might twenty-five years ago have been considered "extraordinary measures" have, one by one, become normalized as new technologies become standard equipment and new treatments routine. Some procedures (for example, bypass surgery, chemotherapy, even immunization) that once required justification are now sufficiently normative to shift the burden of justification to those who opt not to use them. Thus the decision whether or not, under what conditions, and to what ends to hospitalize becomes fraught with moral complexities as well as economic pressures.

To those who share Berry's skepticism about the advantages of hospitalization, one of the most pressing concerns is the hospital bureaucracy's tendency to depersonalize care and diffuse responsibility. This trend, exacerbated in teaching hospitals beholden to a vast scientific superstructure, imposes its own educational and economic agendas on those involved in patient care. Such bureaucracy comes under sharp critical scrutiny in a number of recent films that feature individuals — patients, family, and medical professionals — laboring to maintain compassionate caregiving in a stratified, market-driven, and litigious environment.

Three of these films, *Awakenings* (1990), *The Doctor* (1991), and *Lorenzo's Oil* (1992), which appeared in quick succession, and a much more recent film, *Wit* (HBO, 2001), offer particularly salient critiques of hospitals, medical education, and the politics of medical research. Although made for the mass market, and in some ways appealing to a public tendency to polarize doctors as heroes or villains (a tendency with a long literary history), these films raise responsible and urgent questions about medical, scientific, and political process. From various points of view, they expose the erosive pressures that arise from competition for research funding, litigation threats, chronic understaffing, byzantine insurance systems, expanding government regulations, and escalating expectations of doctors with access to a techno-wonderland of treatment options. Each of the films acknowledges the complexity of serving the different vested interests of patients, caregivers, and administrators, all of whom struggle with competing responsibilities.

Seeing Past the Bottom Line

Awakenings, directed by Penny Marshall and based on an autobiographical work by neurologist Oliver Sacks, follows the fortunes of Dr.

Institutional Impediments   167

Malcolm Sayer (Robin Williams) as staff physician in a chronic care hospital that houses severely mentally and physically impaired patients. The patients include victims of an encephalitis lethargica epidemic, some of whom have been unresponsive — essentially asleep — for years. Coming from pure research, where his recent efforts to extract one decagram of myelin from four tons of earthworms failed, Dr. Sayer appears singularly ill prepared to work with human beings — either patients or colleagues. He is socially awkward, naive about institutional politics, inexperienced at caregiving, and by nature a solitary whose work is his life. Despite these indications of misfit, the hospital hires Dr. Sayer because it desperately needs a staff doctor and he desperately needs a job.

Ironically, his "successful" interview is the first in a series of comic scenes where hospital administrators and Sayer's immediate supervisor, Dr. Kaufman (John Heard), are represented as obstructionists whose fixed ideas impede creative research and effective caregiving. On the basis of their conversation with him, they have every reason to believe that Sayer will be an incompetent caregiver, but they hire him out of economic expediency that seems likely to put patients' welfare at risk. The comedy is broad (at the mention of patients, Sayer asks with some alarm, "When you say people, do you mean living people?"), but the point is painfully sharp: care is often market driven, and patients' welfare subordinated to perceived constraints of time and money. Dr. Sayer, in a sense, shares the marginal status of the patients; his colleagues take neither his expertise nor their illnesses seriously beyond minimal commitment to basic maintenance. As one of the nurses puts it, "We call this place the garden . . . because all we do is feed and water." Sayer also shares with "the plants" a sense of imprisonment; shots of him banging an old window open to lean out for air, or edging through a squalid room crowded with wheelchairs and drab furniture, convey an atmosphere of entrapment, narrowness, and dead ends, both architectural and ideological.

After an initial struggle to fit in, Dr. Sayer turns out to be more trouble than his supervisors imagined. His tireless scientific curiosity leads him to raise disturbing questions that the chief medical officers would rather leave alone. "What are all these people waiting for?" he asks, as he surveys the rows of catatonic figures in wheelchairs and beds. The question itself suggests one of two possibilities: either they're just waiting to die, or they're waiting for a cure. But neither this question nor subsequent ones about their possible states of awareness elicit a serious response. Sayer's queries are routinely met with amused tolerance, less amused skepticism, or impatience. Thus a second indictment of the hospital administration is leveled: those in charge have not only stopped asking scientific and medical questions themselves but also actively suppress such curiosity in subordinates, preferring to conserve institutional resources and their own energy by counting on routine damage control to prevent crisis and keep the institution functioning.

The questions become more profound as Dr. Sayer continues his independent observations. Attempting a necessarily one-sided exam of a catatonic patient, Lucy, he notices that she is capable of intentional movement when he finds her leaning toward glasses he has dropped on the floor. Experimentally he tosses her a ball. She raises her hand to catch it, showing no other response. He reports this finding immediately, calling his colleagues in to show them how she can catch a ball. They dismiss the movement as a reflex. "I'm sorry," Dr. Sayer answers. "If you were right, I'd agree with you." In his efforts to articulate a possible explanation, he muses that in a certain way, having no access to her own will, "She borrows the will of the ball!" At this bit of whimsy, most of the white-coated jury, who have arranged themselves impassively around Lucy's wheelchair, leave. The supervisor, Dr. Kaufman, remains long enough to quip, "Let us know if she catches anything else."

Only Nurse Costello (Julie Kavner), who becomes Dr. Sayer's institutional mentor and sympathetic sidekick, encourages him. "I just wanted to say to you," she comments as the others leave, "I preferred your explanation. And I'll look after things for you until you've settled in." Other staff members represent a range of attitudes: some of the nurses have reduced their labors to entirely perfunctory tasks; one appears to be curious, but skeptical, of Dr. Sayer's efforts to investigate what has for years been a closed case. In effect, the institutional ethos has been shaped by the attitude represented at the top of the hierarchy. Efficiency, cost cutting, and basic maintenance dominate. The staff practices defensive medicine: pleases the trustees, prevents litigation, and pacifies families.

But Sayer continues to behave as an independent scientist. Manifestly incompetent at organizing his professional environment, he carries disheveled stacks of paper, forgets things, writes notes on his hand or on the cuff of his lab coat. Yet with intense care for detail, he observes and puzzles over patients' behaviors, forming hypotheses as he tracks minute changes from one day to the next. The laissez-faire attitude of his supervisor turns to Sayer's advantage, since it leaves him free to fish through ancient files and to hang around the dismal recreation room by day and over patients' beds by night watching for signs of life on a devastated human landscape. Close-up shots of Dr. Sayer leaning over a face, a microscope, or a document testify to the meticulous scrutiny he brings to bear on whatever piques his curiosity, and how the "passions of the mind" sustain him in an environment of professional burnout.

Going through the copious records of catatonic patients, Sayer finds reports that end in "No change of therapy recommended." Symptoms are repeatedly characterized as "atypical." "You'd think," he muses, "that at some point all these atypical somethings would add up to a typical something." The remark suggests an investigative mind-set that contrasts sharply with the noncommittal observations on the charts. Exhausted from research, he goes home, falls asleep, and suddenly wakes with an idea that sends him racing back to the hospital to search for the common denominator that escaped his notice: all these "sleepers" suffered from encephalitis in the 1920s. Since no one else is around with whom he can share his epiphany, Sayer explains it to the startled night janitor — a move that reinforces his wholesale disregard of status, rank, or even interest in his eagerness to share what he knows. Both the comedy and the pathos of this misplaced collegiality lie in the way it testifies to the indifference of professional colleagues.

Other epiphanies come by similarly odd means. Using a Ouija board to see if he can get Leonard (Robert De Niro) to spell his name, Sayer realizes that the patient is attempting to spell out a message. At this point Sayer is hot on the trail, a medical detective with a definitive clue. He'll take information from anywhere he can get it. Leonard's mother visits daily, but no one bothers to question her until Dr. Sayer invites her to tell her story: "I'd like to know more about your son." In his attention to her point of view, he practices a kind of medicine his colleagues have forgotten — or never knew — thinking widely, curiously, and connectively about a medical mystery, slow to dismiss any available information as medically irrelevant. Such a practice takes time. Sayer spends more hours tracing down an old doctor who treated the encephalitic patients during the original outbreak. The retiree has film footage of tests he ran on patients that suggest a connection between encephalitis lethargica and Parkinson's disease. Like Leonard's mother, he has a story worth telling, but heretofore no willing audience.

After attending a conference on Parkinson's (where he once again makes a "fool" of himself asking questions out of turn), Sayer forms the hypothesis that leads to a plan of treatment: L-Dopa, which works on Parkinson's victims, might work on these patients, frozen in their timeless state. Once again, he has difficulty finding a colleague with whom to discuss his hypothesis. When he corners the conference speaker in the bathroom to ask his assessment of the drug's efficacy with the postencephalitic patients, the chemist replies with something approaching a sneer, "I'm just a chemist, doctor. You're the physician. I'll leave it to you to do the damage." When Sayer appeals to Dr. Kaufman for permission to use the drug on patients, the supervisor objects, "You know better than to make a leap like that. You want there to be a connection. That doesn't mean there is one." A brief negotiation ensues:

> "What I know is that these people are alive inside."
> "How many did you think I'd let you put on it?"
> "All of them. Some. One."
> "One. With the family's consent. Signed."

The one is Leonard. He "awakens." In amazement, Sayer begins the campaign to administer the drug to all the postencephalitic patients.

At this point, money becomes the object. Once again the bureaucratic powers take the position that nothing can be done. But the nursing and maintenance staff stage both a protest and a vote of confidence, donating personal funds toward a supply of the experimental drug. The movie, of course, simplifies the process of approving experimental protocols, cutting to Sayer's heartwarming speech before hospital trustees, who pull out their pocketbooks on the spot. Still, the point is reiterated that institutional burnout atrophies curiosity, diminishes hope, and leads to cynicism. The project of healing the sick, or even of maximizing function among the impaired, gives way to an essentially sterile and self-referential version of institutional management. The hospital, rather than its patients, becomes the primary object of concern.

Such slippage is classic. Sociologist Peter Berger (1967) explicates the dynamic in his study of the life cycle of ecclesiastical institutions, *The Sacred Canopy*. His conclusions apply neatly to hospitals: as they become more bureaucratic, acquire more layers of structure, generate more differentiated functions and hence more regulation, institutions begin to defeat their original and deepest purposes and divert their efforts to the survival of the institution. Sayer's supervisor does not, in fact, appear as an entirely unsympathetic character, but rather as someone caught in this institutional dynamic. As the treatment begins to work, he takes an interest and makes further concessions. Still, this interest is motivated largely by the benefits the institution might reap from such dramatic success.

As the drug takes effect, the staff come to observe patients more often and take an interest in Sayer's experiment — to a point. Unfortunately, the therapeutic window begins to close as side effects appear. Leonard begins to lose first his physical coordination, then his awareness. Given a free hand to experiment with dosages, Sayer tries urgently to reverse the downward curve, but eventually all the patients regress. In the midst of this trajectory, Leonard meets with the hospital's governing board to request permission to go for a walk by himself, but he runs into their very reasonable hesitation. They decide against taking the risk, citing "insufficient data." They can't be legally responsible for what happens to him. "We need time to evaluate things," they tell him. Although Leonard has by this time been established as a highly functional patient, viewers must also concede the dilemma facing those who assume responsibility for patients' welfare.

But Leonard doesn't. He starts off on his own anyway, defiant and determined, only to be wrestled to the floor by hospital personnel. Dr. Sayer intervenes, insisting, "He's not a mental patient." The correction is poignant; not everyone there would make this distinction. Patients in this facility receive no benefit of the doubt and have no room to negotiate. Leonard spreads his resentment to other patients; he recruits a small group of men to protest for patients' rights. Sayer and Kaufman, briefly united in an effort to contain further disruption, watch as Leonard desperately campaigns for his freedom. But soon Kaufman reverts to his adversarial role; he blames Sayer for what has become a major disruption: "I have twenty psychotics up there refusing to eat" (figure 1). As his losses grow more egregious, Leonard agrees to allow Dr. Sayer to use him as an experimental subject, to film him, interview him, and learn from his encroaching defeat. Conscious of his own lapses, he takes a certain desperate pride in using his periods of alertness to document his case in detail. The recognition that he can contribute to medical research animates him with a poignant and ultimately tragic enthusiasm. One of the most moving lines in the film is uttered by Leonard in the midst of a seizure: "Go get the camera!" he pleads with Sayer. "Learn! Learn!"

The film chronicles both medical triumph and disappointing reversal in a moving and provocative way, representing better than many commercial films the complexities involved in medical research, although the dynamics of decision making, the legal and psychological consequences of experimentation on human subjects, and the dilemma of hospital administrators with limited resources are seriously oversimplified. Although Sayer appears to have considerable freedom, includ-

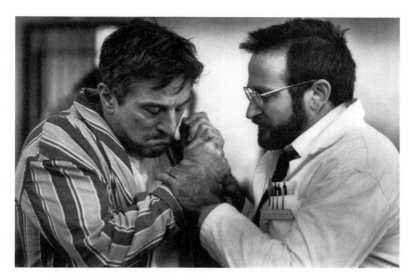

1. Dr. Sayer (Robin Williams) breaks through institutional
barriers to establish contact and eventually a relationship with Leonard
(Robert De Niro), who has been in a sleep state for decades.

ing a great deal of discretionary time to observe the patients in whom
he's taken an interest, viewers receive little help in understanding the
whole context of competing duties, divergent needs, or unreliable
funding sources. (We know from the opening credits that "Bainbridge"
Hospital is located in the Bronx in 1969, but beyond a few shots of the
immediate neighborhood, we receive no clues as to the wider context
in which it operates.) The simplistic representation of the hospital
foundation as rich people who, moved by a speech, can suddenly fund
a major experiment does little to enhance understanding of the complexities of grant writing, regulation, and institutional accountability.
By making the unconventional doctor a hero, the film implicitly rele-
gates those who limit him to the status of antagonists — at best distracted and indifferent, at worst hostile to truth seeking and healing.

The underlying message, that people involved in running large, un-
derfunded institutions burn out, remains. Those focused on economic
accountability can fall prey to intellectual atrophy. Their scientific curiosity can give way to a limited view of therapeutic possibility, since
they are unable to disengage from economic realities long enough to
entertain radical reframings of problems. In this film, the humanity of
Nurse Costello and the compassionate curiosity of Dr. Sayer appear as
exceptions that prove the grim rule that institutional medicine gradu-

ally ceases to be life giving, and not all can maintain their will to heal against its erosive force.

Hoist on Whose Petard?

That same message is foregrounded in *The Doctor* (directed by Randa Haines), which opens in the operating room of a large, well-appointed hospital in San Francisco where a cardiac surgical team is at work. The opening credits roll by over a visual background of a body on the table, chest cavity open, in which gloved hands are carefully at work, accompanied by voices telling jokes, commenting crassly on minor fumbles, making flirtatious banter, telling lawyer jokes. ("Oh, look at that. Made him bleed." "Oh, boy, he's a gusher." "Ooh. I hate blood." "This guy's aorta's in big trouble.") Some are singing along to "Big Girls Don't Cry." As in the widely aired *M*A*S*H* series, to which the scene might be a direct allusion, the surgeons are doing their job with precision, but their behavior suggests complete irreverence for the life that hangs in the balance on the table. As the surgeon removes his bloody hands from the patient's chest, he calls, "Closing music, Joe," whereupon we hear a drawling country music piece, "Why Don't We Get Drunk and Screw?" It would be hard for a viewer not to be seduced into chuckling along; the vision of teamwork and camaraderie has, despite the appalling irreverence, immediate appeal. The only critical note is struck by a nurse, Nancy, who will not sing along.

As he peels off his gloves, leaving a subordinate to close, Dr. McKee (William Hurt) gets a call to look at a patient who is still under anesthetic. The attending physician (dubbed "the rabbi" by his more cynical colleagues) is talking quietly with the patient. We learn that he has published a paper on awareness in unconscious states that has made him the butt of many jokes. Dr. McKee's skepticism about this practice is evident, even as he gives his opinion on the patient at hand. Thus, within the first five minutes, the movie gives us the basic information that the staff tolerates a great deal of crass behavior on the part of physicians, especially surgeons, in the upper ranks of the hospital hierarchy. Among colleagues, respect goes to those who manifest both technical skill and cynical detachment from the emotional and personal dimensions of their work with patients. Those who understand their work as healers more broadly, or who manifest authentic emotional involvement, are subordinated and even feminized by association with the female nurses whose traditional role has been to provide the nurturing presence not required of doctors.

Leaving the hospital, Dr. McKee drives (too fast, in a sporty convertible) to the office of an older doctor, a colleague and friend of his father's, to get his own throat checked. Their brief interview is laced with the language of professional brotherhood — comments on the cost of being "married to a doctor's wife," queries about "business in the big league," which are met with "We're killin' 'em." Here again, we recognize a slightly jarring conjunction of professional courtesy and mutual support with dismissiveness about patients masquerading as professionalism. The dismissiveness becomes more egregious in a subsequent scene where a post-op breast cancer patient, obviously distressed, sitting half-clothed on an examining table, asks Dr. McKee whether her scar will disappear. She is concerned about how it will affect intimacy with her husband. McKee's reply continues to develop him as someone whose capacity for empathy has almost entirely atrophied: "Tell your husband you look like a *Playboy* centerfold. And you have the staple marks to prove it."

One cause for such hardness of heart is that Dr. McKee is living on overload. He rushes from one site to another, accompanied by staff subordinates, his beeper, his car phone. His conversations are brief and usually close with an ironic spin. He forgets social appointments, makes only perfunctory efforts to connect with his wife, Anne (Christine Lahti), and conducts much of his relationship with his son by phone. Not until McKee coughs up blood does he allow his wife to persuade him to get his own condition thoroughly checked. Clearly, his not-so-benign neglect extends to himself; such neglect, like his cavalier attitude toward patients, is valorized under the banner of professionalism.

Indeed, in the following scene, McKee's own condition seems to give him no pause about his attitude. He tells a cluster of interns, "There's a danger about feeling too strongly about your patient. . . . A surgeon's job is to cut. You've got one shot. You go in, you fix it, and get out. Caring is all about time. When you've got thirty seconds before the guy bleeds out, I'd rather you'd cut straight and care less." With the same group, he proceeds to a patient's bedside, where he interrupts a priest to deliver a short explanation of the patient's condition, making no effort to address either patient or priest personally. This hard edge is offset by the aura of competence and confidence Dr. McKee projects. Viewers are repeatedly caught in the crosscurrents of their own value judgments as the film keeps raising questions: What, in fact, do we expect of physicians? How much do patients as well as professional subordinates collaborate in assigning them inordinate responsibility and inordinate power? And how can such elevation not result, at least occasionally, in the kind of inflation depicted in Dr. McKee, whose position at the top of the hospital pecking order is both powerful and precarious?

At this point two major issues of the story are on the table: the problem of curing without caring (and how institutional hierarchy generates this behavior) and the corresponding problem of the physician's self-destructive overcommitment. A third issue is introduced when a colleague of McKee's accosts him in the break room to tell him that he's being threatened with a malpractice suit. It is evident from the colleague's description of the case that his own negligence was involved, but he expects his partners to cover for him — indeed, he takes it for granted that this is a benefit of membership in the professional guild. While this subplot receives little development, it becomes an ethical touchstone later in the movie when McKee, having radically altered his perspective, finds it impossible to be a witness for his colleague.

The problem of collegiality receives a different spin when McKee goes to see a female ENT "man" who is, in fact, an attractive woman. "She does great throat" is the crude assessment of his fellow male surgeons — a comment that prompts us to recognize a parody of sexual aggression in the ensuing encounter where the roles are reversed as the woman penetrates the passive man, jabbing her instruments down his reluctant throat. In her waiting room, McKee mutters restlessly, "What am I doing, sitting here like one of the herd?" When he finally, resentfully, enters her examining room, expecting preferential and even deferential treatment, she doesn't even shake hands. She is, ironically, his kind of doctor — efficient, direct, and barely civil. She is not interested in him. She doesn't explain the examining procedures as they get more invasive and technical. With an image of his throat glowing on two screens, McKee is kept in an undignified position, tasting bitter anesthetic spray, holding his tongue with a gauze strip.

After an awkward silence, she puts her instruments away and announces, "Doctor, you have a growth." To McKee's stunned "What?" she replies simply, "Tumor, laryngeal. Here on the vocal chord?" "I know what laryngeal is," he reminds her. She enumerates the tests she'll want and schedules a biopsy for the next day. Not a soothing word is offered. In a later scene, when radiation has failed and a partial laryngectomy has to be scheduled, he asks for a morning surgery, rea-

2. Dr. Jack McKee (William Hurt) encounters bureaucracy from a new angle of vision as a patient in the hospital where he practices surgery.

soning that she will be in less than her best form if she has to operate on him in the afternoon. Her reply is withering: "I am the doctor, and you are my patient, and I am telling you when I am available." At that point he decides against her and opts in favor of the "rabbi," whose practice of talking with patients under anesthetic suddenly seems appealing (figure 2).

These scenes develop a theme of gender discrimination raised earlier in McKee's encounters with two women patients and with his wife. He seems incapable of imagining or reckoning with the women's fears, frustrations, or emotional needs. In the scenes with the female ENT specialist, the issue is turned to a new angle. Because she is a woman, her dismissive behavior has to be read differently from his. Both are system related; both are results of medical education of the kind McKee has been dispensing, emphasizing technical expertise, efficiency, and detachment. But he has a "sense of humor," and she does not. He, one cannot help but recognize, can afford it. She, on the other hand, has learned her aloofness as a strategy against just such sexist attitudes as those McKee and his partners exhibit.

In subsequent encounters with personnel in oncology, the special treatment McKee feels he has a perfect right to expect is still not forthcoming. He experiences the admitting procedure prior to his battery of tests as an insult:

"Name?"

"Dr. McKee."

"First name?"

"I've been an attending surgeon on this staff for . . . years. I've been sitting here for thirty minutes."

Like his sudden anonymity, the proffered wheelchair is a humiliation. Although the orderly insists ("If you fall over in the hospital, the hospital is liable!"), McKee persists in his refusal of the chair. He objects to not having a private room. There are none left. He wants to wait. His doctor feels the biopsy is urgent. The fact of a roommate distresses McKee. The actual roommate comically makes matters worse by his complaints about doctors, assuring McKee, "They're lying half the time. I can tell. I'm a cop." Thus in one conversation after another, McKee is frustrated and bewildered by his sudden loss of status. When a nurse appears, McKee greets her with deepening irony: "Do you suppose you could get me a thinner sheet? I'm not sure everyone can see through this one."

Leaving the hospital after tests, he submits to the wheelchair. Humiliation has begun to humble him. At the hospital the next day, McKee finds his way to radiation therapy down a long, sterile hall—a scene reminiscent of Kafka's Joseph K wandering in bureaucratic hell. Still attempting to cope with apprehensions by means of humor, McKee responds to the MRI technician's query about whether he is claustrophobic by quipping, "Only in cramped spaces." At every stage of radiation therapy, McKee continues to demand special treatment, objecting to duplication of forms, to tardiness in appointments, to being passed like a buck from one technician to another, to cavalier performance of unsettling procedures that remain unexplained. In radiation, when he asks, "Shouldn't there be a lead apron?" the technician replies casually, "You don't need it." Even after radiation has started, McKee attempts to continue working. Although advised to stay home, he argues, "I don't want to lose ground on the stats." As his veneer of professional assurance erodes, a kind of desperation becomes visible. Without the routines and institutional rituals that reinforce his sense of being in control, he is disoriented, scared, and emotionally confused.

At his second radiation session, McKee meets the cancer patient who will change his attitude, practice, and self-understanding. McKee has just shouted at a harried receptionist about being kept waiting. To her "I'm sorry. I don't make the rules," he snarls, "Let's just drop 'I'm sorry' from the conversation. Let's just assume every sentence begins with that." Seating himself beside a young woman wearing a hat, he is surprised to hear her speak up: "She's just doing her job. If you want to shout, go shout at a doctor." Ironically, despite the offensiveness of his tone, McKee's complaints are clearly justified and generate a sympathy with patients' common frustrations that he has not yet brought fully to consciousness.

During the ensuing conversation, the young woman, June (Elizabeth Perkins), tells him about her brain tumor, and about the difficulties of obtaining timely tests and treatment. McKee, uncomfortable, replies that it's "difficult to comment." She returns, "Oh. Yeah. Well. It's a club, isn't it?" In another waiting room scene, she pulls him up short again: "Tell them you're a big doctor. Cut in line." No one has yet challenged him so forthrightly. The ENT specialist, though she challenged his professionalism, did so as a professional peer, competing for authority. Even his wife has learned to give way to his priorities. Only June calmly disregards his hard-won status with a healthy indifference grounded in her experience as a cancer patient. Her own priorities have been radically rearranged, and she doesn't have time for institutional game playing.

Subsequent conversations with June move McKee to new awareness, especially as he begins to experience some of the deeper distresses of patienthood. To the young woman's explanation that her MRI was postponed because of the expense, he replies, "The system stinks. Insurance companies tell us what we can and can't do." The irony that he himself is a full participant in this system of privilege appears to be lost on him. But as time passes, he gets to know other cancer patients; they become his community. He begins to take in the wisdom that June's illness has taught her: "I don't want to rush past anything anymore. I can't." "Do you pray, June?" he asks her in an extraordinary moment of vulnerability. "Is that what holds you together?" and she responds simply, "I pray, meditate, eat chocolate. I go dancing."

When McKee returns to work after a successful laryngectomy, performed by the "rabbi" who talks him through it, he is transformed. He suddenly wants to know the names of his patients. He takes time to sit on a bed and explain to a heart transplant candidate, "It may take a little while before we have a heart to harvest." When the patient hugs him, he hardly knows how to respond. From this touching scene, we cut to McKee reassuring the patient and his family on the day of the transplant. The scene is replete with visual cues that reinforce our sense of McKee's changed state of mind. Where in earlier scenes the background has been largely white walls, metal, and lights, we see him now surrounded by ordinary people in a softened environment of plants, blankets, and brightly colored clothing. In the OR, he puts on Latin American music, honoring the taste of the Latino patient. As he preps the man, he tells him, "Your wife will be delighted. . . . It's a beautiful heart." Although such total transformation may partake of sentimental fantasy, Hurt is convincing, and the conversion story compelling. A brush with mortality does change people, and until doctors become patients themselves, empathy may require a leap of imagination beyond what can be formally taught. This limitation is exacerbated by the many ways in which institutional structures and customs reinforce doctors' distance from those they work with. The stratified world of the hospital may work directly against compassionate healing. Those like the rabbi who maintain their humaneness may do so in spite of, rather than with the help of, the system they inhabit.

In the final scenes, we see McKee as educator, teaching what he has so recently learned. When a medical student describes a patient as "the terminal" in a room down the hall, he barks, "Call another patient terminal, and that's how you'll describe your career." Of course, it's hard to miss a certain irony in his reforming zeal; his tone of complete command remains, and a certain lack of sympathy seems to have been displaced from patients to students, though in a worthy cause. As the students gather in a crowded hall, he instructs them to strip and put on hospital gowns, assigns them to rooms, and announces that for the next three days, each will be allocated a disease, sleep in a hospital bed, eat hospital food, and undergo appropriate tests. He delivers a speech about how patients feel frightened, embarrassed, and vulnerable, how they are sick and want to get better. Despite his self-righteous posture of the newly converted, the film leaves the viewer with hope for the possibility of reform in medical education and practice, if not by radical restructuring, then by the quiet infiltration of human encounters which at their most authentic can subvert institutional suppression and survive the deadening effects of bureaucracy.

Remapping the Maze

The problem of hospital bureaucracy is framed more widely in *Lorenzo's Oil* (directed by George Miller). Like *Awakenings*, this film is based on a true story of qualified medical success achieved in the face of institutional obstructions. Like *The Doctor*, it shows how professional hierarchy fortifies itself against the unconventional approach, the unfundable project, or the "unqualified" practitioner who challenges institutional norms. Although the tendency of scientists to ignore anomalous results is shown to be problematic, the film does not descend to stereotyping; some of the scientists are compassionate human beings who take large risks to help determined parents find a cure for their son's "incurable" disease.

Lorenzo (played by several remarkable children who represent him at various stages of his disease) is a trilingual child of an American mother and Italian American father who works for the World Bank — Augusto and Michaela Odone (Nick Nolte and Susan Sarandon). Lorenzo has lived in Africa for much of his short life when the film begins with an opening shot of a young African man carving a knife and a background of African vocal music, a setting that contrasts sharply with the long succession of sterile, high-tech institutional environments in which much of the subsequent action takes place. Shortly after returning to the United States, Lorenzo's symptoms start to show up. He throws tantrums at school, acts wild and destructive at home, falls and needs stitches. On his first trip to the hospital, a gentle female doctor sews him up, suggesting that his overattentive parents "lighten up" — the first of many admonishments that the Odones should adjust their attitudes. When Lorenzo falls again, the same doctor tests him and finds his stats normal. This sequence of disruptions and accidents makes the point that much guesswork is involved in diagnosis. Because Lorenzo's "stats" are normal, doctors postpone diagnosis. The parents' concerns and observations are subordinated to what can be measured and documented.

The child's symptoms continue. In the hospital a second time, a new doctor speculates that it could be anything, perhaps a hearing problem. A third visit produces another doctor who tells Lorenzo he'll run tests and "get to the bottom of this." All the doctors are kind. All the responses are uncertain. Then we see a series of hi-tech test scenes where Lorenzo is hooked up to one machine after another in sterile rooms, his anxious parents watching from behind glass. Separation increases and conversation diminishes as technology takes over. Although the reasons for this progression are obvious, the change of ambience is dramatic, reflecting a deepening sense of the parents' disempowerment as institutional protocols and technology drive more decisions.

Just after the testing scenes, the camera cuts to an aerial view of an Easter Mass, priests processing in white albs with candles. The usual analogy between medical hierarchy and priests, between hospital and church as institutions exercising similar authority and ritual practices, is established in this shot and several like it, reinforced by ecclesiastical music, including, somewhat ironically, Mozart's *Ave Verum Corpus* (Hail the True Body). As in the more recent film *Wit*, where poetry provides a grounding point for reflection on terminal illness, *Lorenzo's Oil* provides a rich repertoire of both visual and musical cues that link the arts to medicine in their common concern with the fundamental human experiences of suffering and death.

Back in the hospital, a sober doctor delivers the shocking news that Lorenzo has adrenoleukodystrophy, a metabolic disease that usually runs a horrifying two-year course of progressive loss of function terminating in death. Little is known about it except that it results from an abnormally high level of fat in the blood due to a defective fat-destroying enzyme. The parents ask for specifics. The doctor explains how ALD strips away the myelin sheath so that messages cease to reach the brain. Is anyone working on it? they ask. "Until ten years ago," he replies, "it was unidentified. Scientists are still trying to understand exactly what it is." As they leave his office, the slow crescendo of Barber's *Adagio for Strings* adumbrates the cycles of hope and defeat to come.

Up to this point, the story follows the pattern of innumerable other stories of catastrophic illness, tracing the steps from health through recognition of symptoms to diagnosis. But here it begins to differ. Lorenzo's parents do not regard science as an impenetrable closed system. The fact that they are exceptionally intelligent, motivated, and wealthy enables them to level an exceptional challenge to the medical/scientific establishment. They begin to study Lorenzo's disease. Living in Washington, D.C., gives them access to large medical libraries, including that of the National Institutes of Health. In a series of close-ups we see Augusto poring over a medical reference book where ALD is described and cases cited. The camera lingers on enlargements of horrifying prognostic terms: blind, deaf, mute, paralyzed . . . ending in "death."

Then the camera cuts to his office at the World Bank. It is now 1984. Recurrent dates flashed on the screen remind us of the documentary character of the story. A call comes in from a world expert on leukodystrophies. He explains that one experimental protocol has been launched based on diet. Already the child's walking and speech are severely impaired, but Dr. Nikolais (Peter Ustinov) suggests that they enroll Lorenzo. "If it's any consolation to you," he explains, "you'll be helping us to slow the progress of this relentless disease." The prospect of aiding scientific progress is cold comfort, but the Odones enroll

Lorenzo and withdraw saturated fats from his diet, since it seems the only strategy available that may slow the cascade of symptoms. Six weeks into the diet, Lorenzo's fat levels continue to rise. The Odones report this but are told, "Wait until the end of the trial. . . . It's too early to tell." The research team wants to run the protocol for six months. In light of the rapid progress of the disease, the Odones, reasonably enough, refuse to wait. Their struggle over whether to submit to the terms of the clinical trial brings up the perennial, much-disputed ethical problems involved in experimentation on human subjects. Opinion on the ethics and terms of such experimentation differs widely from one country to another and remains unsettled (Payer 1996).

The Odones next contact the ALD Foundation, a group with five hundred member families (figure 3). They attend an ALD family conference in July 1984, which, to their disappointment, seems mostly an elaborate exercise in group therapy rather than information gathering. When the program degenerates to collecting recipes for a newsletter about the institute diet, Michaela speaks up to declare that the diet isn't working. She looks around the unresponsive audience from the back of a large hall while onstage the facilitating couple register instantaneous disapproval. Undeterred, Michaela asks, simply, "Is the diet working?" Although a few nod acknowledgment, the now irate leader, Mr. Muscatine, breaks in, "This is not the way we do things here," and continues, patronizingly, "The medical folks call this kind of evidence anecdotal." Having regained control of the crowd, he offers a simplistic argument for clinical trials, insisting on the importance of full cooperation. "So what you're saying," Michaela replies, "is that our children are in the service of medical science." But the conundrum is lost on the listeners as Mr. Muscatine turns hastily to welcome a doctor to the podium. The Odones walk out, shocked by parents who have invested so heavily in institutional protocols and procedures that they have blinded themselves to possibilities not already defined and approved by the medical bureaucracy.

Having distanced themselves from the support group and rejected hospital treatment, the Odones set up hospital equipment in their home and commit to caring for Lorenzo there. The domestication of the hospital bed, IV lines, respirator, humidifier, and other cumbersome equipment by piles of books, stuffed toys, musical instruments, and colorful blankets suggests how great a role the beautiful and the familiar might play in the welfare of both patient and caregivers. As Lorenzo's ability to communicate dwindles, his parents sing and tell stories. As in Berry's story about being brought home to die, the do-

3. Michaela and Augusto Odone (Susan Sarandon and Nick Nolte) attend a meeting of parents with children suffering from ALD and are shocked to encounter subservience to the medical authorities they are challenging.

mestic setting here seems the appropriate site for care. Although the value of hospital care is not dismissed, its limitations are evident. Of course, their choice would not be an option for most people; the Odones' personal resources are many times greater than those of most families, so their story cannot in all respects serve as a model.

Moving from the quiet of home, the camera cuts to the NIH library, where Augusto again bends over books and photocopied articles. It is September 1984. Lorenzo is still on the apparently useless diet, his blood fats still rising. Explaining the paradox to Michaela, Augusto fills a kitchen sink with water from two faucets, one representing input of fats from food, the other input of fats by biosynthesis. "Why," he asks didactically, "when we eliminate saturated fats, does the level go up?" Michaela observes in one of her rare moments of amusement, "I married a plumber." Augusto's reply is a telling comment on what constitutes good science: "You married a man with a simple mind who asks simple questions, that's all." Although the film tends to obscure the fact that professional scientists may be working with similar dedication on the same issues, it repeatedly leads us to reflect on the nature of research, suggesting that humility like Augusto's is essential to good science. The simple questions are the hard ones, the simple diagrams often a way to make visible the deep structures that lead to answers. And Augusto's conversations with Michaela, like Dr. Sayer's with whomever he can find to listen, testify to the importance of community, collegiality, and partnership in research. In the context of conversation, questions get answered, ideas reframed, and assumptions tested.

Fittingly, therefore, the next library scene shows Michaela herself, now a full research partner, scanning a microfiche. In a report on fatty acids in rats, she finds a key to the paradox: in the absence of dietary fats, the body compensates by overproducing them. As she shares her discovery with Augusto, we receive another comment on the nature of scientific research: "I found that article by accident. I'm sure I could have missed it. And it was written by a Polish biochemist." Here and there one person at a time is working on a piece of the jigsaw, without much view of the whole. While major public health threats may gather disparate research into more efficient combined efforts, much science is conducted in such isolation, and many results remain inaccessible to those to whom they might be most relevant because of the scattered venues and differing constraints on scientific discourse (Payer 1996, chap. 1). Electronic communication has modified this fact somewhat, but the issue of intellectual community remains vexed, as intellectual property arguments and disputes over rights to protected knowledge continue to demonstrate.

When the Odones return to Dr. Nikolais with their findings, convinced that pooling information could launch more definitive research, they meet with the disheartening objection that the disease is too rare to be of interest to major funders. While no one can exactly be blamed for recognizing economic exigencies, the tragedy of market-driven medicine is once again foregrounded, and the Odones leave the doctor's office having run into another wall in the medical maze. By this time, viewers will have noticed how consistently hospitals and doctors' offices are settings for discouragement and defeat, and how often discovery and renewed hope come in the seclusion of home and library. This polarization, while it romanticizes the parents' independence, does underscore the possibility of lay participation that far exceeds most patients' conditioned notions of their roles and rights.

Still unwilling to accept defeat, the Odones pull together an unorthodox conference in which they plan to participate. Dr. Nikolais hesitantly cooperates. Ironically, the Muscatines of the ALD Foundation refuse support, citing their absolute respect for medical authority. Sweeping past objections, the Odones launch into private fund-raising.

Michaela organizes the food; one renegade ALD parent brings baskets of fresh vegetables. Thus the first world symposium on ALD is held in November 1984, with the Odones in attendance as translators — a role that not only attests to their practical usefulness but works as an analogue to the way they continually "translate" the language and methods of professional science into lay terms. At the conference, scientists' stories are mostly acknowledgments of failure. But a Japanese doctor introduces a way to manipulate fatty acids. A Canadian doctor knows the relevant Polish article about pigs. A thread of possibility emerges. One tentatively reports that he has tried oleic acid, derived from olive oil, with good results. This raises a dilemma: olive oil is forbidden in the institute diet. Pure oleic acid is toxic, and its triglyceride form is not available. The process of extraction is expensive; no one has tried producing it because there is no market.

Determined to breach the next barrier, Michaela makes calls until she finds a chemist willing to provide the extract; his company has been testing oleic acid as an industrial lubricant. So another door opens, reiterating the point that much scientific work is serendipitous, and that solutions often come from unexpected quarters. The Odones buy the one bottle available and take it to Dr. Nikolais for advice. He objects to the experiment on the grounds that they cannot know to what extent Lorenzo can metabolize fat. "I am a scientist," he reminds them, "and I am of absolutely no use to you whatever unless I can maintain my objectivity." Augusto's reply is characteristic: "I am a father, and no one can tell me what dressing to put on my child's salad." Nikolais muses, then replies, "You realize, of course, that any collaboration of mine would have to be unofficial." With that disclaimer, he proceeds to discuss dosage with the eager father, who is next seen measuring the precious oil into a feeding tube. This moment, along with many others, emphasizes how much the pursuit of knowledge within educational, medical, economic, and regulatory systems depends on those who keep one foot outside those systems, challenge them, and even defy or subvert them.

A month after he begins taking the oil, Lorenzo's fat levels are down, but tension builds as the slow processes of research and testing take their inevitable and maddening time. Despite deepening qualms, Augusto trusts hunches and claims the frightening freedom to act on them. When the Muscatines accuse him of arrogance, he points out the etymology of the word: "Arrogance, from *arrogare:* to claim for oneself. . . . I claim the right to fight for my kid's life."

But the professional scientists cannot make the same claim. When in

January 1985 Augusto tries to report a dramatic drop of Lorenzo's blood fat levels to the ALD Foundation, he is summarily dismissed on the grounds that it is too early to draw a conclusion. Moreover, he is asked not to share his good news. The Muscatines hold their position: "We take our guidance from the advisory board." Michaela points out that the advisory board "has another agenda." Ignoring her, they insist, "Our parents suffer enough without being made the victims of false hopes." Insisting that the Muscatines have no right to keep them from sharing information, the Odones plead, "[The doctors] are not gods." Mrs. Muscatine adopts her last line of defense, a powerful rationale for her own choices: "Has it occurred to you that maybe he doesn't want to be around anymore?" There is no arguing with this. It is the bottom line over which the two couples part company. Their differences are axiomatic. In light of Lorenzo's actual struggle, now nearly two decades long, many might find themselves siding with the Muscatines on this point. In the film, however, their conservatism appears as defensive and intransigent timidity.

That timidity provides a foil for Michaela's headstrong courage as she confronts ever more galling crises. In the scene following the argument, the home nurse reaches her own limit, declares, "I'm not comfortable with this situation," and gives notice. One by one, the professional caregivers feel forced to abandon what seems a quixotic journey into uncharted moral territory. Even Michaela's sister joins the growing ranks of those who consider that it might be better to let Lorenzo die. As if to prove the sister's point, Lorenzo's next seizure drives them to the emergency room, where the doctor tells a distraught Augusto, "I don't think you'll have to endure it much longer." While many scenes in the movie might be identified as climactic, this one shows the parents closest to capitulation. The question has come to a head: how long does one allow a loved one to suffer?

The question remains open as the Odones take Lorenzo home and hire another nurse. Augusto returns to the library to review everything he can find on fatty acid metabolism. A close-up shot shows him asleep over his books, when he wakes with an epiphany: "It's the same enzyme! . . . If we keep it busy making one of the monounsaturates, it won't make the other." This can be done by adding erusic acid, a derivative of grape seed oil, to the oleic acid they are using.

Once again the response from Dr. Nikolais is discouraging: "Erusic acid creates cardiac problems in rats." Because of possible deleterious side effects, he explains, human studies cannot be justified. "If something goes wrong, what then?" he asks. It's an old question. They must take their own risks. Michaela's acerbic response again pits parental devotion against scientific caution: "I suppose the risk-reward ratio is not attractive enough for you." Nikolais explains, "Your responsibility is merely towards your own child. My responsibility is to all those who suffer from it now and in the future." He concludes that though he shares their anguish, "I will have nothing to do with this oil." "We are not asking," Michaela icily replies, "for your anguish or your applause. We are asking merely for courage." But they are asking for more than that, and Michaela's heroism is thrown into further question.

The Odones return to the original Cleveland chemist to persuade him to isolate the extract of grape seed oil, but he refuses, unwilling to take the legal or medical risk. "We need a sympathetic collaborator," Augusto explains to him. The term has ominous overtones. When the chemist replies that no one in the country would take on the liability involved in the project, the Odones circulate a paper about their research abroad. Finally an old British chemist agrees to take on the job. He is near retirement. He has little to lose.

Once they put Lorenzo on the combined oils, his blood levels sink until they test normal. Then the Odones, in an underground move, share the oil with another ALD parent, who becomes a companion in their struggle. The doctors want more study before abandoning the dietary protocol. "So the other kids have to wait?" Augusto muses. "We know what to do about that, don't we?" And then, "So we leave science to its own concerns, huh?"

By February 1987, Lorenzo is swallowing for himself, and Dr. Nikolais announces at the ALD parents' meeting that the doctors are "preparing a protocol" and hope to persuade the government to fund it and insurance companies to approve it. But the parent with whom the Odones have shared their oil spills the beans and announces that the Odones have brought in a successful treatment from England, that it's a mixture of two cooking oils, that it's not dangerous, and that her son has been using it, and his blood levels are normal. She compares the situation of ALD patients to the AIDS patients who militantly overrode FDA restrictions on AZT. The announcement opens a Pandora's box of problems, both practical and moral, for official experimenters.

As more time goes by, Augusto continues his studies of the nervous system, pursuing obscure remyelination studies in the hope of restoring function. He raises funds for research, despite continuing objections that "that's not how science works." And, ruefully, he asks Michaela, "Do you ever think all this work may have been for somebody else's kid?" The answer comes in the film's concluding shots—a moving series of one-line testimonies (to a background of Mozart's *Ave Verum*) by healthy-looking boys and parents who announce their names and how long they've been using Lorenzo's oil.

At the time the film was completed in 1992, Augusto had been awarded an honorary medical degree; Lorenzo was fourteen years old, had recovered eyesight, and could communicate by computer. The actual facts of the case, of course, are far more ambiguous than the film leads one to believe. When Michaela Odone died in June 2000, she had spent sixteen hours a day with Lorenzo almost without interruption for the remaining years of her life, and he had regained very little function beyond what is alluded to in the film. Available statistics suggest that the oil works only in about 50 percent of ALD cases when they are caught early. Although certainly heroic, the Odones' story is one of very qualified victory. It is not clear how to assess the trade-offs or the costs. It is not clear that life is worth living on the terms made possible by such radical interventions. It is not clear that the slow processes of medical research ought to be hurried, though what slows them needs to be critically assessed by those both inside and outside the system. Although the film version does not do full justice to these ambiguities, it does raise useful questions about the relationship of the scientific/medical establishment to individuals whose needs lie outside the parameters of standard care and for-profit research. And it offers a hope worth fostering that the medical bureaucracy and scientific establishment are not impenetrable.

Walls of Words

Medicine and science are, however, well fortified. Given their prestige, public money, and educational prerequisites, laypersons less equipped than the Odones have little hope of challenging those establishments successfully. Among the powers that physicians and researchers exercise, language is not the least. The recent film *Wit* (directed by Mike Nichols), which Emma Thompson and Mike Nichols adapted from Margaret Edson's play of the same name, trains a harsh light on the uses and abuses of privileged discourses in doctor-patient negotiations. Medical jargon, medical "histories," and clinical dialogue all come under explicit critical scrutiny in this film by the patient-protagonist-narrator, Dr. Vivian Bearing (Emma Thompson), eminent professor of English literature, specialist in the sonnets of John Donne.

As a highly regarded professional and wordsmith herself, Dr. Bearing pays acute attention to the host of medical terms and clinical euphemisms she encounters after being diagnosed with advanced metastatic ovarian cancer. The opening words, uttered by her oncologist, Dr. Kelekian (Christopher Lloyd), whose impassive face fills the frame, are simple enough: "You have cancer." The explanation that follows, during which the camera alternates close-ups of speaker and listener, is rapid-fire, highly technical, and unalleviated by any expression of sympathy or reference to feeling. He describes the nature and status of the tumor, the rationale for the experimental protocol he recommends, and the likely side effects of treatment, all without reference to the emotional impact such news would be likely to have.

Dr. Bearing, neither alarmed nor intimidated, responds to Dr. Kelekian as a fellow professional whose competency equals his. She demonstrates no emotion. She assures him she understands the diagnosis and its implications. She agrees that she is tough enough (a term that recurs with deepening irony as her treatment goes on) to withstand the most potent treatment available. She even commiserates with him about the laxity of students who don't understand the importance of thoroughness. The one word she questions him about is his use of the term "insidious." "Insidious" he explains, means undetectable at an early stage. "Insidious," she replies, means "treacherous." The exchange sets a keynote for ensuing scenes in which it becomes increasingly apparent that in the world of this teaching and research hospital, ordinary words are pressed into specialized service, and the variegation of lively speech gives way to words that cut, laserlike, through layers of ambiguity and felt reference, losing much of their efficacy to do anything more than denote and instruct. The ironic relationship between Dr. Kelekian's use of "insidious" and Dr. Bearing's extends to many other exchanges in which medically trained technicians use jargon, euphemisms, or borrowed terms, oblivious to their deeper or wider meanings.

Throughout the film, Dr. Bearing comments in lengthy asides on what she regards as degenerate and unimaginative uses of language among caregivers who, with one exception, seem incapable of grasping irony, ambiguity, or allusion, and who rely on stock questions ("How are you feeling today?") in such inappropriate circumstances as to render them comical, were there anyone there to laugh. As a trained reader of the metaphysical poets, she is attuned to the very slippages that make language rich with both comic and tragic possibility — to the many times we say more than we mean, misspeak serendipitously and truly, find a phrase that reaches the analytical mind by way of the imagination. She knows how to "yoke opposites" and takes wry plea-sure even in painful ironies. Yet she, like the doctors and medical stu-dents who surround her with their hard-edged practicality, is a product of an academic system whose competitiveness, elitism, and hierarchy compare closely to the structures and stringencies of the medical re-search environment. She is, after all, a scholar, trained by "the great E. M. Ashford," who holds fast to her own "uncompromising schol-arly standards" and has held students to them as well, sometimes at the expense of human kindness.

A succession of early scenes shows Dr. Bearing being quizzed on her medical history by three different caregivers, none of whom seems capable of imagining or attending to her point of view. When the first, after getting her name, queries cryptically, "Doctor?" she answers, "Yes, I have a Ph.D." Annoyed rather than amused, he explains: "*Your* doctor?" When the nurse in radiology again asks her to state her name for yet another chart, she quips, "Lucy, Countess of Bedford," only to be met with the flat rejoinder "I don't see it here." Her humor is lost on them, her name only a device for locating the many charts on which statistics will be recorded.

Ensconced in the hospital for treatment, Dr. Bearing's two most frequent interlocutors are Jason (Jonathan Woodward), a research fel-low who once took her course in metaphysical poets (to prove he could get an A) and Susie (Audra McDonald), an African American nurse. The two characters are opposites in almost every respect. Jason is an ambitious, driven, highly competitive achiever whose passion is cancer research but whose social skills are severely limited by his inability to see a situation in terms of any but his own frame of reference. He makes the requisite efforts to be pleasant with Dr. Bearing but fails to provide a convincing show of sincere interest in the person behind the disease. Even his admiration for her seems self-directed; he thinks of her authority in the classroom as a hurdle he managed to clear. Susie, on the other hand, located significantly lower on the institutional totem pole, is the only medical professional who sustains both eye contact and conversation with Dr. Bearing. She asks authentic ques-tions and waits for answers. She makes judgments about Vivian's needs by consulting her. She empathizes and comforts. Although this polarity reinforces unhelpful stereotypes of the professional, scientific, male doctor and nurturing, earthy, female nurse, both script and perfor-mances complicate and ironize the contrast. Jason, who fumbles sim-ple human transactions, misses nuances, and finally makes a humiliat-ing medical mistake, has much to learn; and Vivian, it turns out, is still his teacher. Susie manages, despite professional subordination, to practice medicine her own way and protect the woman she sees as her patient from institutional harm. She talks with her. In a moment of pain, she breathes with her. She does as she is told but remains after the doctors depart to do more. She is sharp-eyed and subversive rather than sweet.

All the conversations in the film, except flashbacks to Vivian's life as child, student, and teacher, take place in the hospital; in all but the first scene, she is bald, clad in a hospital gown, on an examining table, a bed, or a wheelchair. The focus remains relentlessly close; we witness her retching and vomiting at uncomfortably intimate range and watch her face become ravaged over time. The close-ups also repeatedly inventory the chrome and glass accoutrements of the hospital rooms. A certain claustrophobia is communicated by entirely visual means. Colorful flashbacks allow us to take the measure of her losses; there is little left in her daily environment to engage the mind, the eye, the imagination, the heart.

Vivian manages to remain intellectually engaged as long as possible during her eight-month ordeal by commenting wryly to herself and the audience on the institutional language and customs she observes from her isolated vantage point. " 'Grand Rounds' is what they call it," she warns us, eyebrow raised, as Dr. Kelekian, Jason, and three other fellows gather at her bedside. Jason abruptly pulls the bedsheet down, her gown up, revealing a long surgical scar, and probes her abdomen as he rapidly recites the facts of her case. When he is finished, still making neither conversation nor eye contact with the patient, Dr. Kelekian quizzes the students: "Side effects?" They enumerate everything but the most obvious — hair loss. When he points out their omission, one cries, "Come on! That doesn't count!" (Vivian assures us it counts rather heavily in the succession of humiliating losses.) Dr. Kelekian finally seeks Vivian's gaze, but only to confirm, as one professor to another, what fools these students be. She obliges him with a concession, but her insult is recorded when she turns to the camera after the white coats are gone and asks, "Wasn't that grand?"

Later, alone in bed, she reasons about her deteriorating condition, which requires extreme precautions: "I'm not in isolation because I have cancer. . . . I'm in isolation because I'm being treated for cancer. Herein lies the paradox." Donne, she muses, would have loved it. He reveled in paradox. "Think of it as a puzzle, I would tell them — as an intellectual game. Or I would have told them, were it a game, which it is not." Paradox, a favorite device of the metaphysical poets, is also a way of understanding and enduring the tensions of conflicting points of view, means, and ends which seem to her to characterize medicine as they do her own profession.

What saves the film from being a commonplace account of a patient suffering indignities at the hands of heartless professionals is not only Vivian Bearing's wit — her capacity to reframe and see the ironies of her situation — but also her self-critical understanding of the ways her own professionalism has been perhaps just as heartless as what she is encountering. She is capable of compassion even for Jason, who ignores, misunderstands, and humiliates her, because, as she puts it, "He is my student. I taught him." "In everything I have been steadfast, resolute," she reflects. "Some would say in the extreme." She has, she realizes, few stones to throw at the medical researchers who will doubtless produce a journal article not about her but about her "peritoneal cavity which, despite their best intent, is now crawling with cancer." Nor does she judge Jason, who innocently, unfeelingly, exclaims, "Cancer's the only thing I've ever wanted!" Even as she gives up any attempt to make him come to terms with her humanity, she sympathizes with his intellectual passion, so like, in some ways, her own. As dramatic monologue, therefore, the film presents the confession and conversion of a woman too highly professionalized, who repents and retrieves the deep human value of her own work by watching how insidiously the intellectual temptations of medicine and the self-protective structures of institutional life have led others into similar self-betrayal. Her capacity for amusement is, finally, the measure of her capacity for compassion on those who watch her suffer without sympathy.

Near the end, Vivian's old professor and mentor, the great E. M. Ashford (Eileen Atkins), visits and reads her a children's story, "The Runaway Bunny," which she muses is a parable of God seeking the lost soul. Listening through a morphine fog, Vivian curls against her and returns to sleep as Professor Ashford kisses her and whispers, "Time to go," and then, "Flights of angels sing thee to thy rest." One might expect this touching moment to be the conclusion, but it is followed, jarringly, by Jason's routine visit to take Vivian's stats. When he finds Vivian not breathing, he calls a code blue. The code team and nurse Susie come running at the same time, the former to rip down Vivian's gown and administer shock treatment, the latter to fight them off, insisting that she was DNR and should not be touched. Jason, watching, finally yells above the pandemonium, "Hey! I made a mistake, okay?" It seems a comment not only on his summoning the team but on his treatment of the old professor who now lies dead, stripped, at the end, of the dignity of a peaceful exit.

At intervals throughout the ninety-minute production, Vivian recites lines from John Donne's "Death Be Not Proud." The poem, like the ecclesiastical music in *Lorenzo's Oil*, reminds her and us of the metaphysical or spiritual universe in which healing takes place, of the reality of death, which no medicine can ultimately defeat, and the promise of eternal life, a powerful human hope. Against that backdrop, the irreverence of hospital protocols and invasive procedures diminishes in urgency and importance, and the question of how we die mirrors something unsettling about how we consent to live out our lives and deal with the ills to which the flesh is heir.

All four of these films, while in some respects oversimplifying or failing to acknowledge a host of economic and legal pressures that hem in scientific research and medical practice, raise important questions about accessibility, accountability, and professionalism. To whom, for instance, should information about new experiments be available, and at what point? What kinds of information protection are legitimate? On what principle should limited attention and resources be distributed? Who assumes the experimental risks and pays the cost of error? When does one invoke the privilege of the "special case"? All these films challenge institutional conservatism that tends to preclude creative approaches to complex problems, raising the ever relevant question of what conditions might both protect the interests of all involved and reward calculated risk taking. All the films deliver a message of qualified hope which, though it sometimes borders on fantasy, may also serve as a needed reminder that even in hidebound bureaucracies where cynicism and despair become occupational hazards, creativity and compassion can survive, and renewal is possible, as it always has been, through the willing and intelligent participation of those with curious minds and caring hearts.

4 Television

Images and Healers

A Visual History of Scientific Medicine

MARC R. COHEN AND AUDREY SHAFER

"All living is interpreting; all action requires seeing the world *as* something." So states the philosopher Martha Nussbaum (1990, 47) in her defense of utilizing literary texts to pursue understanding of "the world's surprising variety, its complexity and mysteriousness, its flawed and imperfect beauty" (3). Images, painted or moving, are also ways of understanding; they are interpretations of contemporaneous life. As that life and our perceptions of it have evolved, so too have the corresponding representational images produced by the arts. Since the nineteenth century, Western medicine has undergone a revolutionary transformation from a field based on traditional, authority-bound teachings to one based on scientific principles of disease and therapy. Through this progression, medicine has evolved from a way of caring to a means of curing, dramatically altering the role of the medical profession and public perceptions of physicians in contemporary society. These developments in the history of medicine are reflected in the changing representation of healers in the visual arts.

While many other visual representations could have been used for this discussion, we selected artistic works on the basis of subject, composition, and adherence to the theme of the healer in scientific Western medicine. The artists of the paintings, etchings, and photographs described here, in their choices of subject, color, mood, light, framing, line, vantage, inclusion, omission, size, and media, offer an interpretation of the healer. And just as diagnostic imaging has shifted from the static (such as flat-plate x ray) to the moving image (such as "fly-through" intraluminal bowel imaging), we conclude this selective journey with an image from television to represent a more current view of healers. We use these images to interpret contemporaneous opinions of the medical profession, of patient desires and expectations, and of the "imperfect beauty" of healers in the scientific era of Western medicine.

Today's physician is a natural resource for treatment of any health condition or emergency, but before the advent of scientific medicine, the relationship between the individual patient and the field of medicine was often a reluctant, and at times uneasy, connection. Physicians were frequently summoned to announce the imminence of death rather than delay it; most hospitals were unsanitary institutions housing desperately ill poor people (G. Williams 1986, 89). Knowledge in early-nineteenth-century medicine was based on traditional theories taught by the previous generation of physicians, not scientific fact. The lack of understanding of disease process meant that the reasoning behind physicians' actions was usually poor, and treatments were designed to affect symptoms instead of underlying conditions. Regardless, even trying to treat symptoms was problematic, as the range of available therapies was often limited to interventions such as "heroic depletion," typically a combination of bloodletting and purgatives (Turow 1989, 4). Given that these treatments were so often unsuccessful, it is hardly surprising that the general public perceived the medical class with skepticism.

Honoré Daumier's 1833 satiric image *The Physician* demonstrates a common perception of contemporary physicians as those who do little to help their patients (figure 1) (Karp 1985, 181). In this representation, a physician sits beneath a bust of Hippocrates and the scythe of Death. Meanwhile a procession of this physician's dead patients march across the foreground, some already in coffins. The doctor is perplexed, unable to understand why his attentions have proven so fruitless. This caricature addresses two pervasive themes — the inadequacies of the medical profession in treating devastating epidemics in newly industrialized cities, and the public's negative attitude about the physician class.

Throughout much of the nineteenth century, a medical practitioner in the United States could "lack an M.D. degree, be unlicensed, belong to no professional society, and not read . . . a medical journal, yet still undeniably be a regular physician" (Warner 1986, 16). Medical institutions promoted a positive image of a medical professional by affirming values such as responsibility, duty, judgment, intellectual achievement, and moral obligation to act in patients' best interests and by instilling such values in their members (Burnham 1982, 1474). As the image of the concerned citizen-physician became more widespread, public perception of the profession improved.

1. Skepticism of prescientific physicians.
Honoré Daumier, *The Physician*. Lithograph, 1833.
Philadelphia Museum of Art. A perplexed early-
nineteenth-century physician watches a parade of his
dead patients led off by devils. The original caption
translates as "Why the Devil! Are all my patients depart-
ing this way? . . . I do my best to bleed them, purge
them, and drug them. . . . I don't understand
anything about it!"

On Christmas Day in 1877, artist Sir Luke Fildes's son lay dying.
Phillip Fildes was attended by Dr. Murray, who, while unable to prevent the boy's death, could at least offer comfort and solace to the
patient and family (Wilson 1997, 90). Fildes later immortalized Murray's dedication in his 1891 work *The Doctor* (figure 2) (Nuland 1992,
94). The physician is seen waiting in vigil, sitting silently with his ill
patient. On the left, a single lamp illuminates the room, highlighting
the faces of physician and patient. In the background are the parents,
yet the child is turned, even reaching, toward the doctor.

The physician in this painting is shown without diagnostic aids, and
a single bottle, perhaps a therapeutic, represents the only available

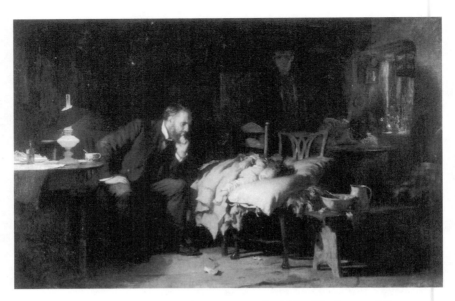

2. The humanistic physician. Sir Luke Fildes, *The Doctor*. Oil on canvas, c. 1891. Tate Gallery, London. A physician, holding vigil by his young patient, epitomizes empathic care.

intervention. This was a time of Cockle's Antibilious Pills and Locock's Pulmonic Wafers (nostrums for indigestion and respiratory ailments such as asthma and tuberculosis), not intravenous drugs and computerized tomography. Physicians had to understand their patients' conditions by learning about the patients themselves. Doctors gleaned patients' habits, lifestyles, and personal histories from interactions in the community and in the homes of ill patients. Yet for all of the physician's seeming inactivity, this painting is not a calculus of despair — while he may not appear to be actively intervening, the doctor embodies the virtues of nurturing, compassion, and understanding.

As medical science progressed, its professional identity came to include more than moral qualities and the use of traditional remedies. The late nineteenth century witnessed a transformation in what Michel Foucault describes as the medical gaze, the combined sensory experience of the observer that informs the physician of the process occurring within the patient (Foucault 1973, 94). With observation and clinical experience came the ability to correlate findings in patients with pathology noted at autopsy. A doctor's ability to look, feel, and listen allowed him (most physicians at that time were male) to "see" beneath the surface of the skin, to begin to understand the underlying disease process, and, accordingly, to act. This projective pathological anatomy, as a mode of medical diagnosis and knowledge not accessible to the layperson or untrained healer, would distinguish the physician as a skilled diagnostician (135–37).

As the traditional role of physician was transformed by incorporating contemporary innovations, the public perception of the medical field also changed (Savitt 1995, 75). The figure of the great physician took on an almost sacred role as keeper and developer of a new knowledge. These exemplars distinguished themselves from the mass of the regular medical profession through achievement, both as academicians and as clinicians. In the arts, such individuals were often rendered in a reverent way, portrayed as dramatic, almost mythic, characters.

In early 1875, Thomas Eakins began working on an imposing 6 1/2-by-8-foot work entitled *Portrait of Professor Gross*, which would later become known as *The Gross Clinic* (figure 3). Eakins's choice of subjects in this work reflects his goal of celebrating both a renowned surgeon, Dr. Samuel Gross, and the achievements of contemporary American surgery. The image depicts a significant surgical advance in the treatment of osteomyelitis, a chronic bone infection. Only recently had it been shown that resection, rather than amputation, was acceptable treatment, and Gross was one of the enthusiastic proponents and researchers involved with this advance (Brodsky 1997, 5). Eakins faithfully rendered the scene complete with modern innovations such as anesthesia, as an ether cloth is draped over the patient's face. The artist is also accurate in noting that Gross had not yet accepted Lister's theories of disinfection and is operating in street clothes without sterile technique. One of the most striking features in this image is Eakins's use of light. Operating theaters were lit by overhead skylight; here an illuminating force comes down from above, falling on two regions in particular: Gross's head and the surgical field. Gross himself practically radiates light, marking him personally as a source of illumination as he metes out wisdom to his students.

He is shown here in the dual roles of surgeon and teacher. As a surgeon probing beneath the surface of the patient's manifestations, Gross elucidates the nature of his patient's somatic complaints (Brodsky 1997, 5). As a teacher, he is the giver of knowledge — one who opens the surgical incision, pushes aside layers of darkness to reveal an inner truth, then imparts that knowledge to others. By emphasizing Gross more than the operating field, Eakins conveys that the enlightenment to be gained in this scene clearly comes from what the professor, not the patient, has to offer.

3. Innovations in surgery. Thomas Eakins, *The Gross Clinic*. Oil on canvas, 1875. Thomas Jefferson University. Light glints from the forehead of the professor-surgeon, who expounds to those assembled in the operating-room theater, including the artist in the first row.

Medical knowledge began to change in the late nineteenth century as physicians refined physical diagnosis skills and scientists developed diagnostic tools and pathological theories of disease (Savitt 1995, 80). Instrumentation and objective evidence supplanted assumptions and philosophy as the main tenets of therapy. As the association between doctors and their technologies became more prominent and complex, visual images of medical professionals now included portrayals of physician-scientists.

In 1888 medical bacteriologist Pierre-Paul-Emil Roux and his assistant Alexandre Yersin demonstrated that injecting animals with cell-free culture medium from diphtheria cultures produced the same effect as inoculating with the bacilli themselves. Their work implied that a toxin, not the bacterium itself, played a vital role in the disease process.

From these observations, Emil von Behring and Shibasaburo Kitasato developed a method of injecting horses with diphtheria toxin, then isolating antitoxin serum from their blood. This serum could then be used in treating humans with the disease, marking one of the major early milestones in bacteriologic therapy (Bynum 1994, 160).

Charles Maurin, an artist working in Paris in the 1890s, was an experienced painter familiar with historical and allegorical works (Karp 1985, 182). In a painting and the etching, entitled *Serum Therapy*, reproduced here (figure 4), he chose to depict the discovery and use of successful therapy against what had been a tremendously fatal disease. Roux is enthroned at the center of the work, with his assistants standing faithfully behind him. Elevated on the right is a horse, the source of the serum, while reviled on the left is a female figure of death, repelled by the therapeutic miracle of antitoxin, as represented by Roux's sweeping gesture (182). The images of lively children pay tribute to the therapy's power by their mere presence, as diphtheria was one of the most significant sources of pediatric mortality prior to vaccination and antitoxin. In a composition reminiscent of Christian themes and the Trinity, Maurin exalts science, scientists, and the promise of salvation that medicine now brings to the afflicted.

Here the subject is not just the physician coming to the aid of a sick patient, or the scientist working diligently in a lab, but the true physician-scientist and the wonders he has brought forth into the world. Even before great numbers of patients had been successfully treated, publicity surrounding the effectiveness of antisera against diphtheria and rabies greatly swayed public opinion in favor of the medical profession (Kaufman 1993, 49). As laboratory research developed effective medical therapies, the physician-scientist came to exemplify the public's ideal healer, and it was this image that appeared in the visual arts.

By the early twentieth century, the power of a physician came to be symbolized by new discoveries and technologies. This was reflected in art by a tendency to emphasize the innovations of medicine more than the practitioners. Raoul Dufy's *The Operation* (c. 1930), while still a surgical scene in the operating room, is entirely different from the late-nineteenth-century images of detailed operating theaters and legendary surgeons (figure 5) (Rousselot 1967, 248). Dufy's focus is on the nature of the procedure only, not the characters involved. Here practice has overtaken the practitioner in importance. Simple lines represent the figures involved, and the once dramatic portraits and facial expressions are reduced to undistinguishing shading around their eyes.

4. The physician-scientist. Charles Maurin, *Serum Therapy*. Etching and drypoint, 1896. Philadelphia Museum of Art. The physician-scientist offers new hope to humanity with the discovery of diphtheria antitoxin.

Some detail is given to the surgeons' hands in the operating field, but even this is hastily sketched. No effort is made to define the doctor's personality through a caring gesture or pained expression, and the relationship of surgeon and patient is sharply defined and distanced. Much as in a real operating room, layers of surgical garb mask the humanity of the figures; sterile dressings hide the patient, his dramatic role reduced to nothing more than an operating field.

As the technology of modern medicine outgrew the resources of the individual physician, the importance of hospitals increased. Large-scale development of modern hospitals boomed in the 1890s following advances in surgery, anesthesia, and aseptic technique (Cassedy 1991, 76). Instead of a place where people were taken to die, the hospital came to represent the forefront of modern medicine. X rays, operating rooms, and diagnostic and therapeutic instrumentation that became fundamental to medical care were more accessible at institutions than offices. Physicians, in turn, became increasingly affiliated with hospitals, depending on institutional medicine and its available technological resources. This access appeared more important than the psychosocial issues concerning the patient, and the clinic evolved into the logical environment for the delivery of modern medicine.

One casualty of the shift from house call to clinic visit was the inti-

5. Anonymity in medicine. Raoul Dufy, *The Operation.*
Drawing, c. 1930. Musée Municipale D'Art Moderne,
Paris. In the twentieth-century operating room, personnel are masked and garbed, and procedure takes
precedence over personality.

macy of the doctor-patient relationship. When a patient presents to a
clinic, he or she is often a stranger. The patient sees others in the
waiting room and knows that the visit is but one bit of a tight schedule.
Both the surroundings and the clinic rituals (check-in, timed visits,
medical record numbers) add to the mechanistic atmosphere. Such
brief interactions, stripped of the personality of the home environment,
necessarily limit the physician's scope of knowledge about a particular
patient.

In his 1926 etching *X-Rays*, artist John Sloan alludes to this new
relationship (figure 6). The physicians in Sloan's work are identified
not by their relationship to the patient but by their use of technology.
Whereas previous representations of physicians may have shown doctors using innovations as part of a bedside routine, these men sit behind
a fluoroscope, completely removed from the patient. They focus on the
technology before them and the answers it might provide, rather than
dealing with the person to whom it is applied. The intimacy between
physician and machine suggests deep reliance; to strip the doctors of
their technology would be to strip them of their professional identities.
The patient's discomfort, due either to drinking a bitter contrast solu-

6. Focus on technology. John Sloan, *X-Rays*.
Etching and aquatint, 1926. Philadelphia Museum
of Art. Technology intervenes between patient and
physician as the fluoroscopic image comes
to represent the patient.

tion or to his isolation from his caregivers, remains unnoticed. The physicians, literally screened off from their patient, see him only as the image on the fluoroscope, not as a human being. Here illumination comes over the physicians, who choose not to share their thoughts, while the patient, despite having a light shining toward him, is figuratively left in the dark, alone. Sloan, who had personal experience in this kind of setting as a result of his own medical problems, conveys a cold sense of isolation that he himself must have felt (Karp 1985, 184). In Sloan's vision, technology has served to eliminate the human interaction between doctor and patient.

Despite technology's effects on the individual patient's experience, well-publicized successes in treatment modalities and public health initiatives brought great respect to the medical field and transformed the social status of the physician. Throughout the 1930s, the doctor in popular media was most often portrayed as an embodiment of the virtues of independence, integrity, dedication, and even patriotism. In comparison with the early 1900s, when doctors survived on meager payments they might collect from their patients, the physician class was now making four times the average income of a working-class man. Public opinion polls showed that regardless of the respondents' own professions, medicine was universally accorded the highest rank in prestige (Raben 1993, 24). This change in status resulted from many factors, including political efforts by physician organizations to codify standards and promote authority, but also because advances in science and medical intervention were perceived as offering significant benefit.

By the middle of the twentieth century, diseases such as pellagra, cholera, malaria, and scurvy had been practically eradicated in the United States. With the use of antimicrobial sulfa drugs in the 1930s and penicillin in the 1940s, physicians began to be able to cure diseases routinely (Kaufman 1993, 149). Society expected an unprecedented amount from medicine — cure, not just care. Medical innovators provided an array of new interventions, machines, and techniques designed to meet these new demands.

To advance the trust between patient and physician, the doctor had to educate his patient, thereby validating the doctor's science. One result was that the public became more aware of what they should expect from the physician, and more aware of shortcomings (Burnham 1982, 1478). By the 1950s, common criticisms revolved around the interactions of the physician, not the effectiveness or competence of his actions. Complaints included "failure to take a personal interest in the patient or his family" and "waiting time in doctor's offices" as well as demands for personal attention (1476). Indifferent attitudes toward patients, epitomized by the move of medicine from the home to the hospital or clinic, was strongly criticized. Patients asked that their physicians listen more, take more time with them, and educate them about their disease, all with expert skill. The public's concept of the ideal physician had been reborn as the old country doctor who can be relied on to be heartfelt, accurate, effective, compassionate, and at times superhuman.

On 20 September 1948, *Life* magazine published a photo-essay by W. Eugene Smith under the title "Country Doctor" (figure 7) (Karp 1985, 185). Smith described the philosophy in his work as an effort to show "life as it is," and his achievements here convey the humanitarian side of an otherwise unheralded rural physician. As photographs, his images are true to reality's details, but Smith's compositions seem to capture the deeper character of his subjects as well. The article chroni-

7. The able generalist. W. Eugene Smith, *Dr. Ceriani Making a House Call.*
Photograph, 1948. Philadelphia Museum of Art. The careworn country
doctor strides to his next house call under a threatening sky.

cles the activities of Ernest Ceriani, a general practitioner working in
rural Colorado. The photographs portray a hardworking man willing
to sacrifice his own comfort for those around him, and the accompanying text lauds him for his tireless dedication, announcing that "his endless work has its own rewards" (W. Eugene Smith 1948). This man
takes few vacations and little personal time — patients always come
first. The article mourns the loss of his type of physician, noting the
trend of medical school graduates to go into specialized and hospital-
based fields. But Ceriani is shown as a true humanist, a capable healer
completely devoted to his community. Walking alone and carrying a
traditional doctor's satchel, Ceriani emerges from the outlying coun-
tryside, selflessly ready to aid his next patient.

In the photograph, Ceriani's powerful character is matched against a
dramatic, sweeping backdrop. The doctor's slight figure is sharply defined by the contrast within the dark sky, but his upright frame keeps a
visual rhythm with the picket fence, incorporating him as part of the
landscape (Karp 1985, 185). The imagery of a solitary and powerful
master of medicine is reminiscent of the almost mythic representations

of the nineteenth-century surgeons such as Gross. But while such allusions might be correct in implying the value of his abilities to his community, Ceriani's practice is firmly a part of his own era. The essay refers to his autoclave and oxygen tent, and other photos depict him perusing x rays or performing surgery. Perhaps Ceriani's most impressive quality is his marriage of the contemporary medical knowledge his profession demands with the traditional interpersonal values treasured by his patients.

Contemporary painting also reflected the ideal of the humanitarian physician, as Andrew Wyeth's 1949 *Children's Doctor* shows (figure 8). Wyeth depicts Dr. Margaret Handy, a pediatrician in Wilmington, Delaware, who had cared for his son during an extreme illness (Nuland 1992, 104). Through use of extraordinary detail, Wyeth evokes a realistic image of compassion and comfort. While her doctor's bag may contain the wonders of modern medicine, it is Handy's inner strength that appears most accessible, a vital quality in any caregiver. The slight fatigue that appears in her face and gesture is familiar to any viewer, and this sympathetic emotion humanizes the capable doctor. As she almost floats into the background, the colors of her clothes blend with the atmosphere of the night. Her ghostlike form represents a powerful healing presence, continuing on to another patient, her work in this scene done.

Although an image can evoke stories, lives, or complex relationships, a static image is a frozen portrayal compared to the narrative potential of film or television. The temporality of any given image in moving pictures highlights evanescence and change. The advent of television, stored media, and Internet technology heralded a new intimacy with images of healers: the personal house call is replaced by the flickering actor-doctor in a box in your living room, and the intimidating hospital edifice is reduced to a brief panorama. Fictional medicos placed in "realistic" settings abound in popular media. Furthermore, no longer is a single artist interpreting the medical enterprise to produce an image: now such images are created by a veritable team of professionals. In sum, the differences between a painting of a physician and an image representing a medical television show are huge, yet both can be used to evaluate contemporaneous interpretations of the physician-healer.

By the mid-twentieth century, medicine was in a golden age of prestige, reflecting scientific advances and high popular regard for the field (Burnham 1982, 1477). It was during this time, with the advent of television and major motion pictures, that the most widely available

8. The compassionate physician. Andrew Wyeth, *Children's Doctor*. Tempera on panel, 1949. Brandywine River Museum, Chadds Ford, Pennsylvania. Women physicians were still a novelty in mid-twentieth-century America, but Wyeth depicts Dr. Handy as a caring individual and not an aberration.

public representations of physicians emerged. One Hollywood franchise, *Dr. Kildare,* enjoyed enormous popularity and developed into a series of films featuring brilliant physicians capable of conquering disease, social ill, and moral conflict. The series reflected a time when medicine seemed to promise a cure for all ills, physical or otherwise. Later representations in the cinema reflected this regard, with doctors appearing in more than one-half of eight hundred films surveyed in 1949 and 1950; an enormous majority of these characters were positive images (1477).

Early television shows like NBC's *Medic* thrived on reality, showing procedures and routines as accurately as possible. *Medic* employed on-set physician consultants, used real operating rooms as shooting locations, and garnered advice and approval from the Los Angeles County Medical Association. Later characters such as Ben Casey and a TV version of Dr. Kildare struck a chord so familiar in some viewers that

Richard Chamberlain, who played Kildare, received 3,500 letters per week from people asking advice, and Vince Edwards, who played Casey, reported that "even real doctors discuss cases with me" (Turow 1989, 69). As the nation's prehospital emergency medical system developed in the late 1960s and early 1970s, NBC responded with a paramedic show called *Emergency!* that kept trends in programming current with those in medicine.

Television today continues to use realism to provide familiar backdrops in medical shows but still tries to find sympathy within viewers by reflecting the public's perceptions and expectations. In the real world, advances in medical technology and economic pressures have coincided with the relative disappearance of the humanist physician. Critics of the health care industry claim that it places emphasis on efficiency, costs, and outcomes, leaving the patient's overall well-being to suffer. During screenings of the movie *As Good As It Gets* in 1997, audiences cheered as Helen Hunt's character delivered (to a kindly doctor making a house call, no less) an impassioned diatribe against HMO greed (Brink 1998, 47). The ideal physician remains one capable of balancing compassion, time, and technology in the atmosphere of managed care, but in reality this person is ever more elusive.

For the sake of commercial appeal and ratings, television characters must embody the same virtues that the viewing public expects in their heroes and, in the case of TV doctors, their physicians. Thus the characters and themes expressed on medical television shows are designed to appeal to the viewer's idealistic side, where quality care and understanding are the hallmarks of the medical establishment. Now, with shows like *ER*, *Gideon's Crossing*, and *Presidio Med*, such characters appear almost nightly on broadcast television. These physicians personify every quality a patient could want: brilliant diagnostic abilities, an unlimited fund of knowledge in all medical subspecialties, and Hollywood-style good looks. In a world of time and economic pressures, these doctors are able to address every concern and comfort nearly everyone around them.

On NBC's show *ER*, a weekly array of trauma victims and ill patients are expertly attended to by a multicultural group of young and beautiful doctors and nurses, all of whom are more dedicated to their work than their personal lives (Annas 1995, 40). The incredibly skilled staff is able to treat all comers with the most considerate of manners, rarely allowing external pressures to interfere with the instantly forged, yet remarkably intimate, doctor-patient relationship. In fact, their abilities to heal may be rivaled only by their degree of compassion. Of note is that at all levels of training, including doctors, the characters claim a wide range of ages and cultural backgrounds. This diversity, not seen in many images of physicians prior to the late twentieth century, reflects both the increased representation of women and nonwhite men in the medical profession and, given the popularity of the characters, an increased public acceptance of them.

The cast photograph displays a mix of sexes, ages, and races (figure 9). The doctors, nurses, and students form a team devoted to patient care; they boldly stare into the camera, relax in their ER garb with stethoscopes slung around their shoulders, and appear ready to scurry along the tiled floor to the next patient encounter. In the ER, these workers deftly handle any needed equipment, navigate the most complex of technological marvels, and perform every indicated technique, yet remain considerate of their patients' personal issues. No procedure or patient is too complicated for them, and they maximize the apparently limitless promises of cure offered by modern medicine. Part of the show's success results from its depiction of a health care system that appeals to the audience (Marin and McCormick 1994, 46–51). Some have called the show's hospital a source of reassurance for a public anxious about their own medical care, noting that this emergency department provides a place where viewers can feel as if they know the staff and believe in the doctors' concern for others (Annas 1995, 40). The minimization of paperwork and financial gatekeeping in the show also makes a tremendous statement about idealized contemporary health care. This is the one hospital in America that hardly ever asks about insurance status. On *ER*, health care is as good and as accessible as it gets, reflecting a viewing audience's dream perception, not reality.

The advent of science heralded a new era in medicine and established a more reliable potential for cure. Advances in diagnosis and pathophysiology led to a better understanding of disease processes. Physicians, whose interventions were no longer limited to the use of heroic depletion, could offer effective therapeutics that improved the lives of the general public. As a result, popular perceptions shifted from ridicule to respect. In the visual arts, physicians were now illustrated in remarkable moments, celebrating personal accomplishments or lauding advances rather than highlighting impotence.

As science proved to be the engine driving medical progress forward, it too was afforded great respect. Popular images celebrated achievement and potential, portraying researchers' dedication to science in a noble and selfless light. But when technology's importance impinged on the interpersonal aspect of regular health care delivery, patients

9. Medicine as pop culture icon. The cast of NBC's *ER*. By the end of the twentieth century, the team approach to health care is the norm, and minorities and women are expected participants. Press release photograph. © Constant c Productions, Amblin Television, Warner Bros. Television, NBC Inc.

grew unhappy, and artists depicted images of depersonalization and isolation. Emphasis moved from the intimacy of the doctor-patient relationship to the efficiency of individual acts of medicine. As the public demanded a general return to humanism and the compassionate physician, celebratory images portrayed the country doctor, capable of handling the intricacies of modern medicine while still being an essential part of the community. Today television reflects trends in attitudes toward both medicine and its practitioners. Modern technology, featured prominently on realistic sets, allows viewers to identify elements from their own experiences with hospitals. Cast composition acknowledges society's considerations for multiculturalism. Meanwhile, the near-miraculous abilities of TV doctors represent the current technomedical expectations of the American health system, while the institutional settings stylize medical care to fit a public idealization.

Medicine has established a record of effective intervention, with new innovations in gene therapy, pharmaceuticals, and surgical procedures offering promises of future improvements — or unwelcome intrusions. In modern times, various media forms, such as television, join the traditional visual arts as part of, and as reflections on, cultural development and contemporary attitudes. Such images echo and interpret the flaws and imperfect beauty, as well as the intimations of grandeur, that the modern healer, steeped in scientific training, represents in the profoundly human enterprise of doctoring.

[The authors would like to acknowledge Daniel Weiss, Ph.D., Chair of the History of Art Department of the Johns Hopkins University, for his generous support of this project. This project was supported in part by the Stanford University School of Medicine Alumni Scholars Fund.]

From *City Hospital* to *ER:*

The Evolution of the Television Physician

GREGG VANDEKIEFT

> Television viewing is a ritual, almost like religion,
> except that it is attended to more regularly. — Gerbner et al.,
> "The Demonstration of Power"

People of a certain age remember the commercial. The image of an actor appeared on the television screen and intoned, "I'm not a doctor, but I play one on TV." Perhaps the most intriguing aspect of that advertisement was what followed: the actor went on to dispense medical advice. That an actor known primarily for portraying a television physician could endorse a pharmaceutical product, with no irony intended, highlights the authority the viewing public grants television doctors.

The impact of television in our society cannot be overstated. The medium of television is a ubiquitous and indelible part of late-twentieth-century American culture and creates, even as it reflects, many of our perceptions of the world around us. In a review of research on television's influence in forming beliefs about social reality, Hawkins and Pingree (1981) stated, "Most studies show evidence for a link between amount of viewing and beliefs, regardless of the kind of reality studied" (349). However, they cautioned that television does not act independently of other societal influences; personal experience, educational background, and exposure to popular media all converge in a complex matrix that helps shape beliefs regarding social institutions. "It would be a considerable overstatement . . . to assign pre-eminence to television as a shaper of culture. However, asserting the opposite — that television's contribution is trivial — likewise misses some important points. . . . Television's influence on individual constructions of reality can no longer be described as direct, but must be viewed as a complex process that takes place within individual contexts" (361–62).

Television's pervasive influence affects the world of medicine no less than other social institutions. Gerbner et al. (1981) asserted, "Although television is only one of the many influences in life, it may well be the single most common and pervasive source of health information" (904). Students and patients enter the world of medicine with expectations potentially shaped as much by television as by personal experience. A conversation I overheard as a new faculty member aptly demonstrates this claim. A group of first-year medical students were discussing which *ER* character they would most like to emulate. One argued, "Benton may be a jerk, but he's *good*. I wouldn't care that I'm not warm and cuddly if I were that good in the O.R." Another countered, "I would rather be like Green — at least he *cares* about his patients." To which the first student replied, "Yeah, but look at what a screwed-up mess he is!" Nowhere in the ensuing conversation did the students discuss their faculty members as role models.

In this essay, I will answer the classic question "Does life imitate art, or does art imitate life?" with a resounding "Yes." Even as television portrays fictionalized, dramatized images of the existing medical culture, its choice of what to portray — and not to portray — simultaneously helps shape public perceptions of medicine that are carried into the clinic and the hospital by patients and trainees. To support this thesis, I will review the evolution of the television physician, placing him (and, only much later, her) within the broader context of the cultural paradigms that shaped the TV doctor.

This review will focus specifically on prime-time fictional dramas and comedies. Although the emerging genre of "reality television" includes medical shows that warrant mention, there has been little analysis of their effect on American culture. Also, physician characters and medical themes remain a staple of fictional daytime serials (soaps), and the influence of these shows merits consideration. Indeed, Gerbner et al. (1981) went so far as to say that "it may well be that daytime serials are the largest source of medical advice in the United States" (903). For the purpose of this review, however, I will limit my focus to evening programming.

The first TV doctor shows, *City Hospital* and *The Doctor*, aired in 1952 and had little impact overall. The initial generation of successful TV doctor shows began in 1954 with *Medic*, starring Richard Boone. During the opening credits, an offscreen narrator proclaimed the doctor as "guardian of birth, healer of the sick, and comforter of the aged." *Medic* aspired to stark realism. Before scripting the pilot episode, the show's creator spent more than two years shadowing doctors at Los Angeles County Hospital; the show was filmed at the hospital (which cost less than building sets); and each episode bore the imprimatur of the Los Angeles County Medical Association (Turow 1989, 32–38).

Medic's relationship with organized medicine may have been its most significant contribution to television medical dramas. At the time *Medic* aired, modern medicine was viewed by many as an almost mystical enterprise. "As writer Evelyn Barkins observed in 1952, 'Most patients are as completely under the supposedly scientific yoke of modern medicine as any primitive savage is under the superstitious serfdom of the tribal witch doctor'" (Burnham 1982, 1475). Medicine in the middle of the twentieth century enjoyed unprecedented prestige and public support. Earlier political and economic victories separated allopathic physicians from other healers, resulting in a near monopoly on mainstream U.S. health care. Scientific advances and the emergence of increasingly sophisticated technology made teaching hospitals centers of high-tech miracles. The new technologies "allowed [physicians] to explore the body with more certainty. . . . Just as significant, they encouraged the patients to feel that the physician had access to bodily changes that patients themselves could not detect. . . . Such capabilities did wonders to increase the legitimacy of 'regular medicine' in the eyes of the rest of society as well as to encourage people's dependence on physicians. . . . And medicine's potential for long-term cultural authority was boosted even further from another direction — by an increased ability to wield political power through the American Medical Association [AMA]" (Turow 1989, 5).

However, at the same time, medicine was facing a wave of external criticism. The dividends of technological medicine came at the expense of the traditional patient-doctor relationship. As health care became increasingly dominated by technical/surgical interventions, empathetic relationships with patients were subordinated to a more efficient, but frequently impersonal, model of technical competence. The scientific model relies on objectivity and reproducible data. Scientific methodology can more readily standardize the human body, in both normal and pathologically disordered states, than the vagaries of individual persons in their full biopsychosocial complexity. Treating diseases supplanted caring for ill patients. As the science of medicine progressed, the art of medicine seemed less essential — even anachronistic. Furthermore, as physicians' incomes rapidly increased, and the profession fought to preserve traditional fee-for-service medicine, many viewed the profession as avaricious and uninterested in public health.

In some circles, however, criticisms of contemporary medicine only reinforced medicine's sanctified social status. Dorothy Thompson observed in 1959, "In a rather profound sense the current attacks on the medical profession compliment it. People, it seems, *expect* more of physicians than they do of any other professional men with the possible exception of the clergy. The medical profession has invited that expectation, and . . . with exceptions that only prove the rule, has deserved it" (Burnham 1982, 1476). Behind the support of such staunch defenders, the medical profession weathered this first wave of criticism without undergoing significant change. That very lack of change would later prove to be a driving force in the incipient bioethics movement.

Not surprisingly, organized medicine was eager to protect and promote its image in the popular media. *Medic*'s relationship with the Los Angeles County Medical Association established a precedent that would repeat itself in later shows: AMA advisers offered an official endorsement of the program in exchange for script approval. This arrangement ostensibly ensured technical accuracy, although the shows already paid independent medical advisers, and the AMA's endorsement enhanced the show's credibility. However, it also allowed those with the greatest stake in projecting a specific, potentially self-serving, image of the profession to exert substantial influence over how television portrayed physicians.

In the mind of the AMA, the viewing public wanted their doctors to be highly dedicated professionals, committed above all to serving patients. That desire was met in the extremely popular shows *Dr. Kildare* and *Ben Casey*, both of which ran from 1961 to 1966. *Dr. Kildare* was a familiar name — the characters were continuations of the extremely popular film series from the 1930s, which was reincarnated as a radio serial in the 1950s. The Kildare films established numerous motifs that shaped how the television series portrayed physicians decades later. Dr. Kildare envisioned medicine as a *calling*, not merely a profession. Kildare's noblesse oblige became a hallmark of early portrayals of physicians — a doctor's personal concerns mattered little compared to the needs of his patients and professional obligations. Indeed, Dr. Kildare sacrificed income and marriage out of a highly idealized conception of professional duty. In practical terms, this meant that little of Kildare's background or personal life emerged on the show. Instead, the cast and their medical home, Blair Hospital, provided consistent characters and

1. Young Dr. Kildare (Richard Chamberlain) gets an earful from an older colleague on the series *Dr. Kildare* (1961–1966).

setting for the enactment of a series of human interest stories in the form of patients and their problems.

The *Dr. Kildare* films also introduced a common motif seen throughout TV doctor shows: the brilliant young protégé and the wiser, older father figure (figure 1). The TV show not only retained the character of Kildare's mentor, Dr. Gillespie, but also cast the Gillespie role before the Kildare role. Casey's Dr. Zorba, Marcus Welby and his young protégé, Stephen Kiley, and Dr. Westphall and Dr. Auschlander, the beneficent attending physicians in charge of the residents of St. Elsewhere, perpetuated this theme.

At the same time that Dr. Kildare was pursuing medical sainthood, *Ben Casey*'s eponymous neurosurgeon was draining a seemingly endless series of subdural hematomas. The two doctors shared high ideals, but their contrasting personalities provided a sort of yin and yang of physician archetypes. Kildare's idealism prompted an insatiable need to please Dr. Gillespie, and his comforting bedside manner put patients at ease. Casey, on the other hand, was gruff and downright disdainful of anyone who stood between him and his unwavering vision of what was right for his patients.

Both series followed the dramatic/heroic format of the first generation of TV doctor shows, which was another legacy from the Kildare film series. The doctors relished being on the edge of life and death. Cures usually required some form of experimental therapy, which could be accomplished only by a breach of protocol by the starring physician — usually in direct defiance of hospital administrators. In one survey of early medical programs, 40 percent of the cases of medical treatment involved situations where "a doctor either (a) performed a treatment that was not normally performed due to its high risk, (b) attempted an experimental treatment that was not yet proven fully reliable, or (c) having alternatives to treatment — one a sure, safe thing and the other risky but, if successful, a complete cure — chose the latter" (McLaughlin 1975, 183–84).

For their part, television physicians relished their role as arbiters of life-and-death decisions and bristled at limitations imposed by anyone outside their hallowed fraternity. Dr. Gillespie proclaimed, "We doctors live with death hovering over our shoulder. . . . There are always risks, unforeseeable risks, but risks that must be taken. Medicine isn't worth practicing if I have to stop myself because of legal risks. Until I am free to proceed on the basis of my knowledge and skill, I am not a doctor. I am a slave to outmoded laws" (*Dr. Kildare*, 1963).

Despite the first generation of TV doctors' heroism, they did periodically lose their patients. This changed in the second generation of medical shows. *Medical Center*'s Joe Gannon and *Emergency*'s paramedics and doctors had astounding success rates — in one survey, 87 percent of the treatments by TV doctors accomplished their goals (Lichter, Lichter, and Rothman 1991, 158). This positivistic approach reflected the optimism of the Kennedy and early Johnson years, when the prevalent belief was that our established institutions were engines of social good and, given proper license and resources, would solve most societal problems through ingenuity and technological process. One journalist noted in 1954 that in this vision of medicine's unlimited potential, doctors should be, "on the one hand, a group of dedicated and white-coated scientists, bending over test tubes and producing marvelous cures for various ailments, and, on the other, equally dedicated practitioners of medicine and surgery, devoting themselves to easing pain and prolonging human life, without thought of personal gain and at considerable self-sacrifice" (quoted in Burnham 1982, 1476).

Joe Gannon also had one foot planted firmly in another tradition of the second generation of TV doctor shows: the inability to recognize traditional boundaries between his patients' personal lives and his professional responsibilities. McLaughlin (1975) noted, "The TV doctor has the power to control the emotions and personalities, as well as the

2. Dr. Welby (Robert Young) and Dr. Kiley (James Brolin) take a break in their busy schedule on the series *Marcus Welby, M.D.* (1969–1976).

health, life and death of the people with whom he deals." In 95 percent of the televised doctor-patient relationships McLaughlin studied, people either were brought closer to one another, worked out a conflict created by the medical treatment, or accepted forces that they realized they could not control. The doctor acted as the "necessary outsider— one who can deal objectively with the facts at hand, interpret and shuffle them, and solve all kinds of problems" (184). McLaughlin concludes, "Television's doctors may not cure their patients, but they can always solve their personal problems" (182).

Certainly no show embodied the necessary outsider better than *Marcus Welby, M.D.* This show ran from 1969 to 1976, much of that time at number one in the ratings (figure 2). By the time Dr. Welby set up practice, the AMA no longer endorsed television shows. Conservative members of the organization were concerned that programs did not *always* project a positive image of the profession and feared the implications of negative portrayals of doctors receiving the AMA seal of approval. They need not have worried: "Television's producers had no intention of creating programs that attacked the legitimacy of the nation's health care professions. Doctors, especially, were the central heroes of TV medicine's struggle against death, and it would be dramatically self-defeating to make them fundamentally unsympathetic" (Turow 1989, 106).

Welby's producers were, however, able to secure the endorsement of the fledgling American Academy of Family Physicians (AAFP). The AAFP was pleased to find one of their own featured as a lead in a medical drama — but even the most optimistic could hardly have predicted Welby's phenomenal ratings success. Just as the AMA had done with *Dr. Kildare* and *Ben Casey*, the AAFP reviewed Welby's scripts to ensure they were medically accurate and portrayed family physicians realistically. Unlike the earlier series, however, the AAFP rarely modified Welby's scripts and seldom intervened in the interest of advancing a broader social agenda. One AAFP reviewer remarked, "The interesting thing to me was how well the writers did. . . . Here I was, a man who'd been a family physician for many years in a small town and taught medicine in the university, and I was impressed with how close the writers got to the spirit of what it meant to do what I do" (Turow 1989, 118).

However, physicians lamented the expectations created by Welby, who, they wryly observed, only took care of one patient per week. Many were concerned that Welby's nearly obsessive attention to individual patients belied the reality of balancing the demands of medical practice. Moreover, they realized that they could not possibly meet Welby's standards. "The upshot, they complained, was that millions of Americans were becoming resentful of their physicians for not living up to the image of the wise and caring physician" (Turow 1989, 129).

TV doctors to this point can be best summarized by the following characterization:

What sorts of norms about medicine are disseminated by these television physicians and their patients? No one has studied the question too rigorously, but the following list probably isn't too far off.

— Doctors are and should be heroic, glamorous figures who regularly — indeed constantly — sacrifice their personal lives and personal relationships for the welfare of their patients.

— The best way — the only conclusive way — to deal with most serious illnesses is surgery.

— Doctors treat one patient at a time. They have the time, the inclination, and the right to become intimately involved in each patient's private life and to mastermind every conceivable aspect of each patient's medical problem.

— Doctors never argue with their patients or among each other about money; they don't especially care if they get paid or not.

—Hospitals are places of high drama and constant personal interaction. Patients are not bored or fed unappetizing food; doctors and nurses are not harried, overworked, exhausted, or abrupt.

—Diagnosis is usually easy; treatment is usually experimental.

—Patients typically hide critical information from their doctors, revealing the key facts only after a highly emotional confrontation with the doctor, which immediately makes them feel better.

—Seriously ill people usually look and behave just like healthy people, except occasionally when they gasp, keel over, and need immediate emergency treatment.

—Apart from high-risk (often experimental) surgery, the key to most medical treatment is sudden insight into one's neurotic relation with one's family and other intimates.

—Most medical decisions are fast, correct, and heroic; a few medical decisions are fast, incorrect, and virtually criminal; no medical decisions are slow, uncertain, or tentative. (Sandman 1976, 381)

At this point, one might expect that progress in the civil rights and feminist movements might have prompted television portrayals that reflected increasing diversity within medicine. Some efforts were made in this direction. In 1979, *The Lazarus Syndrome* was developed from physician Michael Halberstam's book of the same name. The decision to cast Lou Gossett in the lead was not so much a decision to have a medical program with an African American star as "a simple case of creative casting." Gossett, an actor whose work in the miniseries *Roots* favorably impressed the show's creators, seemed well suited to portray the lead character despite, rather than because of, his minority status. To better appeal to mainstream audiences, they "decided that Gossett would play a physician who just happened to be black, and not a slum-bred black, at that" (Turow 1989, 191–92). The show failed. Although opinions varied as to why, given the herd mentality of network programmers, the show's failure inevitably resulted in reluctance to take the risk on a program with a lead character who was not a white male.

For the time, TV and the dominant culture would continue to see doctors who were heroic, young, male, and white (J. MacDonald 1985, 151–52; Turow 1989, 174–82). Minority and woman actors were relegated to nonphysician or background characters, such as Welby's office nurse, Consuela. Women, in particular, were additionally constrained by classic stereotypes. The dramatic tension most commonly confronted by women physicians centered on how to balance a romantic life with the demands of the profession. Men, these characterizations implied, were better equipped to ignore their personal needs in order to honor their professional commitments.

The post-1960s, post-Watergate milieu brought an escalating level of cynicism toward all forms of the Establishment, including medicine and science in general. So it would seem that the next generation of TV doctor shows would demand a less forgiving realism. However, programmers felt that viewers were not really ready for a truly unsettling portrayal of medicine's shortcomings. At least, that was the conclusion following the failure of *Medical Story*, a short-lived series in the late 1970s that intentionally showed the uglier side of medical bureaucracy. Although the format worked for police dramas, such as *Police Story* (which *Medical Story* sought to emulate), "illness hits too close to home to allow viewers to identify with beleaguered physicians fighting the system. . . . They didn't like to think of themselves as pawns in struggles within the medical bureaucracy and between doctors and lawyers" (Turow 1989, 189). Even in an era in which major institutions and traditional authority figures were routinely questioned, the viewing public was not ready for such a harsh exposé of medical culture. Like the old adage about law and sausage, potential patients apparently preferred that the unappealing machinery of medical bureaucracy remain out of sight — and presumably out of mind. Deconstruction of the heroic physician character would need to evolve along a different path.

Into this environment came the surgeons of the 4077th Mobile Army Surgical Hospital (MASH). *M*A*S*H*, which premiered in 1972, was a spin-off of Robert Altman's highly acclaimed 1970 film by the same name — a pitch-black comedy set in the Korean War that simultaneously satirized the military, religion, and medicine. Released at the height of the Vietnam War, the film was a trenchant commentary on what many perceived to be U.S. neocolonialism. The show required that the material be substantially cleaned up and sweetened to accommodate television's standards and viewers' tastes. Altman felt that the show not only eschewed the film's bleaker sensibility but in doing so betrayed the film's spirit. "The series was done for commerce, not art. . . . Having an Asian war in the living rooms for more than a decade is an insidious kind of propaganda filled with easy liberal statements" (Turow 1989, 212).

Unlike preceding medical shows, *M*A*S*H* made the doctors the dramatic centerpiece of each show (figure 3). The setting limited dramatic opportunities for patients, who were nearly all wounded soldiers undergoing surgery. When patients' issues were addressed, they were

3. Tense moments for members (David Ogden Stiers, Loretta Swit, Mike Farrell, and Alan Alda) of the 4077th on the series *M*A*S*H* (1972–1983).

generally a dramatic catalyst for doctor-centered plot developments. The show's star character, Hawkeye Pierce, represented a new image for TV doctors — an iconoclast who drank heavily, womanized, and lacked the typical accoutrements of professional demeanor. Frank Burns represented a subtler milestone for TV physicians: here was the first regularly recurring physician character who was incompetent, arrogant, greedy, and uncaring toward his patients. Previously, quacks had been granted no more than a one-shot guest appearance, often for the express purpose of buttressing the moral message of that particular episode. Yet despite all their flaws, Hawkeye, Trapper, B. J., and the other "good guys" of *M*A*S*H* were still fantastic surgeons whose dedication to their patients, including enemy wounded, was unlimited. Beneath Hawkeye's frat house personality lay a physician whose fundamental professional ideals differed little from those of Kildare or Casey.

In 1982, the premiere of *St. Elsewhere* finally ushered in the next stage of the TV physician's evolution. Because programmers are driven by ratings success, the notion that imitation is the sincerest form of flattery is simple pragmatism when developing new shows. *M*A*S*H*'s unique formula seemed almost inimitable; however, the program's comedy and irreverence certainly seemed replicable and could possibly be integrated within a dramatic series. In the early and mid-1980s, *Hill Street Blues* was a causing a stir. The show portrayed police work with a gritty realism, including filming with handheld cameras, and integrated a mordant sense of humor within its generally serious subject matter. Rather than a central character, *Hill Street* used a large ensemble cast.

St. Elsewhere was intimately linked to *Hill Street Blues* (Thompson 1996, 75–80). Both shows emerged from the same production company, and many of the same creative personnel contributed to both shows. Although *St. Elsewhere* was widely perceived as "*Hill Street Blues* in a hospital," the show's origins were actually in an earlier medical drama, *Operating Room*, whose similarly themed pilot predated *Hill Street Blues*. Programmers still did not trust that audiences would accept an unflattering portrayal of medicine, so *Operating Room* was never picked up. NBC executive Fred Silverman decided to first introduce the format in the more reliable police drama. "Let's try it as a cop show first . . . and if it works we'll try it with doctors" (76). The idea that culminated in *St. Elsewhere* was, in effect, instrumental in the development of *Hill Street Blues*, rather than derivative. "At some basic level, then, *St. Elsewhere* wasn't so much '*Hill Street Blues* in a hospital' as *Hill Street* was '*Operating Room* in a police station' " (76).

Both shows targeted a sophisticated audience, relying on inside references and sly humor that rewarded viewers who possessed an awareness of popular culture identified as "teleliteracy" (86). *St. Elsewhere*'s use of intertextuality (82–83) and complicated narrative structure — both within individual episodes and over the course of the program's run — also gave television credibility as a legitimate artistic medium (89–92). Despite its consistently mediocre ratings, *St. Elsewhere* received numerous awards and was widely regarded as introducing a more intelligent type of television programming. NBC went so far as to place a two-page ad for the show's finale in *TV Guide* that boasted, "*St. Elsewhere*: Where TV Went to Get Better" (93; see figure 4).

A key factor that made *St. Elsewhere* different was its lack of miracles. The doctors were good, but patients still died, sometimes as the result of physician errors. Also, the show was set in a seedy inner-city hospital rather than in a state-of-the-art facility. Some situations and characters were bizarre. Victor Ehrlich, a barely adequate surgical resident, was crude, narcissistic, and misogynistic. His conversations fre-

4. The multiethnic, multigenerational male and female
cast of *St. Elsewhere* (1982–1988).

quently concluded with the other party using the recurring tag line
"Ehrlich, you're a pig." Wayne Fiscus had an affair with a pathologist
who insisted on making love on a slab in the morgue among sheet-
draped cadavers. Peter White was a rapist and a drug addict, but still
an adequate doctor. He met his demise when a staff nurse, realizing he
was the hospital rapist, meted out some vigilante justice by shooting
him in the testicles with a .357 revolver before administering the coup
de grâce with a bullet to a more lethal, though less unsavory, portion of
his anatomy. Elliot Axelrod was obese and bumbling. Wendy Arm-
strong was a bulimic who committed suicide. Bobby Caldwell was a
promiscuous plastic surgeon who contracted AIDS in a heterosexual
liaison at a time when medical researchers were still debating whether
female-to-male transmission of HIV even occurred. And poor Jack
Morris. His wife slipped in the shower and died from the head trauma,
but her heart was transplanted into one of Jack's patients. Her death

From *City Hospital* to *ER*   227

left him alone to raise their son. After he survived nearly being expelled from the residency for incomplete disclosure of poor grades from his offshore medical school, his moonlighting job at a prison clinic went bad when he was taken hostage during an inmate uprising and repeatedly raped by a convict Jack had previously angered. The final episode concluded with a vintage postmodern twist: the closing scene revealed that the entire series was, in fact, merely the imaginings of an autistic child.

Routinely adopting such soap operatic story lines, *St. Elsewhere* was the first generally successful medical series to depict the paradoxically lurid yet realistic goings-on within the hospital, albeit often in a highly sensationalized manner. This warts-and-all depiction, combined with the emphasis on the deviant and idiosyncratic, provided a more cynical and less squeamish generation of TV viewers a voyeuristic "insider's view" into a dysfunctional medical culture. A hallmark of the show was its popularity with medical personnel, who found its candor and willingness to look behind the curtain to be a refreshing departure from the whitewashed images of previous TV doctor shows.

However, this frankness was not universally popular; in addition to the traditional barrier (i.e., laypeople preferred not to know that their physicians might actually have feet of clay), the program's subversive willingness to kill off both patients *and* their doctors and nurses unsettled many viewers. Television critic Jeff Borden commented, "My parents finally gave up watching *St. Elsewhere*. . . . They would follow the story line for weeks and really get involved with the characters only to watch them die. They told me they were tired of going to bed depressed" (K. Edwards 1984, 782).

In the decade following *St. Elsewhere*, new TV doctor shows came and went, but none were different enough to constitute a fourth generation of the television physician. The shows of that era remained within the thematic framework of the earlier models, mostly using the medical context merely as a plot contrivance for a standard situation comedy or drama rather than as a central element of its dramatic focus. *Northern Exposure*'s Joel Fleischman, boy wonder *Doogie Howser*, and *The Cosby Show*'s Clifford Huxtable were all characters in prototypical sitcoms; their identity as a physician was of peripheral importance. J. Fred MacDonald (1985) observed that Cosby's Dr. Huxtable "has become the most successful black physician in the history of television. Yet he seldom is seen at the hospital, and rarely seems to practice medicine. Like a black Ozzie Nelson, Dr. Huxtable really has no job except to be the father of a comedic family" (151).

For that matter, even the more relevant shows — by the admission of the producers of *St. Elsewhere* and *ER* — placed medical realism secondary to the dramatic or entertainment needs of the show (Okie 1986, 15, 17–18). Technical advisers from the time of *Medic* struggled to reconcile medical realism with dramatic license. Most advisers were sympathetic to programmers' needs. Pediatrician Phyllis Wright commented, "I now know that the most difficult chore for my TV employers is to get good scripts. . . . There are still times when I complain that a particular script is just too far out medically, only to be gently reminded by the producers that we are 'not making a documentary film'" (Turow 1989, 65).

However, doctors seemed unable to view even the most insipid of these shows as innocuous. In the late 1980s, *Doctor, Doctor*, a puerile sitcom, lampooned medicine in the manner that the films *Airplane* and *Animal House* spoofed commercial air travel and college fraternity houses. The editor of *Post-graduate Medicine* found this portrayal to be an egregious offense to the profession and wrote a scathing editorial elucidating his outrage. Although most letters in response to his editorial endorsed his position, at least one reader was unimpressed: "*Doctor, Doctor* will do no more harm to the practice of medicine. If anything, *Marcus Welby, MD* has done more harm . . . because it has led the public to believe that doctors can do anything for anyone at any time of the day or night. . . . A lot of the public's dissatisfaction with medicine is caused by the fact that they expect Marcus Welby but instead they get the situation spoofed on *Doctor, Doctor*" (Messmer 1991, 36, 39).

The argument that doctors do more harm by criticizing the surface context of the genre, while missing the deeper social implications of how television's underlying assumptions reflect public perceptions and expectations of the medical profession, warranted a much more robust discussion than ensued. TV critic Jeff Borden summarized, "Television has been very kind to physicians. . . . In fact, the biggest problem the real-life physician may have with his larger-than-life television image . . . is trying to live up to it" (K. Edwards 1984, 783).

Most recently, physicians find themselves living up to the doctors of *ER* (figure 5). Most physicians would not find living up to the personae of *ER*'s physicians as daunting as trying to keep up with their frenetic pace. *ER*, which premiered in 1994, does not represent a fourth generation of TV doctor show as much as a phenomenally popular hybrid of the second and third generations. Its story line is character driven, but the characters driving its narrative continue to be the doctors, not the patients. Like *St. Elsewhere*, *ER* and its less popular rival *Chicago Hope* use an ensemble cast. Although the doctors follow the heroic archetype to a limited extent—more so on *Chicago Hope* than on *ER*—the doctors are still given to human shortcomings. Without the constraints placed on earlier programs by organized medicine's review panels, and in the aftermath of *M*A*S*H*'s and *St. Elsewhere*'s deconstruction of the medical establishment, both shows fearlessly take on the most controversial topics of the day—often matching plotlines to recent headlines. Less noticed, but perhaps more significant, *ER* has unselfconsciously scripted key characters who are minorities, women, and gay—and not limited them to historical two-dimensional stereotypes. *ER*, unlike *Chicago Hope*, has been phenomenally popular with medical students, as well as practicing physicians and medical educators (Durso 1995, 19–22).

The success of *ER* and *Chicago Hope* gave even those who traditionally disdain television reason for pause. George Annas (1995) lamented, "Yes, God help us, the contemporary bioethicist must watch TV to understand how Americans see bioethics issues and how they might usefully be explored in public forums" (40). Annas ascribed *ER*'s success to its "fast-paced, MTV-formatted . . . [amalgam of] three of America's four favorite subjects: sex, violence, and youth."

However, "The real star of this show is the fourth American standby, money; and it is money's remarkable absence that makes it the star" (40). This criticism could aptly be applied to medical shows from *Medic* onward. Although TV doctors occasionally grappled with the issue of social justice, the theme was never sustained and rarely given extensive or thoughtful consideration. Throughout the history of medical shows, patient care was typically delivered as if resources were unlimited, and when the issue was raised, the message most typically conveyed seemed to be that only money-grubbing hospital administrators (the fallback "black hat" characters in medical dramas) believed in fiscal restraint.

The absence of economic factors in television medical dramas was not purely by accident. In the early days, when AMA advisers still reviewed scripts, any plots that seemed sympathetic toward socialized health care (which, to the AMA, included Medicare) were greeted with greater hostility than scripts with technical inaccuracies. The medical establishment was deeply invested in preserving the traditional fee-for-service model of health care reimbursement and went to great lengths to impede televised scenarios that might sway public sympathies otherwise. Despite technology's depersonalizing influence on the patient-

5. The original cast of *ER* (1994–present), the most popular prime-time show on American television.

physician relationship, where finances were concerned, it was implied that the only ethical approach to patient care was unconstrained advocacy for whatever an individual patient needed. TV physicians were allowed to have their cake and eat it too.

What will be the next stage in the evolution of medical programming? The recent trend toward "reality programs" offers one possible direction in which the TV physician might evolve. *Hopkins 24/7* was popular with medical students and certainly influenced expectations of their own training, but its broader impact on the public's perceptions of medicine remains less clear.

Newer shows such as the drama *City of Angels* and the comedy *Scrubs* seem to be a continuation of third-generation medical shows. *Scrubs* has a loyal following within the medical professions, who see their own training experiences reflected in the show. Like *M*A*S*H*, the show depicts a frequently unflattering view of medicine through the lens of comedy, which softens the critique. Many physicians find that they could not bear to see their own brutal training experiences depicted too literally, but a comedic portrayal makes *Scrubs* tolerable viewing (seemingly affirming the *Medical Story* producers' postmortem on why the public rejected an otherwise high quality program).

From *City Hospital* to *ER*   231

Some observers maintain hope that medical dramas might, in fact, serve as moral narratives. Candace Gauthier correlates the scenarios on *ER* and *Chicago Hope* to Martha Nussbaum's notion that literature enhances perception of moral particulars via aesthetic distance. "Medical drama provides an opportunity for the perception of particulars in terms of choices within the health care context and their consequences for oneself and others. This form of narrative engages the viewer emotionally as well as cognitively. It develops and exercises the moral imagination through identification with the characters portrayed, especially patients and their loved ones" (Gauthier 1999, 23).

Although traditional medical series may implicitly provide moral narratives, the demands of winning the weekly ratings wars will most likely limit conscious efforts in this direction. However, the recent HBO production of the award-winning play *Wit* successfully and self-consciously blended drama, entertainment, and moral dilemmas in one package. As a premium cable channel, HBO can — like independent filmmakers — produce such one-shot works on their artistic merit alone, satisfied that critical acclaim and the video rental market can confer success regardless of the ratings. However, feature films, even made-for-TV (or cable) movies, are distinctly different entities than a weekly TV program.

An additional asset of the medical drama is its ability to transcend place and time (Shale 1984, 776). Witness the success of *Dr. Quinn: Medicine Woman* (set in the Wild West) and the enduring popularity of *Star Trek*'s Dr. McCoy (who practiced aboard a spaceship). It is worth noting that each subsequent *Star Trek* series has included the ship's physician as a central character. *Star Trek: Voyager* might have depicted the ultimate evolutionary development for TV physicians. In lieu of an actual person, limited by human subjectivity and fallibility, *Voyager*'s Doc Zimmerman was a holographic image generated by a computer program that contained all medical knowledge ever compiled by the United Federation of Planets, up to the year 2371. Because of the limitations of available computer space, a simple personality protocol was created, leaving Doc Zimmerman with a brusque and humorless bedside manner. Yet as a highly sophisticated computational unit, his data analysis skills were impeccable.

It would be interesting to know how Kildare's and Casey's AMA reviewers would assess Doc Zimmerman. Although the AMA currently has little authority to shape medical programming, organized medicine remains a political force. Turow integrates organized medicine's social responsibility and television's capacity to shape social beliefs to suggest that medical leaders could use the medium (perhaps by cultivating medical dramas as moral narratives) to shape debate over the future of U.S. health care and promote more equitable access to health care (Turow 1996, 1240–1243).

Regardless of the next evolutionary step for the television physician, the American public apparently remains fascinated by the inherent drama in medicine, and television programmers will capitalize on that fascination as long as their efforts are rewarded with ratings success. Viewers will also develop perceptions and expectations for medicine shaped, at least in part, by television. As younger viewers age and make career choices, they may well enter medicine expecting to be initiated into the profession they saw portrayed on television. And as my medical students' conversation exemplifies, physicians in training will turn, at least in part, to fictional role models to help them mark out their own professional pathway. Given physicians' discomfiture with the expectations created by Marcus Welby some thirty years ago, perhaps a fitting coda is to reflect on the cyclical nature of television and culture. In 2001, the American Academy of Family Physicians considered a resolution proposing that the AAFP support the development of a new Welby-like television program to enhance the image of the family physician and to draw talented, idealistic young people into the profession. The goal, apparently, is to have art imitate life just enough that a future generation of physicians will be programmed to make their lives, and their profession, imitate art.

The Fat Detective

Obesity and Disability

SANDER L. GILMAN

The definition of a disability seems to be rather clear. The World Health Organization, in its 1980 *International Classification of Impairments, Disabilities, and Handicaps*, makes a seemingly clear distinction between impairment, disability, and handicap. Impairment is an abnormality of structure or function at the organ level, while disability is the functional consequence of such impairment. A handicap is the social consequences of an impairment and its resultant disability. Thus cognitive or hearing impairments may lead to communication problems, which in turn result in isolation or dependency. Such a functional approach (and this approach is echoed in American common and legal usage) seems to be beyond any ideological bias.

When, however, we substitute "obesity" for "cognitive impairment" there are suddenly an evident and real set of implied ethical questions in thinking about disability. What is obesity? While a set of contemporary medical definitions of obesity exist, it is also clear that the definition of those who are obese changes from culture to culture over time. Is obesity the end product of impairment, or is it impairment itself? If it must begin with an impairment, what "organ" is "impaired"? Is it the body itself? Is it the digestive system? Is it the circulatory system? Or is it that most stigmatizing of illnesses, mental illness? Is obesity the result of an addictive personality (where food is the addiction)? Is addiction a sign of the lack of will? Or is "addiction" a genetically preprogrammed "error" in the human body, which expresses itself in psychological desire for food or the mere inability not to know when one is no longer hungry? Is the impairment of obesity like lung cancer in that it is the result of the voluntary consumption of a dangerous substance? Or is food "addictive" like nicotine, or is it merely an interchangeable sign in society for those things we all desire but most of us can limit? Surely it is not possible to go without food as one could go without cigarettes. Is the obese person mentally or physically disabled? On the other hand, can you be obese and mentally stable? Is the social consequence of obesity isolation or a central place in the society? Are you in the end treated like a social pariah or Santa Claus?

The study of obesity in its cultural and social contexts provides a wide range of interlocking questions about the cultural construction of disability. The role that gender plays is one further variable in the study of the cultural representation of the obese body. Recently, Steven Shapin (1998) wrote a striking essay on the eating habits of skinny philosopher-scientists. His argument is that, at least in the West, there is a powerful myth about the need for such men to have a "lean and hungry look" (in spite of Caesar's and Shakespeare's distrust of such men). That all of Shapin's examples are men is not incidental. Our collective fantasy of the appropriate body of the male thinker stands at the center of Shapin's work. In this essay I want to ask a corollary question: what happens to the image of the "thinking male" when that male body is fat, even obese? Shapin's point, of course, is that Sir Isaac Newton, that proverbial thinker reputed to have forgotten whether he had eaten his chicken or not, actually died hugely bloated. There is a great disparity between the way we imagine that bodies should look and function and our mythmaking about them. In complicated ways, as Irving Kenneth Zola has indicated, detective fiction is a complex mirror of late-nineteenth- and early-twentieth-century popular culture (Zola 1983, 1987). And the fat detective is the antithesis of the lean philosopher.

The fat detective reflects in complex ways how general as well as medical culture shifted its image of the thinking body in the late nineteenth century and the early twentieth. What is there about the representation of a fat, thinking body that makes a fat detective a different category than a thin philosopher? This tale is rooted in a certain notion of the body and its relationship to thought. The image of the fat detective can be found well before the nineteenth century and continues, as many of us have seen, in the overweight title character in the recent BBC detective series *Cracker*, Dr. Eddie Fitzgerald (played by Robbie Coltrane) (figure 1). Dr. Eddie Fitzgerald, nicknamed Cracker, is an out-of-work forensic psychologist who occasionally helps the Manchester police "crack" hard-to-solve cases by interrogating or "cracking" suspects and witnesses. But the central quality of this character is his own nervousness, his own sense of himself as a misfit, his own marginal status as a professional. His oversize body seems symbol-

1. The oversize misfit. Dr. Eddie Fitzgerald (Robbie Coltrane) in the BBC series *Cracker*.

ically to represent this sense of emotional fragility. But it also evokes his mode of inquiry. His approach seems to be empathetic rather than analytic; he feels with and for the victims and even with the criminals, rather than being a "pure intellect" uncovering the criminal. One can note, however, that when ABC unsuccessfully remade *Cracker* for American television and moved its setting to diet-conscious Los Angeles, the svelte Robert Pastorelli was called in to play the protagonist, now called Gerry Fitzgerald. The character was the same; only the body was different. The viewers' response was equally different. Unlike the popular acclaim accorded to the British series, the "thinner" American version was simply not attractive to its intended audience.

The fat detective's body is a different sort of male body than that of the skinny philosopher. Huge, ungainly, sedentary, it houses the brain of a detective. But it is a different sort of detective than the strong, hard-boiled or the thin, ratiocinating one. It is a body out of all moderation. It is not a "modern" body, if by modern we imagine the body as trained, lithesome, strong, active, and thus supremely masculine. Such an obese body seems more feminine, but certainly not female; it is expressive of the nature of the way that the detective seems to "think." His thought processes strike us as intuitive and emotional rather than analytic and objective. In other words, the fat detective's body is feminine. The ratiocinating detective, such as Edgar Allan Poe's C. Auguste Dupin, thinks with his brain. The hard-boiled detective (such as those of Dashiell Hammett's Sam Spade, at least in Humphrey Bogart's rail-thin depiction) thinks with his fists. Our fat detective thinks with his gut, for it is the visible fat which marks his body. This is quite a different version of the ratiocinating detective such as Sherlock Holmes, whose "kingdom is his study and his weapons are intellectual — logic, memory, concentration. He traps criminals in the corridors of his own mind rather than in a back alley at midnight. He is a cultivated gentleman, whose recreation is the library" (Anderson 1984, 113). The fat detective is a countertype to this intellectual detective. He seems to think, but he is primarily intuitive and empathetic; he needs his fat as a shield from the world. His physical immoderation becomes a means of showing both his vulnerability and his strength. He is sedentary rather than active; his intellectual gifts feed his intuition.

As has been noted, of all the figures central in the shaping of our collective fantasy about what the detective's body looks like, the most important figure is Arthur Conan Doyle's Sherlock Holmes (Rauber 1972). Created in 1887, whip-thin, addicted to cocaine rather than food, always ready to head off on a chase at the drop of a clue, Holmes remains the exemplary rational detective (Smead 1991). His regular feats of observation stun his rather dull-witted companion Dr. John Watson, but all rely on the ability causally to link "facts" following the model of analytic thinking he learned in medical school from Dr. Joseph Bell (R. Thomas 1991). Again it is the scientist, but here the scientist as activist, who makes the perfect intellectual detective. He often sinks into a stupor, aided by his tobacco and cocaine. But this detective also goes out into the world gathering facts. Holmes roams the length of Europe — all the way to Tibet — for knowledge. His is the explorer's body, Sir Henry Morton Stanley's body, as well as that of the detective.

But there is another Holmes in these tales: Holmes's older and wiser brother Mycroft, who is introduced in 1892 in the *Strand Magazine*'s publication of "The Case of the Greek Interpreter" (Sobottke 1990; Pasley 1985; Beaman 1976; Propp 1978). Mycroft is huge and sedentary. "Mycroft Holmes was a much larger and stouter man than Sherlock. His body was absolutely corpulent, but his face, though massive, had preserved something of the sharpness of expression which was so remarkable in that of his brother" (Conan Doyle, n.d., 294). Mycroft's intelligence glimmering in his eyes (the mirrors of the soul) seems over-burdened by his primitive body. There is something quite archaic about

The Fat Detective 237

it; he has "a broad fat hand, like the flipper of a seal" (295). He is not quite a sloth, but close enough.

Mycroft is the better brother, as his younger sibling grudgingly admits. Holmes states that "he was my superior in observation and deduction. If the art of the detective began and ended in the reasoning from an arm-chair, my brother would be the greatest criminal agent that ever lived" (293). What makes Holmes the better is that he is willing to use his powers in the world. Mycroft in the end is merely an amateur sleuth, not really a consulting detective. And the amateur nature of his undertaking is seemingly tied to his lack of desire to pursue truth to its bitter ends: "What is to me a means of livelihood is to him the merest hobby of a dilettante" (294). Here the quality of the amateur is central. These are not the professional detectives whose world is the world of action, but the amateur whose interests include other models of the world besides that of rational detection. This is the model that eventually evolves into the string of fat detectives that culminate in *Cracker*. Such detectives of the 1890s and the turn of the century are imagined as thinking differently. They are related to the figures of Sherlock Holmes, but they do seem to think in a different manner. They appear to think through their bodies, but this is deceptive. Their bodies provide an image of obesity, which masks their sharp powers of observation and deduction.

The model of the primitive body that thinks, and thinks in an intuitive way, becomes one of the models for the detective in the course of the twentieth century. Other versions of the fat sleuth followed Conan Doyle. In 1911 G. K. Chesterton began the publication of his Father Brown tales (O. Edwards 1989; Raubicheck 1993). Here the question of belief and the body of the fat amateur detective are again linked. The priest's body is represented as chubby; his response to the murders he investigates is intuitive rather than rational. Indeed, Chesterton saw the Father Brown stories as a means of furthering his Anglo-Catholicism, seen in England, even after Cardinal Newman, as a form of the irrational. The squat body of Father Brown represents the innate seeking for truth beyond logic. He is the embodiment of the idea of thought and faith being aspects of one truth. It is a truth to be found by those who are able to see it, not necessarily by those ordained by the state to seek it.

By 1934 and the publication of Rex Stout's first Nero Wolfe mysteries, the tradition of the fat detective as a countertype had been well established (Isaac 1995; Gerhardt 1968). In 1929 there was Duddington Pell Chalmers, the obese detective hero of John T. McIntyre's *The*

Museum Murder, as well as Gerald Verner's Superintendent Budd, "the stout detective," "who is fat, lazy, graceful on his feet," "prone to shut his eyes while thinking," and "not susceptible to feminine beauty" (McAleer 1977, 552). Like Father Brown, celibate by definition, Nero Wolfe's body too is not a sexualized body — any more than is that of Mycroft Holmes. Yet this feminizing quality of the male body mask a life of passion. In the course of the Nero Wolfe mysteries, we learn of his earlier romantic attachments. All of these took place at a point before the present bulk both inhibited and freed the detective from the power of physical passion.

In Rex Stout's first novel, *Fer-de-Lance* (1934), the hard-boiled associate of Wolfe, Archie Goodwin, notes the almost archaic form of the shape of Wolfe's body like the early-twentieth-century fantasies of Neolithic man: "Wolfe lifted his head. I mention that, because his head was so big that lifting it struck you as being quite a job. It was probably really bigger than it looked, for the rest of him was so huge that any head on top of it but his own would have escaped your notice entirely" (Stout [1934] 1984, 2). Wolfe's body is not only fat; it is huge and archaic in its form.

Wolfe's fat is the fat that protects: "I said to him something I had said before more than once, that beer slowed up a man's head and with him running like a brook, six quarts a day, I never would understand how he could make his brain work so fast and deep that no other men in the country could touch him. He replied, also as he had before, that it wasn't his brain that worked, it was his lower nerve centers" (2). Wolfe, unlike Archie, thinks with his guts: "I am too sensitive to strangers, that is why I keep these layers over my nerves" (164). In *Over My Dead Body*, Wolfe claims that his fat isolates his nerves: "I carry this fat to insulate my feelings. They got too strong for me once or twice and I had that idea. If I had stayed lean and kept moving around I would have been dead long ago" (Stout [1939] 1994, 119). One of the best commentators on the Wolfe novels observed: "Upholders of order are our romantic heroes, and Wolfe qualifies under that category. His daily schedule is as much an insistence on order as a tribute to it: similarly, Wolfe's fat, his gruffness, and his seclusion betray his struggle to insulate himself from emotions, to harness them, to grant them a place, but a smaller one than they claim. Reason then is a goal; it is also a process, a struggle. The Wolfe novels value it as both" (Anderson 1984, 23). The archaic body struggles with its basic emotional nature. And fat is the weapon that enables Wolfe to succeed as a detective.

But one must note that the very act of thinking for Wolfe is a thinking with his body: "Wolfe looked up again, and his big thick lips pushed out a little, tight together, just a small movement, and back again, and then out and back again. How I loved to watch him doing that! That was about the only time I ever got excited, when Wolfe's lips were moving like that. . . . I knew what was going on, something was happening so fast inside of him and so much ground was being covered" (Stout [1934] 1984, 4–5). The pursed lips are the organ of eating but also the organ of thought. Here the parallel to the rest of the lineage of fat detectives is clear. The body has its own life and its own rules. It complements or contradicts the rational mind and provides the means by which fat detectives set themselves off from all other scientific observers.

The popularity of Nero Wolfe began a rather long series of spin-offs of fat detectives in the mass media beginning with Dashiell Hammett's Brad Runyon from 1946 to 1950 on ABC radio. The announcer opened the show with the following observation: "He's walking into that drugstore . . . he's stepping onto the scales . . . (snick! click!) Weight: 237 pounds . . . Fortune: Danger! Whoooo is it? The . . . Fat Man!" The oversize actor J. Scott Smart, who actually outweighed his character by more than thirty pounds, played him on radio. World-weary, Runyon was a cross between Wolfe and Sam Spade. The first episode, written by Hammett, was *The Black Angel*, which was broadcast on 26 November 1946. The body of the fat detective on the radio could only be evoked by the image in the listener's mind. As such, his bulk became part of the fantasy of the obese body as heard rather than seen. Rex Stout's Nero Wolfe himself became part of the invisible world of the fat detective on the radio. In 1982, the Canadian Broadcasting Corporation tried its hand at bringing back old-time radio with thirteen one-hour episodes of Nero Wolfe, all based on novellas or short stories written by Stout. The svelte Mavor Moore played the bulky Nero Wolfe, but all the listener heard was the voice of the fat detective.

A more visible world of the fat detective played itself out on television. In 1981, NBC had a TV series based on novellas and short stories by Rex Stout, which starred William Conrad as Nero Wolfe (figure 2). Conrad, whose voice was well known from his role as the lanky sheriff on radio's version of *Gunsmoke*, went on to play Frank Cannon, a tough, expensive, overweight private detective (Gunning 1995). Directed by George McCowan, *Cannon* began a highly successful run in 1971, which concluded only in 1976. According to the plot, the key to Cannon's character lies in the fact that his wife and infant son died in an automobile accident, after which Cannon placed all his energy and considerable weight into his new profession of private detective. In 1987 Conrad continued a version of the Nero Wolfe character in *Jake and the Fatman*, produced by Ron Satlof and Fred McKnight, in which his role as J. L. "Fatman" McCabe was much more sedentary. He was transformed into a slovenly former Hawaiian cop turned Honolulu district attorney. From the Fatman to Cracker, the space of the fat detective comes again to be one filled with the emotional, elemental, intuitive, and empathetic.

Certainly the key figure in the contemporary representation of the fat detective is to be found on ABC's *NYPD Blue*. He is Detective Andy Sipowicz, played by Dennis Franz (figure 3). Since premiering in 1993, the show has centered itself on this character. Cocreators Steven Bochco and David Milch, along with executive producers Mark Tinker and Michael Robin, continued Franz's character from one who had appeared in Bochco and Milch's earlier success, *Hill Street Blues*. Franz had played Lt. Norman Buntz from 1985 to 1987. But Buntz was merely a "tough cop." In Sipowicz the darkness and complexity of the figure were clearly related to his sense of self as a detective. Sipowicz was portrayed as a recovering alcoholic, the father of a son he had neglected (and who is killed in the course of the show), a man of open emotions and clear prejudices. He is a muscular man gone to fat. It is because of, rather than in spite of, these flaws that he is able to be empathetic with his colleagues and generally to have insight into his own character. The flaws in his character, represented by his overweight body, make him into a better detective. Franz had played in two short-lived detective series (*Beverly Hills Buntz* [1987] and *NYPD Mounted* [1991]) in which the complexity of the fat character was lacking. It was in *NYPD Blue* that he was able to develop his role as a detective, self-consciously using his fat body as an image for his flawed character. Bocho and Milch used this quite self-consciously in the series. The body size of the character was literally exposed in a nude scene, one of the first on commercial television, in which Franz was photographed from the rear. Dennis Franz's body became the key for the figure of the fat detective. His mode of approach is that of the hard-boiled detective, the muscular detective gone to seed, but his fat body is also seen as an external sign of his empathetic nature. (During the 1999 season, the character loses his second wife to a shooting and begins to lose weight as he needs to see himself as both a single father and a part of a new social scene.)

The image of the giant, hulking, primitive body, which responds seemingly intuitively in a stimulus more basic than rational thought, remains a powerful cultural commonplace. It is only the appearance of

2. Actor William Conrad played three different overweight detectives on the following television series: *Nero Wolfe, Cannon,* and *Jake and the Fatman.*

(below) 3. The muscular man gone fat. Detective Andy Sipowicz (Dennis Franz) in *NYPD Blue.*

the fat detective that leads us to assume his "primitive" state. In a cartoon drawn by Scott Adams, the creator of *Dilbert*, a baby dinosaur comments to Dogbert: "My dad says that good is what you know in your heart. He says evil is a bad gut feeling." Dogbert replies, "Well, of course, your dad's brain is so tiny that his other organs have to pitch in like that." The baby dinosaurs replies, "Maybe I shouldn't learn about life from a guy who counts with his toes." And Dogbert concludes, "And thinks with his guts" (S. Adams 1995, 82). This is the way that fat detectives seem to think — but, of course, we know better.

Michel Foucault, in *The Use of Pleasure*, wrote that there has always been a contrast between pleasure and the rational in the West: "The relationship of the logos to the practice of pleasures was described by Greek philosophy of the fourth century. . . . Moderation implied that the logos be placed in a position of supremacy in the human being and that it be able to subdue the desires and regulate behavior. Whereas in the immoderate individual, the force that desires usurps the highest place and rules tyrannically, in the individual who is *sophron*, it is reason that commands and prescribes" (Foucault 1990, 86–87). What happens when desire becomes a means of thinking, an alternative mode of intelligence? The immoderate, according to the Greeks, could never rationally think. Our fat detectives seem to do well in this department, for their job, always well done, is to solve the case. And that they do with elegance and grace — not in spite of, but because of, their bulk. Their bodies, however, also represent their mental status. Their masculinity seems both compromised and expanded by the bulk of their bodies. Are they the ultimate "new man" in their sensitivity and their seemingly intuitive intelligence? For the fat detective, the question is not whether he is physically or emotionally impaired, or whether he has a social handicap because of this impairment. What is clear is that the functional consequence of his impairment, his obesity, is not a *disability* but an *advantage*. It is what frames his ability to function as a "thinking machine." Such texts provide complexities for any study of disability and its social reading in modern culture.

[This essay is dedicated to my friend and colleague Laura Otis.]

Dissecting the Doctor Shows

A Content Analysis of *ER* and *Chicago Hope*

GREGORY MAKOUL AND LIMOR PEER

In the midst of continuing debates about health insurance, a patients' bill of rights, the Human Genome Project, and stem cell research, people are flocking to their television sets to watch medical dramas unfold. *ER*, NBC's hour-long weekly drama series set in a Chicago hospital, has been a top-rated dramatic series since its inception in 1994. It has also won several Emmy and Screen Actors Guild Awards, the People's Choice Award as favorite television dramatic series, and a George Foster Peabody Award. What do people see on shows like *ER* (NBC), often called doctor shows, when they tune in? What messages are conveyed to them about doctors, patients, and the American health care system? How important are these entertainment-oriented depictions in shaping people's understanding of the medical arena? This essay is designed to address these broad questions in the context of two popular doctor shows: *ER* and *Chicago Hope* (figures 1 and 2).

Previous studies document that the doctor in dramatic television programs has most often been portrayed as "a powerful, almost omnipotent, healer who performs his duties above and beyond normally expected capacities" (McLaughlin 1975, 184). Joseph Turow (1989) discerned a slow shift from that model, which was predominant throughout the 1970s, to one that puts more emphasis on doctors' personal problems. Still, the doctor shows tend to glorify physicians and their healing power, portraying them as unrelenting advocates for their patients. Doctors often take risks and break the rules — defying authority is a recurrent theme — if they believe it is for the good of their patients.

Television's glamorization of doctors and health care has led to claims that doctor shows provide an inaccurate picture of medicine. For instance, a study about the portrayal of cardiopulmonary re-

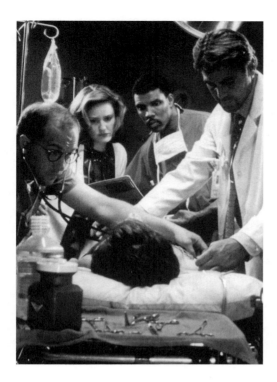

1. Television shows such as *ER* portray medicine as drama and doctors as human.

2. Medical programs such as *Chicago Hope* often focus on issues of professionalism.

suscitation (CPR) on *ER*, *Chicago Hope*, and *Rescue 911* found that survival of an acute trauma is much more likely on television than in actuality (Diem, Lantos, and Tulsky 1995). A physician complained in *Time* magazine that *ER* presents an outdated picture of emergency medical care, with "untrained medical students doing procedures they would never be allowed to perform in a real emergency room" (Zoglin 1994, 76). A book entitled *The Medicine of "ER"* (Ross and Gibbs 1996) is entirely devoted to deconstructing this television series by laboriously explaining not only the jargon of *ER* but also the real-life chances and costs of events that take place in the show. In his seminal analysis of doctor shows, Turow (1989) found discussion of economic and health policy issues limited and inadequate. Despite attention to such issues on the more recent crop of doctor shows, Rapping (1995) argued that "the real issues of health care are strangely missing or invisible" (37). It is time to take a close look at how doctors, patients, and health care issues are portrayed on these programs.

Much of the research on doctor shows warns that a misleading picture of the health care system is detrimental because it leads to unrealistic expectations. Taking his cue from cultivation analysis, Turow (1996) explained that "the patterned nature of TV's images, often viewed over the course of people's lives, leads many people to develop expectations of those institutions that are similar to TV's portrayals" (1241). "What viewers come away with," he added, "may lead them toward false expectations, and they may increasingly blame doctors for decisions that others make and enforce" (1240). The authors of the CPR study cautioned that misrepresentation on doctor shows "undermines trust in data and fosters trust in miracles" (Diem, Lantos, and Tulsky 1995, 1581). However, a survey conducted in the United Kingdom about the effects of television drama on the public's impressions of psychiatrists found no evidence to "support the idea that watching the drama resulted in misconceptions about the real world of psychiatric medicine" (Sancho-Aldridge and Gunter 1994).

This interest in the conceptions and expectations that may be generated by doctor shows is not limited to an academic audience. Indeed, Neal Baer (1998), a writer and producer for *ER*, stated that "*ER* has an obligation to depict medicine accurately. Many of our viewers watch the show for the medical stories, and according to a Kaiser Family Foundation Survey, around 12% seek medical advice based on something they've seen on the show" (855). Since many people are forming, and acting on, impressions of doctors, patients, and health care issues they see on the screen, it is important to monitor the type and tenor of health-related entertainment television content (Sharf and Freimuth 1993).

Theoretical Background and Research Questions

This study fits within the framing paradigm, an area of inquiry concerned with the presentation and interpretation of information. A concept borrowed from social psychology, frames are knowledge structures that define features and relevant attributes of some stimulus domain (Croker, Fiske, and Taylor 1984). These preexisting categories determine how we remember old information and how we process new information. We naturally activate frames to help us simplify, organize, and process the world "without confronting each situation anew" (Jamieson 1992, 166). Framing is the process of selection and emphasis that we use to understand an event or a problem, which then invokes a particular set of responses to that event or problem (see also Entman 1992).

While framing analysis has traditionally been applied to news content (e.g., Gitlin 1980; Herman and Chomsky 1988; Jamieson 1992; Patterson 1994), we think it can and should be applied to entertainment content for three reasons. First, the distinction between news and entertainment content is increasingly problematic. The blurring of the lines between these genres is most apparent in news programs about entertainment (e.g., *Entertainment Tonight* and *A Current Affair*), but it also exists in traditional news shows that are now run by entertainment departments *(e.g., Good Morning America)*. In addition, there has been a steady rise in the number of reality-based shows, from *Cops* to *48 Hours* and, more recently, from *Survivor* to *Fear Factor*. When television presents entertainment content as news, the public has little reason to perceive it as distinct.

Second, entertainment content should be considered for framing analysis because it works in conjunction with news content to form our understanding of reality (Shoemaker and Reese 1996). Entertainment content often provides relevant information that is not present in the news. The doctor shows, for example, provide a behind-the-scenes look at what doctors do. The news, in contrast, may tell us about developments in the areas of policy decisions, structural improvements, labor relations, or budgetary problems, but it is incapable of presenting in detail "what it's really like." Thus entertainment content often complements and reinforces news content. News programs draw on entertainment shows as well, sometimes offering a glimpse of how the shows are made, presenting the "real" story behind an entertainment story line or making purposeful attempts to enhance public health.

Third, there is good evidence that entertainment content is as influential as news content in shaping our perception of reality, suggesting the value of exploring entertainment content in terms of the frames it employs. Studies on how we experience television in everyday life (e.g., Kubey and Csikszentmihalyi 1990; Myerowitz 1985) point to its ability to mold our understanding of our culture as well as ourselves. In the context of the medical world, Turow (1996) argues that "highly viewed [dramatic] TV presentations of medicine hold political significance that should be assessed alongside news. . . . Every week they act out ideas about the medical system's authority to define, prevent, and treat illness" (1240).

In sum, extending framing analysis to the entertainment arena focuses attention on both producers and audience members by raising questions about the nature of decisions that enter into the production of particular content (see Gitlin 1985), as well as the interpretation of that content. Thus the framing paradigm provides an opportunity to bridge a long-standing gap: as Shoemaker and Reese (1996) have argued, too much mass media research focuses either on content or on effects, and not enough on the "process through which the mass media shape social reality" (258). In this essay, we analyze the content of two television drama series, *Chicago Hope* and *ER*, using framing analysis as a foundation for explicating how doctor shows are likely to influence perceptions of doctors, patients, and health care issues. Two research questions drive this investigation:

1. How are health care issues, doctors, and patients portrayed on *ER* and *Chicago Hope*?
2. What are the primary frames highlighted by *ER* and *Chicago Hope* regarding medicine, doctors, and patients?

Methods

Data collected for this study involved all episodes of the 1996–1997 season of both *ER* (twenty-two episodes) and *Chicago Hope* (twenty-four episodes). Sixteen students from Northwestern University coded the videotaped episodes after an introduction to mass communication in the context of health and medicine, as well as intensive training in content analysis. Training consisted of introducing the students to the coding categories and rules, going through a process of clarification and standardization, having everyone code and discuss sample episodes, and creating a system for cross-checking and quality control.

The students were divided into two teams, one working on portrayals of physicians and patients (Physician-Patient Team) and the other focusing on medical and health care issues (Issues Team). Within each team, students worked in pairs, which allowed immediate cross-checking and maintained reliable application of the rules regarding both unitizing and coding. Inter-rater reliability was uniformly high (Kn .90). Two pairs of coders watched each episode, one pair focusing on issues, the other on physicians and patients. Questions and insights were discussed at weekly team meetings.

Units of Analysis

Scenes were the units of analysis. A scene was defined as an action or interaction focusing on one topic or situation. Scenes usually ended with a cut to another physical setting. In some cases, a change in action or interaction, but not necessarily location, marked a transition to a different scene. All videotapes were time coded, which allowed the running time to be viewed on-screen. Each scene was numbered chronologically, and coders recorded the exact time the scene began (inpoint), the time it ended (outpoint), and the general nature of the scene (e.g., woman in labor rushed into trauma room). The Physician-Patient Team and Issues Team coding sheets for all episodes were double-checked to ensure consistency of scene numbers and synchronization of inpoints and outpoints. The following is a detailed description of the data collection process for each team, as it reflects the research questions outlined in the previous section.

Collection of Issues Data

Coders on the Issues Team collected data on up to two medical and health care issues found in each scene, the themes relating to these issues (i.e., how were the issues discussed), and whether any characters gave a long and opinionated speech about an issue. Issues were defined as topics that transcend the characters in the scene and have either policy, social, political, or economic implications. Further, issues were coded only if they were explicitly discussed (i.e., more than just mentioned in passing). There was no preset list of issues. Rather, the list evolved as new issues appeared in the show, and by the completion of the study, there were ninety-nine issues in all. To facilitate interpretation and presentation of data, the issues were grouped into thirteen broader categories: business/administration; controversial procedures; education/training; equality; ethics; HIV/AIDS; patients' issues; personal health/medical problems; personal life of physicians; professionalism; public health/drugs and alcohol; public health/social problems; public health/violence (see appendix).

Every effort was made to standardize the list so that recurrent issues could be coded consistently. For example, a scene on *ER* in which nurses discuss the difficulty in treating patients due to lack of space would be coded as "operating constraints" — an issue already identified when, in a previous episode, there was a scene in which doctors lament about shortage of supplies. Such standardization was achieved through weekly meetings in which coders discussed issues that arose in the episodes they viewed and coded. To enhance accuracy of the standardization and coding processes, coders provided scene-specific detail and context for each issue by noting themes. For instance, the issue of "insurance" includes "treating a patient regardless of insurance status" and "HMO not paying for a costly procedure" as themes; the issue of "HIV-infected staff" encompasses the themes of "possibility of infecting patients" or the "reaction of coworkers." Attention to themes also provided the level of detail needed to group issues into the thirteen broad categories mentioned here and listed in the appendix.

After viewing and coding an episode, members of the Issues Team completed episode summary sheets in which they recorded all the issues that appeared in the episode, as well as the themes that animated these issues, and whether or not there were any speeches. Coders also used this summary sheet to describe the main story lines in the episode and note any comments about the episode.

Collection of Physician and Patient Data

For each scene in which at least one physician appeared, coders on the Physician-Patient Team recorded *physician mode* by choosing from six possibilities: *caring* (primarily concerned for the patient's feelings, comfort, and family), *curing* (focused on the patient's physical condition and treatment), *administrative* (chief role was as a manager of resources, including other health care workers), *business* (focused on budget concerns, insurance problems, or other monetary issues), *education* (primarily involved in role as a teacher or learner), and *personal* (dealt with issues in personal life apart from role as a caregiver). If there were multiple modes in a scene, the predominant one was selected.

To measure the extent to which the physician was involved with patient care, four items were coded for each scene: (1) whether any tests, treatments, or procedures were mentioned; (2) whether any tests, treatments, or procedures were shown or displayed in any manner; (3) whether the physician was dealing with a patient in any way, such as treatment, counseling, or observing; (4) whether there was any dialogue at all between the physician and the patient. For patients who were conscious but unable to talk (e.g., infants), discussion with family members were counted as physician-patient dialogue. If a physician was dealing with the patient in any way, then one of three models was selected for the physician-patient relationship (after Szasz and Hollander 1956): *active-passive* if the physician decided or did everything in the encounter because there was no opportunity or no possibility for discussion (e.g., the patient was unconscious or suffered major trauma and the physician had to act swiftly and independently to remedy the situation); *guidance-cooperation* if the physician gave orders that the patient was expected to follow (i.e., there may have been discussion, but not the kind that involved the patient in decision making); *mutual participation* if the physician and patient both contributed to a decision about tests, treatments, or procedures.

After viewing and coding an episode, the coder pairs completed episode summary sheets in which they used one to three adjectives to record their impressions of each physician and patient who appeared on the show. These adjectives were collated at the end of the study, and redundant descriptors (e.g., "smart" and "intelligent") were combined to facilitate interpretation of data.

Results: Portrayals

Portrayal of Health Care Issues

There were 1,102 scenes in the 22 episodes of *ER*, an average of 50 per episode (SD = 9.72), and 958 scenes in the 24 episodes of *Chicago Hope*, an average of 40 per episode (SD = 6.67). The mean running time for episodes of both shows was approximately 43 minutes. To avoid cluttering the text, we make statistical comparisons only where relevant.

Issues were illustrated in fewer than one-third of the scenes on either show: 24.5 percent on *ER* and 32.3 percent on *Chicago Hope*. As

Table 1. Health Care Issues in *ER* and *Chicago Hope*[a]

Issue	*ER* ($n = 270$)	*Chicago Hope* ($n = 309$)
Professionalism	30.4%	35.0%
Business/administration	24.1%	27.5%
Ethics	21.9%	25.9%
HIV/AIDS	13.3%	0.0%
Violence[b]	6.3%	3.6%
Controversial Procedures	3.3%	11.3%

[a]Scenes are the unit of analysis (total number of scenes: *ER* = 1,102; *Chicago Hope* = 958). This table includes only scenes in which at least one issue was observed, and only issues observed in at least 5 percent of the scenes from either show.
[b]While violence often brought people to the hospital, it was only coded as an issue if discussed as such in the scene. For instance, "22 year old, GSW [gunshot wound] to the chest" would not be coded as an issue, but a discussion of drive-by shootings would.

shown in table 1, the two shows are parallel in terms of the three most frequently presented issues: professionalism (e.g., personal life affecting the job), business/administration (e.g., operating constraints), and ethics (e.g., end-of-life decisions). Note that HIV/AIDS was an issue that appeared on *ER* that season—primarily in the story line about Jeanie Boulet, an HIV-infected health care worker—but not on *Chicago Hope*.

Portrayal of Physicians

Table 2 presents a summary of the images associated with the nine physician characters who regularly appeared on *ER* and the nine who regularly appeared on *Chicago Hope*. At least one physician appeared in 86.6 percent of the scenes on *ER* and in 97.5 percent of those on *Chicago Hope*. Rather than focus on the qualities associated with individual characters, this table offers a broader perspective, indicating the range of qualities evident in the physician portrayals. Again, there is a rough parallel between the two shows in terms of the most frequent images: sensitive/ethical, vulnerable/struggling, insensitive/indifferent, and competent/expert. The characterizations are by no means one-dimensional: Some physicians (e.g., Benton on *ER* and McNeill on

Table 2. Doctor Images on *ER* and *Chicago Hope*[a]

Image	*ER* $(n = 209)$[b]	*Chicago Hope* $(n = 188)$[b]
Sensitive/ethical	22.5%	19.7%
Vulnerable/struggling	15.6%	18.1%
Insensitive/indifferent	8.6%	7.4%
Competent/expert	8.1%	9.6%
Stern/stubborn	8.1%	2.1%
Happy/positive	5.3%	2.1%
Arrogant/selfish	5.3%	5.9%
Levelheaded/calm	3.8%	5.9%
Angry/frustrated	2.9%	5.9%

[a]Coders recorded their impressions of the nine physicians who regularly appeared on either show in the 1996–1997 season. In *ER,* the characters were Donald Ansbaugh, Peter Benton, John Carter, Maggie Doyle, Dennis Gant, Mark Greene, Abby Keaton, Doug Ross, and Kerry Weaver. In *Chicago Hope,* the characters were Kate Austin, Diane Grad, Dennis Hancock, Billy Kronk, Jack McNeill, Daniel Nyland, Aaron Shutt, Phillip Watters, and Keith Wilkes. Images are included in this table only if they comprised at least 5 percent of the doctor descriptions from either show.
[b]The *n* for each group is the total number of adjectives across all episodes (total number of episodes: *ER* = 22; *Chicago Hope* = 24).

Chicago Hope) were associated with all four of these qualities. As illustrated in table 3, physicians on both shows were most often either dealing with their own personal issues and problems or functioning in a curing, problem-solving mode. The curing mode often involved mention or explicit display of tests, treatments, or procedures (table 4).

Portrayal of Patients

In contrast to the high frequency of scenes in which a physician appeared, table 4 indicates that patients were seen relatively rarely and talked with even less. On both *Chicago Hope* and *ER,* the coders recorded instances of physician-patient dialogue during approximately 16 percent of the scenes in which a physician appeared. As shown in table 5, when patients did appear in a scene, *ER* most often portrayed

Table 3. Doctor Modes on *ER* and *Chicago Hope*[a]

Primary Mode	*ER* (*n* = 954)	*Chicago Hope* (*n* = 934)
Personal	30.2%	37.6%
Curing	29.9%	25.4%
Business/administration[b]	19.0%	17.6%
Caring	14.2%	17.7%
Education	6.7%	1.8%

[a]Scenes are the unit of analysis (total number of scenes: *ER* = 1,102; *Chicago Hope* = 958). This table includes only scenes in which a physician appeared.
[b]The categories of Business and Administration were combined.

Table 4. Tests, Treatments, Procedures, and Doctor-Patient Interaction on *ER* and *Chicago Hope*[a]

Tests, Treatments, Procedures	*ER* (*n* = 954)	*Chicago Hope* (*n* = 934)
Mentioned in the scene	43.4%	32.8%
Shown in the scene	28.7%	16.9%
Doctor-Patient Relationship	(*n* = 954)	(*n* = 934)
Doctor is dealing with a patient	36.0%	29.0%
Doctor is talking with a patient	16.1%	16.6%

[a]Scenes are the unit of analysis (total number of scenes: *ER* = 1,102; *Chicago Hope* = 958). This table includes only scenes in which a physician appeared.

them as crazy/irrational (13.3 percent), anxious/afraid (10.8 percent), demanding/annoying (10.1 percent), or unconscious/dead (10.1 percent). While *Chicago Hope* did not have as many patients that seemed crazy/irrational (3.1 percent), the show had more demanding/annoying patients (17.7 percent). Table 6 summarizes the data on models of the physician-patient relationship, the most frequently seen of which was active-passive. *Chicago Hope* had nearly twice the proportion of examples of mutual participation (i.e., shared decision making), reflecting a greater opportunity for such interaction outside of the emergency room.

Table 5. Patient Images on *ER* and *Chicago Hope*[a]

Image	*ER* (*n* = 158)[b]	*Chicago Hope* (*n* = 96)[b]
Crazy/irrational	13.3%	3.1%
Anxious/afraid	10.8%	10.4%
Demanding/annoying	10.1%	17.7%
Unconscious/dead	10.1%	9.4%
Sweet/naive	5.1%	7.3%
Naive/confused	5.1%	3.1%
Angry/violent	5.1%	2.1%
Content/cooperative	1.9%	7.3%
Strong/determined	1.9%	5.2%
Abused/neglected	0.0%	5.2%

[a]Coders recorded their impressions of the patients who appeared on either show in the 1996–1997 season. There was a total of 99 patients on *ER* and 58 on *Chicago Hope*. Images are included in this table only if they comprised at least 5 percent of the patient descriptions from either show.
[b]The *n* for each group is the total number of adjectives across all episodes (total number of episodes: *ER* = 22; *Chicago Hope* = 24).

Table 6. Models of the Physician-Patient Relationship on *ER* and *Chicago Hope*[a]

Model	*ER* (*n* = 343)	*Chicago Hope* (*n* = 271)
Active-passive	56.3%	44.3%
Guidance-cooperation	20.1%	15.1%
Mutual participation	18.1%	33.9%
Cannot judge from scene[b]	5.5%	6.6%

[a]Scenes are the unit of analysis (total number of scenes: *ER* = 1,102; *Chicago Hope* = 958). This table includes only those scenes in which a physician was dealing with a patient.
[b]The model could not be judged unless decisions about tests, treatments, or procedures were made.

Our goal was to conduct a systematic and unbiased examination of how health care issues, doctors, and patients were depicted on two health-related entertainment television programs, *ER* and *Chicago Hope*, during the 1996–1997 season. Rather than limiting our view to portrayals of specific groups, illnesses, or procedures, we sought concrete data on a broad range of topics so that we could use framing analysis as a tool for seeing the "big picture." This approach allows us to address some important questions regarding the process of constructing reality via television: What do these shows tell us about health care issues, doctors, and patients? What choices do these shows make with regard to these topics? What do they emphasize?

Medicine as Drama

With regard to health care issues, *ER* and *Chicago Hope* frame medicine as drama. That is, providing medical care — and living the life of a medical care provider — is presented as interesting and exciting, intense and emotional. Consequently, the mundane and routine aspects of medicine are largely de-emphasized. In a recent interview, *ER* coproducer Neal Baer (1998) explained that he and other writers for the show create episodes by identifying "beats" (i.e., core story lines), which are typically emotional (for instance, Carter [an intern] clashes with Benton [a surgeon] over their differing views of surgery), and only then "discuss possible medical stories that will illustrate the emotional beats" (855).

That drama is the primary frame may hardly be a surprise, since both programs are in the business of entertaining people, and producers and network executives will naturally invite us to perceive medicine in ways that serve their interests. Thus while the people behind the shows are aware of other frames, the medicine-as-drama frame tends to supersede them. Consider the tension between entertainment and education, again, candidly expressed by Neal Baer: "We debate amongst ourselves whether the show's thrust is entertainment or education. I like to think of it as good storytelling. By telling compelling stories the audience will learn new things about medicine and disease and they will be entertained too" (855).

What is interesting about the medicine-as-drama frame is the impact it has on the choice of issues and how they are portrayed. In both *ER* and *Chicago Hope*, professionalism was the most frequently presented issue. This broad category of issues refers to doctors' and other medical staff members' conduct on the job, in terms of their integrity, competence, and ability to care for their patients, as well as in terms of how they relate to each other in their roles as professionals. This issue fits neatly within the medicine-as-drama frame — not only does it provide story lines rich with conflict, but it also focuses attention on the individual doctors, thus personalizing medicine. In Baer's words, "We attempt to show the doctors' and nurses' personalities through their interactions with each other and with patients. How they make decisions and deal with conflict illustrate who they are as characters" (855).

Business and administration (a category including issues related to the business aspect of medicine, administration and management, as well as insurance coverage) and ethics (a category including ethical dilemmas relating to patients' autonomy, confidentiality, and consent, but also to "right action" by doctors and medical staff) were the second and third most frequent issue raised in *ER* and *Chicago Hope*, respectively. Clearly, these categories also provide ample opportunity for conflict and drama, especially in today's climate of a changing health care system. As James Hart, supervising producer of *Chicago Hope*, reveals, "we try to explore issues of ethics and morality every week" (letter to G. Makoul, 22 April 1997). In sum, the medicine-as-drama frame dictates that certain issues will come up primarily as triggers for drama and conflict, while others will be less likely to emerge. This point was reinforced by Annas (1995): "organ transplant stories will always be more compelling than stories about preventing automobile accidents" (43).

Doctors as Human

With respect to physicians, the frame used by *ER* and *Chicago Hope* is that physicians are human. As the data show, the most frequent doctor mode is personal; the personal life of the doctor (i.e., the person) is paramount. The data also show that doctors are presented as multifaceted, vulnerable, and fallible. Our evidence supports Turow's 1989 observation that doctors are no longer portrayed as omnipotent healers. And so, during the 1996–1997 season, we see *ER* intern John Carter struggle with feelings of inadequacy, though he is highly skilled at connecting with patients on an emotional level. We see *ER*'s Dr. Peter Benton transform from a hard-nosed surgeon to a softer person with emotions and feelings. Given the public's growing sophistication, the doctor shows need to offer both a compelling picture of medicine and a textured sense of character if they are to sustain audience interest. This presentation of doctors as human is entirely consistent with the overarching frame of medicine as drama, given the potential it holds for exploring internal conflicts.

Patients as Trouble or Troubled

If drama in general, and human drama in particular, is driving these shows, our data on patient images make it clear that this drama revolves mostly around doctors. As mentioned earlier, not only are patients seen infrequently on the shows, but when they do appear, they are often portrayed as crazy, irrational, anxious, demanding, annoying, unconscious, or dead. This may be partly due to the context of these shows, as much of the action involves trauma care and surgery. Still, the frame used by *ER* and *Chicago Hope* is that patients are trouble or troubled. Moreover, when dealing with patients, physicians are more likely to be portrayed in a curing mode (i.e., focused on the patient's physical condition and treatment) than in a caring mode (i.e., concerned for the patient's feelings, comfort, and family).

Doctors most often assume an interpersonally powerful role, as evidenced by the predominance of the active-passive model in our data, while patients are in a passive position. This, again, emanates from the medicine-as-drama frame but stresses the fact that the drama occurs within, and in relation to, doctors. Some have argued that the focus on doctors — their sorrow, their guilt, their relief, and their joy — rather than on patients is grossly misplaced (see Rapping 1995). While this particular portrayal of patients may serve the demand for drama in the shows or provide suitable background for the unfolding stories about doctors, it also raises questions about the messages these shows sent during the 1996–1997 season, particularly about patients.

Conclusion

The frames operating on both *ER* and *Chicago Hope* are that medicine is drama, doctors are human, and patients are trouble or troubled. The parallel observations regarding portrayals of issues, physicians, and patients in *ER* and *Chicago Hope* suggest that these frames are robust. The doctor shows are powerful tools of socialization in terms of both medical and moral issues, a point also argued by Gauthier (1999). For one audience in particular—medical students—these shows may even be seen as an informal curriculum (Baer 1998; O'Connor 1998; Ostbye and Keller 1997; Stern 1998). In a related study, we found that the frames resonate with medical students and affect the way they think about the medical world (Makoul et al. 1998). The combination of framing analysis and content analysis offers insight into the content, context, and possible effects of these doctor shows. With more doctor shows in the future, it will be both interesting and important to determine the extent to which these same frames are prescribed. In any case, it is likely that the doctors will occupy center stage, with issues revolving around them, patients playing supporting roles, and viewers tuning in to watch and, for better or worse, learn.

Appendix: Issues in *ER* and *Chicago Hope*

Business/Administration
Closing of hospitals/mergers
Cost of procedures/supplies
Cutbacks in staff
HMOS
Hospital policy and administration
Hospital safety
Insurance
Malpractice/lawsuits
Managed care
Management issues
Terms of employment
Operating constraints
Profitability
Waiting time in ER

Education/Training
Choosing residency/specialty
Resident/career training
Stress as a resident

Ethics
Autonomy
Assisted suicide
Confidentiality
Consent
DNRs/advance directives

End-of-life decisions
Ethics
Futile treatment
Limits of medicine
Organ transplant priorities
Patient confidentiality
Patient dumping
Protecting doctors
Quality of life
Right to know
Refusal of treatment
Right to terminate care
Truth telling

Patients' Issues
Care of family/relatives
Demanding patients
Doctors as patients
Grief and death
Vulnerability

HIV/AIDS
HIV/AIDS
HIV-infected staff
Needle stick

Controversial Procedures
Cryogenics
Experimental
Intubation
Marijuana for medical treatment
Research
TPA
Triage
Transplant

Personal Health/Medical Problems
Blood-borne pathogens
Serious long-term illness
Fractures
Mental disability
Neonatal/risky pregnancy

Public Health/Social Problems
Child custody
Foster care and adoption
Homelessness
Incest
Poverty
Teen pregnancy
Sexually active teens
Single mothers
Working parents

Public Health/Drugs and Alcohol
Alcoholism/alcohol/DUI
Drugs
Drug overdose

Public Health/Violence
Abuse
Battery

Child abuse
Crime
Domestic abuse
Gunshot wound
Rape
Violence

Equality
Gay issues
Gender issues
Geriatric care
Nursing homes
Prejudice
Race issues

Professionalism
Access to drugs
Attachment/detachment
Coworker romance
Competition/advancement
Competence/excellence
Criminal wrongdoing
Equal treatment for patients
Honesty/lying/forgery
Impairment (drugs, etc.)
Interprofessional relations
Perceptions of doctors
Personal life affects the job
Physician/staff error/negligence
Political correctness
Service to patients

Personal Life of Physicians
Physician personal issues

[We thank Dr. Neal Baer, coproducer of ER, James Hart, supervising producer of Chicago Hope, and Mary Jane Twohy, director of broadcast relations at Northwestern University, for their help and encouragement during the early stages of this project. We are also grateful for the diligent coding and insightful comments of students on both Northwestern campuses, as well as the data entry and management efforts of the staff at Northwestern University Medical School's Program in Communication and Medicine.]

5 Documentaries

Reproductive Freedom,

Revisionist History, Restricted Cinema

The Strange Case of Margaret Sanger and *Birth Control*

MARTIN F. NORDEN

The years immediately before World War I witnessed a dramatic surge of interest in reproductive health topics that had been veiled in secrecy and misunderstanding during the Victorian era. Despite opposition from the Catholic Church and other guardians of public morality, a growing number of people now spoke and wrote openly about issues such as venereal disease, contraception, and abortion, and no one better epitomized the new spirit of the times than the American birth control advocate Margaret Sanger.

Seeking to undo what she described in *Woman and the New Race* (1920) as "the enslavement of women through unwilling motherhood" (72), Sanger pursued many strategies for disseminating contraceptive information to disadvantaged women. One of her lesser-known projects was a 1917 feature-length film with the simple but at the time controversial title *Birth Control*. This film, which Sanger cowrote with Frederick Blossom and John Lopez and in which she played herself, was a dramatized reenactment of her struggles as a nurse turned birth control activist. This early docudrama was censored immediately on its release and is presumed lost,[1] a situation that has forced scholars to discuss the film solely on the basis of extratextual materials such as eyewitness accounts and judicial opinions (Brownlow 1990, 47–50; de Grazia and Newman 1982, 15–17, 186–88; Goldstein 1988; D. Kennedy 1970, 88; Schaefer 1999, 172–73; Shull 2000, 213; Sloan 1988, 86–90). This study goes beyond these earlier efforts by integrating contemporaneous journalistic and legal materials with a key document discovered at Smith College's Sophia Smith Archive: a heavily detailed scene-by-scene scenario of *Birth Control* that had been entered into the legal record as part of a deposition. Although obviously not an ideal substitute for the film itself, the scenario does yield considerable insight into *Birth Control*'s form, content, and structure. For example, it includes all of the film's title cards (those devices commonly inserted into silent-era films to relay dialogue and narration), as well as descriptions of its settings, characters, and actions. In addition, the scenario occasionally suggests the shot selections employed in the film. Importantly, this item is *not* a screenplay (which may be likened to a proposal for a film) but a descriptive document based on the film itself. It was treated as a surrogate for the film in the various *Birth Control* court cases, and significantly, no one involved in these cases ever claimed that it misrepresented the film. Although Sanger would lament in *My Fight for Birth Control* (1931) that her "simple story of birth control was silenced and destroyed forever" through censorship (198), I hope to revive it, in a sense, by reconstructing its key moments. These moments, as I shall argue, reflected Sanger's desire to redefine herself and her work to American mainstream society. I also hope to provide a framework of understanding for *Birth Control* by tracing Sanger's experiences as they informed the film's content and structure, her efforts to bring it to the screen, and the litigious turmoil that ensued.

Early Influences and Career

Born Margaret Louisa Higgins on 14 September 1879 in Corning, New York, Sanger grew up under impoverished circumstances that later framed her activist agenda. The sixth of eleven children, young Margaret often spent time observing the Corning families that lived along the Chemung River and the socioeconomic gulf that divided them. As she remembered it, she soon began associating family size with quality-of-life concerns:

> Corning was not on the whole a pleasant town. Along the river flats lived the factory workers, chiefly Irish; on the heights above the rolling clouds of smoke that belched from the chimneys lived the owners and executives. The tiny yards of the former were a-sprawl with children; in the gardens on the hills only two or three played. This contrast made a track in my mind. Large families were associated with poverty, toil, unemployment,

drunkenness, cruelty, fighting, jails; the small ones with cleanliness, leisure, freedom, light, space, sunshine. (Sanger 1938, 28)

Sanger's parents exerted an exceptionally strong influence on her during those early years, if in highly divergent ways. Her father, Michael Higgins, an Irish immigrant and stonemason, was a labor organizer who greatly admired the Socialist leader Eugene V. Debs. Although Higgins was not particularly effective as a political activist (Sanger remembered him more as a talker than a doer), he instilled in her a sense of independence and outspokenness that eventually became her defining quality. "It was from him I learned the value of freedom of speech and personal liberty," she would write many years later (Sanger 1931, 6). Higgins, who frequently clashed with Catholics on issues such as obedience to Rome and the use of reason, often admonished his daughter to "do your own thinking" when it came to religious matters (9). His advice collided with the example set by Sanger's mother; Ruth Purcell Higgins, a staunch Catholic, stoically abided her multiple pregnancies despite a case of chronic tuberculosis that left her weaker with each passing year. Sanger watched helplessly as her mother withered from the combined effects of consumption and frequent pregnancies. Shortly after her mother's death in 1899 at age fifty, Sanger enrolled in a nursing school and eventually specialized in obstetrics.

Sanger completed her degree in 1902 and later that year married the architect and political dilettante William Sanger. She commenced a nursing career and, mindful of her father's opinion that Socialism was, in her words, "Christian philosophy put into practice" (Sanger 1918, 23), also began exploring leftist politics with her husband while living in Yonkers, New York, and later New York City.

Sanger joined the New York City branch of the Socialist Party around 1910 and focused much of her activism on the demystification of reproductive health issues. Sanger gave sex education lectures to Socialist Party women in 1910 and 1911, and her talks proved so popular that the editors of the daily Socialist newspaper *The Call* invited her to write a series of weekly essays. Titled "What Every Girl Should Know," Sanger's column dealt with abortion, venereal disease, masturbation, and other sexual topics in language unusually explicit for the time.

When it came to one-on-one nursing care for women in need of birth control advice, however, Sanger often felt compelled to bite her tongue; under New York state law, only physicians could dispense such information, and then only to men and only for preventing the spread of venereal disease. During her many speaking engagements throughout her career, Sanger often expressed regret at remaining silent on the subject during that time and frequently cited the following story, which represented a turning point in her life. In the summer of 1912, she was called on to assist a male doctor ministering to Sadie Sachs, a twenty-eight-year-old European Jewish immigrant who lived with her husband Jake and their ever-expanding family in a lower Manhattan tenement. Sachs, like Sanger's mother, had grown weaker with each pregnancy, and she had reached the point where another birth might prove fatal. She begged the physician for birth control advice, but he refused and instead gave her this nugget of wisdom as a send-off: "Tell Jake to sleep on the roof!" (Sanger 1931, 53). Sachs turned to Sanger after the doctor's departure and pleaded with her for the information, but Sanger felt obliged to follow the law and reluctantly refused to help. Sachs died about three months later from a septicemic infection that set in after an abortion, and for Sanger, the woman's death was an epiphany. "It was the dawn of a new day in my life," she wrote. "I was resolved to seek out the root of evil, to do something to change the destiny of mothers whose miseries were as vast as the sky" (Sanger 1918, 92).[2]

Sanger, newly invigorated, developed strategies on a number of fronts. She toured the country, giving lectures about birth control, raising funds for her educational cause, and helping set up local birth control organizations. In March 1914, she founded *The Woman Rebel*, a radical periodical that bore the slogan "No gods, no masters" and that argued for the autonomy of women, by force if necessary (Sanger 1920, 214). She began making plans for *The Birth Control Review*, a monthly magazine that she eventually launched in early 1917 with the assistance of Frederick Blossom, a young Socialist from Cleveland. Perhaps most significantly, Sanger opened a birth control clinic, the first in America, on 6 October 1916 in the Brownsville section of Brooklyn, New York. Established specifically for indigent women (women of means were pointedly turned away), the storefront clinic attracted as many as five hundred clients before police arrested Sanger and shut down the facility ten days later. Released on bail, she reopened the clinic on 14 November and was promptly rearrested on charges of dispensing contraceptive devices and information in violation of Section 1142 of the New York State Penal Code and of "maintaining a public nuisance" in the form of her clinic. Out on bail once again, Sanger could not help but think about the publicity value of her arrests and the shape that publicity might take.

Sanger's trial did not begin until 29 January 1917, and during the interim, she explored the possibility of creating a film based on her travails as a birth control activist. Sanger had loved playacting as a girl — "I rather fancied myself as an actress," she wrote of her childhood (Sanger 1938, 13) — and the idea of playing herself in a movie appealed strongly to her. As she recalled the situation about twenty years later, she believed that such a film would help promote her clinic and other aspects of her work:

> One of the early essays of education was a moving picture dramatizing the grim and woeful world of the East Side. Both Blossom and I believed it would have value, and I continue to be of the same mind. He had not approved of the clinic and had declined to have anything to do with it, but was eager to join me in capitalizing on the ensuing publicity. Together we wrote a scenario of sorts, concluding with the trial. Although I had long since lost faith in my abilities as an actress, I played the part of the nurse, and an associate of Blossom's financed its production. (251–52)

With additional support from the National Birth Control League (Chesler 1992, 164), Sanger and Blossom wrote and filmed much of their movie, which they tentatively titled *The Woman Rebel*, from November 1916 through January 1917. They then screened a rough cut of *The Woman Rebel* for independent film producer B. S. Moss in the hope that his company would distribute and promote the film throughout the United States. Recognizing the film's potential and, in particular, the built-in publicity provided by the internationally famous Sanger, Moss authorized his corporate attorney to begin negotiating with Sanger to organize a cross-country tour of the film with Sanger as featured speaker. As a part of the deal, Moss would establish a subsidiary called the Message Photo-Play Corp., which would handle all the details of the film and the tour ("Moss Gets Mrs. Sanger," *Variety*, 30 March 1917, 22). The Moss-Sanger negotiations were almost concluded, and the film about two-thirds completed, when Sanger was convicted of distributing birth control literature and contraceptives and was sentenced to a thirty-day term in the Queens County Penitentiary. Sanger surely had a mixed reaction to her conviction; it meant the loss of personal liberty for a month but also represented untold promotional value for her cause. Indeed, when she resumed work on the film soon after her release on 6 March, she and Blossom filmed a scene that served as the film's conclusion: Sanger behind bars, followed by a title card that read: "No matter what happens, the work shall go on." At a time when newsreels were in their infancy and audiences often had to wait months to see moving-image reproductions of news events, *The Woman Rebel*, Sanger and Blossom hoped, would seem blown into theaters by current headlines.

Sanger and Blossom made their film as timely as possible but were quite aware that they were amateurs fumbling their way through their first production. To give their film a competitive edge in the marketplace, they recruited John Lopez, known in the movie business as a finishing specialist, to rewrite all the narration and dialogue conveyed through the film's title cards and also fine-tune the film in other ways (New York Supreme Court 1917b, 24–25). The film that emerged from the combined efforts of Sanger, Blossom, and Lopez — newly retitled *Birth Control* — was now ready for an audience.

Sanger as Martyr

As represented in the film's scene-by-scene scenario (New York Supreme Court 1917b, 68–96), *Birth Control* neatly divided into two parts, both of which underscored Sanger's victimization. The first section, titled "The Martyrdom of Progress," was the shorter of the two and attempted to find Sanger's place within the general history of people, particularly women, persecuted for their ideas. As the first title card in this section proclaimed: "Each great advance in civilization has had its martyrs — unselfish men and women with inspired ideas so far in advance of the times that they were repaid with sneers and persecution usually by the very ones they sought to help." Joan of Arc happened to be a prominent media image during the World War I years, and Sanger wasted little time associating herself with that historical figure.[3] As the next title card noted, "These Martyrs of Progress were often Women. Think back to Joan of Arc, exalted figure of history, inspired and led by God, who was burned at the stake because she lifted the heel of the oppressor from her beloved country." After suggesting that mothers themselves can be considered martyrs "under man-made regulations — as old as Society itself," this series of title cards concluded with one that explicitly linked Sanger with the Maid of Orleans: "To the aid of those mothers comes America's most recent

Joan of Arc, who, for her IDEA — Birth Control — has willingly accepted persecution and imprisonment."

The second segment, "The Story of Margaret Sanger's Fight Against Society's Prejudice," followed a more conventional narrative approach that centered on a mock-journalistic investigation replete with flashbacks. This section began with a newspaper reporter asking Sanger, playing herself, the following question: "Mrs. Sanger, will you tell me how the Birth Control Movement started in this country?" Ignoring the important early work of activists such as Emma Goldman and the National Birth Control League's Mary Ware Dennett, Sanger in effect claimed sole credit by noting that the movement began with "a pitiful tragedy in which I blindly played a responsible part": the Sadie Sachs story, which Sanger significantly revised for the film.

Shifting into a flashback, *Birth Control* showed Sachs, renamed "Helen Field," lying on a bed and about to give birth amid conditions of extreme poverty (figure 1). Although Sanger would later report that Sachs had only three children and that the husband was employed as a truck driver (1938, 90; 1931, 51), a title card heightened Field's abject circumstances by indicating that the infant was her seventh child and that her husband was out of work. A later scene showed that she had recovered somewhat with the help of Sanger but was still in dire need of birth control information. "Tell me what to do," Field pleaded with her doctor. "God knows I don't want to bring any more helpless little children into this hard life." Unlike the physician who actually treated Sachs, this doctor wanted to give the vital information but cited his inability to do so under prevailing law. After his departure, Field held out her hands to Sanger. "You're a woman — won't you help me?" she begged. With both women in tears, Sanger left the room without imparting the information.

As Sanger continued her interview, she noted that Field became pregnant again and, unwilling to go through another potentially fatal childbirth, opted for an abortion. As a title card put it: "Realizing that she again faced maternity, and knowing the probable consequences, she had sought help of a malpractitioner — as so many ignorant women in her plight do." She died as a result, and as Sanger told the reporter via several title cards: "That night her face came before me — as on the day I refused her aid — her pitiful appeal rang in my ears accusingly," and "then and there I resolved to devote my life to helping women like Helen Field."

The film then turned to another, more extensively fabricated story line involving Andrew McDade, a well-to-do fellow who made his

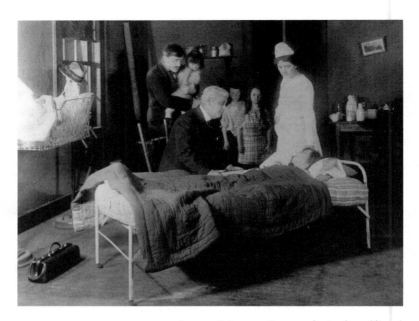

1. A nurse (Margaret Sanger, playing herself) and
a doctor attend to the dying Helen Field in this publicity photo for
Birth Control (1917). Sophia Smith Collection, Smith College.

living helping wealthy people get their names in the newspapers as
public benefactors. The film showed him reading an article in the *New
York Times* about Sanger's arrest and then phoning a rich matron
named Mrs. E. Percy Fakleigh to say that he had found "a fine opportunity for you to bring your noble efforts against the terrible teachings
of this Sanger woman." He later addressed a small gathering of Fakleigh and her friends and told them about Sanger's horribly corrupting
nature. He convinced them to give him money "to fight the forces of
evil" that Sanger represented and later hired two women detectives to
ferret out incriminating evidence against Sanger. One of them, disguised as a scrubwoman, found a document in Sanger's office titled
"Plans for Clinic" and hid it inside her clothing just as Sanger entered
to conduct an interview with another newspaper reporter.

Unaware of the skulduggery that had just occurred, Sanger and the
reporter discussed class differences and their relationship to birth control. The title cards that reflected Sanger's dialogue were intercut with
highly contrasting documentary images of the sedate, upper-class Riv-
erside Park area, where few children lived ("uptown"), and the slums
of the lower East Side, which overflowed with children ("down here").

Sanger then told the reporter about her plans to open a clinic but was unable to find the document in her office.

The next scene showed McDade receiving the purloined sheet from his detective. He and the detective then traveled to the front of Sanger's home, where the detective intentionally fell and pretended to twist her ankle. Sanger came out and, being the good nurse that she was, attended to the woman's injury. Sanger then escorted her into her residence, which the film also represented as Sanger's clinic, while McDade's second detective waited outside and spied on the women entering it.

After witnessing the clinic's activity, the detective who faked the injury had second thoughts about her involvement in McDade's plot to ensnare Sanger and later resigned. "I feel that to proceed against her would be outrageous," she wrote in a letter to her erstwhile employer. McDade, meanwhile, had gone to the police and informed them about Sanger's activities. The police raided the clinic and led Sanger away in handcuffs. The film concluded with images of Sanger in prison.

Promotional Plans and Critical Response

Believing that a ready market existed for their film, Sanger, Blossom, and their associates at the Message Photo-Play Corp. spared no hyperbole in their promotion of *Birth Control*. Advertisements for the film's New York–area premiere proclaimed it the "most startling of all screen dramas" and "an absorbing five reel photodrama [containing] three hundred scenes that tensely grip and profoundly stir. . . . Every woman in the world will demonstrate to see it." Believing their film censorship proof, except perhaps for its title, Sanger and Blossom prepared interchangeable posters and other advertising materials that would enable movie distributors and theaters to promote the film under either its original title or the less incendiary label *The New World*. Sanger made a strong pitch to movie exhibitors about the film's potential as a commercial product; "To announce it is to pack the house," she advised in a two-page advertisement in the 30 March 1917 issue of *Variety*. Confident that the country was ready for "Margaret Sanger's message for the million millions," she announced in the *New York Times* on 28 March 1917, a mere three weeks after her prison release, that she would embark on a nationwide tour with her film shortly after the New York premiere in early May ("Mrs. Sanger to Tour with Her Film," 11).

Birth Control received a significant boost during the first week of

The Strange Case of Margaret Sanger and *Birth Control* 271

April when the National Board of Review, a censorship agency based in New York, approved the film without any reservations. As a *Variety* writer reported on 6 April 1917, the film's "delicate subject was handled with such deft touch and intelligence that the censors passed the picture without so much as an elimination of a sub-title, not to speak of a scene" ("'Birth Control' Passed," 21). The NBR censors' views were echoed by reviewers for the trade press, who lauded the film's effectiveness as both drama and propaganda tract. A critic for *Variety* noted that "the average observer is electrified with the intense convictions of the propagandist [i.e., Sanger], taken hither and thither throughout New York's teeming child streets, to the almost childless precincts of the informed wealthy, and shown the lesson of sex temperance" ("Review of *Birth Control*," 13 April 1917, 27). *Birth Control* "has been handled with great care and contains story interest sufficient to hold the attention through five reels of film," wrote Margaret I. MacDonald (1917) in *Moving Picture World* (451). Her view echoed that of the *Variety* reviewer, who suggested that the film "holds the interest throughout and has its suspense just like a well ordered dramatic production should. . . . There is not a suggestive scene in the picture, and every player who appears in the acting portion is convincingly real" (27).

With the NBR's approval and several glowing reviews in hand, Sanger began selecting cities for the tour that would commence after the New York debut. She and Moss chose Cleveland as the first stop, as it had recently been the site of a highly popular birth control play — *Her Unborn Child*, by Howard McKent Barnes — and therefore provided the proper "psychological environment to intelligently present the Sanger theory," in the words of a *Variety* reporter ("News of the Film World," 20 April 1917, 19). The stage was set for the triumphant opening of *Birth Control*, or so Sanger believed.

Litigious Aftermath

The tour never materialized, however, as *Birth Control* suddenly ran into strong opposition on several fronts. It ran afoul of the Brooklyn branch of the Motion Picture Exhibitors' League, which voted unanimously not to show the film because its membership was, in its words, "opposed to the use of the screen for such purposes" and believed that "themes of this nature hurt the industry" ("Exploiting Falsehood and Boycotting Truth" 1917, 10). Sanger criticized the Brooklyn exhibitors for their hypocrisy — they condemned *Birth Control* but had raked in profits the previous year from films with abortion themes such as *Where Are My Children?*, *Race Suicide*, and *The Unborn* — but to no avail (10).

A far more serious blow came when Sanger attempted to exhibit *Birth Control* in Manhattan. She was scheduled to present the film at the Park Theatre on 6 May 1917 at 2 P.M., with continuous showings until 11 that evening. Unfortunately, the crowd that lined up in front of the Park on Columbus Circle to see the film and hear Sanger speak was turned away; the city's license commissioner, George H. Bell, had informed the Park's manager Lawrence Anhalt that he would revoke the theater's license if the film was shown.

Bell, who took as the source of his authority a 1913 New York City law that dealt with the physical conditions of movie theaters (de Grazia and Newman 1982, 15), had been quick to squelch other controversial films, including *The Black Stork*, *The Burning Question*, and *Womanhood* only a few weeks before. He noted that many people and organizations, including the Catholic Theatre Movement, had protested the possible exhibition of *Birth Control*. Bell, who had not actually seen the film but relied on reports from his representatives, told a *Moving Picture World* reporter that his actions should not be viewed as a judgment on the rightness or wrongness of birth control information (" 'Birth Control' Barred," 19 May 1917, 1098). Nevertheless, Bell did state elsewhere that "we felt that it would be a bad thing, particularly in these war times, to permit the exhibition of a moving picture advocating the limiting of birth. It was also our opinion that the theatre ought not to be used to exploit something that is against the law" ("Birth Control 'Movie' Barred from Public," *New York World*, 7 May 1917, 9).

The Birth Control League hastily arranged a special private screening of the film at the Park to an audience of about one hundred. As a reporter for the *New York Tribune* described it on 7 May 1917, "several persons who witnessed the private screening last night arose at its end and expressed surprise at the Commissioner's action" ("Commissioner Forbids Mrs. Sanger's Film," 7).

Sanger and her colleagues immediately made plans to fight Bell's action. On behalf of the Message Photo-Play Corp., attorney Jonah J. Goldstein applied for an injunction restraining the commissioner, claiming that Bell's refusal to allow the film's exhibition constituted an abuse of his discretionary powers. As a part of the case, the company collected affidavits from community members who had seen the film at the private screening. One such person, a high school teacher and executive committee member of New York City's Civic Club named Henrietta Rodman, stated, "I do not regard the picture as immoral or indecent" (New York Supreme Court 1917b, 13), while Rev. Harvey Dee Brown testified that the film was "absolutely clean and white, from first to last. There can be no honest objection to it from the standpoint of morals" (20). Ray Perlman, a longtime Manhattan social worker, wrote that the film was "if anything, a mild portrayal of the facts as they exist and there is nothing to injure the mind of any young person viewing it. The film merely suggests that such teaching would be of benefit to the countless women who suffer through having too large families, and the manner of suggestion, as shown in the picture, is clean, fair and in no way either suggestive or immoral. By no stretch of imagination can the picture be branded as immoral or indecent" (15).

Such sworn statements may have influenced Justice Nathan Bijur, who ruled in favor of the plaintiffs. "The subject of birth control is plainly one in which the public has an interest and concerning which two conscientious and opposite views may properly be held," he wrote. In an unusually progressive opinion for the time, Bijur suggested further that *Birth Control*

> may not properly be interpreted as more than an attempt to present a dramatic argument in favor of the change in an existing law, and that, while its form, its force, and its good taste may furnish ground for an honest difference of opinion, there is nothing in it which can reasonably be viewed as against morality, decency or public welfare. It affords, therefore, no basis for the exercise of any discretion on the part of the Commissioner. It is a measured and decent exercise of the right of free speech, guaranteed by our Constitution and essential to our national wellbeing, and as such is beyond the power of the Commissioner of Licenses to forbid.[4] ("Upholds Mrs. Sanger Film," *New York Times*, 7 June 1917, 10)

The satisfaction that Sanger took from Bijur's ruling was short-lived, however; in the following month, a New York state appellate court reversed Bijur's order restraining Bell. In so doing, the court cited a legal precedent of which Sanger and her attorneys were apparently unaware and with high irony had unwittingly endorsed. Months before, Sanger had stressed the commerciality of her film to movie exhibitors in an effort to persuade them to contract with Message Photo-Play; for instance, she noted in an advertisement in the 30 March 1917 issue of *Variety* that they could "clean up a quick profit" if they showed her film because of all the publicity she had generated during the past year. This emphasis—an intriguing one for a Socialist-minded person to make—came back to haunt Sanger when Bell's attorneys, led by E. Crosby Kindleberger, argued that the film was essentially a commercial product and, as such, did not enjoy First Amendment protection under current law. The court agreed; citing a 1915 case in which the U.S. Supreme Court ruled that films were items of commerce pure and simple (the now-famous *Mutual Film Corp. v. Industrial Commission of Ohio* decision), the appellate court framed the dispute primarily in terms of business practices: "We are not concerned with the freedom of speech guaranteed by the Constitution," it wrote. "We have to do with the question of revoking a license, which is not property, but merely a temporary permit to conduct a business" (*New York Supplement* 1917, 341).

Kindleberger successfully argued a number of other points, underscoring the following "objectionable ideas or incidents" depicted in the film:

1. The implied safety of intercourse between unmarried persons;
2. The fostering of hatred of the rich by the poor;
3. The improper exhibition of a woman in child birth;
4. Encouraging crime by making a martyr of a deliberate breaker of the Penal Law;
5. Praising the hysterical enthusiasm of the birth control advocates. (New York Supreme Court 1917a, 6–15)

Of these points, the most damning was the concern that the film might inflame relations among the classes. According to Kindleberger, *Birth Control* promoted the idea that rich people did not want poor people to possess birth control information because the rich needed large numbers of workers for their homes and factories. He found the following line of dialogue, which McDade directed to Mrs. Fakleigh and her peers, to be particularly egregious: "Why, if the lower classes do not continue to have children who will act as your servants—who will perform the labor in the industries over which you of the Superior Class rule?" Indeed, the court was not nearly as concerned about issues of sexuality and morality with regard to birth control as it was about the possibility that the film would create further divisions among upper and lower classes. Bell's lawyers contended that *Birth Control* "would have a tendency to arouse class hatred, as it tends to show that the rich have small families and favor the poor having large families," the court wrote (*New York Supplement* 1917, 341), and that argument proved sufficient for upholding Bell's decision to ban the film.

The court's action effectively buried *Birth Control*, a point that Sanger curiously neglected to acknowledge in her autobiographies; she merely stated that the film exhibitors, "fearful lest the breath of censure wither their profits, were too timid to take advantage" of Bijur's ruling (Sanger 1938, 252). Sanger did hold out some optimism that the film would still be publicly exhibited. An untitled article appearing in the December 1917 issue of *The Birth Control Review* about six months after the controversy noted "the splendidly libertarian opinion handed down by Judge Nathan J. Bijur" that was later reversed by "a more conservative court" and went on to say that "this does not mean that the picture has been definitely closed to the public. A final appeal has been made to the Supreme Court, and it is hoped that this highly educational film will be exhibited before long" (10). Nothing came of the appeal, but as history has shown, the suppression of *Birth Control* did little to hinder or diminish Sanger's decades-long struggle to educate people on the need for pregnancy prevention.

Conclusion

Although no copies of *Birth Control* are known to exist, it is possible to infer a number of things about the film, and Sanger's plans for it, from its scenario. For instance, I would argue that Sanger used *Birth Control* to try to redefine herself to her society, and, further, that the film reflected the contradictions that inevitably arise in such undertakings. It is important to remember that Sanger had been connected with radical causes for years; for example, as a Socialist Party regular, she had led a highly publicized evacuation of immigrant children from Lawrence, Massachusetts, to New York City in 1912 while their worker parents went on strike against the Lawrence textile mills (Chesler 1992, 75). In addition, she asserted that she had founded the periodical *The Woman Rebel* in 1914 "to proclaim the gospel of revolt" (Sanger 1920, 214). When the United States became militarily engaged in World War I, however, many radicals began scaling back their activities for fear of reprisals from federal authorities, particularly after learning of the arrest and conviction of prominent peers such as Emma Goldman, Eugene V. Debs, and Bill Haywood (Chesler 1992, 160–62). Sanger was no exception; haunted by the political failures of her well-meaning father, she desperately wanted to avoid being associated with losing causes in the public eye and was quite willing to bend with the times. Although *Birth Control*'s visualization of Sanger's arrest and imprisonment might on its surface link her with other radicals, the film was primarily an expression of her wish to move away from the political fringes and toward middle-class values.

I offer several observations in support of this claim. First of all, the film made no mention of Sanger's past radical associations and instead heavily emphasized her individualized victimization, a "martyrdom" made all the more personalized and domesticized by the suggestion that she ran the clinic out of her home. (In actuality, Sanger's clinic was rented storefront space used solely for the purpose of advising impoverished women.) Sanger further obscured her earlier political life by dropping the film's original title, *The Woman Rebel*, in favor of the phrase that had by then become virtually synonymous with her work.

Birth Control reflected Sanger's desire to migrate toward the mainstream in other ways. Within the context of America's expanding involvement in World War I and growing uneasiness with foreign-born citizens and residents, a prominent name change in the film suggested that Sanger may have wished to disassociate herself from European immigrants; the character based on Sadie Sachs, the Jewish immigrant who had died from septicemia, bore the considerably more WASPy sounding moniker "Helen Field." In addition, the film provided a relatively sympathetic representation of Sachs/Field's doctor in an apparent bid to win the medical establishment to Sanger's cause. According to Sanger's oft-repeated story, the attending physician was a well-meaning but callous fellow who not only admonished Sachs to eschew life-threatening pregnancies by having her husband sleep on the roof but also made light of her sexual proclivities. "Any more such capers, young woman, and there will be no need to call me," he told her. When Sachs asked him how to avoid becoming pregnant again, the doctor allegedly responded with a chortle: "Oh, ho! You want your cake while you eat it too, do you? Well, it can't be done" (Sanger 1931, 52). In *Birth Control*, however, the doctor took a very different tone. "I'm very, very sorry, Mrs. Field, but the laws forbid me to give such information," he said in his sole commentary in the film. Well aware that doctors were exalted figures among the middle class, Sanger decided it was worth the risk of weakening her film's moral imperative and changed him from inconsiderate and jocular to understanding and conciliatory.

Despite the film's de-emphasis of politics beyond the personal level, one aspect of Sanger's radical past was prominently on display in the film: the highly negative portrayal of the rich. Years later, in perhaps another attempt at reinventing herself, Sanger claimed that she had developed the idea of recruiting wealthy women to her cause while waiting out her term in the Queens County Penitentiary:

> The answer was to make the club women, the women of wealth and intelligence, use their power and money and influence to obtain freedom and knowledge for the women of the poor. These laws must be changed. The women of leisure must listen. The women of wealth must give. The women of influence must protest. Together they must bring about a change of laws and convert public opinion to the belief that motherhood should be conscious and volitional. This, then, was the new plan I was to act upon. (Sanger 1931, 191)

The film belied this retrospective view, however; it presented club women, as represented by Mrs. Fakleigh and her friends, to be anything but helpful. Indeed, *Birth Control* attributed Sanger's persecution mainly to such women's vanity and pretense (as Mrs. F's "fakely" name would suggest) and to those who pandered to their desire for publicity. In addition, Sanger and her biographers never noted anyone in her life who resembled the well-heeled Andrew McDade figure, characterized in a title card as "a cunning parasite who fattens upon the ambitions of Social Climbers by starting 'Up-lift Leagues' in which they may shine publicly." Historical and journalistic accounts indicate that a plainclothes policewoman did enter Sanger's clinic to witness the activities firsthand and later led the raid ("A woman — the irony of it!" wrote Sanger [1931, 159]), but none imply that the policewoman's actions had been prompted by reports from wealthy people and their privately hired detectives. If nothing else, *Birth Control* showed that the rich represented an easy target not only for dyed-in-the-wool Socialists but also for those like Sanger who wanted to redirect their efforts to middle-class audiences. As reflected in the appellate court's decision, however, *Birth Control*'s representation of class proved to be a principal factor that led to the film's suppression.

Although she took issue with other arguments against the film,[5] Sanger remained conspicuously silent on the objections to the film's representation of class differences. Instead she blamed the film's censorship squarely on her (and her father's) old nemesis: the Catholic Church. As she wrote about a year after the censorship and subsequent trials: "Then there was the preparation of a birth control film play, depicting the needs of birth control in American life among the poor. Again the [Catholic] Church exerted its influence openly; the film was forbidden to be shown" (Sanger 1918, 4). Although Catholics were certainly instrumental in the film's suppression, Sanger may have had something else in mind here; it is possible that, in the interest of shedding her radical image, she refused to take the class argument "bait" and instead framed the dispute primarily as a moral and religious issue. (It is a position made all the more interesting by the fact that the film cloaked Sanger in Joan of Arc imagery in an apparent attempt to undercut the Catholic Church's criticism.) If Sanger harbored any hope of reviving *Birth Control* by reconceptualizing its opposition in this way, however, she would soon discover that the film's ill-disguised class arguments permanently obviated any such possibility.

Birth Control was a complicated text full of inspired moments and patent contradictions, with the reasons for its undoing equally complex. Although the film remains lost to the ages, its written traces suggest that it was an intriguing repackaging of one of America's most famous social activists. It was and is a vivid reminder of the passions that can be aroused when bioethical concerns intersect with the media.

Notes

1 Still images from the film have proved almost as difficult to find, and I am grateful to the archivists at Smith College's Sophia Smith Collection for helping me find the one reproduced in this essay. Two additional photographic stills (including one showing Sanger under arrest and being led away by the police) may be found in "An Honest Birth Control Film at Last!" *Birth Control Review*, April–May 1917, 11.

2 In her reconstruction of the anecdote, Chesler (1992) noted the possibility that Sachs never actually existed but was a composite of the many women Sanger tried to help (63).

3 American filmmakers were particularly interested in using Joan for propagandistic purposes during World War I, then under way. Films such as *Joan the Woman* (1916), *Womanhood, the Glory of the Nation* (1917), and *Joan of Plattsburg* (1918) appropriated the Maid of Orleans to support their anti-German propaganda. In addition, *Joan of Arc* (1914), a film produced by France's Eclair company, enjoyed a revival in the United States in 1917. For descriptions of the three American films, see Hanson 1988, 474–75, 1063.

4 Bijur's opinion is reprinted in full in "A Decision for Liberty," *Birth Control Review*, June 1917, 2, 8. For a detailed analysis of the opinion, see Goldstein 1988, 193–95.

5 For example, see "Is That So, Dr. Emerson?" *Birth Control Review*, June 1917, 6.

Continence of the Continent

The Ideology of Disease and Hygiene

in World War II Training Films

CHRISTIE MILLIKEN

> [Education] is a process by which the minds of men are
> keyed to the tasks of good citizenship, by which they are geared to the
> privilege of making a constructive contribution, however humble,
> to the highest purposes of the community. — John Grierson,
> "Education and the New Order"

In the beginning of *For Your Information* (1944, RCAF Medical Branch, Associated Screen Pictures), a sex hygiene film made for the women of the Royal Canadian Air Force, a male voice-over (Corey Thompson) establishes a dialogic relationship between the imagined film spectator and the text. As a series of images depicts women in service marching and saluting, working in munitions factories, mess halls, nursing stations, Red Cross depots, and so on, the voice-over intones: "*You* are now doing valuable work on active service, thereby releasing large numbers of men for fighting on the front line. And especially on the home front, *you* women of the RCAF serve that men may fly." Such an introduction, an inducement to a gender-specific (and often service-specific) audience, is typical of World War II training films. The gender specificity shows up in various ways of attributing disease to the "other" sex. For example, training films produced for male recruits attribute the source of venereal disease infection to "dirty women," while films produced for enlisted women do precisely the opposite — declaring sex with diseased men as the scourge to avoid.

While all sex hygiene training films advocate individual self-control, they position the problem as a far greater battle for men, whose sex drive is assumed to be higher, and who also, under particular pressures coincident with wartime activities, may be more in need of "pleasurable releases." An exchange between two characters in *Pick-Up* (1944, U.S. Army Signal Corps) highlights this and other concerns. Corporal Green (the film's "protagonist") meets an attractive young woman (Ann) at the train station, where he goes to purchase a ticket for an upcoming furlough. After a casual conversation, Corporal Green (Johnny) invites Ann out to a juke joint, where they drink and dance late into the evening. Eventually, things heat up, Ann gets nervous, and Johnny says, "Hey, look, I've been around. We like each other, don't we? What's wrong with being nice? There's a war on, honey; we've gotta do everything faster." Ann expresses her stereotypically gendered position: "I know, but a girl has to have *some* self-respect." Self-respect is precisely what Ann does not have, the film suggests, since she infects Johnny with gonorrhea, forcing him to cancel his furlough and consequently miss his last opportunity to see his family and his girl back home before going overseas for combat. This little morality tale ends with a close-up of our depressed, beleaguered (but cured) soldier going off to war — paying the price of his misjudgment. The narrative never addresses the moral issue of Johnny's infidelity to his girlfriend back home, nor does it return to Ann and her fate. Nevertheless, the medical officer who advises Johnny makes the textual interpretation of her behavior clear: "Most of you men have sense enough to let the women who look like real tarts alone. It's the clean kids that worry us. That's our problem today; to keep you men from playing around with the *so-called* nice girls."

Although maintenance of self-respect is a recurring theme and issue for women in these training films, it never has the same resonance for men, who are typically positioned as victims of diseased female bodies (most notably in the case of willing engagement with pickups or prostitutes), but who themselves are not deemed "disreputable" as a result of contracting a venereal disease. While obvious differences exist between the films geared to men and to women, several things unite them. Not only do most of these films typically engage both fictional (a moral story of one or several characters who encounter disease) and nonfictional narrative principles (charts, statistics, animated sketches, photographs), but the primary source of knowledge offered in the films comes through medical expertise and the deployment of war metaphors in the delivery of their pedagogical message. For example, the montage imagery and patriotic marching music beginning *For Your Information* shift to a doctor's office where a male officer/medical

1. Medical officer/pedagogue (played by Jack Ralph) directs his lesson
to the camera/spectator from behind his desk in *For Your Information*.
From the test tubes and microscopes pictured here, the film shifts
into images of charts, statistics, and microscopic images of
disease. Courtesy National Archives, Ottawa.

doctor (played by Jack Ralph) offers the justification for the lesson the
viewer is about to receive: "In order to win this war, we must not only
fight our enemies on the battle fronts, but also on the home front. We
have to fight not only a visible one, but an invisible one. This is not an
enemy in the form of troops or tanks or guns, but it is an enemy
destructive and dangerous to our war effort. The enemy which we all
face is 'venereal disease' " (figure 1).

The juxtaposition between images connoting political patriotism
and the doctor's office as classroom are devices commonly deployed
for the sex education that these films provide. While one can easily
look at these training films today and see how dated, propagandistic,
and (sometimes) downright naive they may seem, they offer important
insights into the fascination with visibility at the heart of medicine's
"visual culture," an argument persuasively presented by Lisa Cartwright (1995) in *Screening the Body: Tracing Medicine's Visual Culture*. These texts also offer insight into social history, military history,
educational theory, nonfiction and fiction film strategies, the history of
medicine (since disease treatments for VD have changed significantly
from the time in which these films were produced), and, of course, the

history (and politics) of sex and gender. If history is a lesson, therefore, the pedagogical imperative offered in these films with respect to the battle against disease may be examined in the context of the historical present as well, since sexually transmitted diseases continue to be an ongoing concern in which parents, teens, adults, children, doctors, educators, and various other governmental *bodies* alike all have enormous stakes. To best understand the pedagogical agenda at work in these films, I will begin by situating them within the ideology of sexual and social hygiene that characterized the Progressive Era.

Hygiene and Contamination: Governance of the Body Politic

While the politics of sexuality is a reflection of both real and symbolic issues, sex is frequently attached to social concerns related to purity/ contamination and control/disorder. Political movements that attempt to change sexual ideas and practices seem to flourish when an older socioeconomic system is in disarray. In this regard, sex education brings into relief the complex interplay of ideologies that negotiate the boundaries of state intervention by highlighting the tensions both within and between political traditions. From the movement toward technological modes of production beginning in the late 1800s, themes of social efficiency become a dominant trope in (and justification for) sex education. The popular rubric of sexual and social *hygiene* is heavily indebted to the social purity and eugenics movements that flourished around this time. *Social* hygiene includes matters such as grooming, etiquette and appearance, human growth and development, eugenics, marriage, and family living and is grounded in a set of standardized practices or discourses which rely on the political economy of the body as defined by its social utility. *Sexual* hygiene, on the other hand, pertains more particularly to body cleanliness, disease, and sanitation. Both concepts share in common the overarching pedagogical presupposition that knowledge of such matters could provide order to social living in an increasingly pluralistic society.

The growth of North American Progressive reform began roughly in the 1880s in both Canada and the United States as an offshoot of the social purity movement and the cultural transformations provoked by industrial capitalism.[1] Commentators characterize the Progressive Era by the profound social, structural, and historical shifts that became standardized as a result of industrialization and its subsidiary effects, including devices such as technologies of verification (statistics, quo-

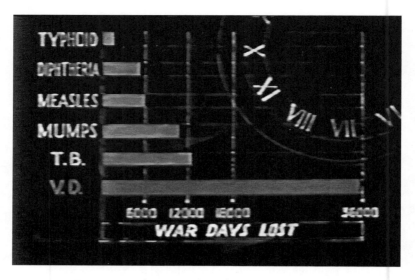

2. Progressive reform's proclivity for scientific efficiency and statistical measure is reflected in this chart from *For Your Information* mapping war days lost to various diseases. Courtesy National Archives, Ottawa.

tas, intelligence quotients, and bell curves were all developed around this time) and processes of governance (including psychological self-governance) (figure 2). Broadly defined, Progressivism is a middle-class response to the vast changes provoked by industrial capitalism. While it is by no means a unified movement, Progressivism may best be understood as a diverse and even contradictory configuration of principles, practices, and ideas for social reformation. These reform ideas attracted a range of thinkers across a broad spectrum of disciplines. For example, though differing markedly in their approach, the two key figures associated with the North American brand of Progressive reform in the context of educational philosophy are John Dewey and William James. Whereas James is noted for his incorporation of the emerging "science" of psychology with Peircean pragmatism into his pedagogical method, Dewey is most famously associated with his 1916 treatise entitled *Democracy and Education*, which argues that the basis for all democratic education must be *scientific*.[2]

Indeed, Progressive reform is most notable for its reliance on science, for its secular rather than religious orientation, for its attempt to represent modern, rational, pragmatic, scientific approaches to understanding and dealing with social problems, and for its unstinting middle-class-ness. It is this acceptance of bourgeois ideology for which critics most frequently attack Progressivism, particularly its acceptance of many traditional conservative values. Nevertheless, in the first fifty years of this century, Progressive reform encouraged an unprecedented degree of state intervention within in a range of social and economic practices. In *Intimate Matters: A History of Sexuality in America*, John D'Emilio and Estelle Freedman (1988) argue that Progressive reform fruitfully addressed a wide range of issues, from the need for playgrounds and housing codes in urban slums to checking the power of monopolistic trusts:

> The Progressive movement embodies sharply conflicting impulses — social order as well as social justice, efficiency along with uplift, faith in the power of education as well as determination to coerce the recalcitrant. Issues of sexual behavior and morality lent themselves to these contrasting tendencies. Some reformers urged education to check the spread of vice and disease, while others organized campaigns of repression. Calls for rehabilitating the victims of commercialized prostitution coexisted with efforts to punish sexual delinquents. Sponsorship of healthful amusements occurred simultaneously with movements of censorship. But, however diverse the program, the Progressive era witnessed the emergence of a full-blown sexual politics. (203–4)

The Progressivist privileging of "scientific" discourses lucidly illustrates Michel Foucault's notion of *scientia sexualis* as the longstanding tradition in Western culture for the justification and proliferation of discourses surrounding matters pertaining to sex and clearly demonstrates a characteristic linking sex education strategies of the period (to this day). Unlike sexual reform efforts of the previous century, which had relied primarily on the logic of moral suasion and the rhetoric of individual *self*-control, many twentieth-century crusaders also sought *state* regulation and intervention to achieve their goals.

With fears of venereal disease achieving epidemic proportions within America's armed forces in World War I, for example, a Commission on Training Camp Activities (CTCA) was created to battle sexually transmitted disease. Modeled on a system of recreational activities created by Canadian camps that Raymond Fosdick (the commission's founder) was sent to study in 1917 just prior to American entry into the war, one of the functions of the CTCA was to provide soldiers with education and amusements to divert their attentions and energies from more "unwholesome" distractions. Part of this agenda included the suppression of prostitution in the vicinity of army camps on both sides of the border. For example, a provision was added to the Defense of Canada Act in

June 1917 making it illegal for any woman suffering from VD in a communicable form to have sexual intercourse with "any member of His Majesty's forces or to solicit or invite any member of said forces to have sexual intercourse" (J. Cassel 1987, 141). Similarly, when the U.S. Congress passed the Draft Act in 1917, it included a provision forbidding prostitution within five miles of all U.S. military posts (Imber 1984, 48).

Structured as a two-pronged attack on VD, the CTCA combined Progressive reform elements of uplift and distraction, coercion, and repression in its efforts to make the military venereal-free. Producing films such as *Fit to Fight* (1918, for men), revised and reissued as *Fit to Win* (1919) and *The End of the Road* (1918, for women), through a complex set of linkages between the U.S. government and the American Social Hygiene Association, the CTCA films reflected the Progressive view of pedagogy, which framed knowledge acquisition as the "educational prophylaxis" to safeguard against disease. The primary agenda of the CTCA was precisely the promotion of leisure activities other than those involving sex. These educational films were largely constructed as morality tales that telegraphed a melodramatic narrative mode as a pedagogical model and were shown to British and Canadian troops as well as to the civilian population after the war. In fact, as Eric Schaefer (1999) argues in *Bold! Daring! Shocking! True!*, these early hygiene films are really the progenitors of a whole tradition of exploitation filmmaking starting roughly from 1919 onward.

According to Stacie Colwell (1992), *Fit to Fight* was the first ever venereal disease film produced with government support. Structured essentially as an army lecture film bracketed by two reels of dramatic material following the fates of five enlisted men, the bookend/lecture footage (which included graphic depictions of the ravages of VD) was cut out, and a new ending indicating the passage into peace was added in order for the film to be theatrically distributed to wider audiences. The narrative essentially gives a cross section of class types and moral positions among five enlisted men who all receive the same instruction on venereal disease from their company commander and react to this instruction according to stereotype. *The End of the Road* depicts a dramatic narrative chronicling the very different trajectories of two young women with respect to their involvement in the war effort and, of course, their encounters with venereal disease. Their fates are counterposed with the good girl receiving proper sex instruction from her mother and becoming a nurse committed to the war effort. The bad girl, shown to have been poorly instructed by a mother who failed to meet her inquiries at a formative stage, goes on to contract syphilis and is eventually educated on the subject of venereal disease by the good girl nurse.

While the pedagogical message of the two films may appear to be grounded in the same principle of hygienic living, there is a fundamental contrast in the underlying message along the lines of gender. *Fit to Fight/ Fit to Win* positions the contraction of VD as profoundly unpatriotic, equating bodily health, moral purity, and fighting fitness on the same plane. *The End of the Road*, while similarly concerned with education, knowledge, and prevention, is concerned with prevention not so much of infection as with sexual activity itself. As Annette Kuhn (1988) says of the film: "it is chastity which is presented as the one sure way of avoiding diseases — and disgrace: for active sexuality, disease and disgrace lie in wait together on the only other road open to women" (52).

Governmentality and Care of the Self

The turn to government intervention in practices of everyday life illustrated by these films and characterizing Progressive reform more broadly is less about a dramatic shift in morality per se than about finding new, alternative procedures to implement specific morals and standards in an increasingly urbanized, industrialized cultural context. In this context, many Progressivists placed enormous faith in the film medium's capacity to instruct and indoctrinate (or perhaps even coerce) large numbers of people with unprecedented efficiency and economy. Moreover, with war mobilization came renewed national attention geared to protecting the health and fighting efficiency of soldiers.

One important factor contributing to the increased use of the film medium during World War II was the rise of the documentary film movement or "the documentary idea"[3] between the two world wars. This is evidenced by the marked difference between these earlier venereal disease educational narratives and the form that would proliferate during World War II, aided by technological advances such as sound, lightweight 16 mm cameras, and the versatility and mobility with projection that the new technology offered. While these training films certainly contain traces of the shock and fear tactics more typical of exploitation films (particularly films made for men), a number of significant differences mark their departure from this tradition. For one thing, training films were short, generally twenty to forty minutes in length, as opposed to the established ninety minutes of feature-length narratives (though exploitation features were generally shorter, as

Schaefer points out). Most pointedly, training films were far from "disreputable" in ways attached to the exploitation genre and were both sponsored and sanctioned by governmental bodies with no profit motive, to be shown and distributed in restricted viewing conditions to restricted audiences. In fact, several of the Women's Army Corps hygiene films were restricted to WAC viewers only.[4]

Since training films were created and viewed within a film culture dominated by Hollywood, a common pedagogical strategy continued to be the thinly veiled narrative that provided dramatic enactment as a means for instruction: a lesson provided by the evidence of experience, as it were. Such films are characterized by what Richard Dyer MacCann (1976) calls a rapprochement between "the factual needs of Washington and the dramatic experience of Hollywood" (136). This so-called wartime wedding of fiction and documentary strategies results from the merging of talent and the unprecedented use of film during World War II to efficiently and economically educate and mobilize large groups of people.

In fact, many companies and independent producers of documentary and educational films gained experience during World War II. The National Film Board of Canada was created in 1939 by John Grierson and participated heavily in the war effort, subcontracting companies such as Crawley Films (Ottawa) and Associated Screen Studios (Montreal) to help production demands that the fledgling organization had neither sufficient equipment nor technical talent to provide. Hollywood's involvement in the war effort is widely known: New York's Astoria Studios (originally a center for Famous Players–Lasky and later Paramount) were taken over by the War Department from 1940 to 1946. The First Motion Picture Unit of the U.S. Army Air Force took over the Hal Roach Studio in Culver City (with studio mogul Jack Warner as head) and used a huge pool of Warner's talent for its training films. Walt Disney's participation in the war effort was sufficient to merit at least one scholarly text, *Donald Duck Joins Up: The Walt Disney Studio during World War II* (Shale 1982). Daryl F. Zanuck (head of Twentieth Century Fox) chaired the Research Council of the Academy of Motion Picture Arts and Sciences, which sponsored the production of a number of training films, and in 1941, he was commissioned as a lieutenant colonel in the Army's Signal Corps, which would oversee the production of more than two hundred training films.

The war effort brought about unprecedented alliances between Canada and the United States, including the exchange of film material, stock footage, combat footage, and captured enemy footage, as well as the circulation of many training films across borders. *For Your Information*, for example, was shown to the U.S. Women's Army Corps and included in the *List of War Department Film, Film Strips, and Recognition Slides* catalog (April 1945) as an official War Department film. While I would not elide the social, political, and cultural differences between these two nations, I want to point out that the mission of these training films — to train, instruct, inform, or indoctrinate against a common enemy — establishes potent alliances between them.[5] Moreover, training films produced in both Canada and the United States reflect very similar ideas about sexual citizenship and deploy equally similar pedagogical tactics to achieve their goals. In sum, while these films are embedded in the rhetoric of patriotism and national values specific to each nation, we can also read them more broadly in relation to pedagogical practices in which the lives, thoughts, actions, and behaviors of individuals and social groups come under increasing scrutiny and management, both in the context of the war itself and in the context of modernity more generally.

Defending the Nation

One of the most famous and most widely circulated training films over which Daryl F. Zanuck presided was John Ford's *Sex Hygiene* (Research Council of the Academy of Motion Picture Arts and Sciences, 1941). Its fame, no doubt, partially stems from its being directed by one of Hollywood cinema's great auteurs, in the same way that Frank Capra's *Why We Fight* series has achieved particular attention. Moreover, *Sex Hygiene* is reputed to have been shown more frequently than any other military training film. For example, in *Film and Propaganda in America*, David Culbert states that in the month of June 1943, of 478 films in release for troops and over 10,000 screenings of all these films, *Sex Hygiene* ranked first with 1,871 presentations in 16 mm format and 294 in 35 mm (Eberwein 1999, 70).

Sex Hygiene begins with a lengthy square-up that takes up almost one-third of the film's duration.[6] The square-up, not unlike those used in exploitation films, contains the justification for the film with a call that appeals to the personal as well as the political. Part of this section reads as follows:

> If our country is to successfully defend our right to live the American way, it needs everyone of you to be in the best possible condition. Any soldier

who willfully or through neglect, fails to maintain his body in this condition is a "shirker" who is throwing an extra burden on his comrades by requiring them to do his work as well as their own. The government is vitally interested in having you return to civil life with a better and stronger body than when you entered the army.

After this extended printed material, we observe a group of men playing pool at a base recreation room and watch their friend "Pete" leave these wholesome activities for a night off base and on the town. His departure is dramatized by an ominous close-up of an eight ball and a dissolve to a phonograph record, after which Pete stealthily emerges from a prostitute's room and picks up a cigar he has conveniently left burning beside a nude female statue. From these not-so-subtle suggestions, we cut back to the base and learn that increased incidents of vD have become a concern and that all soldiers have been ordered to see a film on the subject. Just prior to the projection of this film-within-the-film, the importance of the topic is reiterated by an army officer who introduces the screening to the enlisted men/spectators. In the film-within-the-film, our teacher is a military doctor (played by Charles Trowbridge) who begins his lecture in much the same manner as the medical officer in For Your Information, only his remarks pertain to the "woeful" ignorance of most men with respect to their own bodies. From a very loose narrative diegesis, the film goes on to name and explain the various venereal diseases, illustrate these illnesses with graphic imagery of symptoms including genital chancres and pus discharging from a penis (a sign of gonorrhea) (figure 3), and a demonstration of soldiers receiving prophylaxis treatment after intercourse. This lesson is juxtaposed with various reaction shots of the soldiers in the audience, demonstrating the film-within-a-film structure here as an early example of what Robert Eberwein (1999) sees as a staple of educational films that literally thematize vision by dramatizing the conditions of reception (4–5).

The graphic depictions of ravaged male bodies (most spectacularly the penis) are characteristic of virtually all of the sex hygiene films produced for men, including Sex Hygiene, Pick-Up, It's Up to You (1943, Royal Canadian Air Force, for men), Easy to Get (1943, Army Pictorial Service), Three Cadets (1944), and The Story of the D.E. 733 (1945, Paramount, produced for the U.S. Navy). It is interesting to note that the aforementioned For Your Information (for women) has nothing so graphic. Part of this has to do with the way in which information is sex segregated: men get information, charts, statistics, and

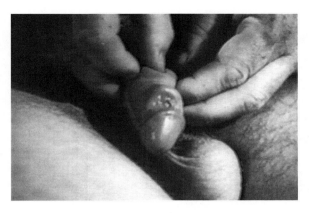

3. The spectacle of the diseased penis pictured here from
Sex Hygiene is a staple of hygiene training films. Courtesy
National Archives and Records Administration.

graphic photographic evidence of how disease affects the male body,
while women receive information about the female urogenital system
and the effects of venereal disease on the female body. Nevertheless,
these differences are also marked by a difference in tone that led one
critic, in an article talking of venereal disease in Canada's armed forces,
to exclaim: "The women's film is a masterpiece in delicacy — just now
copies of it are on loan to the U.S. Navy to be shown to the WAVES. The
airmen's film is about as delicate as a sock in the jaw, and has something of the same impact" (B. Fraser 1944, 29).

While these differences have been offered as a critique of the implied
sexism in what is often referred to as the "gentler" sex, one more
logical reason for this difference has to do precisely with the gender
specificity of the information provided. In *"They're still women after
all": The Second World War and Canadian Womanhood*, Ruth Roach
Pierson (1986) argues that this "potentially harmful protectiveness"
avoided the explicit vernacular of films directed to men and relied on
anatomical drawings and diagrams of the female sex organs rather
than on photographic evidence. Pierson claims that the protectiveness
accorded to women is rooted in a "lingering equation of female purity
with ignorance" (201). Yet this criticism effaces one of the central
"problems" with female anatomy vis-à-vis the spread of venereal disease. The fact that women's sex organs are internal means that women
frequently had absolutely no awareness of infection, since they could
carry and potentially spread disease with no symptoms. While images
of secondary and tertiary syphilis symptoms can be marked on the

Continence of the Continent   291

4. A stunned officer shakes his head at the images of disease before him in *Sex Hygiene*. Courtesy National Archives and Records Administration.

female body and depicted in photographs/footage in films for women (hair loss, skin rashes, crippling), they remain invisible on the external parts of the female genitalia and cannot be documented and offered up as evidence. The hiddenness or invisibility of signifiers of infection in the female body is addressed in the training films geared to men in all kinds of troubling ways (figure 4) and foregrounds the misguided specularity presumed at the interface between ignorance and knowledge (i.e., "She may look clean, but . . ."), which gets played out in endless dichotomizing between the visible/knowable and in the invisible/unknowable (hence mystifying and frightening), between pure and impure, inside and outside.

This gulf between the visible and invisible highlights one of the central problems of sex education, particularly via audiovisual texts, which must negotiate the evidentiary status of the visible (the knowable) at the same time that they must caution against these fundamental precepts of knowledge acquisition. In other words, the visible can be misleading; the signifiers of a healthy body do not always connote what one thinks; the human eye alone cannot be trusted. What is needed is the support of expertise, here in the form of medical science — microscopy, blood tests, radiography, and the like — to explain and contain the "problem" of female difference.

While it is logical to frame the scientific justification for these works (and for sex education more generally) in the context of Foucault's ideas about the history of sexuality, another interesting position from which to view these films is from his notion of *governmentality*, a neologism Foucault created to describe the shift from older states of justice in the Middle Ages to the consolidation of administrative state practices during the fifteenth and sixteenth centuries. Foucault describes this evolution as a series of tactical shifts that make possible the continual definition and redefinition of what we might call the *mentality* of government, what is within the competence of the state and what is not, the notion of public versus private, and so on. Governmentality, then, is the broader configuration of discourses characterized by the shift from an art of government or governmental rationality (as Foucault calls it) toward political science beginning in the eighteenth century. In this regard, governmentality is "the ensemble formed by institutions, procedures, analyses and reflections, the calculations and tactics that allow the exercise of the very specific albeit complex form of power, which has as its target *population*, as its principal form of knowledge *political economy*, and as its essential technical means *apparatuses of security*" (Foucault 1991, 102; italics mine).

Since governmental interest in issues related to venereal disease and hygiene was precipitated by the fear of large numbers of military personnel potentially being rendered ineffective by disease, we might understand the proliferation of sex and hygiene instruction during the two world wars in relation to the phenomena of population and governance. Under the rubric of national defense (or, to use Foucault's term, "apparatuses of security") and the preservation of national identity and values (since the war effort necessitated an emphasis on community over individuality), sex education became implemented and standardized to an unprecedented degree via discourses surrounding population and its control — how it is measured, organized, statistically arranged, and categorically defined within a range of power/knowledge systems.

Much educational material produced during the era is clearly embroiled in conflicting ideas about the social meanings and moral evaluation of sexual behaviors characteristic of Progressivism's conflicting ideologies. In World War I, for example, the American Social Hygiene Association consistently equated venereal disease with immorality, vice, and prostitution by presenting America's fighting men as innocent victims of disease and simultaneously scapegoating prostitutes as the guilty spreaders of infection. Declaring avoidance of prostitutes as a litmus test of patriotic zeal, this rhetoric reflects the tendency to define social problems through statistical calculation, making a vast and often grossly exaggerated compendium of detailed information about commercialized vice and lost manpower due to its ravages.

Other U.S. training films, including *Pick-Up* (1944), *Easy to Get*

(1944, a film for African American soldiers), and *Three Cadets* (1944), all incorporate narrative strategies to chronicle the fate of enlisted men with respect to their sexual practices and experience of disease. At the same time, the films' use of medical diagrams, images of diseased genitalia, and statistical instruction about VD and prophylactic use consistently performs an erasure of the boundaries between fictional and nonfictional modes. One of the consequences of this conflation is how constructions of nationhood and national identity become enmeshed with gendered identity. This collapse of nation and gender vis-à-vis pedagogical practices in which *care of the self* is imbricated in ideological agendas attempts to construct uniformity and purity as constitutive of sexual (and national) citizenship. Because sex education is always a gendered debate, it is not surprising that considerable scapegoating goes on in these training films, which operate under a facile strategy that posits education as a confrontation between ignorance as innocence and knowledge as power. Such dichotomizing allows for the typical distinctions made between virgins/good girls/wives on the one hand and whores/pickups/victory girls (also referred to as "patriotutes") on the other.

The Story of D.E. 733 is, in many ways, typical of many films produced by Hollywood studios in service of the war effort. Early in the film, the executive officer of the ship (MacGregor) reports on the "failure" of his ship to endure battle. From here a flashback structure is deployed, which offers MacGregor's voice-over reflections on the doomed fate of the *D.E. 733*, chronicling the dramatic (and fatal) consequences of a ship manned by too many naval officers rendered "impotent" by disease and unable due to loss of manpower to avoid a torpedo attack.

MacGregor declares that the problems besetting the *D.E. 733* were not in the design of the ship but rather in a failure of his pedagogical method. Urged by the ship's doctor to lecture his crew on the travails of venereal disease just before one of their port stops, MacGregor lists the "factual" and "statistical" characteristics of chancres, bacterial infection, prophylaxis, syphilis, gonorrhea, and condom use, promoting continence as the best and only sure method to stay healthy. Of course, the crew largely ignores this rhetoric. After their port stop, various officers visit the ship's doctor in a montage sequence that provides graphic display of a wide variety of consequent venereal diseases that besmirch the men. When reprimanded by the ship's captain, MacGregor is offered an alternative pedagogical trope. After stating that venereal disease is neither a medical nor a moral problem, the captain declares that "it's a line problem" affecting everyone on ship. He bluntly dismisses the officer and then suddenly beckons him back, saying, "Oh, MacGregor, do you know why men call a ship a *she?*"

> . . . . .because men at war suffer the loss of a woman's companionship. We're lonely for women. We need a woman, so we make our ship one. A substitute. If you want to be psychological, a love object. The love a man would ordinarily give a woman he gives a ship. I want you to tell the crew that when a man brings disease aboard this ship, he is endangering her as though she were his wife.

As this conversation ends, warning bells ring, and the ship is eventually unable, owing to loss of manpower, to prevent an enemy attack. The phallocentrism of the torpedo's invasion of the ship only emphasizes the crudity of the metaphor and illustrates the highly problematic conflations that collapse gender with nation via the motherland, displaying an absurdly dated conception of femininity as simultaneously vessel, receptacle, and dutiful (not to mention sanitary) wife in need of protection. What is of particular interest in the context of governmentality, however, is the ship captain's overt suggestion to deflect attention away from sexual hygiene as either a medical or moral problem, and to reflect on it in terms of manpower and patriotism (population, political economy, and apparatuses of security). The lesson to be learned is neither medical nor moral; "It's a line problem," says the captain. Of course, we all know otherwise.

Racial Others

The problem of patriotism takes on a markedly different connotation in *Easy to Get*, a training film made for African American soldiers. Eberwein (1999) identifies the film as "a disgraceful reminder of the segregation of the troops during World War II" and chastises its racial politics for using a white male voice-over offering commentary on the "ignorance" of the characters in the film (74–75). While I can hardly disagree with the former point, the latter is somewhat less convincing. For one thing, the theme of ignorance, as I have argued, is a recurring theme in all of these films, based, as they are, on knowledge acquisition. Moreover, training and other educational films characteristically use a voice-over commentary either to explain or to ascribe motives and psychological complexity to behavior, as is the case with *Pick-Up* and *It's Up to You*. There are a number of reasons for this, not least of which is the economic advantage it affords to the whole film production process.[7] Beyond this, I would argue that the use of African American role models as incentive marks a curious departure in the politics of this film as compared to the others mentioned here. While *Easy to Get* uses a typical melodramatic, fictional component that follows the fates of Corporal Baker and Private Anderson as they contract disease (from a friendly girl-next-door "pickup" and a prostitute respectively), the film introduces real-life figures in the film's final minutes.

After a montage sequence highlighting the achievements of several African American athletes at the 1936 Berlin Olympic games, one of these athletes, Ralph Metcalf (now in the army himself) speaks to the audience in direct addresses about the need to remain responsible and disease free. After this, the voice-over introduces Paul Robeson, described as enjoying "the respect and recognition of the entire world. From his college days when he was an all-American end through his great career as singer, actor, and world traveler, Mr. Robeson has done as much for our people as any man alive. Listen to him" (figure 5). While precisely who "*our* people" refers to remains unspoken, the montage sequence (and the film itself) suggests that this means the African American men for whom the film was made. That Robeson goes on to make a plea for the spectator to heed the advice of the film and remember his responsibilities "to *our* communities, *our* families and *ourselves*," rather than to *the nation* more generally, is suggestive. Indeed, the rhetoric of *Easy to Get* may be read as outside (or on the margins) of national/patriotic inducements in its efforts to proffer allegiance to a group constituted/imagined by race perhaps *because* the experience of racism and segregation that the film's existence makes so apparent may complicate such a call in the first place. In other words, the appeal to an imagined black community could be viewed as a greater incentive to a group patriotic enough to fight for a democracy that has failed to make good its promise of equality to them. This pedagogical tactic may indeed be a strategic one that can be read retrospectively as prefiguring the shift to identity politics and an increased emphasis on individual self-interest that characterizes later sex education strategies that evolve out of identity-based politics, particularly beginning in the 1960s.

If history is a lesson, the pedagogical imperative operative in these works should be considered in the context of the historical present as well—to issues pertaining to race, sex, gender, class, and beyond. In the wake of penicillin's highly efficient remedy to treat many venereal diseases (several of which, historically, had rather dire consequences

5. "Mr. Robeson has done as much for our people as
any man alive. Listen to him," commands the voice-over
in *Easy to Get*. Courtesy National Archives and Records
Administration.

to physical and mental health), contemporary sex education may be
viewed with respect to these older discourses. Indeed, one might argue
that AIDS education is a history lesson in the repetition of discourses
that have similarly run the gamut of both medicalizing and moralizing.
The war rhetoric characteristic of educational pamphlets, campaigns,
and videos produced in the 1980s (both with reference to drugs and
AIDS) provides a curious parallel between these two sex education
fronts. Of course, a crucial difference is the way in which the emphasis
of contemporary concerns circumscribing a "queered" nation shows
the degree to which attention has been deflected from specifically (and
assiduously) heterosexual conjugality to a broader range of practices
(and discourses). However the history of sexuality is interpreted, whatever governmental tactics are used to deploy the rules and regulations
that define it, and whatever imagery is used to textualize its practices
and whatever pedagogical model is used to deploy information — all of
these works continue to show that the very real experience of sex is
hardly a private affair.

Notes

1 For a brief summary of the movement see Fendler 1998, 51–53.
2 An elaboration of the impact of both James and Dewey on Progressive
   reform in education can be found in Bowen 1981, 408–39.
3 As is famously known, "documentary value" is a term coined by John

Grierson in a review of Robert Flaherty's film *Moana* for a New York newspaper in 1926. That documentary films or "films of fact" date back to the beginnings of cinema is widely acknowledged, and the 1920s saw a significant rise of interest in the "documentary idea," which, in turn, had a profound impact on the form, structure, and use to which the film medium would be put during World War II by both Allied and Axis powers.

4   The War Department List of War Department Films names four such titles, including *For Your Information, Strictly Personal* (1945, 36 min), *Fight Syphilis* (1944, 19 min), and *The Magic Bullet* (1944, 31 min). Since the latter two titles were distributed to other war departments, one may assume that the common practice of altering the films for a female audience was the reason for their segregation. Unfortunately, I have been unable to see these prints and to solve this question definitively, and I can only speculate as to why these films were restricted from male viewers other than that they were assumed to be too graphic and lurid and may arouse prurient rather than more "legitimate" interest.

5   Some critics distinguish between training, incentive, and indoctrination films, a point that I will not belabor here. That these films were made precisely as a form of war propaganda is often elided by those who associate that word with information generated exclusively by the enemy (here Axis) regimes. Others, notably John Grierson, quite willingly accept their wartime work as precisely a form of government propaganda. For more on these debates see Barsam 1973; Ellis 1989.

6   Eric Schaefer (1999) describes the square-up as a typical device used in classical exploitation (69–71). Square-ups are prefatory statements about the social or moral ill that the exploitation film is ostensibly geared to illustrate or combat. The square-up offers a justification — pedagogically speaking — for the existence of the film itself. While the square-up is used throughout the decades in more "respectable" sex education films, square-ups are certainly more prevalent in the 1930s and 1940s.

7   For a short article outlining the general characteristics of training films see Meltzer 1945. Meltzer notes a particular trend for the AAF films (produced in Culver City) late in the war to shift to live dialogue, something made apparent in *Three Cadets* (1944).

"Invisible Invaders"

The Global Body in Public Health Films

KIRSTEN OSTHERR

> Tropical parasites causing disease seem unrelated to the
> everyday living of most Americans, but two things — World War II and
> global travel — have brought them together. — Ralph Chester Williams,
> *The United States Public Health Service, 1798–1950*

This essay borrows its title from the science fiction film *Invisible Invaders* (1959), in which an "invisible" race of aliens threatens to conquer earth in retaliation for human efforts to explore outer space. In this film, as in many alien invasion films of the 1950s, the status of vision and visuality is centrally thematized; the aliens are not actually invisible, but neither are they wholly visible, and the search to determine the boundary between the seen and the unseen provides the central narrative drive of the film. Significantly, this cinematic preoccupation with the borders of the visible extends far beyond Hollywood, infecting varied realms of postwar American culture. In fact, by appropriating the title of a science fiction film to introduce my discussion of a postwar public health film, *The Silent Invader* (1957), I mean to emphasize the intersections (not disconnections) between postwar medical, scientific, and popular cultures. The "silence" and "invisibility" attributed to the postwar invaders are belied by the omnipresent representations of unsanctioned national and bodily border crossings in this period. Rather than creeping undetected across geopolitical and subjective boundaries, the imagined invaders announced their presence everywhere, through audiovisual representations of the ideology of world health. In this discourse, bodily invasion is collapsed with geopolitical invasion, and both are conceptualized as processes of contagion. By promoting international border surveillance as the solution to the global flow of (contaminated) bodies, information, and commerce that characterizes postwar globalization, the discourse of world health espouses an impossible task: to represent visually the invisible paths of transnational contagion. Thus the technologies of transportation and communication that enable postwar globalization to occur simultaneously facilitate the spread of invisible contagions and enable the use of surveillance imaging meant to halt their spread.

As technologies of instruction, education, and discursive production, the motion pictures produced by international health surveillance organizations (such as the United States Public Health Service, the Centers for Disease Control, and the World Health Organization) participate in a discourse on modernization and global sanitation — in other words, on world health. With their emphasis on the problem of visually representing disease, and the attendant paranoia-inducing problem of avoiding infection by "invisible invaders," these films are obsessively preoccupied with the maintenance of organic and national bodily boundaries, the threat of penetration or dissolution of those boundaries, and the conceptualization of the body as the site of a privileged form of knowledge. Starting with a historical account of the role of audiovisual technologies in the practice of disease surveillance, this essay will examine several representative articulations of the discourse of world health, arguing that the "invisibility" of contagion is consistently made visible through representations of the spread of disease that construct a scientifically authoritative form of realism by supplementing documentary footage with nondocumentary techniques of animation and special effects.

A Brief History of Global Health Surveillance

The desire to monitor, regulate, and visually represent the spread of contagious disease in the public sphere has driven the pursuit of public health since its earliest days. The history of global health surveillance dates to at least 1851, when the first International Sanitary Conference took place in Paris to coordinate maritime quarantine requirements intended to prevent the spread of plague, yellow fever, and cholera in Europe (WHO 1976, 8). The perceived need for such an organization was linked to the development of transportation and communications technologies, whose reduction of temporal (and perceived spatial) distances led to the increased potential for the rapid spread of communicable diseases.[1] After several more meetings of the International Sanitary Conference, a permanent committee — the Office International d'Hygiène Publique (OIHP) was established in 1907. The OIHP coexisted with two other international health organizations — the Pan American Sanitary Organization (founded in 1902) and the Health Organization of the League of Nations (created in 1923, in the aftermath of World War I) — until the World Health Organization (WHO), created by the United Nations in 1948, unified and absorbed the activities of all three organizations (WHO 1976, 8–16; R. C. Williams 1951, 441–42; Brockington 1975).

The Communicable Disease Center (now the Centers for Disease Control, or CDC), based in Atlanta, Georgia, also developed out of World War II. In the postwar period, a heightened public concern over the position of the United States in relation to an imaginary global map of world health was answered by the transformation of the United States Public Health Service (USPHS) agency, Malaria Control in War Areas (MCWA), into the permanent institution of the CDC in 1946 (Etheridge 1992, xv–xvi). In the late 1940s and early 1950s, the CDC transitioned from working on specialized projects in war areas to addressing a broader range of contagious diseases threatening peacetime national security. As with the return of troops after the Spanish-American War and World War I, the global travels of servicemen during World War II raised concerns about the invasion of United States soil by "exotic," invisible diseases carried within the bodies of returning soldiers. The enormous expansion of air travel in this period exacerbated these fears, and consequently training programs in the control of communicable diseases also expanded during the postwar period (R. C. Williams 1951, 398). Among other projects, the CDC developed a training program for public health field-workers that acquired global significance as it attracted an international array of students. The program made extensive use of audiovisual materials to ease the language problems attendant on opening the program to participants from around the world, and these films served a variety of ideological and logistical purposes, including instructing field-workers in methods of epidemiological surveillance, popularizing hygiene techniques among U.S. schoolchildren, mobilizing mass campaigns for smallpox vaccination and eradication in West Africa, and instructing male soldiers and civilians in methods of preventing the spread of venereal diseases (Etheridge 1992, 24, 56).

By establishing clinical sites and field offices in previously colonized countries, the CDC and WHO began incorporating local populations into a global system of knowledge, charting the intersections of contagion, physical bodies, and geographic locations onto a global map of hygienic modernization. The films produced by these organizations thus occupy important positions in the transnational spread of Western capitalist hegemony, with its attendant discourses on the importance of bodily surveillance and control. The CDC's transnational reach is epitomized by one of its prominent programs, the Epidemiological Intelligence Service (EIS), created in 1951 to gather information on diseases around the world and to provide expert assistance to health-related crisis zones and "infectious disease emergencies" anywhere on the planet, on request (Duffy 1990, 279). The benevolent internationalism of the EIS disguised its strategic importance to Cold War surveillance activities; funding for the service was secured, in part, to ensure United States preparedness for the potential development of biological weaponry during the Korean War (Mullan 1989, 139). The global scale of the CDC's (and WHO's) pursuit of public health created an enormous demand for personnel trained in specialized health surveillance techniques, which presented, in turn, the need for a universal language of international communication. The shortage of experts available to respond to the suddenly urgent demands of world health prompted the CDC's investment in efficient and mass-reproducible technologies of instruction: the transnational dissemination of training in the techniques and ideology of world health could only be accomplished through the use of audiovisual aids (R. C. Williams 1951, 401). Consequently, the medium of film attained a uniquely privileged status in promoting world health during and after World War II.

Audiovisual materials also played a crucial role in the CDC's prehistory as the MCWA — the organization first employed instructional films to rapidly train a huge staff in the techniques for eradicating malaria-bearing mosquitoes during World War II (Etheridge 1992, 7). After the war, CDC training films were in such high demand that the organization launched its own production studio, as the postwar assistant surgeon general proudly proclaimed in his history of the USPHS:

> The most complete and up-to-date equipment available for production of superior films, filmstrips, and slide series has been installed in the audiovisual production services of the center and well-trained technicians in this field have been employed. A film library is maintained which lends training films and filmstrips to health agencies and schools throughout the world. (R. C. Williams 1951, 402)

The CDC's prestige as a preeminent postwar global health surveillance organization was defined as much by a mastery and distribution of audiovisual technologies of representation as it was by CDC's "control" of infectious diseases. Furthermore, the CDC's media empire reached both scientific and popular audiences; the USPHS also produced a series of health education motion pictures "for the information and guidance of the general public" during the postwar period (407). The popular visibility of institutions of public health is perhaps best represented by the massive nationwide polio immunization drives of the early 1960s, which were assisted by film campaigns using Hollywood stars to promote vaccination and charitable giving (Gould 1995, 85). When new headquarters were constructed for the CDC in 1960, an entire building was dedicated to the audiovisual unit, containing two large soundstages, numerous darkrooms, and a state-of-the-art sound department (Etheridge 1992, 111).

By the mid-1960s, the Audiovisual Unit of the CDC was no longer part of the Center's Training Branch — it had become a separate unit of the U.S. Public Health Service and was renamed the National Medical Audiovisual Facility (NMAV). In 1967 President Johnson secured an enormous budget for the NMAV by selling the program to Congress as the way "to turn otherwise hollow laboratory triumphs into health victories" (Etheridge 1992, 135). The perceived need for the USPHS to demonstrate the relevance of its activities to the general public through popularized motion pictures that explain those "otherwise hollow laboratory triumphs" is particularly revealing when considered in relation to contemporaneous events in the mass media. The sharply critical "Vast Wasteland" speech delivered in 1961 by Newton Minow, chairman of the FCC, prompted the development of a new era in television production, and during this time, "quality" shows and "relevant" programming were meant to replace the mindless drivel that Minow claimed had characterized television programming up to that point (Watson 1994, 22). Television's widely noted attempt to provide socially and politically conscious programming for a presumably intelligent audience affected other spheres of cultural life as well; President Johnson's effort to link scientific progress with social progress through the films produced by the NMAV indicates a recognition, on the part of federal policy makers, of the close association between audiovisual modes of entertainment and audiovisual modes of education. As the following film analysis will show, this ideological intersection parallels the formal and stylistic intersection of public health and Hollywood modes of representation.

While events such as the influenza pandemic of 1918 established the importance of the USPHS to national security during World War I, World War II dramatically expanded the institution's role in promoting a national ideal of physical fitness — an ideal that is captured in both public health and Hollywood films. The increasing involvement of the USPHS in different realms of social life, combined with the new medical techniques and antibiotics developed during World War II, led to greatly enhanced social prestige for the fields of medicine and public health in postwar American culture (Duffy 1990, 269–73). The increasing prominence of institutions of public health, and the proliferation of audiovisual technologies in daily life (such as the expanded use of films and filmstrips in education and industry after World War II, not to mention the new availability of television), combined to disseminate the imagery of world health throughout popular culture.[2] The films produced by postwar health surveillance organizations were especially important elements of the discourse on disease, bodies, and the nation for two key reasons. First, moving images had been of central importance to the practice and popularization of medicine since cinema was invented, and in the postwar period, this importance only expanded as electronically generated images and sounds increasingly permeated everyday life. Second, a founding and ongoing problem of public health has been how to constitute the public sphere as an arena of bodily regulation, when the discipline's primary object — the spread of contagious disease — is "invisible" to the naked eye.[3] To underscore the interconnections of public health and mass culture in postwar American life, I will consider a representative public health film, broadcast on television in an effort to warn the largest possible audience about the impending invasion of the United States by Asian influenza.

The Silent Invader presents the problem of world health through a dialectic of visibility and invisibility, articulated through two generically characteristic representational strategies. First, the spread of infectious disease is conceptualized as a problem of global proportions through the linkage of contagion with transnational communication and transportation technologies, whose assistance in monitoring and spreading disease is demonstrated on animated epidemiological maps of the world.[4] The mutually reinforcing conditions of universal surveillance and universal contagion produce a model of globalization that absorbs the United States into the seemingly unstoppable flow of infections and defines world health as an untenable contradiction. This stalemate is resolved through the second representational strategy: the construction of a visual icon of disease that enables the displacement of contagion onto sources outside of the United States, even while infectious agents continue to move freely across national boundaries. By locating the origins of disease in so-called Third World countries, and invoking documentary images of the inhabitants of those nations as visible evidence of the presence of invisible contaminants, public health films such as *The Silent Invader* recuperate the seeming hopelessness of globalization by quarantining diseased bodies within the spatially and temporally distant locales of an imagined premodern world.

On animated maps of the global spread of disease, and in documentary footage that codes nonwhite bodies as disease carriers, the actual contaminant (whether germ, bacteria, or virus) remains invisible. What is made visible is not concrete scientific evidence of invisible contagion but rather a socially legible — albeit entirely artificial — collapse of the invisible onto alternate forms of representing disease. The constant oscillation between these two modes of representation produces a realism that attempts to attain documentary veracity or indexicality ("seeing is believing") while nonetheless relying heavily on entirely simulated renditions of reality. Thus we arrive at a key contradiction in the audiovisual discourse of world health: the aim of global health surveillance is to visually map the spread of contagious disease and thereby to sustain the imaginary geopolitical map that authorizes the United States and Western Europe as subjects of scientific knowledge, consigning the "precivilized" world to the role of lab specimen. However, the inherent instability of the relationship between the observer and the observed leaves the practice of surveillance always inadequate to the task of preventing "foreign elements" from entering U.S. national/bodily borders. Despite (or perhaps because of) this contradiction, the medium of film is mobilized by health surveillance organizations as a technology of visualization that can capture images of germs that are invisible to the naked eye and then re-present them to a mass audience, training an entire nation of viewers in the techniques of disease surveillance. The instructional power of public health films ostensibly derives from their status as scientific documentations of reality, and yet these films cannot actually capture unmediated scenarios of contagion without displacing the invisible contagion onto artificially constructed visual images.

The Silent Invader is introduced as "an up-to-the-minute report on Asian influenza," brought to home viewers by the Westinghouse Broadcasting Company, the University of Pittsburgh, the American

Medical Association, and the United States Public Health Service. Opening in a newsroom setting, featuring a white male announcer standing behind a desk, in front of a world map, the program immediately launches into a visual montage of "man's battles with nature." This sequence emphasizes the combat mentality suggested by the program's title, as military invasion of national borders is conflated with viral invasion of bodily borders. The montage begins with the influenza pandemic of 1918, noted in the voice-over while documentary footage of World War I troops on the march is displayed on the screen. In the next sequence, various scenarios of natural disaster lead into footage, apparently shot in Southeast Asia, of a long line of men and women walking and being carried through what appears to be a makeshift hospital or refugee camp, with UNICEF jeeps in the background of the shot. Over this series of images, the voice-over announces:

> Unlike the battles of nation against nation, or humanity against the forces of nature, when man has often had an opportunity to prepare himself, the battles against disease throughout the centuries have often found man in the unfortunate position of having to combat this enemy only after it had infiltrated his community and infected much of the population.

At precisely the moment when the discursive tone shifts from the agentless "acts of God" series of natural disasters to the more insidious language of "infection" and "infiltration," the images of nonwhite bodies appear on-screen (figures 1 and 2).

The linkage of disease and national/racial otherness is underscored not only by the documentary convention of the authoritative voice-over, employed here to interpret the visible bodily surfaces of the "Asians" as infectious, but also by the emphasis on global health surveillance as a strategy for delineating the boundaries of modernity according to a geopolitical hygienic hierarchy. Over the display of "diseased" Asian bodies, the voice-over continues:

> You've recently become aware of a pandemic, or a worldwide epidemic, which originated in the Far East and is now known as Asian influenza. Because of the alertness and efficiency of the United States Public Health Service and the World Health Organization, a detection system, similar to that of the aircraft spotting, has been established throughout the world, and has enabled us to recognize and follow the progress of Asian influenza as it circles the globe.

The assertion that geopolitical boundaries can define the distinction between healthy and diseased, modern and premodern, national iden-

1. Scenarios of "infection." *The Silent Invader*, Westinghouse/ USPHS, 1957.

2. Diseased bodies. *The Silent Invader*, Westinghouse/USPHS, 1957.

tities, is both affirmed and denied by the discourse of world health. The very concept of world health is founded on a view of the world as a collection of discrete national bodies, inextricably interconnected by global transportation and communication networks that prevent any nation from functioning in isolation. This geopolitical web facilitates the spread of disease, even as it promotes the fantasy of universal boundary surveillance and control. The plotting of documentary images of diseased bodies onto epidemiological maps thus performs the crucial function of linking disease with racially marked bodies that occupy geographic locations outside of the national borders of the United States. Through this displacement, bodily invasion becomes national invasion, and the project of world health becomes a world war between modern, sanitary countries and disease-ridden, "premodern" societies.

After informing the audience that "health authorities expect an outbreak this fall and winter in the United States," the moderator introduces a professor of public health, who, after acknowledging the impossibility of locating the true origins of the epidemic, nonetheless points out the locations of Hong Kong and Singapore on a world map, indicating that these are the original sources of the disease that now threatens the United States (figure 3). Cutting to documentary footage of streets crowded with pedestrians in those locales, the voice-over narrates the epidemic spread of disease to Formosa, Borneo, and Japan, and from the major shipping areas of these places to widely dispersed locales (figure 4). The first known "invasion" of the United States was carried on ships from Australia heading toward San Francisco, with the first case entering U.S. national borders "only six weeks after the disease first appeared in China." The progress of contagion is tracked in detail on three consecutive epidemiological maps of influenza spread across the entire country in June and July 1957, providing a visual aid to the narrator's ominous diagnosis of U.S. vulnerability to global contagion (figure 5).

Despite the public health professor's role as the voice of scientific authority, even his narration of the spread of Asian influenza is undermined by the virus's representational instability, its oscillation between visibility and invisibility. On the one hand, the narrator admits that it is impossible to accurately trace the spread of contagion, or to impose quarantine, because a carrier of the invisible virus may not manifest visible symptoms for days or weeks after infection. On the other hand, the entire program is dedicated not only to identifying the origins of the disease in so-called underdeveloped locations outside of the United States but also to conceptualizing viral contagion as military invasion, thus promoting a racialized form of national defense that chillingly recalls anti-Asian xenophobia during World War II.[5] Postwar public health films such as *The Silent Invader* articulate the dialectic of visibility and invisibility through a historically specific form of realism that seeks to produce authentic representations of invisible contagion but can only produce simulations of that elusive object. This tension also structures Hollywood representations of invasion and contagion; in science fiction alien invasion films, visuality is constituted through an oscillation between documentary stock footage and special effects.

World Health in Popular Culture

If postwar American culture was preoccupied with the boundaries of visibility, then one would expect this concern to be manifested in a

3. The global spread of "Asian influenza." *The Silent Invader*, Westinghouse/USPHS, 1957.

4. The vectors of contagion. *The Silent Invader*, Westinghouse/ USPHS, 1957.

5. Epidemiological map, "Influenza Spread, July 1957." *The Silent Invader*, Westinghouse/ USPHS, 1957.

wide range of representational arenas. And indeed, the stylistic inter-section that does exist between scientific and popular cultural forms reveals an ideological overlap: the ability to visually represent the invis-ible amounts to the ability to prevent the invasion of national/bodily boundaries, whether by foreign diseases or extraterrestrial aliens. As noted earlier, the Hollywood mode of representing national bound-aries under siege is linked to a generalizable (not solely cinematic), historically specific epistemological formation: the global development of the concept of world health, as implemented by international health surveillance organizations dedicated to simultaneously producing sys-tems of knowledge about bodies and disease and policing the bound-aries of nation-states (and continents), across whose borders con-tagions threatened to spread. The centrality of physical and national borders to public health and science fiction films reveals the linkage between imagery of invasion and anxieties about globalization—a linkage that highlights the permeability of generic boundaries between educational and entertainment cinemas, and the consequent absorp-tion of the discourse of world health into popular culture, through the dialectics of visibility and invisibility.

Instead of answering the public health question of whether a subject is healthy or diseased, the central narrative problem for science fiction films is determining whether a subject is human or alien. To answer either of these questions requires visual access to the invisible interior of the body, and it is precisely this preoccupation with imaging the body's inner space that links the public health project of investigating the body with science fiction's obsessive representation of that body's invasion from outer space. While public health films like *The Silent Invader* narrate the spread of invisible contagions by intercutting doc-umentary footage with epidemiological maps, Hollywood films like *Invisible Invaders* represent the spread of alien invasion by intercutting stock footage with special effects. This strategy for investing narrative fiction film with "scientific" authority is so generically definitive that the film most often cited as inaugurating the science fiction film genre, *Destination Moon* (1950), is almost invariably described in terms of its "realism" and "documentary feel."[6] The film's use of documentary stock footage at key narrative moments (such as the rocket launch) establishes a convention that will pervade science fiction throughout its golden age in the 1950s.[7] The importance of documentary-style con-ventions to the emergence of science fiction—a genre whose literary predecessors were known for their fantastical, not factual, treatments of reality—points to a tension that describes both public health and science fiction films: between privileging "the real" and constructing entirely artificial conceptions of reality.

Moreover, by framing the dialectic of visibility and invisibility in the context of globalization, science fiction cinema reinforces the linkage of national/bodily invasion with world health, as a brief overview of *The War of the Worlds* (1953) will demonstrate. This film opens with stock documentary footage of the two world wars, using a newsreel-style montage and voice-over to contextualize the third world war within the mass-mediated archive of twentieth-century history. Cutting from the newsreel-style opening to a rapid credits sequence, the film recommences at the opposite pole of realism; an animated sequence displays the different planets in earth's solar system, and a voice-over explains that the Martians are invading earth in search of an atmosphere suitable to their survival. This oscillation between the historical and the imaginary is particularly striking given the film's efforts to ensure its reception as an authentic documentation of the real. Capitalizing on the widespread panic that ensued in response to Orson Welles's radio broadcast of "War of the Worlds" in 1938 (played as an emergency news bulletin reporting the invasion of earth by flying saucers), the film promotes its own plausibility through the newsreel framing device, which is reasserted throughout the film via intermittent voice-over announcements serving as plot exposition. Alternating between documentary footage of war and special effects of alien spacecraft (and their occupants), this film performs the same oscillation that postwar public health films enact, both engaging in the self-contradictory discourse of globalization (figures 6 and 7). By the end of the film, the alien destruction of earth, which has been sensationally represented through stock war and natural disaster footage, seems inevitable—all but two of the main characters have been killed off, and the romantic couple has been separated. Almost all hope is lost, when the deus ex machina—contagious disease—saves the day: the destruction unexpectedly comes to a halt, and the voice-over explains:

> The Martians had no resistance to bacteria in our atmosphere to which we had long since become immune. Once they had breathed our air, germs which no longer affect us began to kill them. The end came swiftly. All over the world, their machines began to stop, and fall. After all that men could do had failed, the Martians were destroyed, and humanity was saved, by the littlest things which God, in his wisdom, had put upon this earth.

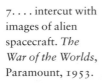

6. Documentary footage of war ... *The War of the Worlds,* Paramount, 1953.

7. ... intercut with images of alien spacecraft. *The War of the Worlds,* Paramount, 1953.

Those "littlest things" were the same invisible germs that postwar global health surveillance organizations were dedicated to investigating and containing.

Although contagious disease is an accidental narrative agent in *The War of the Worlds,* the control of invasionary forces by institutions of public health is a recurring feature of numerous science fiction films of the 1950s. In fact, the United Nations and the World Health Organization had been so rapidly assimilated into the postwar social imaginary that by simply invoking these institutions, a film could immediately frame its particular disaster in the context of both scientific realism and globalization.[8] For instance, a newsreel-style voice-over similar to the framing device in *The War of the Worlds* also structures *Invisible Invaders,* and at the film's conclusion, after the invaders have been conquered, the heroes are celebrated at a special meeting of the United Nations. Over documentary exterior shots of UN headquarters and interior shots of the assembly hall, intercut with studio shots of the film's cast, the reportorial voice-over intones the moral of the story: "Earth had been on the brink of disaster. But out of the holocaust of war, in which a dictatorship of the universe had been defeated, a lesson had been learned. The nations of the world *could* work and fight together, side by side, in a common cause." Ironically though, before the triumphant globalization sequence takes place (earth's inhabitants band together to defeat the enemy from outer space), a distinct but equally iconographic sequence occurs: the transportation and communication networks that provide an essential infrastructure for globalization break down. Thus, before the regulatory agents of globalization (the UN, WHO) can rescue humanity from alien colonization, the foundations of their power have already been undermined.

Similarly, before the World Health Organization saves the day in *The Silent Invader*, the film demonstrates the impossibility of halting the spread of invisible contagions across national boundaries, precisely because of their rapid movement through modern transportation technologies. In public health and science fiction films, contagion metastasizes from local infection to global catastrophe; once the first town is colonized, the alien/viral invasion will spread, literally and figuratively, like a highly contagious disease, across the entire country and planet. The telephone, telegraph, highway, and airport provide the sole sources of salvation, but at the critical narrative moment, the technology fails, the network is already controlled. And therein lies the deep contradiction of the audiovisual discourse of world health: it simultaneously denies the possibility of visually representing (and thereby containing) the invisible contagions that circle the globe and celebrates the fluidity of commerce that is attained through features of postwar globalization such as jet airplane travel, television, and satellite communications.

Whether the invisible is contagious disease or alien invasion, postwar media cultures strive to surpass the boundaries of visibility. Anxiously oscillating between the indexical and the artificial, the cinema of world health attempts to invest the filmed image with an authoritative form of realism through scientific surveillance and mastery of the public sphere and the private body. But the global benefits of hygienic modernization are not easily captured by audiovisual technologies of representation; documentary images can reveal their truths only through the assistance of special effects. Thus scientific authority is generated through recourse to artificiality. And as contemporary cultural productions attest, the impossibility of visually representing invisible contagions continually propels the dialectic of world health and global contagion.

1 The year 1851 was also the one in which the first undersea telegraph cable was laid (Mattelart 2000, 11). On the intersecting histories of public health and immigration, see Kraut 1994; R. C.Williams 1951; Duffy 1990; Wolf 1982.

2 As Richard K. Means and others have demonstrated, audiovisual aids were used extensively in public schools and other commercial and institutional settings only *after* World War II. See Means 1962; Essex-Lopresti 1998; K. Smith 1999.

3 See Cartwright 1995 for an excellent discussion of the early scientific uses of cinema, including microcinematography.

4 For a history of epidemiological cartography, see Thrower 1996. For other postwar public health films that represent global mapping, see *Prevention of the Introduction of Diseases from Abroad* (1946); *Hemolytic Streptococcus Control* (1945); *The Eternal Fight* (1948); *Fight Syphilis* (1941); and *The Fight against the Communicable Diseases* (1950). Another important form of public health animation consists of microscopic images of infectious agents, used to illustrate the presence of contagion in seemingly harmless social exchanges. This representational strategy has been employed since the earliest actualities were produced; in the interest of brevity, its familiarity will be taken for granted here. The "microscopic" form of animation can be found in *The Science of Life* (1922–1924); *Tsutsugamushi: Prevention* (1945); *Fight Syphilis* (1941); *Know for Sure* (1941); *To the People of the United States* (1944); *They Do Come Back* (1940); *Hospital Sepsis: A Communicable Disease* (1959).

5 For a discussion of representations of Asians in popular culture, see Lee 1999; Marchetti 1993.

6 Ironically, considering its celebrated "realism," *Destination Moon* won an Academy Award for Special Effects in 1950 (Hardy 1995, 125).

7 For a discussion of the role of stock footage in *Destination Moon*, see Knee 1997, 75–76. On the use of stock footage in exploitation films, see Schaefer 1999, 42–95; McCarthy and Flynn 1975.

8 Susan Sontag noted this convention in "The Imagination of Disaster," her essay on science fiction cinema (Sontag 1966, 210).

The Medium Is the Message

Documenting the Story of Dax Cowart

THERESE JONES

> This is just the first time they got caught beating
> somebody on video. It was very unethical, you know. — H.R.,
> quoted in Jewelle Taylor Gibbs, *Race and Justice: Rodney King*
> *and O.J. Simpson in a House Divided*

Jolted awake by the piercing scream of sirens and the harsh illumination of a helicopter spotlight just after midnight on 3 March 1991, George Holliday, the thirty-three-year-old manager of a plumbing company, grabbed his brand-new Sony Betacam and turned it on an unfolding drama. What Holliday saw through the lens of that video camera was a large black male surrounded by more than twenty Los Angeles police officers pushing him to the ground. After one officer launched darts from a taser gun to stun the man, three others began brutally beating and savagely kicking him, all the while shouting racial epithets. Throughout the eighty-one-second videotape, the four police officers inflicted a total of fifty-six baton blows on the defenseless suspect, Rodney King, who sustained a fractured skull and eye socket, broken cheekbone and leg, facial nerve damage, and severe bruises and burns all over his body. What Holliday captured with that video camera was a "virtual lynching in full view of a public crowd, an unprecedented record of violence and victimization in late twentieth-century America" (Gibbs 1996, 30). In just eighty-one seconds of electronic reality, more than two hundred years of racial conflict were condensed, and this time, the world could bear witness. This time, according to one writer, "there was an eye witness who was unbiased and wouldn't suffer from fear of reprisals" (Owens 1994, 17). This time, according to Senator Bill Bradley, "it was clear-cut: fifty-six times in eighty-one seconds. That's what Americans saw" (Gibbs 1996, 34).

However, the jurors in Simi Valley, California, simply did not believe the unbiased and unintimidated eyewitness, the clear-cut videotape provided by George Holliday. What they saw was very different from what other Americans saw being aired repeatedly and relentlessly on television. Perhaps the images had become too familiar, the brutality too codified; perhaps, according to legal scholar Barry Scheck, the prosecutors overestimated the power of the videotape (Gibbs 1996, 40). Turning the strongest piece of evidence against the victim, the defense team mounted frame-by-frame still photographs made from the videotape and created a different narrative, effectively decontextualizing the violence and deconstructing the entire encounter between Rodney King and Los Angeles police. The resultant "not guilty" verdict indicated that what the jurors saw, what they believed, was that the beating of Rodney King had been justified.

What does the brutal assault on the black, male body of Rodney King have in common with the terrible suffering of the burned, male body of Dax Cowart nearly twenty years earlier? The most obvious similarity is the medium of videotape, which, in 1991, captured a scene that confirmed the popular view of the LAPD as a "congenitally brutal force given to victimizing minority citizens" (Boyer 2001, 64) and, in 1974 with *Please Let Me Die*, transformed the private ordeal of a patient into a "celebrated 'case study' in medical ethics and human meaning . . . a classic among professionals concerned with the treatment and care of the hopelessly ill and the helplessly deformed" (Kliever 1989, xvii, xv). The most obvious difference is the technical quality of the respective videotapes. The accidental footage of the Rodney King incident lacks the stylistic flourishes, the edited constructs of space, time, metaphor, and psychology of *Please Let Me Die* and the later *Dax's Case*, which combine to tell the story of a twenty-six-year-old burn victim who insisted that his right to die be acknowledged and respected both during the course of his lengthy treatment and long after his successful rehabilitation.

Documentary footage and film serve as a discursive form like no other in that viewers bring to videotaped incidents such as the case of Rodney King or the case of Dax Cowart the assumption of historical accuracy, and they leave reeling from the affective power of such images. Film scholar Bill Nichols points out that seeing brutal violence or terrible suffering in documentary engages us quite differently than in other representations: "This is not a simulation. There is no getting up, dusting off, and going on as if nothing had happened. The imprint of history registers on the flesh" (Nichols 1993, 190). And it demands a response.

Thus, while technically different, the videotapes concerning Rodney King and Dax Cowart are similar in that there arose from both cases a moral and political imperative to seek redress on behalf of the victim or to manufacture justification on behalf of the institution. Both cases have become crucibles in which to test the ethical codes of the respective professions of law enforcement and clinical medicine. If the beating of Rodney King can be both condemned and justified under the credo "to serve and protect," so also can the treatment of Dax Cowart be both argument against, and justification for, the practice of "it's for your own good." Both cases have become part of what Tod Chambers calls the "shared narrative folklore" of their professions (Chambers 1999, 4). While cops can simply say, "Rodney King," to warn or balk against charges of police brutality and racial profiling, bioethicists can simply say, "Dax," to illustrate or indict medical paternalism's trampling of patient autonomy. And finally, both cases serve as contemporary examples of political torture in that perpetrating violence on citizens and inflicting pain on patients are the antitheses of the respective social contracts of law enforcement agencies and health care providers.

Conspicuously absent in most of the response from bioethicists to the story of Dax Cowart is an analysis of the medium in which that story is performed and presented: documentary. That the case has become a "classic" is by virtue of the very existence and accessibility of the videotapes *Please Let Me Die* (1974) and *Dax's Case* (1985), yet few commentators have either carefully scrutinized the construction of the audiovisual texts or critically examined their own reactions to them. As Chambers notes, the presumption among bioethicists is that real cases, whether they are in print or on videotape, are "impartial, theory-free and guileless" (Chambers 1999, 7). In this essay, I will describe in some detail the elements of *Please Let Me Die* and *Dax's Case*, organizing my discussion around what Nichols identifies as the three definitions of documentary: the point of view of filmmaker, text, and viewer (Nichols 1991, 12). As regards the viewer, I will rely on the discourse thus far generated by bioethicists to show that their engagement with, and assessment of, Dax's story was largely determined by the medium in which they first encountered it. My project takes up philosopher Michel Foucault's invitation to recognize the extent to which an object such as documentary is not only constructed but also reconstructed by discursive participants or interpretive communities —

more often than not, reconstructed less dramatically and less destructively than was the case in Simi Valley, California.

Please Let Me Die (1974)

Sorry, man, it was an accident. — unidentified hospital staff,
Please Let Me Die

In the summer of 1973, after graduating from college and serving three years as a jet pilot in the air force, Donald "Dax" Cowart was critically injured in a propane gas explosion that killed his father, who was also Dax's partner in a successful real estate venture. Dax sustained primarily third-degree burns over 68 percent of his body; both eyes were blinded by corneal damage, both ears mostly destroyed, both hands so badly burned that the distal parts of the fingers required amputation and so badly deformed that they appeared as "useless, unsightly stubs" (figures 1 and 2) (White 1975, 9). Within minutes after the accident and throughout the days, weeks, and months of excruciatingly painful treatment such as repeated skin graftings and daily immersions in the household bleach and water mixture of a Hubbard tank for infection control, Dax consistently and coherently stated that he did not want medical care, that he did not want to live.

In April 1974, Dax was admitted to the University of Texas Medical Branch Hospitals (the third care facility since the accident), where he adamantly refused to give consent for corrective surgery on his hands and persistently demanded to leave the hospital and return home to die. Despite his protests, the tankings were continued, and Dr. Robert B. White was called in as a psychiatric consultant to determine the patient's competency. Finding Dax to be "mentally able to make a rational and informed decision" but feeling "deeply troubled" about the circumstances (White 1989, 15), White first conferred with a colleague, who agreed with the initial evaluation, and next obtained permission from Dax and his mother, Ada Cowart, to do a videotaped interview "for educational purposes for medical students and doctors in training" (Robert B. White, telephone interview with author, 7 May 2001). That videotaped interview functions as the structural centerpiece of the thirty-minute documentary *Please Let Me Die*.

As a producer of educational documentaries, White already had what he described as a "longtime collaboration" with the staff of the Medical

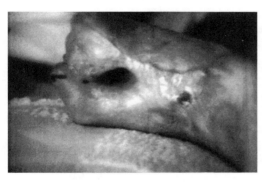

1. Dax Cowart. *(below)* 2. Close-up shot of Dax's left hand. Both from *Please Let Me Die*, University of Texas Medical Branch.

Illustration Department at UTMB, who themselves had "years of experience making medical training films" (White interview). That lengthy and regular working relationship would prove valuable throughout the process of taping and editing *Please Let Me Die*. White recalled that the camera work, so unusual and so powerful, was primarily an intuitive process that required little or no discussion before or during the taping about camera distance, height, or angle: "We worked almost automatically together" (White interview). The results are nearly seamless segments of videotape in which the techniques of the direct cinema or cinema verité mode, such as long, handheld shots and the use of available light and ambient sound, convey an aura of truthfulness, create an effect that what we see is what occurred spontaneously before the camera with little or no authorial intervention and modification.

However, just as the final words of the documentary — the apology quoted from an unidentified staff person in response to Dax's anguished scream during treatment — strike the viewer as both shockingly inadequate and poignantly ironic in the context of such a devastating human catastrophe, so also can those words serve as a reminder

The Medium Is the Message   319

that this documentary about the victim of an accident is itself no accident. The very choice to retain a line that White disclosed was "picked up in the editing" and to use it at the end of the film is significant (White interview). It unmasks the fundamental process of selection and combination at work, a process that produces meaning whether it occurs in language or in image, as well as the informing structure of narrative fiction that was, according to White, the overarching production value: "What we wanted to do was tell the story best" (White interview). However, the question that is neither easily nor simply answered is "Whose story is being told?"

The opening credits of the videotape identify both the pragmatic rationale for the project—the diagnosis of depression—as well as the institutional system within which the project was produced, codified, interpreted, and disseminated: "Videotape Library of Psychiatric Disorders. The University of Texas Medical Branch at Galveston." Most substantive discussions of documentary not only deconstruct the simplistic notion of its observational purity (Winston 2000, 9) and privileged access to the real world (Wayne 1997, 78) but also denote documentary as, first and foremost, an institutional formation whose very discourse reflects our cultural preference for "nonfiction, nonnarrative, instrumental knowledge and 'hard' science [which] complement the engine of progress" and whose very practice reveals the "discursive formations, language games, and rhetorical stratagems by and through which pleasure and power, ideologies and utopias, subjects and subjectivities receive tangible representation" (Nichols 1991, 5, 10). Consequently, *Please Let Me Die* may very well be challenging the institutional tradition it is representing with the videotaped performances of medical paternalism, clinical neglect, and patient dehumanization, but it does so sanctioned by, and in dialogue with, that very tradition. As postmodern theorist and critic Jean-François Lyotard writes:

> An institution . . . always requires supplementary constraints for statements to be declared admissible within its bounds. The constraints function to filter discursive potentials, interrupting possible connections in the communication networks: there are things that should not be said. They also privilege certain classes of statements whose predominance characterizes the discourse of the particular institution: these are things that should be said, and there are ways of saying them. (Lyotard 1984, 17)

I would argue that the very exercise of videotaping Dax Cowart within a clinical environment and among hospital personnel—a setting so discrete and so disconnected from the outside world that, as Chambers

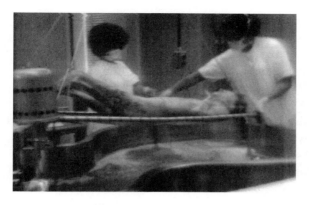

3. Daily immersion in the Hubbard
tank for infection control. *Please Let Me Die*,
University of Texas Medical Branch.

notes, people are transformed into particular, predetermined roles, and their actions have significance only within the setting itself (Chambers 1999, 78–79)—both reifies the dominant power of the institution of medicine and reenacts the objectification of the medical gaze.

Moreover, documentary itself has become an institutional practice informed and guided by its own history, codes, rituals, and ethics. The tension of competing interests or constraints—filmmaker/physician and subject/patient—can be illustrated with the production history of the opening scene of *Please Let Me Die*, in which masked and gowned hospital personnel are preparing Dax, who is naked and immobilized, for immersion in the Hubbard tank (figure 3). While there are some significant close-up shots in this scene, which I will discuss below, camera angle and distance are predominantly eye-level and medium shots. Thus the single image of a helpless patient being attended to by faceless and voiceless staff, the "micronarrative," immediately becomes intellectually recognizable and emotionally familiar placed within images of the "macrocontext" of the clinical setting (Wayne 1997, 89). In addition, the visual construction forges a common linkage between environment and behavior, so that the cold, mechanistic sterility of the hospital both determines and explains what bioethicist Howard Brody describes as the "strikingly callous disregard" of its staff (Brody 1992, 75). Throughout the scene, a radio blares the discordant and disorganized sounds of rock music and the intrusive and ironic chatter of a commercial jingle for Royal Crown Hairdressing, a conditioner for hair and scalp. The overall effect, according to Brody, is that "the place

The Medium Is the Message   321

seems more like an automobile repair shop than a sanctuary for suffering humanity" (75).

Yet White recalls that had he arrived on time for the videotaping, the profoundly effective and affective aural component would simply not have been there: "It was just dumb luck that it was taped that way" (White interview). White was aware that the radio played continuously in the room because the day-to-day experience of caring for suffering patients, often increasing their pain, was "so difficult for the staff that the radio was on for *their* sake, to make *their* work easier," and it was his intent to silence it (White interview). When he realized what had happened, White made the decision to include it because "it was grotesquely fitting," a choice influenced more by a filmmaker's consideration of aesthetic and emotive impact than by a staff physician's concern for either the disingenuous representation of colleagues or the collateral exploitation of a patient.

The events and situations, the actions and issues, of documentary texts take their shape from and through four organizational patterns that Nichols defines as modes of representation: observational, expository, interactive, and reflexive (Nichols 1991, 32). The dominant mode of *Please Let Me Die* is observational, which stresses the nonintervention of the filmmaker and the reliance on editing to enhance the impression of real time (38). Also called direct cinema or cinema verité, this mode is characterized by synchronous images and sounds recorded at the moment of observational filming, such as the opening scene just described, which afford the viewer an opportunity to look in on and overhear the lived experience of others. Four major segments of *Please Let Me Die* are linked with three transitional segments. The first and second segments exemplify the techniques and characteristics of observational documentary while the third segment employs voice-over commentary, a conventional feature of the expository mode. The final segment of the video is a hybrid, combining voice-over commentary and a cinema verité ending.

The first shot of the opening segment is an overhead close-up of rippling water in the Hubbard tank, after which the camera steadies at the conventional eye level in a medium shot to establish setting and circumstance. The second close-up shot comes quickly but not unexpectedly, as the camera has been following the busy and efficient hands of the staff as they remove the bandages that protect the raw and mottled flesh of Dax's body. The second close-up of his scarred feet begins a pattern that will become a kind of hallmark technique of the documentary: the camera moves in to isolate a part of the body, loses focus, gains focus, and remains on the object for a period of time. For example, there will eventually be sixteen close-up shots of Dax's severely injured and shockingly disfigured hands throughout the videotape, a visual effect especially distressing and disorienting to viewers.

In a legal and ethical analysis of the case based solely on *Please Let Me Die*, scholar Robert Burt's own visceral and emotional reactions to the images do not simply color his argument but essentially construct it: our desire to care for a gravely ill or horribly injured person is intertwined with our wish to obliterate him from sight. Because Dax is "terribly maimed," "wholly helpless," "hopelessly remote," and "quite awful to see," Burt believes that he must sense "the revulsion (however involuntary) that his appearance inspired in those who saw him" and be "struggling with the question of whether he deserved to live" (Burt 1979, 1–10). To illustrate, Burt cites Dax's response to White's question about what actions he was taking to secure his release from the hospital: "I'm trying to exhaust every legal means I can find. And I'm working through attorneys and so far I haven't had much luck. It's something that . . . attorneys, at least ethical ones, don't want to touch" (9–10). Burt's interpretation of this comment is Dax's awareness that people would not want to touch *him*, "that others would find him repellent, contemptible, and [wish] him dead" (11). As Chambers notes, Burt's perspective on the case becomes as distorted and as surreal as the unfocused and unsettling close-up shots of Dax's hands (Chambers 1999, 145). The elision of the original remark — from not wanting to touch Dax's *case* to not wanting to touch Dax's *body* — says much about the cumulative power of the graphic images of hands.

Although never explicitly commenting on the number or type of camera shots, bioethicist Sally Gadow writes eloquently about how Dax's virtual loss of his hands creates a situation of altered embodiment that is a condition for morally problematic treatment (Gadow 1989, 154). The clarity of her discussion owes much to the descriptions of how hands receive, enter, and alter the world by deflecting intrusion, wielding tools, or covering nakedness. Her verbal imagery obviously originates in the visual experience of seeing hands that are unable to do any of those things, and her ethical analysis is informed by the empathic experience of observing someone who can neither fend off nor return the gaze of others, including her own: "Exactly because of his inability, [Dax] provides to others almost unlimited possibility . . . through their reconstruction of his body" (155).

More often than not, the recurring close-up shots of Dax's hands are prompted by White's questions regarding actions and choices. Nowhere is the disjunction between autonomy as voluntary choice and autonomy as freedom of action so well represented than through and with these images. For example, during his off-camera account of the accident, White describes what happened just seconds before the explosion: "When you switched the key to the 'on' slot, the whole landscape just went up in one big ball of fire" (Burt 1979, 174). It is then that the camera moves for the first time to Dax's left hand, leaving the viewer to wonder if what is being isolated in the frame and being presented in the shot could ever have engaged in such fine motor skills. These visual emblems of Dax's complete and utter helplessness become even more significant when White questions him about his refusal to sign a consent form or his desire to take his own life. The camera returns again and again to the objects that bear little or no resemblance to hands capable of turning a key, signing a paper, or committing suicide.

In their brief discussion of *Please Let Me Die*, James Childress and Courtney Campbell foreground the conflict between acknowledging Dax's capacity for effective deliberation resulting in voluntary choice and confronting his inability for physically enacting that choice. They posit that because Dax was not autonomous in the sense of free action, "it might be argued that the continuation of treatment was essential to restore his autonomy" (Childress and Campbell 1989, 32). Such a viewpoint would not only serve to justify the unwanted actions of his caregivers but could also serve to explain Burt's ambivalent reaction to the case. Chambers points out that the "separation between the eye and the ear that occurs in *Please Let Me Die*" accounts for the contradiction between Burt's assessment of Dax's competence, which is derived from the aural perspective of the video and his analysis of Dax's regression, which is driven by the visual perspective (Chambers 1999, 145).

The transition from the last shot of the first segment, in which the half-naked, half-submerged body of Dax Cowart floats in the Hubbard tank, is the still photographs of a smiling and dashing pilot posed jauntily at the nose of a jet and at the door to a cockpit. The third and final photo in this series is a close-up profile shot reminiscent of images of the actor James Dean. Here again, the effect is both distressing and disorienting in that the still photographs from Dax's past life seem to be more dynamic and more alive than the actual videotape of his present existence. Stanley Johannesen analyzes the effect of what he identifies as a crucial point in the film's narrative treatment in which the "shroud is whipped aside," unveiling the body of Dax before the accident costumed in the regalia of an American male fantasy: "What does seem clear about the logical structuring of the images in the film is that when the massively damaged body, now stark naked, has allowed us to substitute embarrassed desire with unembarrassed curiosity, we are willing to take the desire to die at face value" (Johannesen 1989, 181).

Johannesen's insight regarding the powerful influence of these juxtaposed images — the "good-looking young man with an excellent future" and the "massively damaged body" — is congruent with Nichols's elucidation of the viewer's experience of observational documentary, which encourages belief and conveys the sense of an unfettered access to the world being represented. The very absence of a filmmaker "clears the way for the dynamics of empathic identification, poetic immersion, or voyeuristic pleasure" (Nichols 1991, 43–44). Thus the immediate and unmediated access to the past, present, and future lives of Dax Cowart provokes in the majority of viewers an impulse to "ditch our ordinary social instinct to skepticism . . . and reach agreement with Dax rather too easily" (Johannesen 1989, 181).

White begins the second segment of *Please Let Me Die*, the interview proper, with the traditional performance of the medical story, the case presentation. His role as expert, as authority, is immediately and definitively established by placing the camera squarely at eye level and framing him head and shoulders in suit and tie with name and credentials. Once his account of the patient moves through the requisite age, gender, and marital status, his description of Dax as "an active, independent person with a mind of his own" is accompanied by, and illustrated with, another series of black-and-white photographs of Dax as a football player, a bronco rider, a jet pilot, a son enjoying outdoor activities such as fishing with his father.

Interview itself is a form of hierarchical discourse that derives from an unequal distribution of power such as interrogation or confession, and when the actual interview commences, the camera position is an overhead shot angled downward, reinforcing the diminishment and subjugation of Dax lying prone in a hospital bed. White's first direct question initiates another visual pattern in the video, this one more conventional, as every time White queries Dax, the camera will continuously zoom in on Dax's face to show the right eye covered by a bandage and the left by skin. The image of Dax's blindness captured by a camera he cannot himself see displays both his desperate helplessness and his terrible exposure. And although White is conspicuously off-camera during most of this segment, the presence of his dominance and control lingers in that his seated position beside the bedside is one familiar to viewers.

The discussion of Dax's request to leave the hospital and go home to die becomes the verbal cue for the third segment of the documentary, a return to the Hubbard tank. Dax's response is certain and clear: "I still want out." Again, the aural expression of willfulness is counterpointed and undermined by the visual representation of powerlessness as what the viewer sees — Dax lying naked in the tank — is contrary to what the viewer hears. What follows as a transitional segment is arguably one of the most ironic and calculated sets of images in the documentary as the camera pans slowly over the caption beneath a yearbook picture of past athletic glory, "Dax Cowart leaps over David Smith for extra yardage," before returning in an overhead shot to the immobile and frail form hanging suspended over the water on the slightly swaying gurney.

The thematic emphasis of the fourth and final segment is pain and suffering. In voice-over commentary, Dax flatly states that "the end result isn't worth the pain involved" as the staff begin the excruciating process of bandaging his legs. There is a medium shot of his naked body followed by a close-up shot of his face contorted in mute agony. Dax's cogent and compelling argument for his own civil liberties is made over a close-up image of his right hand, which is raised in a feeble and futile gesture of protest. In a technical replication of the opening scene that creates visual symmetry and narrative coherence, sound becomes once again synchronous with image as the documentary comes to a close. The noise of the radio is now replaced with Dax's increasingly anguished pleas to go easy. However, the staff remain anonymous and silent until his final cry elicits the muttered apology.

In *The Birth of the Clinic*, Foucault identifies the "perception of resemblances" as one feature of the structural transformation from classical to clinical medicine: "The pictures resemble things, but they also resemble each other" (Foucault 1973b, 6). In reading the images in documentary, we bring with us two kinds of "inculcated conceptual schema": those we use everyday to differentiate between things (a hand? not a hand?) and those specific to cultural artifacts (Wayne 1997, 85). Being alert to the processes of perceiving resemblances and distinguishing differences can illuminate various samples of the viewer response to *Please Let Me Die*. For example, Burt is the first commentator on Dax's case to make an explicit connection between the videotaped depiction of his treatment and the collective nightmare of Nazi persecution: "His entire skeletal frame was starkly emaciated, looking as if he were a survivor of a Nazi concentration camp" (Burt 1979, 8).

Gadow's reliance on the shared cultural experience of either witnessing the documentary record of concentration camps and mass graves or seeing the feature films on the Nazi experience is implicit in her discussion of Dax's story as a case of political torture. And Johannesen foregrounds intertextuality in his discussion, writing that the "example of Nazi Germany so haunts the modern consciousness" that the viewer of *Please Let Me Die* is in danger of unconsciously reacting to these images of forced dehumanization in a clinical setting without consciously remembering that Dax Cowart was not really a victim of ideology, not really a victim of medical experimentation. Simply put, the viewer is in danger of "attending to the wrong lesson" (Johannesen 1989, 174–75). The second documentary, produced a decade later, will present a meticulously constructed argument in an effort to ensure that whatever the outcome for Dax, those watching it will attend to only one lesson: that he ought to have been allowed to die.

Dax's Case (1985)

> It was not the future that I was concerned with;
> it was the present. — Dax Cowart, "Confronting Death"

Viewers of *Please Let Me Die* are usually more than a little concerned and curious about Dax Cowart's future. The documentary ends without any resolution, without any closure. Was Dax successful in his efforts to refuse treatment? Or did he eventually change his mind? Despite his certainty of not wanting "to go on as a blind and a cripple," was he ever minimally rehabilitated? Unanswered questions such as these prompted freelance journalist Keith Burton, who saw the videotape in a bioethics seminar in 1979 at Southern Methodist University, to meet Dax and get the rest of the story. Burton then embarked on a five-year project to produce *Dax's Case*, an hour-long video spanning the time from the summer of 1973 to the fall of 1984 (Burton 1989, 12).

In addition to the filmmaker, other commentators whose writings are collected in a volume under the same title, *Dax's Case*, write of the need to know what happened after *Please Let Me Die* (Burton 1989, 1; Kliever 1989, xv; King 1989, 97). As Nichols points out, when "the 'ordinary' matter of individual death . . . reaches an order of magnitude that requires comment" in a documentary film, viewers expect that while the empathic identification with a character might remain tenuous as it is in fictional film, the intellectual engagement with the issue will gain in prominence and ultimately be mediated by the rhetoric and conventions of objectivity (Nichols 1991, 30). Thus in *Please Let Me Die*, the human elements of the personal story that create the dynamic of narrative suspense underpin the ethical and political issues of the medical story that create the dynamic of problem solving. Our expectations, our felt needs, arise from this emotional and intellectual complex and remain unmet at the end of *Please Let Me Die*. The production of the second documentary attempts to gratify the desire to know what happened as well as to provide an answer to the puzzle. The mode of documentary best designed to relay information, advance argument, and offer solution is the expository mode, the dominant textual form of *Dax's Case*. Its technical features include the use of evidentiary editing, which establishes rhetorical continuity by bringing together the best possible testimony in support of a point and the use of direct address, which efficiently advances the argument and effectively creates an impression of objectivity. Both techniques are prominently displayed in *Dax's Case*. For example, scenes from *Please Let Me Die* are juxtaposed to illustrate Dax's narrative account of the events, his story, and to emphasize the key points of his argument, his case. Further, his commentary as well as the recollections and opinions of others involved (his four treating physicians, his mother, his lawyer, and his friend) are spoken directly to the camera, which is placed in a conventional eye-level medium shot.

Kliever describes the overall effect as that of a "clash of perspectives and sentiments through vivid scenes and conflicting interpretations of Cowart's accident, treatment and rehabilitation" (Kliever 1989, xvi). However, as Chambers notes, the individual segments are edited so that they only appear to be in dialogue with one another; they only appear to clash and conflict. In reality, the videotaped comments are discrete bites that Dax consistently revises or persuasively refutes "to present an argument and a perspective apart from that of the participants" (Chambers 1999, 151). The best visual and rhetorical model for *Dax's Case* is not that of a collage (Winslade 1989, 115) or an interrogation (Kliever 1989, xvii) but rather that of a courtroom drama with its pattern of testimony, rebuttal, and summation. The legal tone and structure are not surprising given that Dax has become a practicing attorney in the years since the first documentary. The two scenes that open the second documentary essentially telegraph his transformation from the naked, helpless patient of the past (the representation of objectification in *Please Let Me Die*) to the professionally costumed, assertive person of the present — the enactment of subjectivity in *Dax's Case*. In fact, the first visual image of Dax in *Dax's Case* is a virtual replication of the first visual image of Dr. White in *Please Let Me Die:* head and shoulders encased in suit and tie above name and credentials. It is an effective beginning to the performance of an individual's visual and verbal usurpation of institutional power, an individual's physical and intellectual assertion of autonomy. And although the viewer will meet Dax's wife and his dog through the course of the videotape, the final image is that of a self-sufficient, self-reliant, and self-contained person sitting all alone, listening to music and sipping a beer.

The expository mode, the primary means of relaying information and making a case on film since the 1920s, inevitably raises the question of voice: is the text speaking more objectively or more persuasively? (Nichols 1991, 34). Persuasion is most readily identified as the dominant trope in a nonfiction film when the project exhibits a singularity of purpose and tone as does *Dax's Case* (Renov 1993, 30). And because the Aristotelian triad of proofs — *logos, pathos, ethos* — are also operative in documentary, the viewer is likely to encounter everything from pie charts that tease the brain to images that tug at the heart such as those extracted from *Please Let Me Die*.

The baseline of persuasion for all nonfiction film, whether it is last night's network news or a propaganda documentary, is the ethical status of the interview subject. In *Dax's Case*, the visual context from which that subject speaks either reinforces or subverts his or her "truth claim" (Renov 1993, 30). For example, Dax himself speaks within various settings that combine to create the visual composition of a dynamic but deliberative life: sitting behind a desk in a fully equipped law office; standing before the backdrop of a pine forest in the unpaved intersection where the accident befell him (the literal and symbolic crossroads in his life); and relaxing before books and stereo in his own study. Ada Cowart's performance is more static, but equally symbolic in that her maternal devotion to the physical and spiritual well-being of her child is enhanced by the domestic accoutrements of a floral sofa, an heirloom clock, and a spinning wheel (the traditional distaff). Although she could never honor her son's request to die, she is presented in a sympathetic and respectful manner.

In contrast are the segments featuring two of the treating physicians, Doctors Baxter and Larson. The environment in which Baxter is taped as he sits in a white coat before a wall of medical slides conveys the kind of clinical detachment and professional neutrality that is most often associated with an old-fashioned and benign medical paternalism. Larson, who opens his interview with a description of Dax as a "difficult patient" whose request to die was not a "reasonable solution," sits before a vivid orange-red wall that reinforces the physician's outrage at what he regards as the open defiance of his professional authority ("It was not a difficult choice for *me*") and the unwelcome challenge to his ethical code ("Don't ask *us* to kill you!").

The singularity of purpose and tone that characterizes the persuasive modality of *Dax's Case* is pictorially represented in the repetitive sameness of the camera shots, making it much less visually arresting and visually interesting than *Please Let Me Die*. As Kliever points out in his preface to the essay collection, *Dax's Case* was primarily designed as a teaching tool and is, in fact, much more accessible and thus more often seen by students and trainees than is *Please Let Me Die*. However, clinical and academic educators frequently edit the hour-long tape, primarily because of its rather monotonous succession of talking heads.

For many bioethicists, what *Dax's Case* has provided is irrefutable evidence to support a critique of medical paternalism and the curative model. For others, it has provided an illustrative fable to meditate on the human experience of suffering and the heroic effort of transformation. And in spite of our learning what happened next, Dax's story is more problematized than simplified by the second videotape, a sentiment that White expresses in an apostrophe to Dax: "You have troubled my mind greatly . . . [you] have made me think about unthinkable problems" (White 1989, 21). The existence of *Please Let Me Die* and *Dax's Case* ensures that we will also remember Dax and will also experience moral uncertainty and emotional uneasiness by virtue of the medium in which we encounter his story.

In *The Evil Demon of Images*, Jean Baudrillard admonishes us to doubt the reference principle of images, "this strategy by means of which they always appear to refer to a real work, to real objects, to reproduce something which is logically and chronologically anterior to themselves. None of this is true" (Baudrillard 1988, 13). However, no question of significance surrounds the videotaped footage of a Dax Cowart or a Rodney King. These are moments that cut through the narrative frames and explanatory nets cast around them, moments that confront the gap between representation and referent and acknowledge the inadequacy of response channeled through the representation itself, despite the enormity of its impact (Nichols 1993, 190–91). These are moments that compel us to look beyond the screen and survey our own cultural landscape in hopes that what we saw really wasn't true after all.

6 Computers

Technologies

Transforming Health Care

X Rays, Computers, and the Internet

JOEL D. HOWELL

Medicine in the United States has changed in amazing ways. Seemingly without end, we have witnessed the introduction of new therapies, new tools, and new techniques for the treatment of disease and the prolongation of life. Computers, in particular, have become a familiar part of human existence. Today we take for granted the notion that computers are helpful for health care and that the Internet is both a source of information and a means for communication. But more has changed than simply the introduction of new tools. It was around the turn of the twentieth century that one of the most significant transformations occurred — the start of the notion, now generally accepted, that science could be, indeed *ought* to be, seen as essential to health care. Now so widely accepted as to be unremarkable, this was at the time quite a radical concept. Throughout most of the preceding years, one could say, as did the noted eighteenth-century U.S. physician Benjamin Rush, that knowing science was simply not an essential tool for an excellent physician. Similarly, our perspective on technology — our widely held belief that technology can be used to improve health care — is itself a rather new proposition.

During most of the nineteenth century, technology was far from a central feature of modern medical care (Reiser 1978). But sometime around the turn of the century, those ideas started to change, aided by the quickly apparent diagnostic utility of the new theory of microbiology, the dramatic graphs and images produced by the invention of new tools such as the electrocardiogram and the x ray, and, a couple of decades into the century, the amazing therapeutic efficacy of new treatments such as insulin. Abraham Flexner's well-known 1910 report to the Carnegie Foundation for the Advancement of Teaching, in which he argued for a more systematic and scientific model of medical education, did not so much create change as reflect what was already coming to be a consensus: that medicine around the turn of the twentieth century had undergone a profound transformation.

Of course, medicine and technology then (and at any other time) can only be understood as part of a larger social context. The United States in the early twentieth century was a land dominated by technology, nonmedical as well as medical. Factories, automobiles, elevators, trains, and airplanes, followed all too soon by the intensive and destructive military technology employed in World War I, all served to emphasize the importance of technology for the American public. Communications technologies such as the telegraph, the telephone, and the typewriter changed how people transferred information from one person to another. No longer did people need to meet face-to-face to share ideas, stories, and business. Given the breadth of technology's impact, it would be a surprise indeed if ideas about medical care did not share in this societal transformation.

Almost a century later came another revolution, centered on a dramatic new means of manipulating and transferring information, an electronic medium that seemed, at first glance, to be completely unprecedented. This essay looks at the historical roots of the Internet. But we might start by wondering if there is any point at all to examining this history. Perhaps the introduction of the Internet is just so new, so dramatic, so revolutionary, so (literally) unprecedented that there is no point to examining what has come before. One hears this argument from time to time surrounding the introduction of a new tool or idea, often heard in the context of someone trying to make a case about the importance of a seemingly novel invention or policy endeavor. Yet even a cursory historical review reveals that we are hardly the first generation to see our own time as one of great change, as one of profound discontinuity with the past. Consider how some of the aforementioned medical innovations entered the stage. In 1882, Robert Koch described the tubercle bacillus and proved that it caused tuberculosis. This discovery was met with widespread amazement and celebration. The methods used to define the cause of tuberculosis were quickly applied to discover the cause of many other diseases caused by many other newly discovered microorganisms, ushering in a radical transformation in the understanding of human disease, with profound consequences for virtually all of humankind. In 1895, Wilhelm Conrad

Röntgen discovered new rays that could penetrate human flesh and produce pictures of the objects therein, images widely reproduced all around the world (and about which I will say more hereafter). In 1921 the team of Fred Banting, Charles Best, John Macleod, and J. B. Collip discovered insulin, a discovery that in early 1922 led to effectively treating people with diabetes, transforming those who had previously seemed condemned to certain debilitation and death into apparently hale and hearty people. Mention of these past events is not meant to suggest that the present is not also a time of unprecedented change. Rather, it is meant to suggest that in those past instances, the scientific and medical world seemed to be rapidly transforming in unprecedented (and sometimes unanticipated) ways. These transformative times have existed before and doubtless will again. Furthermore, in each of these examples, the public reaction (as well as the expert experimentation) was firmly grounded in what had come before.

How should we think about technology as an object of study per se? Historians of technology have made it clear over the past several decades that to study the history of technology, we need to appreciate that "technology" is best understood as being not only a fixed object, an artifact. Technology is also the information needed to use that artifact. In addition, we can conceptualize technology as being a system, an articulated means of arranging people, information, or machines. That system can (and must) encompass a broad swath of human activity.

Part of what gives a new technology broad scope is the way it is considered, and reacted to, by a wide range of the public. It should not be seen as surprising that the invention of dramatic new technologies has usually evoked some sort of a response from society at large. Part of that reaction came from the mass media. Part of that reaction came from the military, from wars and plans to fight more wars. The reaction to each technology has always been a function of the specific set of social circumstances within which the new technology is developed and used. The public reaction, in turn, shapes the way each technology is applied. Thus an inevitable interaction exists between the development of the new technology and public reactions to it.

Historical analysis is of more than merely academic interest, as it often helps us grapple with contemporary issues. As we examine the past, we find that some things that may seem new are, in fact, rather old. Even as we celebrate the grandeur of our newly found powers and seemingly unprecedented knowledge, even as we amaze ourselves with the latest, smallest, fastest device for accessing the Internet from our office, our car, our home, we should take pause and realize that we have been here before. Not exactly here, no; but as we ponder the meanings of this new world, we should consider that this is not the first time (nor is it likely be the last) that a new technology has been seen as transforming the world.

The history of the x ray is, arguably, the most dramatic and fundamentally transforming invention of the twentieth century, if one is willing to place the periodization of the century back five years from the traditional starting date. I will discuss in this essay other technologies that helped lay the groundwork for reactions to the digital computer, used initially as a tool for information processing and only quite a bit later (and somewhat surprisingly, for many who were involved in its development) as the centerpiece for a new and innovative system of communication.

Introduction and Use of the X Ray

In 1895 Wilhelm Röntgen described a new type of ray that could pierce through flesh as well as other solid substances. He called the new rays "x rays" because he did not know what they were made of. On New Year's Day, 1896, he sent a picture of his wife's hand to his friends and colleagues; the world has not been the same since. This event had an impact on both lay and professional conceptualizations of health that is hard to overestimate. In the first year of its existence, the x ray was the subject of more than one thousand medical articles and almost fifty books, a truly phenomenal amount of attention, especially in a world with far fewer medical journals than at the turn of the twenty-first century.

Not only in medical journals was the x ray an ubiquitous sight. One is hard-pressed to go far in any popular publication from 1896 without seeing images of the new rays. This widespread public exposure resulted from the ray's characteristics combined with a fortuitous combination of recent inventions that made the x ray the first medical image to be available in essentially the same form to medical and lay observers alike. At least four reasons made this the case. First, x-ray images were not particularly detailed. While certain subtleties took time to learn how to appreciate, the image was far less complex than, say, the view of an abdomen opened to permit removal of an inflamed appendix, appendectomy being one of the bold new operations current at the same time. The x-ray image was, after all, a shadow and as such did not include the subtleties of color that might distinguish viable from nonviable tissue, or bright arterial blood from the darker-hued venous. Second, as a photograph, the x-ray image was static. Unchanging. No blood oozed. Medical and nonmedical people alike could ponder the image at leisure. Third, the x ray was, as was its reproduction, two-dimensional. When putting the image into a magazine, one did not have to try to represent a three-dimensional perception on a two-dimensional page (as of an opened abdominal cavity). Finally, at around the same time as the x ray's invention, new technology made it possible for popular magazines easily to print black-and-white images. Given the opportunity to include x-ray pictures, most magazines took advantage of the chance to include the new, modern pictures, publishing scores to amaze and delight the eye. Those pictures served to make the x ray part of a change in cultural perceptions of the body that was far more pervasive than merely within the medical world.

Not only changing specific conceptions of the body, the x-ray machine served as the leading edge for the idea that science and technology should be seen as central for health care. I have elsewhere examined in detail how and why the x-ray machine came to be symbolic of modern health care, how it became a part of everyday care for patients, and how it paved the way for what we now see as modern scientific medicine (Howell 1995).

Notwithstanding the dramatic impact of the x ray, I found that its use was not nearly as immediate as some other histories might suggest. It is certainly true that the machine attracted a phenomenal amount of attention. By 1900 use of the x-ray machine was widely described in the standard medical literature as being essential for the diagnosis of fractured bones, as well as several other diagnoses. But how much was it actually being used? To answer that question, I examined more than six thousand systematically selected case records from hospitals in the United States and England, choosing well-established, financially secure hospitals that owned an x-ray machine and employed someone to run the device. In spite of the enormous outpouring of public interest, it was not until almost three decades after the machine's invention that the x ray finally became a part of routine medical care. This observation led to an obvious question: why did it take so long for this seemingly powerful new technology to become an integral part of the health care system? There were several reasons.

Use of the x-ray machine not only required a new set of tools and tubes but also demanded transformation in the fundamental nature of social interactions between providers of health care. Part of that change within an increasingly complex system involved both the need to manage information for clinical care and the (newly important) need to maintain a complex set of financial records. Information technology transformed both the scientific and health care environment. During the early twentieth century, mechanical tools such as the typewriter and the Hollerith card (the precursor to the IBM punch card), as well as conceptual tools such as standardized forms and graphs, were actively imported into medicine from business; those tools transformed health care in ways that continue to reverberate even today and formed the basis for the subsequent development of computer systems. Seeing the history of the x ray as including the history of business technologies also exemplifies the broad way in which many historians of technology have come to define technology itself.

Given the wide public discussion of x rays, it is not surprising that patients were aware of this new development and that issues soon arose concerning the relationship between patient, physician, and x ray. Some of the issues that were raised a century ago are still very much with us today as we work through the appropriate medical use of the Internet. One question had to do with ownership. While early on, x-ray images were made and sold by a wide range of individuals, including photographers, physicists, and even pharmacists, physicians argued with increasing success that to use the new device adequately required some degree of medical sophistication possessed only by physicians. This led to questions about the standing of the image, knowledge, and the patient. Did the patient consult the early-twentieth-century physician to purchase a picture? Or to seek a consultation? Whose x-ray image was it, anyway? Physicians were eventually able to argue successfully that patients consulted physicians for an expert opinion, not to purchase an image. Similar issues of patient data ownership have persisted throughout the century and have recently gained added salience as a result of the ease with which information can be transmitted over the Internet. Who should be allowed to use patient data for purposes such as research? Who owns the data?

Another issue surrounding early x-ray use had to do with effects on the patient-physician relationship. Physicians had previously obtained almost all of the information necessary to care for a patient either from the history — talking to the patient — or from the direct laying on of hands during a physical examination. Examination using tools such as a stethoscope distanced the patient from physician only slightly; they still shared the same basic space. Now, with the x ray, the diagnosis became instrumentally mediated, done at a distance. The image was taken and interpreted far away from the patient. This distanced patient from physician, creating a space that increased with the use of all manner of additional imaging and laboratory tests that soon followed on the 1895 invention of the x ray. There were several effects of this distancing. One was that patients may have felt less connected with their physician, less trusting. Another is that physicians may have started to lose some of their diagnostic skills that were based on direct contact with patient. Today's use of the Internet may also distance patient from physician, with the ultimate consequences at present unknown.

During the early twentieth century, the health care system came to include the need for not only increased information coordination but also increased physical coordination. The new technologies of the telephone and the automobile played a role in enhancing use of technology such as the x ray as well as in changing the very nature of health care. The x-ray machine was relatively immobile, and being able to transport patients via automobile to have an image obtained made it possible for the device to be applied to a wider range of injured people. These two devices were quite self-consciously seen as new technologies that were described and discussed in great practical detail in the medical literature ("Satisfaction in Automobiling" 1912). Both were essential elements in the transition from home-based outpatient care to office-based outpatient care

Communications Technologies

At about the same time as the x ray was invented, a number of other devices came into existence. They were seen in some instances as being part of the same system as the x-ray machine, or as sharing some of the same characteristics. In most instances, however, they were more reminders for Americans in the late nineteenth century and the early twentieth that theirs was a faster-moving and more intensive age. This idea helped to frame the overall stage into which technologies would be understood and utilized, as well as setting the stage for the even more rapid form of communication that was to become the Internet.

Before the introduction of the telegraph to the United States in 1844, the speed at which information could travel was limited to the speed at which a human being could travel, whether on horseback or on foot or on the relatively new railroads, carrying information to tell or carrying letters to read. The telegraph enabled information to flow much faster than ever before, albeit only where the telegraph lines existed. The information also traveled only in a coded form, which required someone at either end who could encode and decode the messages. As a result, telegraphy was relatively expensive. Nonetheless, its speed made it an intensively used means of communication, especially for railroads and some other industries.

In 1876 the telephone, invented by Alexander Graham Bell, enabled communication via voice, not by coded signals, yet at the same speed as the telegraph. In order for the telephone to be an effective means of communication, a set of economic and technological problems needed to be solved. In 1878 the first telephone exchange was built in New Haven, but automatic switchboards were not a significant part of the system until the 1920s. By 1900, 1.5 million telephones were in service. Once it became operational, the telephone allowed for easier coordination among an increasingly specialized group of physicians and other health care providers. Previously, patients could only find out if a physician was available for consultation by traveling to her or his office. Once there, they often were directed to yet another house, where the physician would be making a house call, perhaps using an automobile if not a horse to traverse the distance. With the telephone, one could call and see if the physician was available and thus coordinate bodies moving at faster speeds and enhance patient care.

The telephone, unlike the telegraph, both provided voice communication and went directly into people's houses. In so doing, the telephone raised concern about the invasion of privacy. It was, after all, an instrument that could ring people up in the "very bosom of their families" ("Scientific Inquisitors" 1896). Questions of privacy gained added salience with the operator placing calls, or with people sharing party lines. The telephone forced the creation of a new set of rules for social engagement, wonderfully described in the Lynds' classic 1929 sociological study, *Middletown*. In some ways, the telephone brought people closer together, allowing a "semi-private, depersonalized means of approach to a person of the other sex." On the other hand, the phone made people farther apart, as instead of visiting — so called "dropping in" — people might now simply ring someone up on the phone.

Other means of communicating were used more locally. In 1876 the phonograph record was invented by Thomas Edison, who designed it as a device to place a spoken message on a telephone line by making indentations on a strip of metal foil. In 1887 Emile Berliner modified the device, which led a decade later to the development of a flat disc that has come to be called a "record." This tool was also seen as a threat to privacy because it could register and reproduce the "most intimate of domestic confidences" ("Scientific inquisitors" 1896). But the device was also used as the basis for dictating machines to be used in offices, allowing for more efficient communication between the people composing the information and the people creating the message, the latter group often using typewriters, of which I have more to say in the next section.

Information-Manipulating Technologies

Tools to manipulate information have always been a part of medical practice. When computers entered the medical world, they could not help but be seen in relationship to the sorts of ways that information had previously been manipulated. Those devices may seem ordinary and unremarkable — and indeed they may be so — but each device has a history, and that history both reflected and shaped a larger context. Even the pencil — seemingly an ordinary and unremarkable device — has a long, rich history that includes decisions about how to get the lead inside the pencil, how to make a pencil that would not roll off the table, how to design an eraser that would work with the available paper. Later came a world of mechanical pencils, which solved questions about how to sharpen the pencil but raised new ones about the manufacturing necessities for both the pencil and the carefully designed lead (Petroski 1990). These decisions were not made with medical record keeping in mind, but they certainly had an impact on the ability of people to keep careful and accurate records.

The typewriter brought a whole new set of issues to the fore, well described by JoAnne Yates (1989, 39–45). There had long been attempts to use machines to produce some sort of written record, but only in the second half of the nineteenth century did typewriters start to become readily available in a form resembling the modern device. Sold by Remington starting in 1874, for prices ranging from $25 to $50, they could only type capital letters. In 1878 Remington started to sell a typewriter that could type lowercase letters as well. Early users of the device included court reporters, lawyers, editors, and members of the clergy, soon followed by businesspeople. The popularity of the machine grew, and by the turn of the twentieth century almost 1.5 million had been sold.

The typewriter was in many ways a direct precursor to the Internet. For one, the typewriter enabled text to be produced at a much more rapid rate of speed. Instead of the 24 words per minute produced by handwriting, a person using a typewriter could reach as high as 120 words per minute with the aid of touch typing, invented in the 1880s. An average speed was more likely to have been in the range of 80 words per minute, still quite a bit faster than handwriting. The typewriter created consistent, readable text and became an essential part of any modern business. Commentary on the introduction of the typewriter seems reminiscent of more recent commentary on the introduction of word processing. "Five years ago the typewriter was simply a mechanical curiosity. Today its monotonous click can be heard in almost every well regulated business establishment in the country. A great revolution is taking place and the typewriter is at the bottom of it" (Yates 1989, 41).

The typewriter created a way of producing a written record that was obviously quite a bit different from handwriting. Designers made decisions surrounding the way the keyboard should look, how the keys were to be laid out, how one would move from capital letters to lowercase. All of these decisions created something that was to be the basis years later for the computer keyboard, something that looks like (but is profoundly different from) the original typewriter keyboard.

Moreover, the typewriter separated the act of creating the information contained in a document and creating the document itself. In so doing, it gave birth to a new type of clerical worker, one whose numbers grew rapidly. U.S. Census figures show a dramatic increase in the number of people employed as stenographers, typists, and secretaries, from not even 50,000 in 1890 to more than .75 million people — mostly women — in 1920. This burgeoning occupational class allowed a clear status and gender distinction between the person who was thinking about the issues (typically male) and the person who was physically creating the document (typically female), a distinction that would reappear at the end of the century as a means of some physicians resisting what they saw as a lower-status task.

In addition, the very physical document that typewriters produced signaled a new, modern way of creating a report. It was clean and legible and, with the aid of tools such as carbon paper, could easily be created in multiple copies, each of which would share at least some of the crispness and sharpness of the original. Like the Internet, using the typewriter required some additional tools and supplies, such as the ribbon and, if one desired, carbon paper. The typewriter was soon taken up by health care institutions, most notably the hospital, where it came to symbolize what was new and modern and the very best about a hospital.

Number-Manipulating Technologies

Businesses in the early twentieth century found themselves having to deal with more and more numbers, often (but not exclusively) financial. Much as the typewriter allowed for faster and more legible creation of text documents, so, too, advances in accounting technology allowed for more efficient creation and manipulation of numerical data. Whereas accountants in the nineteenth century had typically done their sums by hand (sometimes in a Dickensian environment), the invention of recording adding machines enabled sums to be done much faster, as well as creating a written record of the results. Money and information could thus be managed in an ever larger set of businesses. The same desire for easily obtainable quantitative information led Herman Hollerith to invent the punched card that bears his name. That input device came to be better known as an IBM punch card, which was used to input information into early computers. Those computers grew out of earlier attempts to manipulate numbers. Other attempts had been made to create a calculating machine, some going back to the early years of the nineteenth century with Charles Babbage's attempt to create a machine to produce tables, which he called a "difference engine." Computing devices were only one facet of new ways of dealing with numerical information. Forms, charts, and cost accounting were also part of the new technology, self-consciously described as new inventions for the modern business owner of the 1910s and 1920s.

While developments of calculating machines had up to this point been driven largely by peacetime finances, some of the next set of changes were motivated by wartime needs, both current and anticipated. During World War II people attempting to use guns carried on battleships, tanks, and airplanes found accurately aiming the devices required that they had to do some fairly intensive calculations. Aiming could be done with a set of complicated tables, but even with the most advanced calculators then available, each table took several months to complete. In 1942 a faculty member at the University of Pennsylvania suggested that an electronic calculator based on vacuum tubes could accomplish the calculations much more rapidly. The suggestion did not bear fruit until after the end of the war (during which time the initial problem had been solved by the brute force solution of simply hiring more people). What eventually was created was termed ENIAC, for electronic numerical integrator and computer. It was large enough to fill a squash court, had more than 17,000 vacuum tubes, and weighed thirty tons. But it could add 5,000 ten-digit numbers in one second, and this set it apart from any calculating device previously created. ENIAC was designed as a general-purpose calculator, one that could be applied to work on all manner of problems. It served as the forerunner of the explosion in computing power that followed, fueled in part by a military striving for world dominance during the Cold War, in part by technological advances such as the transistor in 1947 and the microprocessor in 1971. Although not the first commercial maker of computers, IBM came to dominate the market, starting with the model 650 computer, introduced in 1953. By renting its computers at deep discounts to universities, IBM made sure that its machines were at the center of the new field of computer science. They succeeded. By the 1960s, IBM computers dominated the market. Punch cards came to be replaced by tape; individual programming replaced by prepurchased programs. Computers became increasingly (and simultaneously) smaller and ever more powerful.

So what existed in the 1950s was a number of (by the standards of the time) very high performance calculating devices. Over the subsequent decades, these devices were not used as much for health care as some thought would be ideal. Writing in the late 1980s, computer expert and historian Bonnie Kaplan identified three historical periods for ideas about how medical computing lagged. Prior to the mid-1960s, concerns were focused on appropriate use of the computer as a research tool. From the late 1960s to the early 1970s, the emphasis shifted from research to patient care. From the early 1970s, the lag was seen to be one having to do with rationalization and social optimization.

But all of this was to soon change. The use of computers was transformed from a collection of data-manipulating devices into the basis for what we have come to know as the Internet, an application broad enough to be part of a book such as this on the media. The story of this most unlikely transformation of number crunching to mass communication has been well told by the historian Janet Abbate. This history is worth sketching out because, if nothing else, it serves as a corrective to the natural (but profoundly ahistorical) tendency to see the present as a natural and logical result of some sort of rational process. To see the computer in the 1960s as some sort of communication device would have been almost inconceivable. The roots of the Internet came from a desire by the U.S. military to rationalize the use of expensive, high-powered computing machinery supported by the U.S. Department of Defense's Advanced Research Projects Agency (ARPA). Designed to allow researchers to use computer facilities at distant sites, the initial network connected computers purchased by ARPA and was known as ARPANET. Another goal of the network was to enable the military to communicate effectively throughout the world, a failing that had come into focus during the 1962 Cuban Missile Crisis. In an attempt to create a robust system, the people who designed ARPANET made use of a new but key innovation called packet switching, which was intended to help the computer network survive an enemy attack. The essential nature of the system was to be decentralized and flexible (although not too flexible — one goal of the network, at least in the early years, was to keep overly inquisitive graduate students away from tinkering with the system). The broad vision of early network pioneers had limits. Systems developers did not see commercial applications as an important part of the nascent network.

Historians have come to recognize the importance of users in shaping technology, and the history of the Internet is no exception. Set up to facilitate resource sharing, the network was to assume a very different role through the development of e-mail. The idea of e-mail was dismissed as unimportant in a 1967 analysis and came along almost by happenstance in the 1970s. Had it not, "the network might be remembered today as a minor failure" (Abbate 1999, 106). The use of e-mail was initially encouraged by financial administrators who were early adopters — those who worked in the system came to learn (as others have since then) that e-mail offered an easy access to people in power. As e-mail came to be a dominant use of the system, ARPANET underwent a radical transformation from a network primarily designed for resource sharing to one increasingly used for all manner of communications.

In the 1970s ARPANET became the Internet. The new system continued to reflect its military origins in the selection of technical means of communications. It also reflected the new availability of personal computers, starting with the world's first personal computer, the Altair 8800, introduced for $379 in 1975. The explosive growth of the Internet as a place for Web browsing came about in a setting of decentralized authority and a tradition of user activism. Once the Internet came under civilian control and expanded accessibility, it grew rapidly, from about 2,000 computers with access to the Internet in 1985 to 30,000 in 1987 and 159,000 in 1989. The expansion was informal and uncontrolled. In 1990 ARPANET was decommissioned and connections shifted over to a system run by the National Science Foundation. Other networks such as USENET joined in, again often with the goal of communication between geographically diverse users. Abbate places the first incarnation of the Web in 1990. Subsequent growth was explosive at the very least. In 1993 there were sixty-two Web servers; a year later there were more than one thousand. The decentralized system permitted nearly constant and unpredictable change. Any numbers that one could provide as evidence for the Internet's popularity would be out of date long before this chapter sees the light of day. Suffice it to say that the Internet has become a ubiquitous part of American society, and there is no reason to believe that this trend will abate anytime soon.

Historical Present and Present History

Having thought a bit about the history of the Internet, we can start to see some historical continuities with what has come before and speculate about the role of the Internet in media communications of the future. Communications technologies have been actively imported into the health care system for some time. It should not be a surprise that the form of a technology dictates, to some extent, what will and can be done with it. In some instances, those technologies came from the worlds of business and finance. In the case of the Internet, the new communications technology came from roots that were more military. With hindsight, one can identify certain characteristics of its origins that had a major impact on the ways that the Internet has been used as a media tool. It is a flexible, decentralized technology, one created at the outset to operate free of any firm, overriding control. The original intent was to protect the system from enemy attack; today's outcome is that media presented on the Internet can be produced by multiple authors. Perhaps one of the most important results of the system was that end users could easily become publishers. "Self-publishing" is easy. Anyone can put up a Web site; anyone call tell his or her story to thousands (or hundreds of thousands, or millions) of people. The stories that result may be very personal and very compelling but also run the risk of being very misleading, in the general genre of "I was saved from cancer by [fill in the blank]." Misleading information abounds; accurate information abounds. Attempts to systematize or standardize medical information on the Internet are under way, but such efforts run counter to the very raison d'être of its original creation.

Another result of the Internet's inherent flexibility is that it can as-

346 JOEL D. HOWELL

sume many forms. It has been easy to add features—multimedia, sound, video—which have added immeasurably to the power of a technology that was barely in existence only a decade ago and that now reaches millions of people worldwide. Remember that e-mail as a network function was initially overlooked, perhaps because people at the time emphasized the primary use of the network as being resource sharing. Who can predict what applications we are overlooking today?

Technologies can be profoundly destabilizing of social relationships. The x ray for a time threatened to take control of medical information away from physicians and give it to photographers or patients. E-mail can destabilize relationships between health care providers and patients. Patients can not only search for information but also search for any sort of media through which to learn. Information about drugs is easy to come by. Medline was once expensive and slow; now it is fast and free. Patients come in to see their physicians with diagnostic criteria in hand. The Internet thus enhances patient autonomy even as it breaks down hierarchies.

The Internet also carries with it some clear advantages for physician-patient communication. Because it doesn't require sender and receiver to be available at the same time, it enables physicians to interact with patients at times convenient to each. It is instantaneous. It is profoundly diversifying. One can send a message to several addresses at once. E-mail is profoundly different from other forms of communication. It exists everywhere at once—you can read and answer e-mail from the office or on vacation, and the person sending it knows not where you picked it up or from where you are answering. On a more mundane but (alas) no less practical note, e-mail goes far to solve problems having to do with faulty handwriting.

Despite what some people see as significant advantages for patients and caregivers alike, some physicians have nonetheless vigorously resisted the use of the Internet for communication with patients. Some are concerned about the lack of reimbursement for time spent reading and answering e-mail, while others are concerned about potential litigation for advice given over the Net to patients unseen. Some physicians may simply be jaded by multiple unfulfilled promises about the future of computing, as in the persistent failure to create effective computer-assisted diagnosis.

But some of the reason for vigorous resistance to the use of e-mail and the Internet to communicate with patients may be rooted in long-term resonances of status differentials that were originally established by the typewriter. The typewriter enabled physicians to dissociate the creation of knowledge from the creation of the document. It soon became the case that dictation, whether taken on steno pads over Dictaphone machines or over a phone line, was something created by a physician and taken by clerical staff, and the physical document was also created, whether (initially) on a typewriter or (much later) on a word processor by someone of lesser status than the physician. The two tasks — creating the knowledge and creating the document — became separated and came to signify different levels of status and skill. Today physicians who are otherwise willing to learn skills of far greater difficulty insist that they do not, cannot, and absolutely will not learn how to type, expressing these views with a passion that bespeaks a more profound concern, that typing is somehow a function of lower status than the exalted one to which they would like to aspire. They are, however, willing to use software that translates speech into text on the computer screen, indicating a willingness to use new technology as long as it resembles the older forms of status hierarchy. This sort of division may not survive. As the Internet becomes part of the societal fabric, it may come to be the case that we will see patients "dragging their doctors along" to the Internet (Kassirer 2000).

The Internet may break down hierarchies of knowledge production, which has heretofore been dominated by a handful of academic, urban medical centers. The health policy expert John Eisenberg refers to electronic records as potentially marking a two-way street, establishing electronic networks of physicians who can then do research on actual practice. This sort of proposed use of the Internet hearkens back to ideas espoused around the turn of the century by the eminent Scottish physician Sir James Mackenzie, who left a prestigious London hospital position for a small Scottish village because he felt that only in smaller communities could one truly make progress in the understanding and treatment of disease. Mackenzie and Eisenberg both have ideas that are reminiscent of the original purpose of the Net, as means of resource sharing.

The Internet may enhance other hierarchies. Availability of the Internet mirrors in its intensity what we already know to be true about many features of American society. There are clear class distinctions around who has access to the Internet and what sort of access they have, be it measured in speed or simply ease of access (it is one thing to have a DSL line at home that is always on; it is quite another to have to go down to your local public library in order to search on-line). There is not a match — nor would one think that there would necessarily be one a priori — between people who are ill and those who have access to the Internet. Older people have more disease; younger people tend more to be on the Net. People with chronic disease tend to be more in need and also tend to be older. But history gives hope — the system may adapt.

There are clear dangers to communication on the Net. Far more goes on in the doctor-patient relationship than merely the conveyance of information from one person to another. Even the very entrance of the physician into the examining room creates a whole set of expectations, a kind of entrance music, well before any words are spoken (Caldicott 1998). That entrance music is silenced by the Internet. Or perhaps it assumes a different form. Technology can change relationships between physician and patient. One concern, raised for the x ray as well as many other technologies, was that technology would distance patient from physician. But some technologies, such as the telephone and the automobile, have brought physician and patient together. Another concern is that physicians would lose their physical diagnosis skills; similar concerns were raised with the x ray. But the x ray could be used to teach anatomy and physician diagnosis; Internet multimedia can help students learn about the heart sounds and the diagnosis of rashes. Technologies are what we create out of them.

There are dangers to privacy through use of the Internet. When you are speaking face-to-face with someone, you not only get all sorts of nonverbal communication; you also know, for sure, with whom you are speaking. Furthermore, you know that your voice, the sounds you are making, will be gone when you finish speaking. An Internet posting may persist far longer than the writer would prefer. Framing of communication on the Internet will present patients and physicians alike with a whole new way of interacting.

During the past century we have come to welcome a world based on science and technology. It has been said that the most profound technologies are those that disappear. Who thinks about computer networks when drawing money out of an ATM, or checking in at the airport, or paying for gasoline directly at the pump with a credit card? That disappearance may be the ultimate fate of the Internet for health care media. The day may soon come when Internet-based media are wholly unremarkable.

During the twentieth century, technology has come to play an ever increasing role in medicine. At the turn of the century, most people, patients and physicians alike, simply saw no relevance of technology for most of medical care. Starting with the x ray, a technology with tremendous transformative power, other technologies have entered the world of health care delivery. This essay has attempted to trace one set of connections among these many ways of looking at medicine, showing how the power of the x ray to change ideas about the relationships between humankind and machines served to set the stage for what was to follow, a world that has eventually come to include powerful computing machines and a network connecting those machines initially designed for one purpose but now routinely used for communication by an increasingly larger segment of society.

The Shape of Things to Come

Surgery in the Age of Medialization

TIMOTHY LENOIR

Media inscribe our situation. We are becoming immersed in a growing repertoire of computer-based media for creating, distributing, and interacting with digitized versions of the world, media that constitute the instrumentarium of a new epistemic regime. In numerous areas of our daily activities, we are witnessing a drive toward fusion of digital and physical reality; not the replacement of the real by a hyperreal, the obliteration of a referent and its replacement by a model without origin or reality as Baudrillard predicted, but a new playing field of ubiquitous computing in which wearable computers, independent computational agent-artifacts, and material objects are all part of the landscape. To paraphrase William Gibson's character Case in *Neuromancer*, "data is being made flesh."

Surgery provides a dramatic example of a field newly saturated with information technologies. In the past decade, computers have entered the operating room to assist physicians in realizing a dream they have pursued ever since Claude Bernard: to make medicine both experimental and predictive. The emerging field of computer-assisted surgery offers a dramatic change from the days of individual heroic surgeons. Soon surgeons will no longer boldly improvise modestly preplanned scripts, adjusting them in the operating room to fit the particular case at hand. To perform an operation, surgeons must increasingly use extensive 3-D modeling tools to generate a predictive model, the basis for a simulation that will become a software surgical interface. This interface will guide the surgeon in performing the procedure.

These developments in surgery date back to the 1970s, when widely successful endoscopic devices appeared. First among these were arthroscopes for orthopedic surgery, available in most large hospitals by 1975, but at that point more a gimmick than a mainstream procedure. Safe surgical procedures with such scopes were limited because the surgeon had to operate while holding the scope in one hand and a single instrument in the other.

What changed the image of endoscopy in the mind of the surgical community and turned arthroscopy, cholecystectomy (removal of the gallbladder with instruments inserted through the abdominal wall), and numerous other endoscopic surgical techniques into common operative procedures? The introduction of the small medical video camera attachable to the eyepiece of the arthroscope or laparascope was an initial major step. French surgeons were the first to develop small, sterilizable, high-resolution video cameras that could be attached to a laparoscopic device. With the further addition of halogen high-intensity light sources with fiber-optic connections, surgeons were able to obtain bright, magnified images that could be viewed by all members of the surgical team on a video monitor rather than just by the surgeon alone. This technical development had consequences for the culture of surgery; it contributed to greater cooperative teamwork and opened the possibility for surgical procedures of increasing complexity, including suturing and surgical reconstruction done only with videoendoscopic vision (Périssat, Collet, and Belliard 1990, 1–5; Dubois et al. 1990, 60–62). French surgeons performed the first laparoscopic cholecystectomy in 1989. A burgeoning biomedical devices industry sprang up almost immediately to provide the necessary ancillary technology to make laparoscopic procedures practical in local hospitals, such as new, specialized instruments for tissue handling, cutting, hemostasis, and many other applications.

Due to their benefits of small scars, less pain, and a more rapid recovery, endoscopic procedures were rapidly adopted after the late 1980s and became a standard method for nearly every area of surgery in the 1990s. Demand from patients has had much to do with the rapid evolution of the technology. Equally important have been the efforts of health care organizations to control costs. In a period of deep concern about skyrocketing health care costs, any procedure that improved surgical outcomes and reduced hospital stays interested medical instrument makers. Encouraged by the success of the new videoendoscopic devices, medical instrument companies in the early 1990s foresaw a new field of minimally invasive diagnostic and surgical tools. Surgery was about to enter a technology-intense era that offered immense opportunities to companies teaming surgeons and engineers to apply the latest developments in robotics, imaging, and sensing to the field of minimally invasive surgery. While pathbreaking developments had occurred, the instruments available for such surgeries allowed only a limited number of the complex functions demanded by the surgeon. Surgeons needed better visualization, finer manipulators, and new types of remote sensors, and they needed these tools integrated into a complete system.

Telepresence Surgery

A new vision emerged, heavily nurtured by funds from the Advanced Research Projects Agency (ARPA), the NIH, and NASA, and developed through contracts made by these agencies with laboratories such as the Stanford Research Institute (SRI), the Johns Hopkins Institute for Information Enhanced Medicine, the University of North Carolina Computer Science Department, the University of Washington Human Interface Technology Laboratory, the Mayo Clinic, and the MIT Artificial Intelligence Laboratory. The vision promoted by Dr. Richard Satava, who spearheaded the ARPA program, was to develop "telepresence" workstations that would allow surgeons to perform telerobotically complex surgical procedures that demand great dexterity. These workstations would re-create and magnify all of the motor, visual, and sensory sensations of the surgeon as if he were actually inside the patient. The aim of the programs sponsored by these agencies was eventually to enable surgeons to perform surgeries such as certain complex brain surgeries or heart operations not even possible in the early 1990s, improve the speed and surety of existing procedures, and reduce the number of people in the surgical team. Central to this program was telepresence-telerobotics, allowing an operator the complex sensory feedback and motor control he would have if he were actually at the work site, carrying out the operation with his own hands. The goal of telepresence was to project full motor and sensory capabilities — visual, tactile, force, auditory — into even microscopic environments to perform operations that demand fine dexterity and hand-eye coordination.

The Shape of Things to Come   353

Philip Green led a team at SRI that assembled the first working model of a telepresence surgery system in 1991, and with funding from the NIH, he went on to design and build a demonstration system. The proposal contained the diagram shown in figure 1, showing the concept of workstation, viewing arrangement, and manipulation configuration used in the surgical telepresence systems today. In 1992 SRI obtained funding for a second-generation telepresence system for emergency surgeries in battlefield situations. For this second-generation system, the SRI team developed the precise servo-mechanics, force-feedback, 3-D visualization and surgical instruments needed to build a computer-driven system that could accurately reproduce a surgeon's hand motions with remote surgical instruments having five degrees of freedom and extremely sensitive tactile response.

In late 1995 SRI licensed this technology to Intuitive Surgical, Inc., of Mountain View, California. Intuitive Surgical furthered the work begun at SRI by improving on the precise control of the surgical instruments, adding a new invention, EndoWrist, patented by company co-founder Frederic Moll, which added two degrees of freedom to the SRI device — inner pitch and inner yaw (inner pitch is the motion a wrist performs to knock on a door; inner yaw is the side-to-side movement used in wiping a table) — allowing the system to better mimic a surgeon's actions; it gives the robot ability to reach around, beyond, and behind delicate body structures, delivering these angles right at the surgical site (figure 2). Through licenses of IBM patents, Intuitive also improved the 3-D video imaging, navigation, and registration of the video image to the spatial frame in which the robot operates. The system employs 250 megaflops of parallel processing power.

A further crucial improvement to the system was brought by Kenneth Salisbury from the MIT Artificial Intelligence Laboratory, who imported ideas from the force-reflecting haptic feedback system he and Thomas Massie invented as the basis of their PHANTOM system, a device invented in 1993 permitting touch interactions between human users and remote virtual and physical environments.[1] The PHANTOM is a desktop device that provides a force-reflecting interface between a human user and a computer. Users connect to the mechanism by simply inserting their index finger into a thimble. The PHANTOM tracks the motion of the user's fingertip and can actively exert an external force on the finger, creating compelling illusions of interaction with solid physical objects. A stylus can be substituted for the thimble, and users can feel the tip of the stylus touch virtual surfaces. The haptic interface allows the system to go beyond previous instruments for minimally

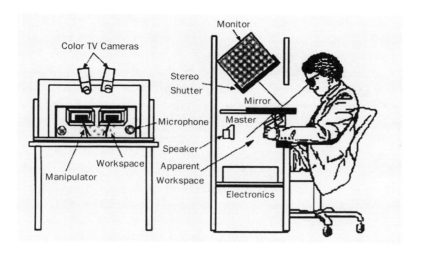

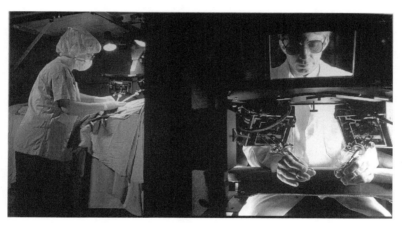

(top) 1. Philip Green, schema for force-reflecting surgical manipulator.
Stanford Research Institute, Menlo Park, Calif., 1992.
(bottom) 2. Philip Green, force-reflecting surgical manipulator. *Time*,
special issue, fall 1996.

invasive surgery (MIS). These earlier instruments precluded a sense of touch or feeling for the surgeon; the PHANTOM haptic interface, by contrast, gives an additional element of immersion. When the arm encounters resistance inside the patient, that resistance is transmitted back to the console, where the surgeon can feel it. When the thimble hits a position corresponding to the surface of a virtual object in the computer, three motors generate forces on the thimble that imitate the feel of the object (figure 3). The PHANTOM can duplicate all sorts of textures, including coarse, slippery, spongy, or even sticky surfaces. It also reproduces friction. And if two PHANTOMs are put together, a user can "grab" a virtual object with thumb and forefinger. Given advanced haptic and visual feedback, the system greatly facilitates dissecting, cutting, suturing, and other surgical procedures, even those on very small structures, by giving the doctor inches to move in order to cut millimeters. Furthermore, the interface can be programmed to compensate for error and natural hand tremors that would otherwise negatively affect MIS technique.

The surgical manipulator made its first public debut in actual surgery in May 1998. From May through December 1998, Professor Alain Carpentier and Dr. Didier Loulmet of the Broussais Hospital in Paris performed six open-heart surgeries using the Intuitive system.[2] In June 1998, the same team performed the world's first closed-chest videoendoscopic coronary bypass surgery completely through small (1 cm) ports in the chest wall (figure 4). Since that time more than 250 heart surgeries and 150 completely videoendoscopic surgeries have been performed with the system. The system was given approval to be sold throughout the European Community in January 1999.

Computer Modeling and Predictive Medicine

A development of equal importance to the contribution of computers in the MIS revolution has been the application of computer modeling, simulation, and virtual reality to surgery. The development of various modes of digital imaging in the 1970s, such as CT (which was especially useful for bone), MRI (useful for soft tissue), ultrasound, and later PET scanning have made it possible to do precise quantitative modeling and preoperative planning for many types of surgery. Because these modalities, particularly CT and MRI, produce 2-D "slices" through the patient, the natural next step (taken by Gabor Herman and his associates in 1977) was to stack these slices in a computer program to produce a 3-D

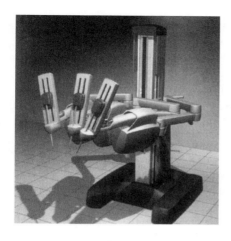

3. Intuitive surgical
DaVinci computer-assisted
robotic unit. Promotional
material, Intuitive
Surgical, Palo Alto, Calif.,
1999.
4. Endoscopic bypass
surgery, Paris, 1999, using
Intuitive Surgical system.
Photograph from Intuitive
Surgical press releases.

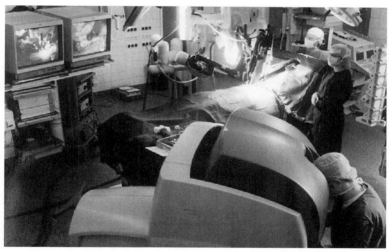

visualization (Herman and Liu 1977, 155–60). Three-dimensional
modeling first developed in craniofacial surgery because it focused on
bone, and CT scanning was more highly evolved. Another reason was
that in contrast to many areas of surgery where a series of 2-D slices —
the outline of a tumor, for example — give the surgeon all the information he needs, in craniofacial surgery the surgeon must focus on the
skull in its entirety rather than on small sections at a time.

Jeffrey Marsh and Michael Vannier pioneered the application of 3-D
computer imaging to craniofacial surgery in 1983 (Vannier, Marsh,
and Warren 1983, 263–73). Before their work, surgical procedures

The Shape of Things to Come 357

were planned with tracings made on paper from 2-D radiographs. Frontal and lateral radiographs were taken, and the silhouette lines of bony skull edges were traced onto paper. Cutouts were then made of the desired bone fragments and manipulated. The clinician would move the bone fragment cutout in the paper simulation until the overall structure approximated normal. Measurements would be taken and compared to an ideal, and another cycle of cut-and-try would be carried out. These hand-done optimization procedures would be repeated until a surgical plan was derived that promised to yield the most normal-looking face for the patient.

Between 1983 and 1986, Marsh, Vannier, and their colleagues computerized each step of this 2-D optimization cycle (Vannier, Marsh, and Warren 1983, 179–84; Marsh, Vannier, and Stevens 1985, 279–91; Knapp, Vannier, and Marsh 1985, 391–98). The 3-D visualizations overcame some of the deficiencies in the older 2-D process. Two-dimensional planning, for instance, is of little use in attempting to consider the result of rotations. Cutouts planned in one view are no longer correct when rotated to another view. Volume rendering of 2-D slices in the computer overcame this problem. Moreover, comparison of the 3-D preoperative and postoperative visualization often suggested an improved surgical design in retrospect. A frequent problem in craniofacial surgery is the necessity of having to perform further surgeries to get the final optimal result. For instance, placement of bone grafts in gaps leads to varying degrees of resorption. Similarly a section of the patient's facial bones may not grow after the operation, or attachment of soft tissues to bone fragments may constrain the fragment's movement. These and other problems suggested the value of a surgical simulator that would assemble a 3-D interactive model of the patient from imaging data, provide the surgeon with tools similar to engineering computer-aided design tools for manipulating objects, and allow him to compare "before" and "after" views to generate an optimal surgical plan. In 1986 Marsh and Vannier developed the first simulator by applying commercial CAD software to provide an automated optimization of bone fragment position to "best fit" normal form (Marsh et al. 1986, 441–48; Vannier and Conroy 1989, 22–32; Vannier 1990, 139–47; Vannier and Marsh 1992, 193–209). Since then customized programs designed specifically for craniofacial surgery have made it possible to construct multiple preoperative surgical plans for correcting a particular problem, allowing the surgeon to make the optimal choice.

These early models were further extended in an attempt to make them reflect not only the geometry but also the physical properties of bone and tissues, thus rendering them truly quantitative and predictive. R. M. Koch, M. H. Gross, and colleagues from the ETH Zurich, for example, applied physics-based finite element modeling to facial reconstructive surgery (Koch et al. 1996, 421–28). Going beyond a "best fit" geometrical modeling among facial bones, their approach is to construct triangular prism elements consisting of a facial layer and five layers of epidermis, dermis, subcutaneous connective tissue, fascia, and muscles, each connected to one another by springs of various stiffness. The stiffness parameters for the soft tissues are assigned on the basis of segmentation of CT scan data. In this model each prism-shaped volume element has its own physics. All interactive procedures such as bone and soft tissue repositioning are performed under the guidance of the modeling system, which feeds the processed geometry into the finite element model program. The resulting shape is generated from minimizing the global energy of the surface under the presence of external forces. The result is the ability to generate highly realistic 3-D images of the postsurgical shape. Computationally based surgery analogous to the craniofacial surgery described earlier has been introduced in eye surgeries; in prostate, orthopedic, lung, and liver surgeries; and in repair of cerebral aneurysms.

Equally impressive applications of computational modeling have been introduced into cardiovascular surgery. In this field, simulation techniques have gone beyond modeling structure to simulating function, such as blood flow in the individual patient who needs, for example, a coronary bypass surgery. Charles A. Taylor and colleagues at the Stanford Medical Center have demonstrated a system that creates a patient-specific three-dimensional finite element model of the patient's vasculature and blood flow under a variety of conditions (C. Taylor et al. 1999, 231–47). A software simulation system using equations governing blood flow in arteries then provides a set of tools that allow the physician to predict the outcome of alternate treatment plans on vascular hemodynamics. With such systems, predictive medicine has arrived.

Medical Avatars: Surgery as Interface Problem

Such examples demonstrate that computational modeling has added an entirely new dimension to surgery. For the first time, the surgeon is able to plan and simulate a surgery based on a mathematical model that reflects the actual anatomy and physiology of the individual patient. Moreover, the model need not stay outside the operating room. Several groups of researchers have used these models to develop "augmented reality" systems that produce a precise, scalable registration of the model on the patient so that a fusion of the model and the 3-D stereo camera images is made. The structures rendered from preoperative MRI or CT data are registered on the patient's body and displayed simultaneously to the surgeon in near to real time. Intense efforts are under way to develop real-time volume rendering of CT, MRI, and ultrasound data as the visual component in image-guided surgery. Intraoperative position sensing enhances the surgeon's ability to execute a surgical plan based on 3-D CT and MRI by providing a precise determination of his tools' locations in the geography of the patient. This procedure has been carried out successfully in removing brain tumors and in a number of prostatectomies in the Mayo Clinic's Virtual Reality Assisted Surgery Program (VRASP) headed by Richard Robb.

In addition to improving the performance of surgeons by putting predictive modeling and mathematically precise planning at their disposal, computers are playing a major role in improving surgical outcomes by providing surgeons opportunities to train and rehearse important procedures before they go into the operating theater. By 1995, modeling and planning systems began to be implemented in both surgical training simulators and in real time surgeries. One of the first systems to incorporate all these features in a surgical simulator was developed for eye surgery by MIT robotics scientist Ian Hunter (figure 5). Hunter's microsurgical robot (MSR) system incorporated features described earlier such as data acquisition by CT and MRI scanning, use of finite element modeling of the planned surgical procedure, and a force-reflecting haptic feedback system that enables the perception of tissue cutting forces, including those that would normally be imperceptible to the surgeon if they were transmitted directly to his hands (Hunter et al. 1993, 265–80).

Surgery demands an interface. The surgeon is on the outside. The targeted anatomy is on the inside. Minimally invasive laparoscopic surgery is typically performed by making a small incision in the patient's body and inserting a long-shafted instrument. At the far end of the shaft is the working tip of the instrument, which contacts the target anatomy inside the patient. At the near end of the shaft is the mechanism (typically finger loops) handled by the surgeon outside the patient. The mechanism outside the patient is the master component that controls the action of the slave mechanism inside the patient. The shaft provides a physical link or interface between master and slave. But

5. Ian Hunter, microsurgical robot. *Presence: Teleoperators and Virtual Environments* 2, no. 4 (1993).

laparoscopic systems have a number of problems. While minimally invasive laparoscopic surgical methods permit smaller entry incisions, the entry point fulcrum inverts hand movements, limits degrees of freedom, and amplifies tremor, making the surgery more difficult. Robotic systems combining virtual reality interfaces with haptic feedback such as Hunter's prototype and a similar system developed by researchers at the University of Washington's Human Interface Technology Laboratory (HIT Lab) can overcome these problems with minimally invasive laparoscopic methods (Oppenheimer and Weghorst 1999). By performing the procedure with a robot, one can numerically remap the relationship between the surgeon and the instruments. The surgeon's head and hand movements are tracked by the system. The system performs inverse kinematic transformations so that the artifacts of the fulcrum point are effectively bypassed, making the surgeon's movements appear to drive the instruments as if he were literally present at the site of the surgical procedure. This provides more direct manipulations resembling those of open surgery while maintaining the benefits of minimal incision. By controlling the articulated endoscope with the surgeon's head movements and feeding the endoscopic image back to a head-mounted display, one gives the surgeon the impression

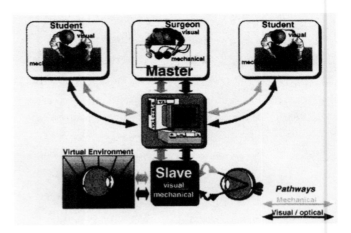

6. Graphic showing "fade in" of student surgeons. I. W. Hunter et al., "A Teleoperated Microsurgical Robot and Associated Virtual Environment for Eye Surgery," *Presence: Teleoperators and Virtual Environments* 2, no. 4 (1993): 271.

of being immersed into the patient's body. Additional scaling transformations and tremor filtering map large movements by the surgeon to smoothed accurate microsurgical movements by the robot.

Immersive robotic surgical interfaces fusing the haptic environment with 3-D stereo camera images fed to a head-mounted display give the surgeon the perspective of being placed inside the patient's body and shrunk to the scale of the target anatomy. Such systems are valuable as training devices. As if in a flight simulator, the surgeon can rehearse his procedure on the model he has constructed of the individual patient. In addition, the model can be used as a training site for student surgeons, copresent during a practice surgery, sharing the same video screen and feeling the same surgical moves as the master surgeon. But such systems can also be deployed in a collaborative telesurgery system, allowing different specialists to be faded in to take the controls during different parts of the procedure (figure 6). Indeed, a collaborative clinic incorporating these features was demonstrated at NASA-Ames on 5 May 1999 with participants at five different sites around the United States.

Such demonstrations point to the possibility in the not too distant future of a new type of operating theater. In place of the all too typical scene of the crowded operating theater with assistants and technicians, we could expect to see a lone surgeon seated at an operating console powered by Silicon Graphics Infinite Reality Engines potentially communicating simultaneously with participant surgeons located at distant sites, with on-line access to virtual reference tools, including a library of distributed virtual objects, and the data banks of the National Institute of Health's Digital Human via the Scaleable Coherent Interface on Fiber Channel at eight gigabits per second. Although seated alone at his console, the surgeon would actually be assisted by a team of surgeons and support technicians in an OR with whom he is virtually present; they would see him as he performs the delicate surgery with them.

The scenario envisioned five to ten years in the future by the National Research Council's Committee on Virtual Reality Research illustrates how future surgeons may be trained to use these surgical interfaces. In a discussion of the use of VR in training heart surgeons, VR researchers describe how haptic augmentation can correct the tremors of the hand as it guides a scalpel over a beating heart:

> Jennifer Roberts . . . is training to become a surgeon and is at her SE [surgical environment] station studying past heart operations. . . . This system includes a special virtual-heart computer program obtained from the National Medical Library of Physical/Computational Models of Human Body Systems and a special haptic interface that enables her to interact manually with the virtual heart. Special scientific visualization subroutines enable her to see, hear, and feel the heart (and its various component subsystems) from various vantage points and at various scales. Also, the haptic interface, which includes a special suite of surgical tool handles for use in surgical simulation (analogous to the force-feedback controls used in advanced simulations of flying or driving), enables her to practice various types of surgical operations on the heart. As part of this practice, she sometimes deliberately deviates from the recommended surgical procedures in order to observe the effects of such deviations. However, in order to prevent her medical school tutor (who has access to stored versions of these practice runs on his own SE station) from thinking that these deviations are unintentional (and therefore that she is poor material for surgical training), she always indicates her intention to deviate at the beginning of the surgical run.
>
> Her training also includes studying heart action in real humans by using see-through displays (augmented reality) that enable the viewer to combine normal visual images of the subject with images of the beating heart derived (in real time) from ultrasound scans. . . .
>
> . . . In all of these operations, the surgery was performed by means of a

surgical teleoperator system. Such systems not only enable remote surgery to be performed, but also increase surgical precision (e.g. elimination of hand tremor) and decrease need for immobilization of the heart during surgery (the surgical telerobot is designed to track the motion of the heart and to move the scalpel along with the heart in such a way that the relative position of the scalpel and the target can be precisely controlled even when the heart is beating).

The human operator of these surgical teleoperator systems generally has access not only to real-time visual images of the heart via the telerobotic cameras employed in the system, but also to augmented-reality information derived from other forms of sensing and overlaid on the real images. Some of these other images, like the ultrasound image mentioned above are derived in real time; others summarize information obtained at previous times and contribute to the surgeon's awareness of the patient's heart history.

All the operations performed with such telerobotic surgery systems are recorded and stored using visual, auditory, and mechanical recording and storage systems. These operations can then be replayed at any time (and the operation felt as well as seen and heard) by any individual such as Jennifer, who has the appropriate replay equipment available. Recordings are generally labeled "master," "ordinary," and "botched," according to the quality of the operation performed. As one might expect, the American Medical Association initially objected to the recording of operations; however, they agreed to it when a system was developed that guaranteed anonymity of the surgeon and the Supreme Court ruled that patients and insurance companies would not have access to the information. This particular evening, Jennifer is examining two master double-bypass operations and one botched triple-bypass operation. (Durlach and Mavor 1995, 25–26)

This scenario builds its vision of the future from systems like Hunter's microsurgical robot. Among the many remarkable features in this account, perhaps one of the most salient for my purposes is the medialization and simultaneous rewriting of human agency depicted. The committee focuses on the utility of the system for teaching purposes. In Hunter's system, multiple participants can be faded in and faded out so that they actually feel what the surgeon directing the robot feels. But here a reverse video effect seems to set in: it is difficult to determine who is in control, robot system or human. A human team clearly programs the robot, but the robot enhances perception and actually guides the hand of the surgeon, correcting for errors due to (human-generated) hand tremor. The guiding hand of the microsurgical system "trains" Jennifer's erratic movements.

Surgery in an Age of Medialization

The microsurgical systems I have sketched here are by no means wild fantasies of techno-enthusiast surgeons. After little more than a decade of serious development, many of these systems are already in use in select areas in Europe, and several have been approved for clinical trials in the United States. To be sure, these developments are by no means a large movement in contemporary medicine; they constitute a fraction of funds spent on medical development. Nevertheless it is intriguing to ponder the conditions that would lead them to be implemented more widely and the consequences entailed for both patients and surgeons were these technologies to become widely adopted. Let's begin by considering the arguments of proponents of the systems and the economic and political pressures that support their efforts.

Proponents of these new systems advance arguments based on claims for cost-saving measures the new technologies permit as a result of less invasive procedures and improved recovery chances of patients due to limitation of blood loss during surgeries that are more accurately planned and more precisely executed. Proponents also point to more efficient use of costly facilities through telepresence and the improvement of training regimes for surgeons. Such arguments question our tolerance for high error rates in surgeries (greater than 10 percent in some areas), whereas in other areas of risk, such as pilot training for commercial airlines, we would find even a 2 percent error rate intolerable. In the case of pilot error, one reason for the low incidence of error is arguably the availability of high-quality simulation technology for training.

A salient feature of contemporary health care is its attention to designing health care plans, diagnoses, and therapies targeted for the individual patient. This coincides with the demand for greater involvement by individuals in decisions related to their own health. The new surgical techniques map onto these concerns for individually tailored therapies. As I have suggested, the new modeling and simulation tools enable the design of procedures based on actual patient data rather than on generic experience with a condition — procedure x is what you do in situation y. Dynamic simulation and modeling tools enable surgeons to construct alternative surgical plans based on actual anatomic and physiological data projected to specific outcomes in terms of life-style and patient expectations. Proponents argue that the new surgical tools take the guesswork out of choosing a procedure specific to the case at hand. Such outcomes not only increase patient satisfaction but reduce costly repetition of procedures that were not optimized on the first pass.

The downside of this greater precision for the patient, of course, is increased surveillance. It is ironic that while the new technology brings the capability to design therapies — including drugs — specifically tar-geted for the individual, hence freeing the individual from infirmity and disease in a way never before imagined, it does so most efficiently and cost-effectively by instituting a massive system of preventive health care from genome to lifestyle. In the age of medialization, your lifestyle is medicalized.

It is not difficult to see how the surgical systems explored here would mesh with such a system. The systems I have discussed deploy anatom-ical overlays and patient-related data as aids to the surgical procedure, but other layers of augmentation can be foreseen. Analogous to the insertion of material constraints, cost factors, and building code reg-ulations in current CAD-CAM design tools, surgical simulators could be augmented with the list of allowable procedures the patient's HMO authorizes, and within this list various treatment packages could be prescribed according to a benefit plan. Currently in a number of states, hospitals and managed care facilities that receive reimbursement from Medicaid dollars are required to treat patients with a prioritized list of diagnoses and procedures, ranked according to criteria such as life expectancy, quality of life, cost effectiveness of a treatment, and the scope of its benefits. The Oregon Health Plan, which first implemented this system, ranked 700 diagnoses and treatments in order of impor-tance. Items below line 587 are disallowed (Kassirer 1995; Boden-heimer 1997a, 1997b). Currently in facilities such as emergency rooms a staff supervisor examines the treatment prescribed by staff physi-cians, and decisions to ignore the guidelines require the prescribing physician to produce a formal written justification. Physicians are re-luctant to confront this additional layer of bureaucracy, particularly since the financial risks incurred by denial of Medicaid funding can be a potential source of friction with the management of the HMO em-ploying them. In the future, the appropriate constraints and efficiency measures could be preprogrammed into the surgical treatment plan-ning simulator.

The new computer-intensive, highly networked surgical systems I have explored also carry consequences for the discipline of surgery and for the agent we call "surgeon." In the age of heroic medicine, the days before the advent of the corporate health care system, surgeons were celebrated as among the most autonomous of professional agents. Society granted these demigods of the surgical wards great status and autonomy in exchange for their ability to bring massive amounts of scientific and medical knowledge to bear in a heartbeat of surgical practice.[3] These guys (since surgeons were overwhelmingly males) had the proverbial right stuff, agency par excellence. But in the telerobotics systems examined here, the surgeon function dissolves into the ever more computationally mediated technologies of apperception, diagnosis, decision, gesture, and speech. The once autonomous surgeon-agent is being displaced by a collection of software agents embedded in megabits of computer code. How is this possible?

Consider the surgeon planning an arterial stent graft before the advent of real-time volume rendering. He used a medical atlas — or perhaps more recently a 3-D medical viewer — in combination with echocardiograms, CAT scans, and MRI images of his patient. At best the surgeon dealt with a stack of two-dimensional representations, slices separated by several millimeters. These were mentally integrated in the surgeon's imagination and compared with the anatomy of the standard human. Through this complex process of internalization, reasoning, and imagining, the surgeon "saw" structures he would expect to be seeing as he performed the actual surgery, a quasi-virtual surgical template in his imagination. The surgeon worked as the head of a team in the operating room with anesthesiologists, and several surgical assistants, but the surgeon mentally planned and executed the surgery himself or herself. No matter how you slice it, the position of the surgeon as an autonomous center of agency and responsibility was crucial to this system.

In the new surgical paradigm, the surgeon first begins with the patient data set of MRI, CAT, and other physiological data. He or she enters that data into a surgical model utilizing a variety of software and data management tools to construct a simulation of the surgery to be performed. An entire suite of software tools enables the construction of such a simulation depending on the type of procedure to be performed. The Virtual Workbench, Cyberscalpel, and various systems for interfacing anatomical and physiological data with finite element modeling tools are all elements of this new repertoire of tools for preparing a surgery. A surgical plan is constructed listing the navigational coordinates, step-by-step procedures, and specific patient data important to keep in mind at critical points. The simulation is, in fact, an interactive hypermedia document.

Voxel-Man provides a particularly clear illustration of this hypertextualization of the surgical body (Höhne et al. 2001). The key idea underlying the approach is to combine in one single framework a computer-generated spatial model linked to a complete atlas with textual description of whatever detail is necessary for every volume element in all the anatomical structures along the path of a surgery. These constituents differ for the different domains of knowledge, such as structural and functional anatomy. The same voxel (volume pixel element) may belong to different voxel sets with respect to the particular domain. The membership is characterized by object labels that are stored in "attribute volumes" congruent to the image volume, including features such as vulnerability or mechanical properties, which might be important for the surgical simulation. Also included can be patient-specific data for that particular region, such as the specific frames of MRI or CAT data used to construct the simulation.

Such intelligent volumes are not only for preparing the surgery, or later for teaching and review. Built into the patient-specific surgical plan, the hypertext atlas assumes the role of surgical companion in an "augmented reality" system. In Hunter's surgical manipulator, for example, various pieces of information — patient-specific data, such as MRI records, or particular annotations the surgical team had made in preparing the plan — appear in the margins of the visual simulation indicating particular aspects of the procedure to be performed at the given stage of the surgery. The surgeon team and the procedures it designs are thus inscribed in a vast hypertext narrative of spatialized scripts to be activated as the procedure unfolds.

Well before we enter the operating room of the future, it is clear that the surgeons are going to be significantly reconfigured in terms of skills and background. Two processes are driving that reconfiguration: medialization and postmodern distributed production. Key to medialization is the externalization of formerly internal mental processes, the literalization of skill in an inscription device.[4] This process is abundantly evident in the introduction of new media technologies in surgery, such as computer visualization, modeling and simulation modules, and computer-generated virtual reality interfaces for interacting with the patient's body. Whereas various aspects of the visualization and presurgical planning took place in the surgeon's well-trained imagination, those mental skills are now being externalized into object-oriented software modules; and the surgeon's delicate manual dexterity acquired through years of training is being coded into haptic interface modules that will accompany, guide, and in many cases assist the surgeon in carrying out a difficult procedure. How will all this affect the heroic subject we have called surgeon? Will that new techno-supersurgeon be an upgrade on the last generation of heroic surgeon? Such a surgeon would undoubtedly have background knowledge in the texts and practices of anatomy, biochemistry, physiology, and pathology, including some traditional practices from earlier generations. But he or she will require familiarity, if not hands-on experience, in new fields such as biophysics, computer graphics and animation, biorobotics, and mechanical and biomedical engineering. He or she will also need to be aware of the importance of network services and bandwidth issues as enabling components of surgical practice. Obviously, it is unrealistic to assume that the last generation's heroic surgeon is going to come repackaged with all these features, any more than next year's undergraduates are going to show up to math class with slide rules. If we have learned anything about postmodern distributed production, it is to expect flat organizational structures, distributed teamwork, and modularization. Thus, given the complexity of all these fields, surgical systems will likely come packaged as turnkey systems. Many surgeons will be operators of these systems, performing "routine" cardiac bypass surgeries implementing predesigned surgical plans from a library of stored simulations owned by the company employing them. I am not saying that surgeons will simply become technicians or that surgery will cease to be a highly creative field. What I am saying, however, is that creativity will be of a different sort as many of the functions now internalized by surgeons get externalized into packaged surgical design tools, just as computer-aided design packages such as Autocad, 3-D Studio Max, or Maya have reconfigured the training, design practices, and the creativity of architects. Some surgeons with access to resources will undoubtedly engage in high-level surgical design work, but that process will be highly mediated in teamwork involving software engineers, robotics experts, and a host of others.

Other specialties connected with surgery will be similarly altered by the medialization of surgery. Consider the impact on radiology. The radiologist has been crucial to the surgeon's ability to carry off such a complex surgery prior to the age of medialization. Like the surgeon, the radiologist has been a highly valued and relatively autonomous agent. As a key professional in the surgical design process, the radiologist would make x rays and more recently CAT, MRI, or various other types of scanning modalities appropriate to the diagnosis of a suspected disease. Examining a dozen or so images, or more recently a hundred or so slices of a CAT or MRI scan, the radiologist would prepare a diagnostic report for the surgeon. Like the similar skill of the physician, the radiologist's diagnosis was heavily dependent on acquiring keen mental skills of observation for detecting artifacts and spotting lesions or other abnormalities that would be the subject of the report. But the relative autonomy of the radiologist and his or her relationship to the diagnostic and surgical design process will certainly change in the near future. As real-time computer-generated imaging becomes the norm, software tools for visualization and automated segmentation of tissues will displace the radiologist as interpreter of the data. Indeed, pressures are already mounting in this direction as the manufacturers of imaging systems such as GE, Siemens, and Brücke install systems that rapidly generate more than one thousand images rather than a few dozen slices. Radiologists are under siege by an explosion of new data. Given the cardinal rule of data processing that valuable data should not go unused, the segmentation of this data into tissues, organs, and other anatomical structures, together with the detection of abnormalities, is becoming a problem for software automation. As automated tools for handling the explosion of imaging data arrive, the radiologist will undoubtedly reorient his or her professional activity and training to focus on new problems, such as construction of surgical simulations. To do so, radiologists will work closely with computer programmers and software engineers. Needless to say, if radiology as a medical specialty survives, the background, types of knowledge, and training of its practitioners will be radically different.

Should we deplore these developments? Many feel that the increase in technical mediation of surgery I have discussed here, together with its attendant changes in organization, financing, careers, and personnel, is one more step in the direction of the dehumanization of medicine by the advance of technology. To many, just describing these systems is in some sense to celebrate them, whereas our role as medical humanists should be to critique and wherever possible resist the technical interface driving a deeper wedge between caring doctors and their patients. While sympathetic to these views, I wonder where we might locate the moral high ground to fashion such a critical framework. The problem, as I see it, is that there is no "there" there to critique. The episodes I have treated illustrate that while the rapidity with which these changes are taking place may suggest creeping technological determinism, this is hardly the case. Each of the technical steps I have described involves negotiations among a large network of actors, machines, and markets.

The technology involved draws simultaneously on military-sponsored research in simulation, networking, and robotics while at the same time depending on imaging technologies driven by price reductions deriving from the entertainment industry, particularly improvements in 3-D computer graphics by leading-edge companies supplying the videogame industry such as Nvidia. The component technologies driving this surgical revolution are rapidly becoming ubiquitous. They are embedded in so many facets of our lives — from the tools of our workplaces, to our cell phones and personal digital assistants, to our means of entertainment — that it is impossible to identify the "good guys" and "bad guys." No less problematic are the values motivating the changes. Who can find fault with the professed goal of expanding the range of operable conditions, reducing blood loss and dangers from infection, and improving recovery times through advanced endoscopic procedures? Or given the enormous costs of health care, who has a problem with the goal of making medical care efficient through training and simulation exercises linked to diagnostic and surgical procedures profiled to meet the needs of the specific individual? Haven't these goals always been the proper motivations of caring, humane medicine?

Perhaps more problematic for identifying a critical high ground is the phenomenon I have called "medialization." By this term I have sought to call attention to the ways in which the medical body is being redefined as the digital body. From stem cells to fully developed organisms, digital media provide the interface for medical intervention. But media are not transparent devices — and new media, with their increased involvement of all the senses, perhaps less so than previous media configurations. Media not only participate in creating objects of desire; they are desiring machines that shape us. Through medialization we come to desire the digital medical body. Media inscribe our situation: it is difficult to see how we can teleport ourselves to some morally neutral ground.

Notes

1 For background on the PHANTOM system, see the information at http://www.sensable.com.
2 For technical reports and news updates on the stages in development and approval of the Intuitive system, see the archive section of the Intuitive Surgical, Inc., Web site: http://www/intuitivesurgical.com.

3   The classic sources on this point are Freidson 1970; Larson 1977; Rosenberg 1987; Starr 1982.

4   André Leroi-Gourhan (1964) and others have pointed out that a key feature in the construction of new media is the externalization of mental processes in an inscription device or system of inscription. The relation of phonetic script to speech is the classical example of this phenomenon, but as Friedrich Kittler and others have pointed out, the process is evident in other inscription technologies. See Kittler 1988; Derrida 1976. For an excellent overview of the problem, see Wellbery 1988.

Medicine.com

The Internet and the Patient-Physician Relationship

FAITH MCLELLAN

Patients who seek medical information from the Internet often pro-
voke strong reactions among doctors. These "wired" patients have
been documented in medical charts as "Internet-positive"; "e-literate"
consumers have been called a threat to doctors ("E-literate Patients"
1999); and one physician doubtless spoke for many others when he
indignantly exclaimed that "armed with the information available on
the Internet, many people may believe they can just be their own primary care provider!" (Scherger 2002).

On the other hand, some physicians welcome this development. The
Internet can relieve them of duties to provide lengthy education and
ongoing emotional support, especially to patients with chronic diseases. These wired doctors see the Internet as a useful clinical partner in
patient management. For them, the medium is not merely a passive
information source but has become an active force in reshaping the
professional-lay relationship. The knowledge it provides is powerful,
creating a kind of "presence" that has been called a third party in the
examining room (Pergament 1999).

Doctors' dichotomous reactions reflect the reality that patients' involvement with the Internet has both drawbacks and advantages. It
remains to be seen whether the Internet is primarily a "threat to [doc-
tors'] clinical autonomy" or "a resource to promote a partnership in
care" (Hardey 1999). Whatever its long-term effects, it is clear that the
electronic medium is changing the patient-physician relationship. The
Internet has called into question seemingly impregnable notions about
the province of professional or specialized knowledge, exclusive access
to which has long been at the heart of clinical practice (Hardey 1999;
Giddens 1991). Because it provides patients with unparalleled access
to information — in many cases, the same information that profes-

sionals have — the Internet has become a leveling force between patients and doctors, tipping the balance of power toward patients.

The Electronic Intersection

Patients, physicians, and the Internet come together in a number of ways. Four uses of the medium have a particular bearing on the relationship between doctors and patients: the Internet as an information resource, as a creator of community, as a communication tool, and as the basis of new technologies, such as telemedicine.

Many laypeople, consulting an eclectic variety of sites before and after doctor visits, use the Internet to get basic information about diseases and conditions. This searching may take place in the privacy of the patient's own home, the atmosphere of which is obviously different from that of the time-pressured clinical encounter. Here patients seek answers to questions they might be hesitant to raise in a face-to-face encounter. Although the scenario is a common dream of creators of electronic patient information, there is little evidence to suggest that doctors and patients consult electronic resources together in the examining room. Anecdotally, this goal is thought to founder on two grounds: doctors' reluctance to consult reference material in front of patients, and the extremely limited consultation time in an era of managed care. Thus patients are more likely to use the Internet as preparation before they see a doctor, or to reinforce information gleaned during the visit. In addition, they may use the Internet to find a doctor, using directories or professional associations, or, more controversially (to physicians, at least), through sites that rate physicians using various criteria, including survey data from patients (D. Adams 2001).

The type of information patients are seeking covers a spectrum. In a survey of randomly selected patients from one primary care practice, 54 percent of patients reported that they had used the Internet to get medical information, primarily for information about nutrition or diet, drug side effects, complications of treatment, or complementary and alternative medicine (Diaz et al. 2002). More significantly for the patient-physician relationship, patients also used the Internet to obtain second opinions. Further, 60 percent of the Internet users believed the information they found was the same as, or better than, information they got from their doctors. Patients said it was more convenient and less expensive to get information on-line. A few offered other explanations, saying that their doctors did not have enough time to educate them, were not open to discussion, or did not understand their concerns (Diaz et al. 2002, 183). Based on these results, Diaz and his coauthors recommended that physicians ask patients, as part of history taking, whether they use the Internet to get medical information, and that physicians be able to suggest Web resources and help patients evaluate the quality of Internet information (a development sometimes called "information therapy" [Chin 2002], "patient informatics" [Bader and Braud 1998], or "consumer health informatics" [Eysenbach 2000]). The authors did not address concerns about the time and resources required to implement their recommendations.

The resources patients use often extend beyond simple background. The National Library of Medicine (NLM), recognizing that patients want reliable sources of quality information, in 1998 created MED-LINEplus, a database of health information for the general public (Lindberg 2001). In addition to information on diseases and conditions (culled from NLM and National Institutes of Health [NIH] sources, among others), the site contains drug information and links to directories of hospitals and physicians, medical dictionaries and encyclopedias. Searchers may also go beyond resources created for laypeople to those aimed at professionals. One resource to which they now have access is MEDLINE, the NLM's database of references to more than 12 million articles in more than 4,300 biomedical journals. Here laypeople have direct access to information written by and for scientists and health professionals.

The professional literature patients are consulting is not limited to research articles in individual peer-reviewed journals. They are also reading, and in some cases contributing to, synoptic resources that synthesize and critique the best available research evidence for clinical practice. The international Cochrane Collaboration, for example, publishes systematic reviews of all randomized controlled trials; these reviews are produced by expert collaborative review groups who, through database and hand searches of the medical literature, evaluate and summarize the evidence that does or does not support prevention and treatment strategies for many health conditions ("The Cochrane Collaboration" 2002). Because one of the Cochrane principles is wide participation, laypeople participate in the review groups. These consumers have also formed a network that translates Cochrane reviews for laypeople and coordinates reviews related to consumers' interaction with health care ("The Cochrane Collaboration Consumer Network" 2002).

In addition, patients are creating a literature of their own, in individual electronic narratives of illness (McLellan 1998), on support group sites, and in collaborative efforts such as DIPEX ("Database of Individual Patient Experiences" 2002), which is organized by condition. DIPEX contains interviews with patients, audio and video clips of patients' stories, and many resource links. By virtue of their involvement with these kinds of electronic resources, patients are no longer mere recipients of information. Instead they have become working participants in its creation.

Patients can also use the Internet to find clinical trials for which they might be eligible, thus bypassing traditional routes of getting to such information. At ClinicalTrials.gov, also a service of the NLM and the NIH, patients can search a large database of clinical research studies. Other commercial ventures, some in partnership with pharmaceutical companies, provide similar databases, which describe protocols and entry criteria and provide contact information so that interested patients can determine their eligibility for enrollment in trials. By using these databases, patients may well know more about the range of available experimental options than do their physicians.

Second opinions are also available on-line. One recently announced service, created as a partnership of several Boston hospitals, enables patients to get a virtual second opinion by having their primary care physician formally request a review of their case by a specialist ("Welcome to Partners Online Specialty Consultations" 2002). An e-consult costs $600 and is not covered by insurance. Further, unlike sites offering similar services, this one uses the patient's own doctor as a funnel: the specialist gives the second opinion directly to the doctor, who discusses the results with the patient. Direct contact with the patient may not be allowed on account of licensing regulations that govern the practice of medicine across state lines.

Finally, patients armed with electronic information may in effect become research assistants to their doctors. An article in the *Medical Journal of Australia* recounts the case of an expectant couple whose fetus was diagnosed antenatally with two different diseases, which when the child was born were changed to a definitive third diagnosis of a rare syndrome. By this time, the Internet-savvy parents had uncovered a great deal of information that turned out to be useless, "which negated the worth of their Internet searches and eroded their confidence in the attendant specialists" (Pemberton and Goldblatt 1998). Their doctors, who were at this point themselves looking for advice on the Internet, used this turn of events to employ the parents as information gatherers. The doctors emphasized to the parents that, owing to their workload, information they forwarded to them had to be selective. The parents then located resources that were ultimately useful for their baby's clinical management; in addition, they were able to e-mail photographic documentation of the baby's condition, reducing the number of required clinic visits. The physician-authors concluded that the Internet provides an avenue for teamwork and collaboration between patients and families and physicians.

These examples demonstrate that the information patients are seeking and creating on-line is of many types and may be used for a variety of purposes that may directly and profoundly affect the patient-physician relationship. Patients are using electronic resources in partnership with physicians, or to supplement or supplant the advice they receive from them, or possibly to bypass a personal physician altogether.

A second way patients are using the Internet is to create community. Support and self-help groups providing anecdotal information, resources for practical help, and emotional outlets are ubiquitous on the Web. This outgrowth of the electronic medium is neither original nor specific to health and medical topics, but it may be an important factor in a clinical relationship. Patients often find such groups independently, but physicians also refer patients to them. The emotional support provided by Internet discussion groups is especially valuable in settings of rare or chronic diseases (Zrebiec and Jacobson 2001). The Internet provides one of the few, and now easiest, ways for affected patients and families to find each other, an evolution that one woman with Takayasu's arteritis says "has transformed the definition of community for the patient with a rare disease" (Patsos 2002).

Unfortunately, on-line support groups may also attract people with considerable psychopathology. There are a number of documented cases of patients feigning illness in electronic forums, a situation that has been termed "virtual factitious disorder" or "virtual Munchausen by proxy" (Feldman 2000, 669).

A third use of the medium for doctors and patients is, not surprisingly, e-mail. However, this communication method has proved more problematic and controversial in medicine than in many other settings. Although one study showed that patients want to be able to e-mail their doctors and would be willing to change doctors to do so (Miller and Reents 2002), many physicians are reluctant to correspond with patients by e-mail, unconvinced that it will improve patient care without becoming an unmanageable (and unreimbursed) administrative burden. In a Harris poll released on 10 April 2002, patients said that in addition to communicating with their doctor, they wanted to be able to ask questions when an office visit was unnecessary, schedule appointments, refill prescriptions, and receive the results of laboratory testing electronically (Taylor and Leitman 2002). About one-third of respondents said they would be willing to pay for these services. A majority of respondents said the availability of electronic services would influence their choice of health plans and doctors.

Doctors are worried about becoming overwhelmed with trivial questions and are concerned that they cannot be reimbursed for the time spent consulting with patients electronically, and that patients in emergent situations will use e-mail instead of appropriate means of emergency contact. From the patient's perspective, though, e-mail communication can be less emotionally burdensome than actually talking with a doctor in person. One oncologist remarked that "many patients will say in print what they won't say to me in person" (Stewart 2002). Indeed, e-mail received in advance of a patient's office visit may help establish a conversational agenda. And as a practical matter, better communication between doctors and patients may lead to decreased litigation (Kane and Sands 1998).

E-mail between patients and doctors raises important questions about privacy and confidentiality that are more significant than for other types of electronic transactions. Physicians are sometimes also counseled to obtain informed consent from patients for the use of e-mail. The informed consent document would describe "permissible transactions and content," anticipated turnaround times, instructions for "escalating" communication (i.e., to a phone call or office visit), indemnification for technical failures, and encryption requirements or waivers (Kane and Sands 1998).

Guidelines that have been developed for the use of e-mail between physicians and patients stress the need to determine whether there are topics that are forbidden (HIV status, pregnancy, sexually transmitted diseases) in electronic communications. Mental health professionals have additional concerns that are extensively explored in their specialist literature (ISMHO 2000; Kassaw and Gabbard 2002). And doctors are not the only ones to be concerned about these issues; patients, especially those using e-mail from employers' accounts, say they worry about privacy. However, the nature of the medium, which seems to promote anonymity (Turkle 1995), causes some people to divulge extremely personal information without regard to the potential for breaches of privacy. A guidelines document warns physicians that they "should be prepared to encounter patients who are sophisticated Internet users, aware of its privacy limitations, who nevertheless initiate unencrypted e-mail discussions of a surprisingly intimate medical nature" (Kane and Sands 1998).

Patient privacy is a recent focus of government as well. Privacy regulations soon to be enacted in the Health Insurance Portability and Accountability Act (HIPAA) are adding to concerns about the use of the electronic medium in clinical relationships. Liability issues, which cause some physicians to shy away from advice provided electronically, are currently unsettled. Some third-party payers are experimenting with reimbursement schemes, in the belief that e-mail communication, especially for the management of chronic diseases, can be cost-effective (Wiebe 2000). In response to these concerns about privacy, liability, and cost, companies are creating new methods of secure on-line communication to facilitate electronic patient-physician "non-visit care" ("Idealized Design" 2002), and HIPAA-compliant systems are rapidly appearing.

E-mail can extend beyond routine transactional exchanges to become a new kind of voice in the patient chart. Despite the lack of visual and aural cues that accompany face-to-face conversation, e-mail can be a valuable repository of "highly specific, descriptive, and sometimes intimate portrayals of patient narrative and physician compassion. . . . [that] will reshape the way basic medical care is delivered" (Spielberg 1998, 1358). For medical-legal reasons, e-mail exchanges need to be printed and filed in the patient's chart, where they function as progress notes and become formal entries in the medical record.

Ironically, physicians who learn to harness e-mail communication may find it an effective tool that allows them to spend more time with patients in face-to-face encounters, or to devote more time to patients with complex problems. E-mail has also been said to facilitate important dynamics of the patient-physician relationship, including "a physician's availability, accessibility, and willingness to listen" (Spielberg 1998, 1358).

A fourth important source of electronic interaction between patients and doctors is telemedicine. The term generally refers to "the use of electronic information and communications technologies to provide and support health care when distance separates the participants" (Field and Grigsby 2002, 423). No longer must the physician see and touch the patient in a face-to-face physical encounter to diagnose, treat, and monitor the patient's progress. Two types of this technology may profoundly affect the patient-physician relationship: remote monitoring in hospital units, and electronic tools for the management of chronic diseases.

One example of remote monitoring is an Internet-based program in a neonatal intensive care unit (NICU) that allowed families to see their hospitalized infant from home, get daily clinical progress reports, send messages to members of the NICU staff, and get educational materials about their infant's condition, tests, treatments, and discharge instructions (Gray et al. 2000). This pilot telemedicine project, reported in the journal *Pediatrics*, demonstrated increased family satisfaction with their care, the NICU environment, and visitation. The authors noted their "paradoxical" use of "a high-tech approach in a high-tech environment to provide a more humane high-touch" (Gray et al. 2000, 1324).

Another development that brings patients and providers together is electronic disease management tools. In partnership with their physicians and other health-care professionals, such as diabetes educators, nurses, and nutritionists, patients can use Web-based systems to record and monitor symptoms and signs of chronic diseases (Mazzi and Kidd 2002). Using electronic tools, patients with diabetes can record blood glucose values, patients with hypertension can enter blood pressure readings, patients with asthma or chronic obstructive pulmonary disease can provide spirometry data, and so forth. Caregivers give feedback to the patient after reviewing these electronic records, which may also provide links to further information, personalized guidance, and methods for communicating with health care providers. Outcomes of these disease management systems may include decreased numbers of hospitalizations, decreased medical costs, and increased patient satisfaction and health.

Physicians' Responses: Wary, Worried, Watchful

Given these examples of the potential of the Internet for clinical practice, what accounts for physicians' relative reluctance to harness the electronic medium along with their patients? One explanation is that doctors have been slow to adopt the technology compared with other professionals and the general public. A 2002 survey by the AMA shows, however, that this trend is changing, with 78 percent of physicians reporting use of the Web, an increase of 24 percent in five years ("AMA Study" 2002). The percentage of physicians who have their own Web site (three in ten) has not changed since 1999. Those surveyed reported their primary reason for having a Web site was to promote their practices and to provide patient education.

The provision of information on physician Web sites is not enough, though, for computer-literate patients. They want medical transactions to be available on-line, just as for other consumer services. These would include e-mail reminders and booking of appointments, updates about their diseases and treatments, and "virtual visits" for a narrow segment of medical problems (Grover et al. 2002). They also want on-line access to, and monitoring of, laboratory tests, and to use e-mail to prevent playing "telephone tag" with receptionists and nurses as intermediaries between doctor and patient (Harris Interactive/AriA Marketing 2002).

The quality of information patients find on-line is a concern for many doctors (Silberg, Lundberg, and Musacchio 1997), some of whom worry that patients cannot understand the information they retrieve, even if it is reliable (Murero, D'Ancona, and Karamanoukian 2001). But at least one survey has concluded that risks to patients from Internet information may have been exaggerated, with patients deriving more benefit than harm (Potts and Wyatt 2002).

In an effort to create quality control, a number of groups have developed codes or guidelines to ensure the quality and reliability of on-line information; a partial list of these includes the Health on the Net Foundation Code of Conduct (HonCODE), Hi-Ethics, and the e-Health Ethics Initiative (Foubister 2000; Internet Healthcare Coalition 2002). There have been calls for a unifying international organization to oversee ethical issues affecting the medical Internet, including fraud, consumer privacy, advertising, and other issues (Dyer 2001).

Further, it is widely recognized that the electronic playing field is not level, with social disparities limiting Internet access to a smaller and more privileged group than the general universe of patients (Eng et al. 1998). Internet use among patients is often correlated with a certain set of social, economic, and demographic conditions, such as younger age and having a computer and Internet access at home (Smith-Barbaro et al. 2001). Patients outside this privileged group may find themselves receiving "a clipped version of the ideal patient-physician relationship" (Spielberg 1998, 1359).

Effects on the Patient-Physician Relationship

Certain features of the electronic medium, that it can be curiously nameless, faceless, "depersonalized," and seemingly anonymous, pose clear challenges to a relationship that is supposed to be marked by care and compassion (Terry 2001) and face-to-face interaction. But the Internet is hardly the first challenge to a personal doctor-patient relationship. Many would argue that the rise of managed care, gatekeeper systems, and the constantly shifting ground of insurance coverage, which causes many patients to change doctors frequently, have been much more powerful forces in the erosion of the traditional therapeutic relationship than the Internet.

The personal relationship between physician and patient is based on trust and mutual obligation. Trust was historically especially necessary because the patient did not share the same intellectual base on which to make treatment decisions. Some twenty years ago, William F. May proclaimed the disparity between the scientific knowledge of doctors and "even their most educated patients" so vast that "patients can only submit themselves to the superior knowledge, authority, good intentions, and technical ingenuity of the doctor" (May 2000, 160–61). Such a stance naturally invested physicians with an enormous amount of power.

Thanks, however, to the transforming force of the Internet, which "blows wide open the medical guild system's historic hegemony on medical knowledge" (Jones 2000), knowledge as power has become a two-way street. Whereas knowledge used to reside only on one side of the relationship, the professional side, now patients have increasingly greater access to that same knowledge, with the result that the balance of power begins to shift. When the balance of understanding tips, so does the balance of power.

Wide access to information also poses a threat to professional identity. If everyone, including those without professional training and education, has access to the same information, what is the nature of specialized knowledge, which, in fact, helps to create professional identity? Doctors have become used to being the gatekeepers to knowledge and decision making, but this model is breaking down as doctors are increasingly bypassed as a knowledge source (termed "disintermediation") and as health care becomes "less hierarchical" (Terry 2001). Some doctors thus see patients' use of the Internet as a challenge to doctors' authority that implies a lack of faith in their professional judgment. They are uncomfortable with the shift from the rather more passive patient to the active information seeker who arrives for a consultation already armed with background (Jadad 1999). Meanwhile the physician in the examining room is likely to be harried and drowning in a sea of professional literature that he or she has no time to read or absorb. Medical information from the Internet simply adds to the impossibility of keeping up with the knowledge explosion.

Still, the physician has a responsibility to interpret his or her knowledge for the patient. Especially in an era that values autonomy, the doctor must focus on the individualized tailoring of that knowledge, ensuring that it is "placed in the service of the values and aspirations of the patient" (T. Kennedy 2001). Ideally, this leads to a model of shared decision making between doctors and patients. Yet the Internet may be pushing these parameters even further: a survey of consumer demand for on-line health information showed that one-third of the respondents rejected a shared-authority model; instead, they believe patients are totally in charge of the patient-physician relationship (Miller and Reents 2002).

With the balance of power and knowledge traditionally skewed in their favor, physicians have long seen themselves in the role of teacher. In an electronic era, physicians who direct patients to Internet resources, both for information and for emotional support, are continuing in this tradition, using the Internet as an educational tool and a patient education opportunity. The potential to personalize Web resources adds additional power to such education, as individual doctors and their practices can tailor patient education materials to the needs of their specific patient population. The ability to create personally tailored, individualized electronic information may actually strengthen the relationship — by reversing "damaging informational asymmetry between patient and physician" (Terry 2001) — particularly if the patient's own physician has had some involvement in the customization. This might be as simple as the physician's having a personal Web site with links to other, evaluated sites useful for patients (Ferguson 1998).

As suggested earlier, in an ideal world — one that almost certainly exists beyond the bounds of an eight-minute clinical consultation — doctors could go on-line with patients during an office visit (Crigger and Callahan 2000, 12). This is a natural extension of the aims of point-of-care electronic clinical decision tools, but it requires resources that may currently be beyond the reach of most practitioners. Practices that maintain their own Web sites with links to vetted and evaluated information are performing this service on a larger and more generalized scale.

But to some, patients' turning to the Internet instead of to their doctors represents both the failure of doctors as teachers and an added burden to do a different kind of teaching, one that may involve, subtly or overtly, pointing out the weaknesses in the patient's Internet-acquired knowledge. Doctors may be forced to spend precious clinical time debunking Internet myths and dealing with misinformation patients have gathered from the Web (Crigger and Callahan 2000, 10). This time may well be better spent in listening to patients' concerns, assessing their values and wishes for treatment, and formulating shared plans. In this way, patients' use of the Internet may actually be an impediment to an effective patient-physician relationship. (There is, however, evidence to the contrary: one Canadian study of patients with cancer and their oncologists showed that neither doctors nor patients believed that information seeking had an effect on the patient-physician relationship [Chen and Siu 2001].)

To deal with misinformed patients, philosopher Thomas D. Kennedy suggests that "physicians may need to teach subversively: less a matter of trying to teach a patient what she may not know and more a matter of convincing her that she is less knowledgeable than she may believe" (T. Kennedy 2001). This warning, however, sounds more like an insecure professional whose identity is under threat than an overburdened physician having to correct inaccuracies.

Kennedy sees the Internet's major effect as creating divisiveness:

> Patients whose confidence that their medical knowledge is growing as, correspondingly, their suspicion of their physicians is deepening, may be conferring with frazzled physicians increasingly skeptical of the presumed knowledge of their patients. . . .
>
> Whether or not the Web genuinely levels the playing field of physicians and patients, it is conducive to the development of a confidence in patients and a dismissiveness in physicians that sets the stage for physician-patient confrontations. . . .
>
> The Internet, which at first appearance promised to transform the relationship of physician and patient to a partnership of equals, has in fact fanned the flames of adversarialism. (T. Kennedy 2001)

Kennedy concludes that the Internet "can be a marvelous tool in our recovery of attentiveness to the goods of health care," but he warns that it is a tool and only a tool. This view, however, fails to adequately acknowledge the powerful social context of the interactions among patients, physicians, and the Internet.

Because of the social dynamics of the patient-physician relationship in which it is embedded, the uses of the Internet for health and medical purposes carry more social and emotional weight than do its applications in other areas of life. The medium can indeed potentially increase the impersonal and remote aspects of care. But ultimately the Internet does not of itself decrease the need for attention to the individual patient, nor does it diminish the positive value of patients and physicians as partners. The professional attributes that create trust—the essential component of the patient-physician relationship—do not have to be harmed by the Internet. Trust should be an expansive quality, one that "creates the moral space necessary to accommodate increasingly well-informed and curious patients who desire an enhanced role in determining their medical care" (Spielberg 1998, 1358).

At present, a number of issues remain to be solved before the Internet becomes a permanent and positive partner in strengthening the patient-physician relationship. Social and economic barriers to electronic access must decrease, in order to give more patients access to information, and Internet usage must become ubiquitous among doctors overall. Outcome studies are needed to better characterize the effects of the Internet on patients and doctors and to suggest avenues for improvement. Reliable, consistent, proven guidelines and best practices for harnessing e-mail and other forms of electronic communication and information will eventually result in accepted norms of practice. When these milestones have been reached, the Internet will be as much a taken-for-granted part of doctor-patient interaction as the telephone. Then chapters like this one will take their place as archival documentation, adding to a long historical record of the constantly evolving relationship between patients and physicians.

Virtual Disability

On the Internet, Nobody Knows

You're Not a Sick Puppy

TOD CHAMBERS

> On the Internet nobody knows you at all, on the Internet
> nobody knows what your race is or your sex. That whole colour
> and sex-blindness is a positive force for a lot of people. They feel
> welcome. Certainly, this goes for people with disabilities.
> — John Gilmore, quoted in Tim Jordan, *Cyberpower*

It could be said that the Internet saved Joan Sue Green's life. At one time she had been a relatively happy twenty-something neuropsychologist living in New York City. But all of that changed when Joan became the victim of a drunk-driving accident. In the accident her boyfriend was killed, and she was left disfigured, physically incapacitated, and unable to talk because of brain damage. Soon she fell into a deep depression and seriously considered taking her own life. But her therapist brought a computer to Joan's apartment, and Joan got on the Internet. Her original Net handle was "Quiet Lady," but as she became more confident in this new world, she changed it to "Talkin' Lady." Soon she was a star on the Internet. As one of the women who knew her recalled, Joan was "a monumental on-line presence who served both as a support for other disabled women and as an inspiring stereotype-smasher to the able-bodied. Through her many intense friendships and (in some cases) her on-line romances, she changed the lives of dozens of women" (Van Gelder 1991, 365). For many, Joan's social rebirth through the Internet clearly demonstrates the profoundly liberating features of this new medium for communication. An MCI WorldCom advertisement states: "There is no race. There is no gender.

There is no age. There are no infirmities. There are only minds. Utopia? No, Internet" (Trend 2001, 183). It is not surprising to discover that of individuals who have access to the Internet, those with disabilities spend twice as much time on-line as do able-bodied users (Grossman 2001, 29–30). And many Net enthusiasts view this new social environment as liberating primarily because it frees users from the constraints of the human body. We encounter others in cyberspace without the kind of prejudices that comes when we meet the body before the person. The Internet thus granted Joan the kind of relationships that might never have been possible in previous forms of communication.

But it can also be said that without the Internet, Joan Sue Green would never have existed. For Joan does not exist outside of cyberspace; she was the creation of a middle-aged, able-bodied, male psychiatrist. He created Joan so that he could experience what it would be like to encounter women as a woman. When this psychiatrist was outed, many of Joan's friends and lovers felt personally violated. Yet if the Internet allows ideas to be free of the social prejudices concerning the body, then how do we explain the social drama that occurred following the revelation of Joan's real-life (RL) identity? It seems clear that Joan was able to inspire others not by her words alone but through her identity as a disabled person who had triumphed over adversity. Suppose the psychiatrist had openly admitted from the beginning that Joan was a fiction; if this had happened, it seems easy to conjecture that Joan's statements would not have been judged credible by this Net community.

The Internet as a medium of communication thus exhibits a fascinating paradoxical nature — the RL body of speakers is simultaneously unimportant and vitally meaningful. This property of Net communication is particularly significant for public discussions about morality and medicine, for recently in bioethics there has arisen a form of identity politics. These changes are perhaps most vividly evidenced in a 1996 protest at Michigan State University. The university's Center for Ethics and Humanities in the Life Sciences that year was holding a conference on the topic of the Americans with Disabilities Act (ADA), but the plans for what was to be a relatively conventional bioethics conference became thoroughly unconventional when it was the site for a demonstration by the disability activist group Not Dead Yet. Why would a disability activist group protest an academic meeting of scholars interested in social morality? Stephen Drake, a Not Dead Yet member, later wrote about the reasons he traveled to Michigan, "spending money and time I could not afford to spend." Drake, who suffered "severe brain damage at birth," was at the time a graduate student studying the issue of language and disability.

> Over the past couple of years, my research efforts and my work have involved communication on the Internet. Among other things, two contradictory issues have caught my attention. One is the increasing concern expressed by people with disabilities in regard to access to health care and access to supports in the community. The other is the growing popularity of the "right to be killed" movement, whose message is that life with a disability is not worth living. (Drake 1996)

Drake went to Michigan State "to join others in my community — the disability community" in denouncing the plan of medical ethicists to discuss the conditions by which euthanasia would be morally permissible. Drake points out that this conference was "especially outrageous" because not one of the speakers was a member of his community, that is, "the group of people the discussions would affect." In other words, it was the identity of the speakers that was particularly "outrageous" to Not Dead Yet, for their lack of membership in the disability community made their statements, even prior to being uttered, suspicious. For one's opinion to be respected, it must be presented along with a presentation of a disabled body. This concern for knowing the bodily identity of the one proposing a particular moral position runs counter to the traditional Western belief that the merit of ideas should be judged outside of their relation to particular persons. In our public discussions about morality and the body, a recent trend has been the advent of a form of identity politics (Elliott 1999). Joseph Shapiro begins his history of the disability civil rights movement by stating baldly, "Nondisabled Americans do not understand disabled ones" (3). Identification with a disabling condition or a disease process grants one unique experiences and in turn special authority in speaking about social issues related to that illness (Chambers 1999).

In Drake's comments on the Michigan conference, he notes the simultaneous increase of concern by disabled people with community access and of support for euthanasia by others. When social discussions turn toward the diseased body in cyberspace, the identity of the speaker, or rather the identity of the speaker's body, becomes a central concern for the audience, for it is the body behind the bodiless communication that lends moral authority to the speaker's message. But how did Drake become aware of these trends? His central research area has been in communication and the Internet. But how does Drake know that those identified as disabled on the Internet are just that? And how does he know that those who express their support for euthanasia are not disabled? How does he know that he is not listening to "Joan" when he cites the opinions of those in the disability community? What follows is an attempt to explore some of the initial problems that this form of illness identity politics will come upon as it uses this new medium of public discourse. We need first, however, to look at the new forms of social identity that have been generated by the Internet. Following this, we will look at how these identities grant new social disguises and thus how they complicate public discussions about the body and medicine that are grounded in the moral authority of particular illness experiences.

Ghosts in the New Machine

With the advent of the Internet, the face-to-face role-playing games of the 1970s (Dungeons and Dragons being the most renowned) were translated into the disembodied world of computer MUDs (multi-user dungeons) (Turkle 1995). MUDs fall into two basic types: "those with adventures or quests that require players to be active and follow through tasks and those that are purely social, offering the opportunity for interaction" (Jordon 1999, 61). Sherry Turkle considers these various MUDs a form of virtual reality, in which rather than the body's sensations being made to feel as if it were in a particular physical dimension, the users of MUDs "immerse themselves in a world of words. MUDs are a text-based, social virtual reality" (181). In *Hamlet on the Holodeck* Janet Murray (1997), with the sensitivity of a literature scholar, recognizes that this text-based virtual reality sounds a great deal like private reading experiences in which one "gets lost" in a book, yet she claims that the digital world has added something new to the traditional imaginative experience of reading a novel, attending an opera, or watching a movie. The cyberworld permits one to put on personae and act with others who are also adopting various personae.

These personae are referred to as "avatars." Computer-generated virtual selves are a key feature in many contemporary visions of the near future. In his classic cyberpunk novel *Snow Crash*, Neal Stephenson (1993) imagines a future where people can inhabit a second life in Metaverse, a simulated world that is a collaborative fabrication of computer hackers. In Metaverse, one's physical self is represented by avatars, "audiovisual bodies." Those lacking the skill or the capital to have a custom-made avatar can purchase an "off-the-shelf" one from a

Virtual Disability 389

Wal-Mart; comically in Stephenson's novel, these generic models are so common that they can be thought to constitute a "new ethnic group." Ostensibly — if one has the talent or the finances — the only limitations in the creation of an identity in Metaverse are the limits of one's own inventiveness, which is the reason that as one travels in this virtual city one "can look like a gorilla or a dragon or a giant talking penis. . . . Spend five minutes walking down the Street and you will see all of these" (36).

While Murray (1997) compares the experience of adopting an avatar to performance activities such as mystery plays and the Renaissance masques, there are some differences between the consciousness that arises during virtual reality and that during performance activities. In performance activities, Richard Schechner (1988) notes, there is always a conscious gap between the "real" and the "performed": "Theater, to be effective, must maintain its double or incomplete presence, as a *here-and-now performance of there-and-then events*" (69). When an actor takes on the role of Hamlet, he does not become a Danish prince, but he does take on a self different from his ordinary way of being. Schechner refers to this as a "not not-not" consciousness; the actor is not Hamlet but the actor is also not not Hamlet. In this gap between the here and now and the there and then, performance becomes a powerful means for society to reflect about itself to itself, so to lose this gap is to sacrifice the unique self-reflexivity that performance can generate. In my example of playing Hamlet, I have used the male gender pronoun "he," and since I am in the habit of using inclusive language, this is something that on the page looks peculiar to me. Yet a performance of *Hamlet* with a woman playing the protagonist would generate a commentary on the gendered aspects of the play, and this kind of self-reflexivity is one of the powerful features of performance activities.

Virtual worlds, however, strive to efface this self-conscious doubleness, so a woman in cyberspace could play Hamlet and do so without necessarily introducing a feminist commentary into the play. The issue of not being able to distinguish reality from fantasy is a frequent theme in cyberpunk science fiction. Often the reader cannot determine if the characters are simply insane (due to their insistence that what is going on around them is not real) or the only sane agents (due to their insight into the inauthenticity of what is going on around them). A good example of this authenticity confusion can be found in David Cronenberg's 1999 film *eXistenZ*, which concerns a virtual reality game about a virtual reality game. At the end of the film, one character turns to the other and asks, "Hey, tell me the truth . . . are we still in the game?" In theater performance, we would question the soundness of someone who jumps onstage to stop Hamlet from killing Polonius, but in virtual reality the aim is often to try and blur the distinction so that we may potentially forget that we are in a simulacrum. Postmodern theorists such as Jean Baudrillard argue that the simulations we create today are beginning to be viewed as "more real" than the things they are supposed to simulate. I may be disappointed if my experience of Bangkok when I physically visit does not conform to the media images I have received prior to the trip; the real city is thought of as less authentic than the simulacrum.

Unlike Stephenson's Metaverse or a holographic environment like the Holodeck first portrayed in the television series *Star Trek: The Next Generation*, the world of MUDs on the Internet is entirely textual. Some Net theorists have argued that the entelechy of cyberspace is not textual but visual; yet putting teleconferencing aside, the present examples of this visual cyberworld tend to promote not the anonymous constructed nature of textual identity (or the visual constructions in the Metaverse) but a type of exhibitionist realism (McLemee 2001). One can imagine a future akin to those portrayed in cyberpunk novels, where physical representations of one's body become an indispensable feature of Internet communication. I suspect that along with such a development would come the ability to create three-dimensional avatars that present an idealized, false, or purely fantastical image of oneself. Of course, at a very basic level such images are still textual, that is, based on the binary language of computers. The textual selves presently created for Internet communication may be thought in the future to be merely the antediluvian examples of more sophisticated textual selves to come. The creation of new forms of self-presentation often also portends novel forms of deception. At this time, cyberspace permits one to create a textual self that is potentially unrelated to one's RL identity.

Some theorists conceive of the Internet as a place of social liberation, where we can encounter people as they themselves wish to be seen. For this reason, Peter Steiner's *New Yorker* cartoon of one dog sitting by a computer and informing another dog, "On the Internet, nobody knows you're a dog," has become a frequently cited joke in discussions about the Net (Steiner 2001). For cyberspace enthusiasts, these textual encounters allow one to put aside social biases that have tended to suppress open communication among people of different body types. Textual identities in cyberspace, however, must still work within prior social conventions. Cameron Bailey (2001) observes that in cyberspace, "one presents oneself in language, as is done in all forms of writing, which require the multifaceted acts of identity construction, selective editing, and telling lies" (336). While faking a textual identity is certainly easier in cyberspace than in RL, one must still adopt an expressive style that will present a particular self. To be viewed as unmarked, that is, "styleless," can only occur if one adopts the style of Standard English, that is, the expression of the speech community of white, formally educated, middle-class Americans. Tim Jordan (1999) points out that while cyberspace relies on different symbolic capital in the creation of identity from that of RL, "the different resources for avatar construction are potential bases for new forms of hierarchy. Style, in particular, forms an important basis for hierarchy with different participants considered more or less important depending on their style. People can be dismissed from serious consideration depending on their style" (80).

Textual identities in cyberspace are also less "real" than the textual identities created in the RL genres of physical manuscripts. In a discussion of reading e-books, Sven Birkerts (2001) observes that the ephemeral quality of electronic language affects the power of the word. Others have noted the evanescent and shadowy bearing of electronic writing, where "losing" data seems different from misplacing a book that one was reading. Computers are not the only technology that produces this discursive ephemerality; in the Ken McMullen film *Ghost Dance*, the philosopher Jacques Derrida is asked if he believes in ghosts, and Derrida responds, "That's a hard question because, you see, I am a ghost" (Bennett and Royle 1990, 138). Derrida has explicitly examined the ontological implications of such odd nonbeings as technological "ghosts" in his study of what he refers to as "hauntology" (Poster 1999). An extreme form of this can be found in William Gibson's 1983 novel *Neuromancer*, the science fiction novel that introduced the term "cyberspace." In this near-future dystopia, the novel's protagonist, Case, asks for help from his friend Dixie "Flatline" McCoy. Case's friend died before the novel begins, but a recording of his personality has been made, and Case is able to interact with this construct: "It was disturbing to think of Flatline as a construct, a hardwired ROM cassette replicating a dead man's skills, obsessions, knee-jerk responses" (77).

The bodily markers that we use to classify and define our world — such as gender, race, and body type — can be re-created in cyberspace, yet these creations are not necessarily consonant with the RL body of the avatar's creator. Turkle (1995) has written about the issue of "virtual gender-swapping" in the MUDS. She notes that among the registered members of a particular Japanese MUD there is a ratio of four men participants to every woman, yet during the game, the ratio of male to female characters is three to one; "a significant number of players, many tens of thousands of them, are virtually cross-dressing" (212). MUDders are able — and seemingly eager — to switch genders in their cyberspace interactions. Some of these virtual cross-dressers claim that their experience interacting as another gender grants them real insights into the way gender affects their own identity. While creating a textual identity is substantially different from RL cross-dressing, assuming a credible front of another gender "requires understanding how gender inflects speech, manner, the interpretation of experience" (213); it is thus a type of performance, which can be viewed as similar to the way that biological transsexuals experience being the other gender through a daily performance of "manness" or "womanness." Turkle observes that "expectations are expressed in visible textual actions, widely witnessed and openly discussed" (214). Identifying oneself as male or female creates expectations by one's audience of the kind of attitudes and beliefs that one will express not only through explicit statements but also through the way those statements are made. Lisa Nakamura (2001) observes that because we do not have access to the real biological bodies of the players in MUDS, "it can be said that everyone who participates is 'passing'" (227).

Turkle also notes that MUDS permit individuals to create parallel versions of their own selves, which allow them to "play out" in a safe environment particular facets of their selfhood. Turkle describes an MIT conference where a graduate student revealed how she had used a MUD to work out her own discomfort with a disability (262–63). This graduate student, who had lost a leg in an automobile accident, created an avatar who was one-legged. This disabled avatar established a romantic relationship with another MUD character, and through her virtual self, this student was able to learn to accept her RL body. The virtual self on the Internet thus permitted her to fashion a new self in the real world. This difference between the two selves can be viewed as equivalent to the concept of an "implied author" in literary criticism. Wayne Booth (1983) argues that readers construct a concept of the author of a work of fiction that may not relate to the real-life author, but the notion of this "person" is a significant aspect in how readers evaluate fiction, especially its moral import. In cyberspace there is also a notion of an implied author behind the avatars, and just as in the reading of fiction, we need to be cognizant that the RL self is as much a construct as the avatar.

The social drama around Joan concerned the relationship between the implied author and the characters created. In fictional discourse, we expect a distance between the narrator and the author. We do not believe that the narrator of *The Fall* shares the worldview and morals of Albert Camus, and, as Booth argues, our evaluation of such works depends on this aesthetic distance. When we consider the narrator's perspective as morally suspect but do not discern a distance from the author, then we may come to view the work itself as morally problematic; this, for example, is the reason that Vladimir Nabokov's *Lolita* has often been judged harshly. In nonfictional discourse, we do not believe that a distance exists between the narrator and the implied author. The moral questions raised about the Joan case can be viewed as similar to the kind of moral distance one expects and depends on to judge literary works. It is important to note that the Joan case occurred in the early years of the Internet, and from the present-day vantage point it may seem naive not to suspect that the person one may be experiencing is not a simulacrum. From the accounts of those, like Turkle, who have done research on these various MUDs, there is a general acceptance (and to some degree expectation) that the people one meets may not relate directly to the biological selves authoring those texts.

Yet a recent case concerning the diary of a cancer patient echoes the moral and epistemological problems raised in the Joan case. "Kaycee," an eighteen-year-old woman living with her mother, created "Living Colours: A Diary of Survival," an on-line journal of her experiences with illness. Kaycee died on Mother's day, but it was soon revealed that Debbie Swenson, Kaycee's "mother," had fabricated this identity (Gunn 2001). The dramatic reaction of readers who had been duped by Swenson are similar to the reactions to the revelations of the implied author of Joan. One can easily warrant the creation of alternative identities in the case of the disabled MIT graduate student and that of the MUD players. Within MUDs, the world encountered is assumed to be fictional; therefore, for a player to be morally outraged when it is discovered that someone is not who they say they are there would be akin to being perturbed when one watches the able-bodied Daniel Day-Lewis receive an Academy Award for his performance in *My Left Foot*. The framing of their discourse as fictional permits the MUDders to play with their identities; one would be puzzled by a participant disturbed by changes in gender and physical being when in many of the games the avatars created include elves, hobbits, and wizards. Changes in gender and able-bodiedness seem trivial in comparison to the alteration of one's species. In the case of the MIT student, I suspect that most people's assessment of her creation of this particular persona would be positive, for she has essentially constructed a "parallel" self in her creation of an avatar.

Unlike MUDs, the world that Joan was participating within was thought to be real or as close a simulation of a real encounter as there can be. The participants in these forums assume that the selves presented are the same selves one would meet on the street and that the ideas and feelings disclosed are sincere expressions of these RL selves. We should then distinguish two types of avatars. The first type of avatar I will refer to as chimerical, for this cyberidentity is a creation thought to be separate and distinct from one's RL identity. The second type of avatar is agnatic; that is, it is parallel or consonant with the RL self. Each of these avatars is judged differently in different social frames. In a MUD, it is assumed that everyone is playing a chimerical avatar, and one would feel a bit like Alice in Wonderland if one responded to the selves encountered in the game as if they were agnatic. In the frame of chat rooms and on-line forums such as a virtual patient support group, however, one assumes that the others are agnatic avatars. So one would expect that unlike the MUD players, if Joan had described herself as a dragon or a giant talking penis, it would be considered a metaphor; if the other members of the discussion believed that Joan was serious about thinking that she was a dragon, then they would want her to get psychiatric help. The MIT graduate student represents a form of agnatic avatar, for she is representing her actual self and constructing novel experiences for that self. This is akin to the use of the subjunctive mood in speech: stating "If I were the president, I would . . ." leads the listener to assume that the "I" of the sentence, which is counter to fact, is essentially the same person as the speaker. This graduate student's avatar can be seen as analogous to the way transsexuals are expected to live as a "woman" or a "man" for a period of time before they can undergo surgery.

This analogy to transsexuals' passing as another gender is worth exploring. What does it mean to live as a man or a woman? The reason for transsexuals to attempt this performance seems important in relation to their ultimate decision of their social gender identification, for performance provides some crucial insights into the entire question of what we expect of transsexuals. Judith Butler (1990) argues that gender is something that is performed for others, and one's identity is created through this performed social script (136). For a transsexual to live as a man or a woman means that he or she has successfully performed a new gender script. From Butler's perspective, gender does not possess an ontological status separate from cultural conventions but is instead fabricated in these ritualized performances of self. In examining the cultural concept of the "female impersonator," Butler concludes that cross-dressing *implicitly reveals the imitative structure of gender itself—as well as its contingency*" (137). In comparison to Schechner's 1988 notion of self-conscious doubleness in the frame of theater performance, the notion of social performance theorized by Butler is closer to the performance of a simulacrum in which there is no RL identity waiting for the curtain to come down on the performance (cf. Goffman 1959). Being able to pass as a woman is to be a woman, so it makes no sense to ask, "Are we still in the game?"—for all the game is all there is.

Drawing on Butler's work, Susan Stryker (2000) queries this dramaturgical gender identity within the disembodied stage of cyberspace through her own identity as a transsexual: "What subjective qualities produced by the flesh persist in a technologized space that stages the body's absence? . . . How might flesh signify when it is not visually performative?" (595). Stryker notes that while the Internet may hide social markers, the participants are "inextricably caught up in other interactive ways where flesh matters a great deal—kinship systems, sexuality-based communities, cities, racial formations, educational institutions" (595). Consequently bodies in cyberspace both do and do not matter. One cultural category that illustrates this is race. Nakamura (2001) notes that when someone identifies his or her race in a MUD description, players tend to respond by claiming that this is "a form of hostile performance," because it destroys the utopian image of cyberspace as free from racial prejudice. Why would one want to introduce racial differences in a social space innately free of such differences? Yet Nakamura observes that in cyberspace "some forms of racial passing are condoned and practised"; she notes the frequency in which players adopt Asian personae, such as Mr. Sulu, Bruce Lee,

Chun Li, and Akira (228). Nakamura characterizes the performance of such "Orientalized theatricality" as "identity tourism." While cyberspace may cloak people from each other, the prejudices of society are still carried into the system. In other words, cyberspace clearly does not spawn a Rousseauian utopia but perhaps may in the name of harmless fantasy license malevolent speech acts without personal accountability.

Authority, Identity, and Avatars

Most of those writing about Joan have focused on the issue of gender switching, but little has been said about the issue of the able-bodied man assuming a persona with a disability. In the discourse surrounding morality and medicine, personal experience is generally accorded special moral authority. In an article examining this special authority, "Ethics and Experience: The Case of the Curious Response," Paul Lauritzen (1996) recounts the various reactions he received in response to "What Price Parenthood," an essay he had written in 1990, in which he was critical of reproductive technology. In this earlier essay, Lauritzen drew on his own experiences with infertility, and he holds that one of the reasons for the positive responses he received after the essay's publication was because his personal story granted him special "authority." After the article was published, he encountered a person at a conference who expressed admiration for the article. During their conversation, Lauritzen revealed that his wife and he had just had a son. While the article had implied that Lauritzen and his wife could not have children, here he was telling of the recent birth of a child. Lauritzen recalls that the man's reaction to this new information was not merely one of dismay but one of hostility. The veracity of Lauritzen's original story was now placed under question, and so was the authority for his position on reproductive technology. It was as if Lauritzen had revealed that the writer of the article were a chimerical avatar. While Lauritzen is critical of the power granted personal narratives in moral argument, others, like Arthur Frank (1995), explicitly laud their presence in social deliberations about morality. Frank has castigated the academic study of bioethics for attending primarily to the ethics cases of health care professionals rather than the narratives of the ill (cf. Arras 1997). Hilde Nelson (2001) has also been a proponent of the importance of "counterstories" in public discourse.

This issue becomes even more complicated as we switch the medium from the personal narratives related through oral and literary forums to cyberspace, where avatars can have illness narratives. I suspect that one of the most troubling features of this issue is not so much that there have been cases where a person tried to pass as a "woman with a disability" or a "cancer patient" but that they successfully passed and could have continued to do so. Of course, deceiving others has long been a part of human interactions, and one merely has to remember that one of the great skills of Homer's hero Odysseus was deception. But often Odysseus required the assistance of the goddess Athena to transform his physical appearance so that he could successfully delude his enemies, and even with this assistance, some could still see through his disguise. Cyberspace as a means of communication grants one the ability to deceive without supernatural assistance, and in permitting bodiless arguments, the Net may unwittingly challenge the persuasive power of the personal narrative in moral deliberation.

Works Cited

Abbate, Janet. 1999. *Inventing the Internet*. Cambridge: MIT Press.

Adams, Damon. 2001. "Doctors Bristle at Quality Web Ratings in Two Cities." *Amednews.com*, 11 June. Accessed 14 November 2002. ⟨http://www.ama-assn.org/sci-pubs/amnews/pick_01/prsb0611.htm⟩.

Alali, A. O., and Gary W. Byrd. 1994. *Terrorism and the News Media: A Selected, Annotated Bibliography*. Jefferson, N.C.: McFarland.

Alexander, Frank, and Sheldon Selesnick. 1966. *The History of Psychiatry*. New York: Harper.

Alpers, A. and Lo B. 2000. "Uses and Abuses of Prescription Drug Information in Pharmacy Benefits Management Programs." *JAMA* 283(6) (Feb. 9): 801–6.

"AMA Hits TV Drug Ads." 1957. *Television Code Subscriber Bulletin*, June, 1.

"AMA Study: Physicians' Use of Internet Steadily Rising." 2002. Accessed 19 November. ⟨http://www.ama-assn.org/ama/pub/article/1616–6473.html⟩.

Anderson, David R. 1984. *Rex Stout*. New York: Frederick Ungar.

Annas, G. J. 1995. "Sex, Money, and Bioethics: Watching *ER* and *Chicago Hope*." *Hastings Center Report* 25(5):40–43.

Arnold, Jean. 1994. "A Clearinghouse Mobilizes against Stigma." *Journal of the California Alliance for the Mentally Ill* 4:50–51.

Arras, John. 1997. "Nice Story, but So What? Narrative and Justification in Ethics." In *Stories and Their Limits: Narrative Approaches to Bioethics*, ed. Hilde Nelson. New York: Routledge.

Awakenings. 1990. Dir. Penny Marshall. With Robin Williams, Robert De Niro. Columbia Pictures.

Ayd, Frank. 1991. "The Early History of Modern Psychopharmacology." *Neuropsychopharmacology* 5:2: 71–84.

Bader, S. A., and R. M. Braude. 1998. " 'Patient Informatics': Creating New Partnerships in Medical Decision Making." *Academic Medicine* 73:408–11.

Baer, N. 1998. "An interview with Neal Baer, M.D., the doctor behind *ER*." *Journal of the American Medical Association* 280:855.

Bailey, Cameron. 2001. "Virtual Skin: Articulating Race in Cyberspace." In *Reading Digital Culture*, ed. D. Trend. Malden, Mass.: Blackwell.

Barnett, Sylvan. *A Short Guide to Writing About Art*. New York: Longman Press, 1997.

Barnhurst, K., and D. Mutz. 1997. "American Journalism and the Decline in Event-Centered Reporting." *Journal of Communication* 47(4):27–33.

Barnouw, Erik. 1978. *The Sponsor*. New York: Oxford University Press.

Barsam, Richard M. 1973. *Non-fiction Film: A Critical History*. Bloomington: Indiana University.

Barthes, Roland. 1977. "The Rhetoric of the Image." In *Image-Music-Text*. New York: Hill and Wang.

Baudrillard, Jean. 1988. *The Evil Demon of Images*. Sydney: Power Publications.

Baughman, James L. 1985. *Television's Guardians: The FCC and the Politics of Programming, 1958–1967*. Knoxville: University of Tennessee Press.

Beaman, Bruce R. 1976. "Mycroft Holmes, Agoraphobe." *Baker Street Journal* 26:91–93.

Bennett, Andrew, and Nicholas Royle. 1990. *Introduction to Literature, Criticism, and Theory*. London: Prentice Hall.

Berger, Peter. 1967. *The Sacred Canopy: Elements of a Sociological Theory of Religion*. Garden City, N.Y.: Doubleday.

Berry, Wendell. 1992. "Fidelity." In *Fidelity*. New York: Pantheon.

Betzold, Michael. 1998. "Brazen Defiance Is Nothing New for Euthanasia Guru Kevorkian." Agence France Presse wire, 23 November.

Bickford, Linda. 1956. "Children Visit Patients By Television." *Hospital Management*. 82(1): 51, 62.

Birkerts, Sven. 2001. "E-Books and the Fate of Reading." *Ruminator Review*, 7.

Blaska, Joan. 1993. "The Power of Language: Speak and Write Using 'Person First.'" In *Perspectives on Disability*, 2d ed., ed. Mark Nagler. Palo Alto, Calif.: Health Markets Research.

Bloom, S. G. 1996. "Health Legacies from Franklin Roosevelt to Robert Dole, or How Medical and Health Care Issues Took Over the Nation's News." *Journal of Health Communication* 1(1):83–97.

Boddy, William. 1990. "The Seven Dwarfs and the Money Grubbers: The Public Relations Crisis of U.S. Television in the Late 1950s." In *Logics of Television*, ed. Patricia Mellencamp. Bloomington: Indiana University Press.

Bodenheimer, Thomas. 1997a. "The Oregon Health Plan: Lessons for the Nation, Part One." *New England Journal of Medicine* 337(9):651–55.

———. 1997b. "The Oregon Health Plan: Lessons for the Nation, Part Two." *New England Journal of Medicine* 337(10):720–23.

Bodroghkozy, Aniko. 1992. "'Is This What You Mean by Color TV?': Race, Gender and Contested Meanings in NBC's *Julia*." In *Private Screenings: Television and the Female Consumer*, eds. Lynn Spigel and Denise Mann Minneapolis: Univ. of Minnesota Press.

Booth, Wayne C. 1983. *The Rhetoric of Fiction*. Chicago: University of Chicago Press.

Bowen, James. 1981. *A History of Western Education*. Vol. 3. London: Methuen.

Boyer, Peter J. 2001. "Bad Cops." *New Yorker*, 21 May, 60–77.

Branigan, Edward. 1984. *Point of View in the Cinema: A Theory of Narration and Subjectivity in Classical Film*. New York: Mouton.

Brink, S. 1998. "HMO's Were the Right Rx: Americans Got Lower Medical Costs but Also More Worries." *U.S. News and World Report* 124(9):47–50.

Brockington, Fraser. 1975. *World Health*. New York: Churchill Livingstone Press.

Brodsky, M. I. 1997. "Portrait of an American Surgeon." *Pharos* 60:4–8.

Brody, Howard. 1992. *The Healer's Power.* New Haven: Yale University Press.

Brown, Bertram S. 1976. "The Life of Psychiatry." *American Journal of Psychiatry* 133:489–95.

Brownlow, Kevin. 1990. *Behind the Mask of Innocence.* New York: Alfred A. Knopf.

Burnham, John C. 1982. "American Medicine's Golden Age: What Happened to It?" *Science* 215:1474–79.

Burt, Robert A. 1979. *Taking Care of Strangers: The Rule of Law in Doctor-Patient Relations.* New York: Free Press.

Burton, Keith. 1989. "A Chronicle: Dax's Case As It Happened." In *Dax's Case: Essays in Medical Ethics and Human Meaning*, ed. Lonnie D. Kliever. Dallas: Southern Methodist University Press.

Butler, Judith. 1990. *Gender Trouble: Feminism and the Subversion of Identity.* New York: Routledge.

Bynum, W. F. 1994. *Science and Practice of Medicine in the Nineteenth Century.* Cambridge: Cambridge University Press.

Byock, I. 1996. "The Nature of Suffering and the Nature of Opportunity at the End of Life." *Clinical Geriatric Medicine* 12(2):237–51.

Caldicott, Catherine V. 1998. "From Balcony to Bedside: Operatic Entrance Music in the Clinical Encounter." *Perspectives in Biology and Medicine* 41:549–64.

Caplan, A. 1995. *Moral Matters: Ethical Issues in Medicine and the Life Sciences.* New York: John Wiley and Sons.

———. 1998. *Due Consideration: Controversy in the Age of Medical Miracles.* New York: Wiley.

Caplan, A., L. Snyder, and K. Faber-Langendoen. 2000. "The Role of Guidelines in the Practice of Physician-Assisted Suicide." *Annals of Internal Medicine* 132(6):476–82.

Cartwright, Lisa. 1995. *Screening the Body: Tracing Medicine's Visual Culture.* Minneapolis: University of Minnesota Press.

Cassedy, J. 1991. *Medicine in America.* Baltimore, Md.: Johns Hopkins University Press.

Cassel, E. J. 1982. "The Nature of Suffering and the Goals of Medicine." *New England Journal of Medicine* 306:639–45.

Cassel, Jay. 1987. *The Secret Plague: Venereal Disease in Canada, 1838–1939.* Toronto: University of Toronto Press.

Chambers, Tod. 1999. *The Fiction of Bioethics: Cases as Literary Texts.* New York: Routledge.

———. 2001. "Theory and the Organic Bioethicist." *Theoretical Medicine* 22(2):123–34.

Chen, Xueyu, and Lillian L. Siu. 2001. "Impact of the Media and the Internet on Oncology: Survey of Cancer Patients and Oncologists in Canada." *Journal of Clinical Oncology* 19:4291–97.

Chesler, Ellen. 1992. *Woman of Valor: Margaret Sanger and the Birth Control Movement in America.* New York: Simon and Schuster.

Childress, James F., and Courtney C. Campbell. 1989. "Who Is a Doctor to Decide Whether a Person Lives or Dies? Reflections on Dax's Case." In *Dax's Case: Essays in Medical Ethics and Human Meaning*, ed. Lonnie D. Kliever. Dallas: Southern Methodist University Press.

Chin, Tyler. 2002. "Information Driveway: Physicians Create Inexpensive Web Sites Offering Health Data to Patients." *Amednews.com*, 4 September. Accessed 9 September. ⟨http://www.ama-assn.org/sci-pubs/amnews/pick_02/bisa0909.htm⟩.

Chodorow, Nancy. 1978. *The Reproduction of Mothering: Psychoanalysis and the Sociology of Gender*. Berkeley: University of California Press.

Clark, David L., and Catherine Myser. 1996. "Being Humaned: Medical Documentaries and the Hyperrealization of Conjoined Twins." In *Freakery: Cultural Spectacles of the Extraordinary Body*, ed. Rosemarie Garland Thomson. New York: New York University Press.

Clements, Mark. 1993. "What We Say about Mental Illness." *Parade Magazine*, 31 October, 3–6.

"The Cochrane Collaboration." 2002. Accessed 13 November. ⟨http://www.cochrane.org⟩.

"Cochrane Collaboration Consumer Network." 2002. Accessed 13 November. ⟨http://www.cochraneconsumer.com⟩.

Colwell, Stacie. 1992. "The End of the Road: Gender, the Dissemination of Knowledge, and the American Campaign against Venereal Disease during World War I." *Camera Obscura* 29:91–130.

Comolli, Jean-Louis. 1977. "Technique and Ideology: Camera Perspective, Depth of Field." *Film Reader* 2:132–52.

Conan Doyle, Arthur. n.d. *The Original Illustrated Sherlock Holmes*. New York: Castle.

Connelly, Julia E. 1994. "Listening, Empathy, and Clinical Practice." In *The Empathetic Practitioner: Empathy, Gender, and Medicine*, ed. Marueen A. Milligan and Ellen Singer More. New Brunswick, N.J.: Rutgers University Press.

Cook, Kay K. 1996. "Medical Identity: My DNA/Myself." In *Getting A Life: Everyday Uses of Autobiography*, edited by Smith and Watson. Minneapolis: University of Minnesota Press.

Courtney, A. and T. Whipple. 1983. *Sex Stereotype in Advertising*. Massachussetts: Lexington Books.

Cowan, Ruth Schwartz. 1983. *More Work for Mother: The Ironies of Household Technology From the Open Hearth to the Microwave*. New York: Basic Books.

Cowart, Dax, and Robert Burt. 1998. "Confronting Death: Who Chooses, Who Controls? A Dialogue Between Dax Cowart and Robert Burt." *Hastings Centre Report* 28(1):14–24.

Crigger, Bette-Jane, and Mark Callahan. 2000. "Patients, Physicians, and the Internet." *Seminars in Medical Practice* 3:9–16.

Croker, J., S. T. Fiske, and S. E. Taylor. 1984. "Schematic Bases of Belief Change." In *Attitudinal Judgment*, ed. J. R. Eiser. New York: Springer.

"Database of Individual Patient Experiences." 2002. Accessed 15 November. ⟨http://www.dipex.org/DIPEX⟩.

Dax's Case. 1985. New York: Concern for Dying.

Day, David M., and Stewart Page. 1986. "Portrayal of Mental Illness in Canadian Newspapers." *Canadian Journal of Psychiatry* 31:813–16.

Dayan, D., and E. Katz. 1992. *Media Events: The Live Broadcasting of History.* Cambridge: Harvard University Press.

"Death by Doctor: Dr. Jack Kevorkian Tapes His Latest Assisted Suicide in an Effort to Get Authorities to Deal with the Legality of Euthanasia." 1998. CBS News, *Sixty Minutes*, 22 November. Transcript.

D'Emilio, John and Estelle B. Freedman. 1988. *Intimate Matters: A History of Sexuality in America.* New York: Harper and Row.

de Grazia, Edward, and Roger K. Newman. 1982. *Banned Films: Movies, Censors, and the First Amendment.* New York: R. R. Bowker.

Derrida, Jacques. 1976. *Of Grammatology.* Trans. Gayatri Spivak. Baltimore: Johns Hopkins University Press.

Dewey, John. 1916. *Democracy and Education.* New York: Macmillan.

Diaz, Joseph A., Rebecca A. Griffith, James J. Ng, Steven E. Reinert, Peter D. Griedmann, and Anne W. Moulton. 2002. "Patients' Use of the Internet for Medical Information." *Journal of General Internal Medicine* 17:180–85.

Diem, Susan J., John Lantos, and James Tulsky. 1995. "Cardiopulmonary Resuscitation on Television: Miracles and Misinformation." *New England Journal of Medicine* 334(24):1578–82.

Doane, Mary Ann. 1981. "Woman's Stake: Filming the Female Body." *October* 17: 23–36.

The Doctor. 1991. Dir. Randa Haines. With William Hurt, Christine Lahti, Mandy Patinkin, Elizabeth Perkins. Walt Disney Studios.

Dorrian, Mark. 2000. "On the Monstrous and the Grotesque." *Word and Image* 16:311–18.

Drake, Stephen N. 1996. "Demand to Be Heard." *Medical Humanities Report* 18(1).

Drumheller, Isabelle R. 1959. "TV Visiting." *American Journal of Nursing* 59 (4):522–23.

Dubois, F., et al. 1990. "Coelioscopic Cholecystectomy: Preliminary Report of Six Cases." *Annals of Surgery* 211:60–62.

Duffy, John. 1990. *The Sanitarians: A History of American Public Health.* Urbana: University of Illinois Press.

Durlach, Nathaniel I., and Anne S. Mavor, eds. 1995. *Virtual Reality: Scientific and Technological Challenges.* Washington, D.C: National Academy Press.

Durso, Christopher. 1995. "Specialized Television." *New Physician* 44(1):19–22.

Dyer, Kirsti A. 2001. "Ethical Challenges of Medicine and Health on the Internet: A Review." *Journal of Medical Internet Research* 3:e23. Accessed 22 August 2002. ⟨http://www.jmir.org/2001/2/e23⟩.

DYG, Inc. 1990. *Public Attitudes toward People with Chronic Mental Illness.* Report prepared for the Robert Wood Johnson Foundation Program on Chronic Mental Illness. April.

Earle, Howard. 1958. "Push-Button Age Hits Hospital." *Today's Health* 36(11): 10–12.

Eberwein, Robert. 1999. *Sex Ed: Film, Video, and the Framework of Desire.* New Brunswick, N.J.: Rutgers University Press.

Edwards, Karen. 1984. "The Small Screen's Larger-than-Life Image." *Ohio State Medical Journal* 80:780–83.

Edwards, Owen Dudley. 1989. "The Immortality of Father Brown." *Chesterton Review* 15:295–325.

Eisenberg, John M. 1999. "Ten Lessons for Evidence-Based Technology Assessment." *Journal of the American Medical Association* 282:1865–69.

"E-literate Patients Upstage Doctors." 1999. *BBC News*, 16 September. Accessed 30 August 2002. ⟨http://news.bbc.co.uk/1/hi/health/449566.stm⟩.

Elliott, Carl. 1999. *A Philosophical Disease.* New York: Routledge.

Ellis, Jack C. 1989. *The Documentary Idea: A Critical History of English-Language Documentary Film and Video.* Englewood Cliffs, N.J.: Prentice-Hall.

Eng, Thomas R., Andrew Maxfield, Kevin Patrick, Mary Jo Deering, Scott C. Ratzan, and David H. Gustafson. 1998. "Access to Health Information and Support: A Public Highway or a Private Road?" *Journal of the American Medical Association* 280:1371–75.

Entman, R. M. 1992. "Framing: Toward a Clarification of a Fractured Paradigm." *Journal of Communication* 43:51–58.

Essex-Lopresti, Michael. 1998. "The Medical Film 1897–1997, Part I: The First Half-Century." *Journal of Audiovisual Media in Medicine* 21(1):7–12.

Etheridge, Elizabeth W. 1992. *Sentinel for Health: A History of the Centers for Disease Control.* Berkeley: University of California Press.

Eysenbach, Gunther. 2000. "Consumer Health Informatics." *British Medical Journal* 320:1713–16.

"Fake TV Doctors Must Go — at Least Half-Way." 1958. *Printers' Ink*, 27 June, 13.

Feldman, Marc D. 2000. "Munchausen by Internet: Detecting Factitious Illness and Crisis on the Internet." *Southern Medical Journal* 93:669–72.

Fendler, Lynn. 1998. "What Is It Possible to Think? A Genealogy of the Educated Subject." In *Foucault's Challenge: Discourse, Knowledge, and Power in Education*, ed. Thomas S. Popkewitz and Marie Brennan. New York: Teachers College Press.

Ferguson, Tom. 1998. "Digital Doctoring: Opportunities and Challenges in Electronic Patient-Physician Communication." *Journal of the American Medical Association* 280:1361–62.

Field, Marilyn J., and Jim Grigsby. 2002. "Telemedicine and Remote Patient Monitoring." *Journal of the American Medical Association* 288:423–25.

Fingal, Wally. 1957. "FCC and FTC Combine Forces in Ad Probe." *Printers' Ink*, 1 March, 65.

Fleischman, Martin. 1968. "Will the Real Third Revolution Please Stand Up?" *American Journal of Psychiatry* 124:1260–62.

Foubister, Vida. 2000. "Developing Rules for the Web." *Amednews.com*, 31 July. Accessed 22 August 2002. ⟨http://www.ama-assn.org/sci-ubs/amnews/pick_00prsa0731.htm⟩.

Foucault, Michel. 1973. *The Birth of the Clinic: An Archaeology of Medical Perception*. Trans. A. M. S. Smith New York: Vintage Books.

———. 1980. *The History of Sexuality. Volume I: An Introduction*. New York: Vintage.

———. 1990. *The Use of Pleasure*. Trans. Robert Hurley. New York: Vintage.

———. 1991. "Governmentality." In *The Foucault Effect: Studies in Governmentality*, ed. Graham Burchell, Colin Gordon, and Peter Miller. Chicago: University of Chicago Press.

Fowler, Gene, and Bill Crawford. 1987. *Border Radio*. Austin: Texas Monthly Press.

Frank, Arthur. 1995. *The Wounded Storyteller*. Chicago: University of Chicago Press.

Fraser, Blair. 1944. "VD . . . No. 1 Saboteur." *Maclean's Magazine*, 15 February, 5, 29–31.

Fraser, J. 1991. *The American Billboard: One Hundred Years*. New York: Harry N. Abrams.

Fraser, Mary. 1994. "Educating the Public about Mental Illness: What Will It Take to Get the Job Done?" *Innovations and Research* 3:29–31.

Freedberg, D. 1989. *The Power of Images: Studies in the History and Theory of Response*. Chicago: University of Chicago Press.

Freidson, Eliot. 1970. *The Profession of Medicine*. New York: Dodd, Mead.

Freud, Sigmund. 1905. "Three Essays on Sexuality." Vol. 7 in *Standard Edition of the Complete Psychological Works of Sigmund Freud*, ed. and trans. James Strachey. 24 vols. London: Hogarth Press, 1953–74.

———. 1909. "Notes upon a Case of Obsessional Neurosis." Vol. 10 in *Standard Edition of the Complete Psychological Works of Sigmund Freud*, ed. and trans. James Strachey. 24 vols. London: Hogarth Press, 1953–74.

———. 1915. "Instincts and Their Vicissitudes." Vol. 14 in *Standard Edition of the Complete Psychological Works of Sigmund Freud*, ed. and trans. James Strachey., 24 vols. London: Hogarth Press, 1953–74.

———. 1918. "From the History of an Infantile Neurosis." Vol. 17 in *Standard Edition of the Complete Psychological Works of Sigmund Freud*, ed. and trans. James Strachey. 24 vols. London: Hogarth Press, 1953–74.

Gadow, Sally. 1989. "Remembered in the Body: Pain and Moral Uncertainty." In *Dax's Case: Essays in Medical Ethics and Human Meaning*, ed. Lonnie D. Kliever. Dallas: Southern Methodist University Press.

Gans, H. 1979. *Deciding What's News*. New York: Vintage.

Garb, Tamar. 1993. "Gender and Representation." In *Modernity and Modernism: French Painting in the Nineteenth Century*, ed. Francis Frascina, 219–90. New Haven: Yale University Press.

Gauthier, Candace Cummins. 1999. "Television Drama and Popular Film as Medical Narrative." *Journal of American Culture* 22(3):23–25.

Gerbner, George, Larry Gross, Michael Morgan, and Nancy Signorielli. 1981. "Health and Medicine on Television." *New England Journal of Medicine* 305:901–4.

Gerbner, George, Larry Gross, Nancy Signorielli, Michael Morgan, and Marilyn Jackson-Beeck. 1979. "The Demonstration of Power: Violence Profile No. 10." *Journal of Communication* 29(3):177–96.

Gerhardt, Mia I. 1968. " 'Homicide West': Some Observations on the Nero Wolfe Stories of Rex Stout." *English Studies* 49:107–27.

Gibbs, Jewelle Taylor. 1996. *Race and Justice: Rodney King and O.J. Simpson in a House Divided.* San Francisco: Jossey-Bass.

Gibson, William. 1983. *Neuromancer.* New York: Ace Books.

Giddens, Anthony. 1991. *Modernity and Self-Identity: Self and Society in the Late Modern Age.* Stanford, Calif.: Stanford University Press.

Gilman, Sander. 1985. "Sexology, Psychoanalysis, and Degeneration: From a Theory of Race to a Race of Theory." In *Degeneration: The Dark Side of Progress,* ed. J. Edward Chamberlain and Sander Gilman. New York: Columbia University Press.

———. 1995. *Picturing Health and Illness: Images of Identity and Difference.* Baltimore: Johns Hopkins University Press.

Gitlin, T. 1980. *The Whole World Is Watching: The Mass Media in the Making and Unmaking of the New Left.* Berkeley: University of California Press.

———. 1985. *Inside Prime Time.* New York: Pantheon.

Glazer, Eliot. 1992. "Medical Marketing Case History." *Medical Marketing and Media* 27:56–60.

Glick, Shimon. 1993. "The Empathetic Physician: Nature and Nurture." In *Empathy and the Practice of Medicine: Beyond Pills and the Scalpel,* ed. Howard Spiro et al. New Haven: Yale University Press.

Glut, Donald F. 1978. *Classic Movie Monsters.* Metuchen, N.J.: Scarecrow Press.

Goffman, Erving. 1959. *The Presentation of Self.* Garden City, N.Y.: Doubleday.

Goldstein, Cynthia. 1988. "Early Film Censorship: Margaret Sanger, *Birth Control,* and the Law." In *Current Research in Film: Audiences, Economics, and Law,* vol. 4, ed. Bruce A. Austin. Norwood: Ablex.

Goldfield, Norbert. 2000. *National Health Reform, American Style.* Tampa: American College of Physician Executives.

Goldfield, Norbert, Celia Larson, Douglas Roblin, David Siegal, and John Eisenhandler. 1999. "The Content of Report Cards: What Health Plan Members, Primary Care Physicians, and Managed Care Medical Directors Think Is Important." *Joint Commission Journal on Quality Improvement,* August.

Goldfield, Norbert, and D. Nash. 2000. *Providing Quality Care.* Tampa: American College of Physician Executives.

Goldsmith, Marsha. 1999. "George D. Lundberg Ousted as JAMA Editor." *Journal of the American Medical Association* 281:403.

Gould, Tony. 1995. *Summer Plague: Polio and Its Survivors.* New Haven: Yale University Press.

Gray, James E., Charles Safran, Roger B. Davis, Grace Pompilio-Weitzner, Jane E. Stewart, Linda Zaccagnini, and DeWayne Pursley. 2000. "Baby CareLink: Using the Internet and Telemedicine to Improve Care for High-Risk Infants." *Pediatrics* 106:1318–24.

"The Great Medicine Show." 1956. *Time*, 22 October, 87–88.

Grierson, John. 1966. "Education and the New Order." In *Grierson on Documentary*, ed. and comp. Forsyth Hardy. London: Faber and Faber.

Grossman, Lev. 2001. "Still Waters Run Deep." *On Magazine*, September, 29–30.

Grosz, Elizabeth. 1996. "Intolerable Ambiguity: Freaks as/at the Limit." In *Freakery: Cultural Spectacles of the Extraordinary Body*, ed. Rosemarie Garland Thomson. New York: New York University Press.

Grover, Fred, Jr., H. David Wu, Christal Blanford, Sherry Holcomb, and Diana Tidler. 2002. "Computer-Using Patients Want Internet Services from Family Physicians." *Journal of Family Practice* 51. Accessed 28 September 2002. ⟨http://www.jfponline.com/content/2002/06/jfp_0602_00570.asp⟩.

Gunn, Angela. 2001. "The Girl Who Wasn't There." *Yahoo! Internet Life*, August, 66.

Gunning, Tom. 1995. "Tracing the Individual Body: Photography, Detectives, and Early Cinema." In *Cinema and the Invention of Modern Life*, ed. Leo Charney and Vanessa R. Schwartz. Berkeley: University of California Press.

Halberstam. Judith. 1995. *Skin Shows: Gothic Horror and the Technology of Monsters*. Durham, N.C.: Duke University Press.

Halpern, Jodi. 1993. "Empathy: Using Resonance Emotions in the Service of Curiosity." In *Empathy and the Practice of Medicine: Beyond Pills and the Scalpel*, ed. Howard Spiro et al. New Haven: Yale University Press.

Hanson, Patricia King, ed. 1988. *The American Film Institute Catalog of Motion Pictures Produced in the United States: Feature Films, 1911–1920*. Berkeley: University of California Press.

Hardey, Michael. 1999. "Doctor in the House: The Internet as a Source of Lay Health Knowledge and the Challenge to Expertise." *Sociology of Health and Illness* 21:820–35.

———. 2001. "'E-Health': The Internet and the Transformation of Patients into Consumers and Producers of Health Knowledge." *Information, Communication, and Society* 4:388–405.

Hardy, Phil. 1995. *The Overlook Film Encyclopedia: Science Fiction*. 3d ed. Woodstock, N.Y.: Overlook Press.

Harris Interactive/AriA Marketing. 2002. "Healthcare Satisfaction Study: Final Report." 28 September. ⟨http://www.harrisinteractive.com/news/downloads/HarrisAriaHCSatRpt.pdf⟩.

Hawkins, Joellen W., and Cynthia S. Aber. 1988. "The Content of Advertisements in Medical Journals: Distorting the Image of Woman." *Women and Health* 14:2:45–59.

Hawkins, Robert P., and Suzanne Pingree. 1981. "Using Television to Construct Social Reality." *Journal of Broadcasting* 25:347–64.

Helffrich, Stockton. 1957. "Interdepartmental Memo to Continuity Acceptance Personnel, 15 May 1957." CART Reports, NBC Files. Madison: Wisconsin Historical Society.

Herman, E. S., and N. Chomsky. 1988. *Manufacturing Consent: The Political Economy of the Mass Media*. New York: Pantheon.

Herman, G., and H. Liu. 1977. "Display of Three-Dimensional Information in Computed Tomography." *Journal of Computer Assisted Tomography* 1:155–60.

Höhne, Karl Heinz. 2001. Voxel-Man 3-D Navigator. Heidelberg: Springer-Verlag.

"How Authentic Is Medicine on Television?" 1957. *Journal of the American Medical Association*, 4 May, 49–51.

Howell, Joel D. 1995. *Technology in the Hospital: Transforming Patient Care in the Early Twentieth Century*. Baltimore: Johns Hopkins University Press.

Hunter, I. W., et al. 1993. "A Teleoperated Microsurgical Robot and Associated Virtual Environment for Eye Surgery." *Presence: Teleoperators and Virtual Environments* 2(4):265–80.

"Idealized Design of Clinical Office Practices." 2002. Accessed 14 November. ⟨http://www.ihi.org/idealized/idcop/index.asp⟩.

Imber, Michael. 1984. "The First World War, Sex Education, and the American Social Hygiene Association's Campaign against Venereal Disease." *Journal of Educational Administration and History* 16(1):47–56.

ISMHO (International Society for Mental Health Online). 2000. "ISMHO/PSI Suggested Principles for the Online Provision of Mental Health Services." Version 3.11. 9 January. Accessed 22 August 2002. ⟨http://www.ismho.org/suggestions/html⟩.

Internet Healthcare Coalition. 2002. "E-Health Ethics Initiative: Draft Code." Accessed 22 August. ⟨http://www.ihealthcoalition.org/ethics/draftcode.html⟩.

Isaac, Frederick. 1995. "Enter the Fat Man: Rex Stout's *Fer-de-Lance*." In *In the Beginning: First Novels in Mystery Series*, ed. Mary Jean DeMarr. Bowling Green, Ohio: Popular Press.

Jadad, Alejandro R. 1999. "Promoting Partnerships: Challenges for the Internet Age." *British Medical Journal* 319:761–64.

Jamieson, K. H. 1992. *Dirty Politics: Deception, Distraction, and Democracy*. New York: Oxford University Press.

Johannesen, Stanley. 1989. "On Why We Should Not Agree with Dax." In *Dax's Case: Essays in Medical Ethics and Human Meaning*, ed. Lonnie D. Kliever. Dallas: Southern Methodist University Press.

Johnson, Timothy. 1998. "Medicine and Media." *New England Journal of Medicine* 339(2):87–92.

Jones, Wanda J. 2000. "Beyond Technology and Managed Care: The Health System Considers Ten Future Trends." *Frontiers of Health Services Management* 16:13–28.

Jordan, Tim. 1999. *Cyberpower: The Culture and Politics of Cyberspace and the Internet*. London: Routledge.

Josephson, Susan. 1996. *From Idolatry to Advertising: Visual Art and Contemporary Culture*. New York: M. E. Sharpe.

Kalbfleisch, Pamela J. 1979. "The Portrayal of the Killer in Society: A Comparison Study." Ph.D. diss., Department of Communication, Michigan State University.

Kane, Beverly, and Daniel Z. Sands. 1998. "Guidelines for the Clinical Use of Electronic Mail with Patients." Prepared for the AMIA Internet Working Group, Task Force on Guidelines for the Use of Clinic-Patient Electronic Mail. *Journal of the American Medical Informatics Association* 5. Accessed 26 August 2002. ⟨http://www.amia.org/pubs/other/email_guidelines.html⟩.

Kaplan, Bonnie. 1987. "The Medical Computing 'Lag': Perceptions of Barriers to the Application of Computers to Medicine." *International Journal of Technology Assessment in Health Care* 3:123–36.

Karp, D., ed. 1985. *Ars Medica: Art, Medicine, and the Human Condition*. Philadelphia: Philadelphia Museum of Art.

Kassaw, Kristin, and Glen O. Gabbard. 2002. "The Ethics of E-Mail Communication in Psychiatry." *Psychiatric Clinics of North America* 25:665–74.

Kassirer, Jerome P. 1995a. "Managed Care and the Morality of the Marketplace." *New England Journal of Medicine* 333(1):50–52.

———. 1995b. "The Next Transformation in the Delivery of Health Care." *New England Journal of Medicine* 332:52–54.

———. 2000. "Patients, Physicians, and the Internet." *Health Affairs* 19:115–23.

Kaufman, S. 1993. *The Healer's Tale*. Madison: University of Wisconsin Press.

Kennedy, David M. 1970. *Birth Control in America: The Career of Margaret Sanger*. New Haven: Yale University Press.

Kennedy, Thomas D. 2001. "Fallout from the Knowledge Explosion: The Physician as Teacher in the Internet Age." *Second Opinion* 6:23–36.

King, Patricia. 1989. "Dax's Case: Implications for the Legal Profession." In *Dax's Case: Essays in Medical Ethics and Human Meaning*, ed. Lonnie D. Kliever. Dallas: Southern Methodist University Press.

Kittler, Friedrich. 1988. *Discourse Networks, 1800–1900*. Stanford, Calif.: Stanford University Press.

Klerman, Gerald. 1984. "The Advances of *DSM-III*." *American Journal of Psychiatry* 141: 539–42.

Kliever, Lonnie D. 1989. Preface to *Dax's Case: Essays in Medical Ethics and Human Meaning*, ed. Lonnie D. Kliever. Dallas: Southern Methodist University Press.

Knapp, R. H., M. W. Vannier, and J. L. Marsh. 1985. "Generation of Three Dimensional Images from CT Scans: Technological Perspective." *Radiological Technology* 56(6):391–98.

Knee, Adam. 1997. "The American Science Fiction Film and Fifties Culture." Ph.D. diss., New York University.

Koch, R. M., et al. 1996. "Simulating Facial Surgery Using Finite Element

Models." *Siggraph 96: Computer Graphics Proceedings*. Annual Conference Series.

Kozloff, Sarah. 1988. *Invisible Storytellers: Voice-Over Narration in American Fiction Film*. Berkeley: University of California Press.

Kraut, Alan M. 1994. *Silent Travelers: Germs, Genes, and the "Immigrant Menace."* New York: HarperCollins.

Kubey, R., and M. Csikszentmihalyi. 1990. *Television and the Quality of Life: How Viewing Shapes Everyday Experiences*. Hillsdale, N.J.: Lawrence Erlbaum Associates.

Kuhn, Annette. 1988. *Cinema, Censorship, and Sexuality, 1909–1925*. New York: Routledge.

Lambertson, Eleanor C., R.N., Ed.D. 1965. "Nurses Have Been Trained to Nurse People, Not Machines." *Modern Hospital* 105(4):144.

Larson, Magali Sarfatti. 1977. *The Rise of Professionalism*. Berkeley: University of California Press.

Lauritzen, Paul. 1990. "What Price Parenthood? Reflections on the New Reproductive Technologies." *Hastings Center Report* 20(2):38–46.

———. 1996. "Ethics and Experience: The Case of the Curious Response." *Hastings Center Report* 26(1):6–15.

Lavasseur, Leanne, and David R. Vance. 1993. "Doctors, Nurses, and Empathy." In *Empathy and the Practice of Medicine: Beyond Pills and the Scalpel*, ed. Howard Spiro et al. New Haven: Yale University Press.

Lawrence, Amy. 1991. *Echo and Narcissus: Women's Voices in Classical Hollywood Cinema*. Berkeley: University of California Press.

Lears, Jackson. 1994. *Fables of Abundance: A Cultural History of Advertising in America*. New York: Basic Books.

Lee, Robert G. 1999. *Orientals: Asian Americans in Popular Culture*. Philadelphia: Temple University Press.

Leroi-Gourhan, André. 1964. *Le geste et la parole: Dessins de l'auteur*. Paris: A. Michel.

Letourneau, Charles U. and William D. Hamrick. 1964. "The Use of Television in Hospitals." *Hospital Management*, May, 54.

Levine, Suzanne C. 1999. "Reporting on Disability." *Media Alliance*. www.media_alliance.org/mediafile/18-4/disability.html. Accessed 10 September.

Levy, Richard. 1994. "The Role and Value of Pharmaceutical Marketing." *Archives of Family Medicine* 3:327–32.

Lichter, S. Robert, Linda Lichter, and Stanley Rothman. 1991. *Watching America*. New York: Prentice-Hall.

"Like Your Doctor?" 1956. *Newsweek*, 13 February, 58.

Lindberg, Donald A. B. 2001. "The National Library of Medicine's Web Site for Physicians and Patients." *JAMA* 285:806.

Lippmann, W. 1922. *Public Opinion*. New York: Macmillan.

Lohr, Kathleen N., ed. 1990. *Medicare: A Strategy for Quality Assurance*. Vol. 1. Washington: Institute of Medicine.

Lorenzo's Oil. 1992. Dir. George Miller. With Nick Nolte, Susan Sarandon, Peter Ustinov. Universal City Studios.

Luhrman, T. M. 2000. *Of Two Minds: The Growing Disorder in American Psychiatry.* New York: Knopf.

Lynd, Robert S., and Helen Merrell Lynds. 1929. *Middletown: A Study in American Culture.* New York: Harcourt Brace Jovanovich.

Lyotard, Jean-François. 1984. *The Postmodern Condition: A Report on Knowledge.* Trans. Geoff Bennington. Minneapolis: University of Minnesota Press.

MacCann, Richard Dyer. 1976. "World War II: Armed Forces Documentary." In *Nonfiction Film Theory and Criticism,* ed. Richard Maran Barsam. New York: E. P. Dutton.

MacDonald, J. Fred. 1985. "Black Doctors on Television." *New York State Journal of Medicine* 85:151–52.

MacDonald, Margaret I. 1917. Review of *Birth Control. Moving Picture World,* 21 April, 451.

MacKenzie, James. 1922. "An Address on Clinical Research." *Reports of the St. Andrews Institute for Clinical Research* 1:11–30.

MacKenzie, R. 1997. "EEOC: Political Asylum." *Richmond Times Dispatch,* 5 May, A12.

McAleer, John. 1977. *Rex Stout: A Biography.* Boston: Little, Brown.

McCarthy, Anna. 2001. *Ambient Television: Visual Culture and Public Space.* Durham: Duke University Press.

McCarthy, Todd, and Charles Flynn, eds. 1975. *Kings of the B's: Working Within the Hollywood System: An Anthology of Film History and Criticism.* New York: E. P. Dutton.

McLaughlin, James. 1975. "The Doctor Shows." *Journal of Communication* 23(3):182–84.

McLellan, Faith. 1998. " 'Like Hunger, Like Thirst': Patients, Journals, and the Internet." *Lancet* 352:Supp. II 39–43.

McLemee, Scott. 2001. "I Am a Camera." *Lingua Franca* 11(1):6–8.

Makoul, Gregory, et al. 1998. "Doctors, Patients, and Health Care Issues in Entertainment Television: A Content Analysis of *ER* and *Chicago Hope.*" Presented at the International Communication Association Annual Conference, San Francisco.

Malmsheimer, Richard. 1988. *"Doctors Only" The Evolving Image of the American Physician.* New York: Greenwood Press.

Marchand, Roland. 1985. *Advertising the American Dream.* Berkeley: University of California Press.

Marchetti, Gina. 1993. *Romance and the Yellow Peril: Race, Sex, and Discursive Strategies in Hollywood Fiction.* Berkeley: University of California Press.

Marin, R., and J. McCormick. 1994. "S*M*A*S*H: A Health Care Program That Really Works." *Newsweek,* 31 October, 46–51.

Marsh, J. L., et al. 1986. "Applications of Computer Graphics in Craniofacial Surgery." *Clinical Plastic Surgery* 13:441–48.

Marsh, J. L., M. W. Vannier, and W. G. Stevens. 1985. "Computerized Imaging for Soft Tissue and Osseous Reconstruction in the Head and Neck." *Plastic Surgery Clinicians of North America* 12:279–91.

Martin, L. J., and R. Hiebert. 1990. *Current Issues in International Communication*. New York: Longman.

Mathiasen, Helle, and Joseph A. Alpert. 1993. "Lessons in Empathy: Literature, Art, and Medicine." In *Empathy and the Practice of Medicine: Beyond Pills and the Scalpel*, ed. Howard Spiro et al. New Haven: Yale University Press.

Mattelart, Armand. 2000. *Networking the World, 1794–2000*. Trans. Liz Carey-Libbrecht and James A. Cohen. Minneapolis: University of Minnesota Press.

May, William F. 2000. *The Physician's Covenant: Images of the Healer in Medical Ethics*. 2d ed. Louisville: Westminster John Knox Press.

Mazzi, Christian P., and Michael Kidd. 2002. "A Framework for the Evaluation of Internet-Based Diabetes Management." *Journal of Medical Internet Research* 4(1):e1. Accessed 14 November 2002. 〈http://www.jmir.org/2002/1/e1〉.

Means, Richard K. 1962. *A History of Health Education in the United States*. Philadelphia: Lea and Febiger Press.

Meltzer, Newton E. 1945. "The War and the Training Film." *American Cinematographer*, July, 230.

"'Men in White' Ad Ban Amplified." 1958. *Television Code Subscriber Bulletin*, July, 1.

"'Men-In-White' Rule Clarified — All Medical References Must Be Documented." 1965. *Television Code News*, January.

Messmer, John J. 1991. "*Doctor, Doctor* Strikes a Nerve." Letter in *Postgraduate Medicine* 89(2):36, 39.

Miller, Justin. 1951. "Inter-Office Correspondence to JM File, 1 November." NAB Files. Madison: Wisconsin Historical Society.

Miller, Thomas E., and Scott Reents. 2002. "The Health Care Industry in Transition: The Online Mandate to Change." Accessed 29 August. 〈http://www.cyberdialogue.com/pdfs/wp/wp-cch-1999-transition.pdf〉.

Milligan, Marueen A., and Ellen Singer More, eds. 1994. *The Empathetic Practitioner: Empathy, Gender, and Medicine*. New Brunswick, N.J.: Rutgers University Press.

Minsky, Rosalind. 1996. *Psychoanalysis and Gender*. London: Routledge.

Mitchell, David, and Sharon Snyder, eds. 1997. *The Body and Physical Difference: Discourses of Disability*. Ann Arbor: University of Michigan Press.

Montagu, Ashley. 1979. *The Elephant Man: A Study of Human Dignity*. New York: E. P. Dutton.

Moynihan, B. A., et al. 2000. "Coverage by the News Media of the Benefits and Risks of Medications." *New England Journal of Medicine* 342(22):1645–50.

Mullan, Fitzhugh. 1989. *Plagues and Politics: The Story of the United States Public Health Service*. New York: Basic Books.

Mulvey, Laura. 1989. *Visual and Other Pleasures*. Bloomington: Indiana University Press.

Murero, Monica, Giuseppe D'Ancona, and Hratch Karamanoukian. 2001.

"Use of the Internet by Patients before and after Cardiac Surgery: Telephone Survey." *Journal of Medical Internet Research* 3:e27. Accessed 28 September 2002. ⟨http://www.jmir.org/2001/3/e27/index.htm⟩.

Murray, Janet H. 1999. *Hamlet on the Holodeck*. Cambridge: MIT Press.

Myerowitz, J. 1985. *No Sense of Place: The Impact of Electronic Media on Social Behavior*. New York: Oxford University Press.

"NAB Out to Unfrock 'Doctors.' " 1958. *Broadcasting*, 23 June, 33–34.

Nakamura, Lisa. 2001. "Race in/for Cyberspace: Identity Tourism and Racial Passing on the Internet." In *Reading Digital Culture*, ed. David Trend. Malden, Mass.: Blackwell.

Nelkin, Dorothy. 1996. "An Uneasy Relationship: The Tensions between Medicine and the Media." *Lancet* 347:1600–1603.

Nelson, Hilde Lindemann. 2001. *Damaged Identities, Narrative Repair*. Ithaca: Cornell University Press.

Nerone, J. 1994. *Violence against the Press: Policing the Public Sphere in U.S. History*. New York: Oxford University Press.

New York Supplement and State Reporter. 1917. 6 August–19 November. Margaret Sanger Papers, Sophia Smith Collection, Smith College, Northampton, Mass.

New York Supreme Court. 1917a. Appellate Division, First Dept. *Brief for Appellant*. Reg. 117, Fol. 490. June. Margaret Sanger Papers, Sophia Smith Collection, Smith College, Northampton, Mass.

———. 1917b. Appellate Division, First Dept. *Papers on Appeal*. Reg. 117, Fol. 490. June. Margaret Sanger Papers, Sophia Smith Collection, Smith College, Northampton, Mass.

Nichols, Bill. 1991. *Representing Reality: Issues and Concepts in Documentary*. Bloomington: Indiana University Press.

———. 1993. " 'Getting to Know You . . .': Knowledge, Power, and the Body." In *Theorizing Documentary*, ed. Michael Renov. New York: Routledge.

"No More 'Men-in-White.' " 1959. *Television Code Bulletin*, February, 4.

Nuland, S. 1992. *The Art of Healing*. New York: Hugh Lauter Levin.

———. 1994. *How We Die*. New York: Knopf.

Nussbaum, M.C. 1990. *Love's Knowledge: Essays on Philosophy and Literature*. New York: Oxford University Press.

O'Connor, M. M. 1998. "The Role of the Television Drama *ER* in Medical Student Life: Entertainment or Socialization?" *Journal of the American Medical Association* 280:854–55.

Okie, Susan. 1986. "Playing Doctor." *New Physician* 35(4):14–15, 17–18.

Olin, Margaret. 1996. "Gaze." In *Critical Terms for Art History*, ed. Robert S. Nelson and Richard Schiff, 208–19. Chicago: University of Chicago Press.

Oppenheimer, Peter, and Suzanne Weghorst. 1999. "Immersive Surgical Robotic Interfaces." *Medicine Meets Virtual Reality (MMVR '99)*. San Francisco.

Osborn, Barbara B. 1998. "New Questions about Crime Coverage: Reporting Violence as a Public Health Issue." *Extra*, 11–12.

Ostbye, T., B. Miller, and H. Keller. 1997. "Throw That Epidemiologist Out of the Emergency Room: Using the Television series *ER* as a Vehicle for Teaching Methodologists about Medical Issues." *Journal of Clinical Epidemiology* 50:1183–86.

Owens, Tom. 1994. *Lying Eyes: The Truth behind the Corruption and Brutality of the LAPD and the Beating of Rodney King.* New York: Thunder's Mouth.

Panofsky, Erwin. 1995. *Meaning in the Visual Arts: Views from the Outside — a Centennial Commemoration of Erwin Panofsky (1892–1968).* Ed. Irving Lavin. Princeton, N.J.: Institute for Advanced Study.

Pasley, Robert S. 1985. "The Greek Interpreter Interpreted: A Revisionist Essay." *Baker Street Journal* 35:106–11.

Patsos, Mary. 2002. "The Internet and Medicine: Building a Community for Patients with Rare Diseases." *JAMA* 285:805.

Patterson, T. E. 1994. *Out of Order.* New York: Vintage.

Payer, Lynn. 1996. *Medicine and Culture.* New York: Henry Holt.

Pemberton, Patrick J., and Jack Goldblatt. 1998. "The Internet and the Changing Roles of Doctors, Patients, and Families." *Medical Journal of Australia* 169:594–95.

Pender, Stephen. 1996. " 'No Monsters at the Resurrection': Inside Some Conjoined Twins." In *Monster Theory: Reading Culture*, ed. Jeffrey Jerome Cohen. Minneapolis: University of Minnesota Press.

Pergament, Deborah, Eugene Pergament, Aimee Wonderlick, and Morris Fiddler. 1999. "At the Crossroads: The Intersection of the Internet and Clinical Oncology." *Oncology (Huntingt)* 13:577–83.

Périssat, J., D. Collet, and R. Belliard. 1990. "Gallstones: Laparoscopic Treatment-Cholecystectomy, Sholecystostomy, and Lithotripsy: Our Own Technique." *Surgical Endoscopy* 4(1):1–5.

Pescosolido, Bernice, John Monahan, Bruce G. Link, Ann Stueve, and Saiko Kikuzawa. 1999. "The Public's View of the Competence, Dangerousness, and Need for Legal Coercion among Persons with Mental Health Problems." *American Journal of Public Health* 89:1339–45.

Petroshius, Susan, et al. 1995. "Physician Attitudes toward Pharmaceutical Drug Advertising." *Journal of Advertising Research* 35:41–51.

Petroski, Henry. 1990. *The Pencil: A History of Design and Circumstance.* New York: Alfred A. Knopf.

Phelan, Jo C., Bruce G. Link, Ann Stueve, and Bernice Pescosolido. 1999. *Public Conceptions of Mental Illness in 1950 and 1996: Has Sophistication Increased? Has Stigma Declined?* Indiana Consortium for Mental Health Services Research.

Phillips, D. P., et al. 1991. "Importance of the Lay Press in the Transmission of Medical Knowledge to the Scientific Community." *New England Journal of Medicine* 325(16):1180–83.

Philo, Greg, Greg McLaughlin, and Lesley Henderson. 1997. "Media Content." In *The Media and Mental Distress*, ed. Greg Philo. Glasgow: Glasgow University Press.

Picard, R. G., and Y. Alexander. 1991. *In the Camera's eye: News Coverage of Terrorist Events*. Washington, D.C.: Brassey's.

Pierson, Ruth Roach. 1986. *"They're still women after all": The Second World War and Canadian Womanhood*. Toronto: McClelland and Stewart.

Pies, Ronald. 1998. *Handbook of Essential Psychopharmacology*. Washington: APA. *Please Let Me Die*. 1974. Department of Psychiatry. Galveston: University of Texas Medical Branch.

Pollock, Griselda. 1991. "Degas/Images/Women; Women/Degas/Images: What Difference Does Feminism Make to Art History." In *Dealing With Degas: Representations of Women and the Politics of Vision*, ed. Griselda Pollock and Richard Kendall, 22–42. London: Pandora.

——. 1999. *Differencing the Canon: Feminist Desire and the Writing of Art's Histories*. New York: Routledge.

Poster, Mark. 1999. "Theorizing Virtual Reality: Baudrillard and Derrida." *Cyberspace Textuality: Computer Technology and Literary Theory*, ed. Marie-Laure Ryan. Bloomington: Indiana University Press.

Potts, Henry W. W., and Jeremy C. Wyatt. 2002. "Survey of Doctors' Experience of Patients Using the Internet." *Journal of Medical Internet Research* 4:e5. Accessed 29 August. ⟨http://www.jmir.org/2002/1/e5⟩.

"Professor Charges 'Distortions, Lies' in Medical TV Ads." 1958. *Advertising Age*, 27 January, 2.

Propp, William W. 1978. "A Study in Similarity: Mycroft Holmes and C. Auguste Dupin." *Baker Street Journal* 28:32–35.

Pulver, Sydney E. 1978. "Survey of Psychoanalytic Practice, 1976; Some Trends and Implications" *Journal of the American Psychoanalytic Association* 26:615–31.

"Query for Tyro Doctors: Show Biz or Bandages?" 1958. *Printers' Ink*, 17 October, 11.

Quill, P. 1993. *Death and Dignity*. New York: Norton.

"Quiz Probe May Change TV." 1959. *Business Week*, 7 November, 28–30.

Raben, E. M. 1993. "*Men in White* and *Yellow Jack* as Mirrors of the Medical Profession." *Literature and Medicine* 12(1):19–41.

Radford, Tim. 1996. "Influence and Power of the Media." *Lancet* 347:1533–35.

Rapping, E. 1995. "Bad Medicine." *Progressive* 59:36–38.

Rauber, D. F. 1972. "Sherlock Holmes and Nero Wolfe: The Role of the 'Great Detective' in Intellectual History." *Journal of Popular Culture* 6:483–95.

Raubicheck, Walter. 1993. "Father Brown and the 'Performance' of Crime." *Chesterton Review* 19:39–45.

"Real Doctors May Be Used to Avoid Ban on TV Medics." 1958. *Advertising Age*, 13 October, 1.

Reiser, Stanley Joel. 1978. *Medicine and the Reign of Technology*. Cambridge: Cambridge University Press.

——. 1993. "Science, Pedagogy, and the Transformation of Empathy in Medicine." In *Empathy and the Practice of Medicine: Beyond Pills and the Scalpel*, ed. Howard Spiro et al. New Haven: Yale University Press.

Renov, Michael. 1993. "Toward a Poetics of Documentary." In *Theorizing Documentary*, ed. Michael Renov. New York: Routledge.

"Review of *Birth Control*." 1917. *Variety*, 13 April, 27.

Riggs, Karen. 1998. *Mature Audiences: Television in the Lives of Elders*. New Brunswick: Rutgers University Press.

Riley, Philip J. 1989. *Frankenstein*. Universal Filmscripts Series, Classical Horror Films, 1. Absecon, N.J.: MagicImage Filmbooks.

Robertson, Tatsha. 1999. "Kevorkian Conviction Alters Scene Little for Right-to-Die Movement." *Boston Globe*, 28 March, A3.

Rosaldo, Michelle Zimbalist, and Louise Lamphere, eds. 1974. *Woman, Culture, and Society*. Stanford, Calif.: Stanford University Press.

Rose, Jacqueline. 1986. *Sexuality in the Field of Vision*. London: Verso.

Rosenbaum, Dr. Edward E. 1988. *A Taste of My Own Medicine: When the Doctor Is the Patient*. New York: Random House.

Rosenberg, Charles. 1987. *The Care of Strangers*. New York: Basic Books.

Ross, A. D., and H. Gibbs. 1996. *The Medicine of "ER": Or How We Almost Die*. New York: Basic Books.

Rousselot, J. 1967. *Medicine in Art: A Cultural History*. New York: McGraw-Hill.

Sancho-Aldridge, J., and B. Gunter. 1994. "Effects of a TV Drama Series upon Public Impressions about Psychiatrists." *Psychological Reports* 74:163–78.

Sanders, Stephanie, and June Reinisch. 1999. "Would You Say You 'Had Sex' If . . . ?" *Journal of the American Medical Association* 281:275–77.

Sandman, Peter M. 1976. "Medicine and Mass Communication: An Agenda for Physicians." *Annals of Internal Medicine* 85:378–83.

Sanger, Margaret. "Exploiting Falsehood and Boycotting Truth." 1917. *Birth Control Review*, April–May, 10.

———. 1918. "Clinics, Courts, and Jails." *Birth Control Review*, April, 3–4.

———. 1920. *Woman and the New Race*. New York: Brentano's.

———. 1931. *My Fight for Birth Control*. New York: Farrar and Rinehart.

———. 1938. *Margaret Sanger: An Autobiography*. New York: W. W. Norton.

"Satisfaction in Automobiling: A Symposium by Physicians on Their Experience with Motor-Cars — How to Secure the Most in Comfort and Help at the Least Expense." 1912. *Journal of the American Medical Association* 58:1049–70.

Savitt, T. 1995. "Self-Reliance and the Changing Physician-Patient Relationship." In *History of the Doctor-Patient Relationship*, ed. Y. Kawakita, S. Sakai, and Y. Otsuka. Tokyo: Ishiyaku EuroAmerica.

Schaefer, Eric. 1999. *Bold! Daring! Shocking! True! A History of Exploitation Films, 1919–1959*. Durham, N.C.: Duke University Press.

Schechner, Richard. 1988. *Performance Theory*. Rev. and expanded ed. London: Routledge.

Schemmel, DeLores J. 1953. "One Nurse Can't Do Everything." *Modern Hospital*, April, 59–61.

Scherger, Joseph E. 2002. "Challenges and Opportunities for Primary Care in 2002." *Medscape Family Medicine.* Accessed 26 August. ⟨http://www.medscape.com/viewarticle/420680⟩.

Schnuck, M. 1992. "The Construction of Risk : The U.S. Media, the Audience, and International Terrorism." Master's thesis, University of Pennsylvania.

Senn, Bryan. 1996. *Golden Horrors : An Illustrated Critical Filmography of Terror Cinema, 1931–1939.* Jefferson, N.C.: McFarland.

Shain, Russell, and Julie Phillips. 1991. "The Stigma of Mental Illness: Labeling and Stereotyping in the News." In *Risky Business: Communicating Issues of Science*, ed. Lee Wilkins and Philip Patterson. Westport, Conn.: Greenwood Press.

Shale, Richard. 1982. *Donald Duck Joins Up: The Walt Disney Studio during World War II.* Ann Arbor: UMI Research Press.

———. 1984. "Saints and Sinners: Images of the Medical Profession in the Movies." *Ohio State Medical Journal* 80:775–79.

Shapin, Steven. 1998. "The Philosopher and the Chicken: On the Dietetics of Disembodied Knowledge." In *Science Incarnate: Historical Embodiments of Natural Knowledge*, ed. Steven Shapin and Christopher Lawrence. Chicago: University of Chicago Press.

Shapiro, Joseph P. 1993. *No Pity.* New York: Times Books.

Sharf, B. F., and V. S. Freimuth. 1993. "The Construction of Illness on Entertainment Television: Coping with Cancer on *Thirtysomething.*" *Health Communication* 5:141–60.

Shoemaker, P. J., and S. D. Reese. 1996. *Mediating the Message: Theories of Influences on Mass Media Content.* 2d ed. New York: Longman.

Shuchman, Miriam, and Michael Wilkes. 1997. "Medical Scientists and Health News Reporting: A Case of Miscommunication." *Annals of Internal Medicine* 26(12):976–82.

Shull, Michael. 2000. *Radicalism in American Silent Films, 1909–1929: A Filmography and History.* Jefferson, N.C.: McFarland.

Shorter, Edward. 1997. *A History of Psychiatry: From the Era of the Asylum to the Age of Prozac.* New York: Wiley.

Silberg, William M., George D. Lundberg, and Robert A. Musacchio. 1997. "Assessing, Controlling, and Assuring the Quality of Medical Information on the Internet: Caveant Lector et Viewor — Let the Reader and Viewer Beware." *Journal of the American Medical Association* 277:1244–45.

Silverman, Kaja. 1988. *The Acoustic Mirror: The Female Voice in Psychoanalysis and Cinema.* Bloomington and Indianapolis: Indiana University Press.

Skal, David J. 1998. *Screams of Reason: Mad Science and Modern Culture.* New York: W. W. Norton.

Sloan, Kay. 1988. *The Loud Silents: Origins of the Social Problem Film.* Urbana: University of Illinois Press.

Smead, James D. 1991. "The Landscape of Modernity: Rationality and the Detective." In *Digging into Popular Culture: Theories and Methodologies in Archeology, Anthropology, and Other Fields*, ed. Ray B. Browne and Pat Browne. Bowling Green, Ohio: Popular Press.

Smith, Ken. 1999. *Mental Hygiene: Classroom Films, 1945–1970*. New York: Blast Books.

Smith, W. Eugene. 1948. "Country Doctor." Photographs for *Life*, 20 September. Accessed 15 April 1999. ⟨http://www.pathfinder.com/Life/essay/country_doctor/index.html⟩.

Smith, Wesley J. 1997. *Forced Exit: The Slippery Slope from Assisted Suicide to Legalized Murder*. New York: Times Books.

Smith-Barbaro, Peggy A., John C. Licciardone, Howard F. Clarke, and Samuel T. Coleridge. 2001. "Factors Associated with Intended Use of a Web Site among Family Practice Patients." *Journal of Medical Internet Research* 3:e17. Accessed 28 September 2002. ⟨http://www.jmir.org/2001/2/e17/index.htm.⟩

Snyder, L., and A. L. Caplan. 2000. "Assisted Suicide: Finding Common Ground." *Annals of Internal Medicine* 132(6).

Sobottke, Thomas M. 1990. "Speculations on the Further Career of Mycroft Holmes." *Baker Street Journal* 2:75–77.

Solomon, M., ed. 1991. *A Voice of Their Own: The Woman Suffrage Press, 1840–1910*. Tuscaloosa: University of Alabama Press.

Sontag, Susan. 1966. *Against Interpretation, and Other Essays*. New York: Farrar Straus and Giroux.

Spielberg, Alissa R. 1998. "On Call and Online: Sociohistorical, Legal, and Ethical Implications of E-mail for the Patient-Physician Relationship." *Journal of the American Medical Association* 280:1353–59.

Spigel, Lynn. 1992. *Make Room for TV: Television and the Family Ideal in Postwar America*. Chicago: University of Chicago Press.

Spiro, Howard, with Mary G. McCrea, Enic Peschel, and Deborah St. James, eds. 1993. *Empathy and the Practice of Medicine: Beyond Pills and the Scalpel*. New Haven: Yale University Press.

Stallybrass, Peter, and Allon White. 1986. *The Politics and Poetics of Transgression*. Ithaca, N.Y.: Cornell University Press.

Starr, Paul. 1982. *The Social Transformation of American Medicine: The Rise of a Sovereign Profession and the Making of a Vast Industry*. New York: Basic Books.

Steiner, Peter. 2001. "On the Internet, Nobody Knows You're a Dog." In *The New Yorker Book of Technology Cartoons*, ed. Robert Mankoff. Princeton: Bloomberg Press.

Stephenson, Neal. 1993. *Snow Crash*. New York: Bantam Books.

Stern, D. T. 1998. "In Search of the Informal Curriculum: When and Where Professional Values Are Taught." *Academic Medicine* 73:S28–30.

Stevens, Rosemary. 1999. *In Sickness and In Wealth: American Hospitals in the Twentieth Century*. Baltimore: Johns Hopkins University Press.

Stewart, James A. 2002. "Patient/Physician Emails: A Blessing or a Curse?" *Oncology Issues* 16:13. Accessed 26 August 2002. ⟨http://www.medscape.com/viewarticle/421477⟩.

Stout, Rex. [1934] 1984. *Fer-de-Lance*. New York: Bantam.

——. [1939] 1994. *Over My Dead Body*. New York: Bantam.

Strasser, Susan. 1982. *Never Done: A History of American Housework*. New York: Pantheon Books.

Stryker, Susan. 2000. "Transsexuality: The Postmodern Body and/as Technology." In *The Cybercultures Reader*, ed. David Bell, David Kennedy, and Barbara Kennedy. London: Routledge.

Surrey, Janet L., and Stephen J. Bergman (Samuel Shem). 1994. "Gender Differences in Relational Development: Implications for Empathy in the Doctor-Patient Relationship." In *The Empathetic Practitioner: Empathy, Gender, and Medicine*, ed. Maureen A. Milligan and Ellen Singer More. New Brunswick, N.J.: Rutgers University Press.

Szasz, Thomas. 2000. "The Case Against Psychiatric Power." In *The Construction of Power and Authority in Psychiatry*, ed. Phil Barker and Chris Stevenson. Oxford: Butterworth.

Szasz, T. S., and M. H. Hollander. 1956. "A Contribution to the Philosophy of Medicine." *Archives of Internal Medicine* 97:585–92.

Taylor, C. A., et al. 1999. "Predictive Medicine: Computational Techniques in Therapeutic Decision-Making." *Computer Aided Surgery* 4(5):231–47.

Taylor, Humphrey, and Robert Leitman, eds. 2002. "Patient/Physician Online Communication: Many Patients Want It, Would Pay for It, and It Would Influence Their Choice of Doctors and Health Plans." *Health Care News*, 10 April. Accessed 19 November. ⟨http://www.harrisinteractive.com/news/newsletters/healthnews/HI_HealthCareNews2002Vol2_Iss08.pdf⟩.

"Television Board Tightens Code's 'Men-In-White' Ban." 1963. *Television Code News*, January.

Terry, Nicolas. 2001. "Access versus Quality Assurance: The e-Health Conundrum." *JAMA* 285:807.

Thomas, Ronald R. 1991. "Minding the Body Politic: The Romance of Science and the Revision of History in Victorian Detective Fiction." *Victorian Literature and Culture* 19:233–54.

Thompson, Robert J. 1996. *Television's Second Golden Age: From "Hill Street Blues" to "ER."* New York: Continuum.

Thomson, Rosemarie Garland. 1996. "From Wonder to Error: A Genealogy of Freak Discourse in Modernity." In *Freakery: Cultural Spectacles of the Extraordinary Body*, ed. Rosemarie Garland Thomson. New York: New York University Press.

Thornton, Joann, and Otto Wahl. 1996. "Impact of a Newspaper Article on Attitudes toward Mental Illness." *Journal of Community Psychology* 24:17–25.

Thrower, Norman J. W. 1996. *Maps and Civilization: Cartography in Culture and Society*. Chicago: University of Chicago Press.

Trend, David, ed. 2001. *Reading Digital Culture*. Malden, Mass.: Blackwell.

Tuchman, G. 1978. *Making News: A Study in the Construction of Reality*. New York: Free Press.

Turkle, Sherry. 1995. *Life on the Screen: Identity in the Age of the Internet*. New York: Simon and Schuster.

Turow, Joseph. 1989. *Playing Doctor: Television, Storytelling, and Medical Power*. New York: Oxford University Press.

——. 1996. "Television Entertainment and the U.S. Health Care Debate." *Lancet* 347:1240–43.

"TV Board Approves '57–58 Code Plans." 1957. *Television Code Subscriber Bulletin*, February.

"TV Told to 'Clean Up This Mess.'" 1959. *Broadcasting*, 7 December, 40–44.

Uhlmann, M. 1998. *Last Rights? Assisted Suicide and Euthanasia Debated.* Washington, D.C.: Ethics and Public Policy Center.

U.S. Department of Health and Human Services. 1999. *Mental Health: A Report of the Surgeon General.* Rockville, Md.: U.S. Department of Health and Human Services, Substance Abuse and Mental Health Services Administration, National Institute of Health, National Institute of Mental Health.

U.S. War Department. 1945. *List of War Department Films, Film Strips, and Recognition Slides.* Washington, D.C.: U.S. Government Printing Office.

Van Gelder, Lindsy. 1991. "The Strange Case of the Electronic Lover." In *Computerization and Controversy*, ed. Charles Dunlop and Rob Kling. Boston: Academic Press.

Vannier, M. W. 1990. "PCs Invade Processing of Biomedical Images." *Diagnostic Imaging* 12(2):139–47.

Vannier, M. W., and G. C. Conroy. 1989. "Three-Dimensional Surface Reconstruction Software System for IBM Personal Computers." *Folia Primatologica (Basel)* 53(1–4):22–32.

Vannier, M. W., and J. L. Marsh. 1992. "Craniofacial Imaging: Principles and Applications of Three-Dimensional Imaging." *Lippincott's Reviews: Radiology* 1(2):193–209.

Vannier, M. W., J. L. Marsh, and J. O. Warren. 1983. "Three-Dimensional Computer Graphics for Craniofacial Surgical Planning and Evaluation." *Computer Graphics* 17:263–73.

Verderber, Stephen, and David Fine. 2000. *Healthcare Architecture in an Era of Radical Transformation.* New Haven: Yale University Press.

Voss, Melinda. 1998. "Covering Mental Health: A Resource Guide for Reporters and Editors." *Columbia Journalism Review*, January–February, 37–44.

Wahl, Otto F. 1995. *Media Madness: Public Images of Mental Illness.* New Brunswick, N.J.: Rutgers University Press.

——. 1999. *Telling Is Risky Business: Mental Health Consumers Confront Stigma.* New Brunswick, N.J.: Rutgers University Press.

Wahl, Otto F., Amy Wood, and Renee Richards. 2000. "Newspaper Coverage of Mental Illness." Manuscript.

Walker, Janet. 1993. *Couching Resistance: Women, Film, and Psychoanalytic Psychiatry.* Minneapolis: University of Minnesota Press.

Wallerstein, Robert S. 1991. "The Future of Psychotherapy." *Bulletin of the Menninger Clinic* 55:421–43.

Ward, Gary. 1997. *Mental Health and the National Press.* London: Health Education Authority.

Warner, J. H. 1986. *The Therapeutic Perspective.* Cambridge: Harvard University Press.

Watson, Mary Ann. 1994. *The Expanding Vista: American Television in the Kennedy Years*. Durham: Duke University Press.

Wayne, Mike. 1997. *Theorising Video Practice*. London: Lawrence and Wishart.

Weibel, Frederick C. 1997. "Edison's Frankenstein." In *We Belong Dead*, ed. Gary and Susan Svehla, 18–27. Baltimore, Md.: Midnight Marquee Press.

Weimann, G., and C. Winn. 1994. *The Theater of Terror*. New York: Longman.

"Welcome to Partners Online Specialty Consultations." 2002. Accessed 12 November. ⟨https://econsults.partners.org⟩.

Wellbery, David E. 1988. Foreword to *Discourse Networks, 1800–1900*, by Friedrich Kittler. Stanford, Calif.: Stanford University Press.

White, Robert B. 1975. "A Demand to Die." *Hastings Center Report* 5:9–10.

———. 1989. "A Memoir: Dax's Case Twelve Years Later." In *Dax's Case: Essays in Medical Ethics and Human Meaning*, ed. Lonnie D. Kliever. Dallas: Southern Methodist University Press.

"White Coats Now on Pro's." 1959. *Broadcasting*, 9 February, 36–37.

WHO (World Health Organization). 1976. *Introducing WHO*. Geneva: WHO.

Wiebe, Christine. 2002. "More Doctors Hit 'Reply' to Patients' Email Queries." *Medscape Money and Medicine* 1. Accessed 26 August. ⟨http://www.medscape.com/viewarticle/408337⟩.

Wilde, Oscar. [1891] 1981. *The Picture of Dorian Gray*. Ed. Isobel Murray. New York: Oxford University Press.

Wilkes, Michael. 1997. "The Public Dissemination of Medical Research: Problems and Solutions." *Journal of Health Communication* 1(1):61–62.

Williams, Guy R. 1986. *The Age of Agony: The Art of Healing, c. 1700–1800*. Chicago: Academy Chicago Publishers.

Williams, Ralph Chester. 1951. *The United States Public Health Service, 1798–1950*. Richmond, Va.: Whittet and Shepperson Press.

Williams, Linda. 1989. *Hard Core: Power, Pleasure, and the "Frenzy of the Visible."* Berkeley and Los Angeles: University of California Press.

Wilson, Mitchel. 1993. "*DSM III* and the Transformation of American Psychiatry: A History." *American Journal of Psychiatry* 150:399–410.

Wilson S. 1997. *Tate Gallery: An Illustrated Companion*. London: Tate Gallery.

Winslade, William J. 1989. "Taken to the Limits: Pain, Identity, and Self-Transformation." In *Dax's Case: Essays in Medical Ethics and Human Meaning*, ed. Lonnie D. Kliever. Dallas: Southern Methodist University Press.

Winston, Brian. 2000. *Lies, Damn Lies, and Documentaries*. London: British Film Institute.

Wit. 2000. Dir. Mike Nichols. With Emma Thompson, Jonathan Woodward, Christopher Lloyd, Eileen Atkins. Avenue Pictures Productions, HBO Films.

Wolf, Eric. 1982. *Europe and the People Without History*. Berkeley: University of California Press.

Wolfe, Sidney. 1996. "Drug Advertisements That Go Straight to the Hippocampus." *Health Letter* 12:4–6.

Woolston, Chris. 2001. "Surviving a Media Onslaught." *Chronicle of Higher*

Education's Career Network. Accessed 19 November 2001. ⟨*www.chronicl-e.com*⟩.

Yates, JoAnne. 1989. *Control through Communication: The Rise of System in American Management*. Baltimore: Johns Hopkins University Press.

Young, James Harvey. 1992. *The Medical Messiahs: A Social History of Health Quackery in Twentieth-Century America*. Rev. ed. Princeton: Princeton University Press.

Zakharieva, Bouriana. 2000. "Frankenstein of the Nineties: The Composite Body." In *Mary Shelley: Frankenstein*, ed. Johanna M. Smith. New York: St. Martin's Press.

Zita, Jaqueline. 1998. "Prozac Feminism." *Body Talk: Philosophical Reflections on Sex and Gender*, 61–84. New York: Columbia University Press.

Zoglin, R. 1994. "Angels with Dirty Faces: Its Doctors Aren't Glamorous and Its Stories Aren't Pretty, but *ER* Is the Season's Surprise Hit." *Time*, 31 October, 75–76.

Zola, Irving Kenneth. 1983. "'Any Distinguishing Features?' The Portrayal of Disability on the Crime-Mystery Genre." *Policy Studies Journal* 15:485–513.

———. 1987. "The Portrayal of Disability in the Crime Mystery Genre." *Social Policy* 17:34–39.

Zrebiec, J. F., and A. M. Jacobson. 2001. "What Attracts Patients with Diabetes to an Internet Support Group? A 21-Month Longitudinal Website Study." *Diabetic Medicine* 18:154.

Contributors

STEPHANIE BROWN CLARK is an assistant professor in the Division of Medical Humanities at the University of Rochester Medical Center in New York, where she teaches medical history, literature, and medicine to medical students and residents. After completing her M.A. (University of Western Ontario), higher diploma in Anglo-Irish literature (Trinity College Dublin), and M.D. (McMaster University) degrees, she received her Ph.D. in medical history and English literature at the University of Leiden in the Netherlands. Her historical and literary interests include physical and mental disabilities in the eighteenth and nineteenth centuries. She has published articles in the *Canadian Medical Association Journal* on biology and William Blake, as well as on sexual assault in literature and medicine.

ARTHUR L. CAPLAN is Robert and Emmanuel Hart Professor of Bioethics, Chair of the Department of Medical Ethics, and Director of the Center for Bioethics at the University of Pennsylvania Medical Center. He has written and spoken extensively on issues such as end-of-life care and genetic engineering. His recent books include *Who Owns Life* and *Am I My Brother's Keeper?* He was a member of the Presidential Advisory Committee on Gulf War Veterans' Illnesses, and Chairman of the Advisory Committee to the Department of Health and Human Services, Centers for Disease Control, and Food and Drug Administration on Blood Safety and Availability.

TOD CHAMBERS is an associate professor of medical ethics and humanities at Northwestern University Medical School, with areas of specialization in culture and medicine, medical ethics, and the phenomenology of religion. His essays have appeared in a variety of journals, including *American Journal of Bioethics*, *Literature and Medicine*, *Journal of Medicine and Philosophy*, and the *Hastings Center Report*. He is the author of *The Fiction of Bioethics*, which examines the rhetorical uses of bioethics case narratives, and the coeditor (with Carl Elliott) of *Prozac as a Way of Life* (University of North Carolina Press). He is presently writing a book about bioethics in the public sphere.

MARC R. COHEN currently practices emergency medicine in Los Angeles while pursuing an appointment as an assistant clinical professor at UCLA. Prior to graduating from the Stanford University School of Medicine, he earned a bachelor's degree in the history of art from the Johns Hopkins University. He continues to actively explore the role of visual arts and imagery within the setting of modern medical practice.

KELLY A. COLE is a Ph.D. candidate in the Department of Communication Arts at the University of Wisconsin, Madison. Her recent presentations include "Quacks, MDs, and the Regulation of Medical Ads on the Air," given at the Radio Conference: A Transnational Forum (2003) and "Exorcising Men in White: An Exercise in Cultural Power," given at the Society for Cinema Studies Conference (1999). She is currently conducting research on the emergence of new broadcast networks in 1990s television.

LUCY FISCHER is a professor of film studies and English at the University of Pittsburgh, where she directs the Film Studies Program. She is the author of *Jacques Tati; Shot/Countershot: Film Tradition and Women's Cinema; Cinematernity: Film, Motherhood, Genre; Sunrise;* and *Designing Women: Cinema, Art Deco, and the Female Form*. She has published extensively on issues of film history, theory, and criticism. Professor Fischer has served as President of the Society for Cinema and Media Studies and has been a recipient of National Endowment for the Arts and National Endowment for the Humanities Fellowships.

LESTER D. FRIEDMAN has a joint senior appointment in the Program in Medical humanities and Bioethics (Feinberg School of Medicine) and Department of Radio/TV/Film (School of Communication) at Northwestern University. The author and editor of numerous books and articles, including *The Jewish Image in American Film, Unspeakable Images: Multiculturalism in American Cinema*, and *Arthur Penn's Bonnie and Clyde*, he lectures frequently on a wide variety of topics related to American media and medical culture. Professor Friedman is an associate editor of the *Journal of Medical Humanities* and has won the National Jewish Book Award.

JOY V. FUQUA is an associate professor in the Department of Communication at Tulane University and the director of the interdisciplinary minor in cultural studies. Her research interests include cultural studies of health, consumer culture, global pharmaceutical industries, and HIV/AIDS. Her book *Healthy TV: Television and Medical Media* (Duke University Press, forthcoming) documents the role of television in the construction of health consumer cultures. She has published articles and given academic presentations on popular culture, television, and representation of sexuality and HIV/AIDS.

SANDER L. GILMAN is a distinguished professor of liberal arts and medicine at the University of Illinois in Chicago and the director of the Humanities Laboratory. A cultural and literary historian, he is the author or editor of more than sixty books, including his most recent monograph, *The Fortunes of the Humanities: Teaching the Humanities in the New Millennium*, and a coedited book, *A New Germany in the New Europe*. For twenty-five years he was a member of the humanities and medical faculties at Cornell University, where he held the Goldwin Smith Professorship of Humane Studies, and, for six years, the Henry R. Luce Distinguished Service Professorship of the Liberal Arts in Human Biology at the University of Chicago. He was president of the Modern

Language Association in 1995 and was awarded the Mertes Prize of the German Historical Institute in 1997 and the Alexander von Humboldt Research Prize in 1998.

NORBERT GOLDFIELD is Medical Director for 3M Health Information System and previously served as Associate National Medical Director for CIGNA Health Plans Inc. He has worked on a number of projects including the development of tools for payment of health services and new methods of measuring quality of care. Many countries throughout the world use these tools for quality management purposes. Dr. Goldfield is editor of *The Journal of Ambulatory Care Management*. His most recent books are *National Health Reform, American Style* and *Physician Profiling and Risk Adjustment*. In addition, he has helped form several volunteer organizations, including Hampshire Health Access and the Palestinian Medical Access Partnership.

JOEL D. HOWELL holds the Victor Vaughan Chair in the History of Medicine at the University of Michigan, as well as appointments in the Departments of Internal Medicine and Health Services Management and Policy. In addition to his medical training, he was a Robert Wood Johnson Clinical Scholar and received his Ph.D. in the history and sociology of science. Dr. Howell is Codirector of the Robert Wood Johnson Clinical Scholars Program and Director of the Program in Society and Medicine. His current research analyzes the health policy implications of factors that have both contributed to, and slowed the diffusion of, medical technology into clinical practice. Dr. Howell's most recent book is *Technology in the Hospital: Transforming Patient Care in the Early Twentieth Century*.

THERESE JONES is an associate professor in the Department of Medicine and the associate director of the Center of Medical Humanities and Ethics at the University of Texas Health Science Center at San Antonio. She is curently designing and implementing a four-year required and integrated humanities curriculum for the School of Medicine. Her publications include *Sharing the Delirium: Second Generation AIDS Plays and Performances*, "As the World Turns on the Sick and the Restless, So Go the Days of Our Lives: Family and Illness in Daytime Drama," and "On Becoming a Medical Humanities Curriculum." She is editor of the *Journal of Medical Humanities* and coeditor of the Literature, Medicine, and Arts Database at New York University School of Medicine. She serves on the external advisory board for the American Medical Association's publication *Virtual Mentor*.

TIMOTHY LENOIR is a professor of history and chair of the Program in History and Philosophy of Science at Stanford University. He is the author of *The Strategy of Life: Teleology and Mechanics in Nineteenth Century German Biology; Instituting Science: The Cultural Production of Scientific Disciplines;* and an edited volume, *Inscribing Science: Scientific Texts and the Materiality of Communication*. With funding from the Alfred P. Sloan Foundation, he is currently constructing a Web project on the history of human computer interaction. Lenoir has been a fellow of the John Simon Guggenheim Foundation and twice a fellow of the Institute for Advanced Studies in Berlin. He was named Bing Fellow for Excellence in Teaching, 1998–2001.

MARILYN CHANDLER MCENTYRE is a professor of English at Westmont College and an associate editor of *Literature and Medicine* and of the Online Database of Literature, Arts, and Medicine. She serves on the Board of the Center for Medicine, Humanities, and Law at the University of California, Berkeley. Her articles on topics in literature and medicine have appeared in *Literature and Medicine*, *Medical Humanities*, *Perspectives in Biology and Medicine*, *Pharos*, and *Academic Medicine*. Dr. McEntyre coedited *Approaches to Teaching Literature and Medicine* with Anne Hunsaker Hawkins.

FAITH MCLELLAN took the bachelor's degree in English from Wake Forest University and the doctorate in the medical humanities (literature and medicine) from the University of Texas Medical Branch. Her dissertation was about narratives of illness that patients are writing on the Internet. She has worked as a medical editor in two academic departments of anesthesiology and at the American College of Physicians. With Anne Hudson Jones, she is coeditor of *Ethical Issues in Publication*. Now serving as president of the Council of Science Editors, she is also active in the World Association of Medical Editors and the United Kingdom's Committee on Publication Ethics. She is currently North American Senior Editor of *The Lancet*.

GREGORY MAKOUL, associate professor and Director of the Program in Communication and Medicine at Northwestern University, oversees communication education for the Feinberg School of Medicine and communication research for the Division of General Internal Medicine. He holds faculty appointments in the Department of Medicine, in Medical Education, and in Northwestern University's Department of Communication Studies. Professor Makoul is a fellow of the Oxford Centre for Ethics and Communication in Health Care Practice and a member of Northwestern's Robert H. Lurie Comprehensive Cancer Center. His research focuses on communication, decision making, and health promotion in medical encounters, as well as communication skills teaching and assessment. He is on the editorial board of both *Patient Education and Counseling* and the *Journal of Health Communication*.

JONATHAN M. METZL is an assistant professor of psychiatry and women's studies at the University of Michigan, where he works as a senior attending physician and teaches courses in gender and health, gender and psychopharmacology, and the history of psychiatry. In addition, Dr. Metzl directs the Program in Culture, Health, and Medicine and is past director of the Rackham Summer Interdisciplinary Institute. He has written extensively on psychiatric medicine and the humanities; his book *Prozac on the Couch: Prescribing Gender in the Era of Wonder Drugs* (Duke University Press, 2003) traces psychotropic medications through American popular culture.

CHRISTIE MILLIKEN is an assistant professor in the Department of Communications, Popular Culture, and Film at Brock University. Her published essays have been included in *Spectator*, *Velvet Light Trap*, and the *Journal of Lesbian Studies*, as well as in book anthologies including *Lesbian Sex Scandals* and *Sugar, Spice, and Everything Nice: Cinemas of Girlhood*. She recently completed a dissertation entitled "Generation Sex: Reconfiguring Sexual Citizenship in Educational Film and Video" at the University of Southern California.

MARTIN F. NORDEN is a professor of communication at the University of Massachusetts, Amherst, where he teaches film. His articles and reviews have appeared in the journals *Wide Angle*, *Film Criticism*, *Journal of Film and Video*, and *Paradoxa*. His essays are also included in many anthologies. He presented a draft of the essay in this volume at the "Women and the Silent Screen" conference held at the University of California, Santa Cruz in November 2001.

KIRSTEN OSTHERR is an assistant professor of English at Rice University, where she teaches film and visual studies. She is currently revising her dissertation, "Cinematic Prophylaxis: Globalization and Contagion in the Audiovisual Discourse of World Health," for publication. She has presented papers on film, race, gender, and sexuality, curated film festival and screening programs, and written art, film, and book reviews. Her recent articles on documentary cinema, contemporary Hollywood, and Spanish film have appeared in *Camera Obscura*, *Senses of Cinema*, and *Cine-Lit*.

LIMOR PEER has an appointment in the Department of Communication Studies at Northwestern University as an adjunct assistant professor, where she teaches courses in communication theory, public opinion, and media and society. Her academic research interests include public opinion methodology, media and democratic theory, and macro-level media effects. Dr. Peer is also a research associate for the Readership Institute at the Media Management Center, Northwestern University. In this capacity she has been working on a large-scale study of the American newspaper industry, with a primary focus on data analysis and interpretation related to content and readership.

AUDREY SHAFER is an associate professor of anesthesia at Stanford University School of Medicine and staff anesthesiologist at the Veterans Affairs Palo Alto Health Care System. She teaches several medical humanities courses, including "Creative Writing for Medical Students" and "Literature and Medical Interventions." Her poems have been published in various literary and medical journals and collected in *Sleep Talker: Poems by a Doctor/Mother* (Xlibris, 2001). Her academic interests include the ethics of anesthesia care, the language of medicine, and communication in the operating room.

JOSEPH TUROW is Robert Lewis Shayon Professor of Communication at the University of Pennsylvania's Annenberg School for Communication. He is the author of more than forty-five articles and seven books on mass media industries, including *Playing Doctor: Television, Storytelling, and Medical Power*; *Breaking Up America: Advertisers and the New Media World*; and *Media*

Today. He has also written about media for the popular press. From 1995 to 1997, Professor Turow was the elected chair of the Mass Communication Division of the International Communication Association. He currently serves on the editorial boards of six scholarly journals, including a new one, *New Media and Society: An International Journal.*

GREGG VANDEKIEFT is on the faculty at the Providence St. Peter Hospital Family Practice Residency in Olympia, Washington, and an associate clinical professor in the University of Washington Department of Family Medicine. He taught at the Michigan State University College of Human Medicine from 1996 to 2001, where he was also Assistant Director of the Program for Palliative Care Education and Research. In addition to his formal medical training, Dr. VandeKieft completed the University of Washington's Certificate Program in Health Care Ethics and received a master's degree from Michigan State University's Interdisciplinary Program in Health and Humanities.

OTTO F. WAHL is a professor of psychology and Director of the Graduate Institute of Professional Psychology at the University of Hartford. He is the author of two books, *Media Madness: Public Images of Mental Illness* and *Telling Is Risky Business: Mental Health Consumers Confront Stigma.* Dr. Wahl has written and presented on the topic of mass media depiction of mental illness for more than twenty years. A recipient of the 2002 Eli Lilly Welcome Back Award for Destigmatization, he also serves on the advisory boards for the National Stigma Clearinghouse and the Rosalynn Carter Fellowships in Mental Health Journalism.

Index

Abbate, Janet, 344–45
Aber, Cynthia S., 17
abortion, in Sanger's film *Birth Control,* 271–79
Academy Awards, 62
Academy of Motion Picture Arts and Sciences, Research Council, 288–89
Adagio for Strings (Barber), 182
Adams, Damon, 374
Adams, Scott, 243
addiction, defined, 234–35
adrenoleukodystrophy, 182, 185–88
Advanced Research Projects Agency (ARPA), 345, 353; development of ARPANET, 345
advertising: content and visual analysis of MCO advertisements, 118–24; cultural trends in, 28–29, 93–108; historical changes in, 110–12; managed care billboard advertising, 109–25; medicine and role of, 8–9, 93–108; medicine man imagery and legislative policy, 94–97; nurses' images in, 74; physicians' images in, 15–34, 215–33; public attitudes toward, 99–101; scopophilia theory and medication advertising, 15–34; television as hospital equipment in, 75–81, 83–92
Advertising Age magazine, 105–6
affect, in physicians, 149–65. *See also* empathy
African Americans: in nursing, 75; service training films for, 295–97; in television medical shows, 223–24
A-H Robbins Corporation, 88

Airplane (film), 229
Alexander, Frank, 34
Alexander, Y., 36
Alpers, A., 17
Alpert, Joseph A., 152, 161, 165
Altman, Robert, 224
American Academy of Family Physicians (AAFP), 222, 233
American Association of Advertising Agencies, 95
American Drug Association, medical advertising and, 105
American Home magazine, 76
American Journal of Psychiatry: advertisements in, 18–25, 35n.4; debates over psychotropic drugs in, 31
American Medical Association (AMA): hospital television systems and, 83; Lundberg controversy and, 6; organization of, 97–98; political influence of, 217–18, 221–22, 230–33; public health films and, 305–6; survey in physicians' Internet use, 380–85; television advertising codes and, 93–108
American Social Hygiene Association, 286, 293
Americans with Disabilities Act (ADA), 59–60, 387–88
Anderson, David R., 237
Anderson, Ratcliffe Jr., 6
Anhalt, Lawrence, 273
"An Honest Birth Control Film at Last!", 279n.1
Animal House (film), 229
Annas, George, 230, 257
antibiotics, development of, 207

"Content of Advertisements in Medical Journals: Distorting the Image of Woman, The," 17

Cook, Kay, 30

Cosby Show, The (television show), 227

cost issues in health care: content analysis of ER and Chicago Hope, 247–51; euthanasia debate and, 41, 45–46; explosion of cost increases, 111–12; in hospitals, 167, 171–74; Internet use in medicine and, 379–85; managed care advertising focus on, 116–25; minimally invasive surgery and, 362–53; surgical technology and, 365–71; in television medical shows, 230–31

Couching Resistance: Women, Film, and Psychoanalytic Psychiatry (book), 17

"Country Doctor" (photo essay), 207–9

Courtney, A., 17

Cowan, Ruth Schwartz, 81

Cowart, Ada, 318, 329

Cowart, Dax, 11, 315–30

Cracker (television show), 235–38

Crawford, Bill, 96

Crawley Films, 288

"Crazy Water Crystals," 96

Crewson, Wendy, 156

Crigger, Bette-Jane, 383–84

crime references: in euthanasia coverage, 43–46; to Kervorkian, 46–54; in mental illness coverage, 57–59

Croker, J., 247

Cronenberg, David, 390–91

Csikszentmihalyi, R., 248

Cuban Missile Crisis, Internet development and, 345

Culbert, David, 289

cultural paradigms: content analysis of ER and Chicago Hope and, 247–60; healer images in medical history, 197–214; impact of television on, 215; medical advertising and, 28–29, 93–108; in medicine,

media and, 1–11; midcentury prestige of health and medicine and, 304–8; obesity and, 235–43; public health films and, 299, 304–8; right to die and, 326–30; role of physicians, 97–98; technology in health care and changes in, 367–71; world health and, 308–13. See also popular culture

Current Affair, A (television show), 247

Cyberpower (book), 386

Cyberscalpel system, 367–68

Dance With Me (film), 163

D'Ancona, Giuseppe, 381

Daumier, Honoré, 198–99

Dax's Case (book), 327–28, 330

Dax's Case (film), 11, 316–17, 327–30

Day, David, 57–58, 62

Dayan, D., 53

Day-Lewis, Daniel, 395

daytime serials (soaps), hospitals and medicine on, 216

Dean, James, 324

Debs, Eugene V., 265, 276

Defense of Canada Act, 285–86

de Grazia, Edward, 263, 273

D'Emilio, John, 285

Democracy and Education (book), 284

De Niro, Robert, 170, 173

Deprol, print advertisements for, 19–25, 35n.4

Derrida, Jacques, 392

Designer TV system, 84

Destination Moon (film), 310–11, 314n.6

detective fiction, obesity in, 235–43

Dewey, John, 284

diabetes: electronic management of, 380; history of research on, 335

"Diary of a Nurse," 92n.1

Diaz, Joseph A., 375

Diem, Susan J., 5, 246

digital imaging, evolution of, 356–59

347–50; patient-physician relationships and, 377–85
embodiment: Dax Cowart story and use of, 316–30; Internet and concept of, 393–98; monstrosity and, 143–45, 147–48; obesity and, 235–39; in *Please Let Me Die*, 323–30; in public health films, 299–300, 304–8
Emergency (television show), 220
emergency medical systems, television images of, 211–12, 244–46
Empathetic Practitioner, The (book), 150
empathy: intellectual component of, 152; in medicine, 149–65, 175–80; right to die and role of, 318–30
Empathy and the Practice of Medicine, 149
End of the Road, The (film), 286–87
endoscopy, evolution of, 352–53
EndoWrist, 354, 356
Eng, Thomas R., 381
ENIAC, creation of, 343
Entertainment Tonight (television show), 247
epidemiological cartography, 304, 314n.4
Epidemiological Intelligence Service (EIS), 302
"epistemology of sight," medicine in film and, 131–32, 134
Equal Employment Opportunity Commission (EEOC): mental illness and employment discrimination research, 59–60
ER (television show), 1, 5, 10; awards, 244; content analysis of, 244–60; physician images on, 211–13, 216–18, 229–33; table of medical issues in, 259–60
Etheridge, Elizabeth W., 301, 303
"Ethics and Experience: The Case of the Curious Response," 397
ethics in media: Kervorkian coverage and, 40–46, 50–54. *See also* bioethics

ETH Zurich, 359
euthanasia: media coverage of, 8–9, 36–54; opinions in disability community about, 386–89. *See also* assisted suicide; right to die
EvenView Corporation, 84
Evil Demon of Images, The (book), 330
eXistenZ (film), 390–91
Eysenbach, Gunther, 375

Faber-Langendoen, K., 41, 45
facial reconstructive surgery, computer modeling for, 358–59
Fall, The (novel), 394
Famous Players-Lasky, 288
Fear Factor (television show), 247
Federal Bureau of Investigation (FBI), television licensing probe, 102
Federal Communications Commission (FCC), 96, 102–3, 303
Federal Radio Commission, 96
Federal Trade Commission (FTC), 96, 103, 106
Fer-de-Lance (novel), 239
Ferguson, Tom, 383
"Fidelity," 166–67
Field, Marilyn J., 379
Fight Syphilis (film), 298n.4
Fildes, Luke (Sir), 199–200
Fildes, Phillip, 199
Film and Propaganda in America (book), 289
films: birth control issues in, 264–74; fictional depiction of medicine in, 8, 9–10, 129–48; health issues in, 1–2; hospitals in, 167–74; medical films, 35n.8; physician images in, 98, 149–65, 174–94; public health films, 299–313; science depicted in, 129–32; training films, disease and hygiene in, 280–97
Fine, David J., 80
First Amendment protections, Sanger's film *Birth Control* exempted from, 275
Fischer, Lucy, 9

Hollerith, Herman, 343; invention of Hollerith card, 338, 342

Holliday, George, 315

Hollywood, influence in service training films of, 288–89

holography, medicine and, 390–98

homicides, coverage of, when linked to mental illness, 57–58

homo bene figuratus, monstrosity and concept of, 133, 137

Hopkins 24/7 (television show), 231

Hospital Progress magazine, 75–76

hospitals: administrative changes in, 74–75; cameras' presence in, 5; deinstitutionalization of, 80–81; film images of, 167–94; gender-based labor divisions in, 74, 81–92; institutional impediments in, 166–94; portrayal in popular television of, 216–33; public/media relations departments in, 4–5; remote monitoring systems, 379–80; television's institutional presence in, 9, 73–92; visual images of, 204–14

Hospitals magazine, 75–76

House Government Operations Committee, 105

"How Authentic Is Medicine on Television?" 98

Howell, Joel, 11

Hunter, Ian, 360–62, 364, 368

Hurt, William, 149, 174

hygiene, ideology of, in World War II training films, 280–97

IBM: computer technology and, 344–46; punch card, invention of, 343

identity: on the Internet, 390–98; monstrosity and, 134, 141–45

illness: empathy and, 161–65; Internet narratives about, 375–76, 386–98

image manipulation, in MCO billboard advertising, 120–24

"Imagination of Disaster, The," 314n.8

immigration, public health and, 301, 314n.1

impairment, defined, 234

Indiana Consortium for Mental Health Services Research, 60–61

infectious disease: documentation of, 304–8; global health surveillance of, 300–303, 314n.1; as narrative agent, 311–13

influenza pandemic of 1918, 304, 306

information, quality of on-line, 381

information technology: impact on health care, 338–39, 341–43; impact on patient-physician relationship, 374–85; quality issues in, 381. *See also* communications technology

information therapy, concept of, 375

informed consent, release forms vs., 5

inscription technology, surgery and, 368–71, 372 n.4

Institute of Medicine, quality of health services analysis, 118

institutional impediments in health care, film images of, 166–94

International Classification of Impairments, Disabilities, and Handicaps, 234

International Sanitary Conference, 300–301

International Society for Mental Health Online (ISMHO), 378

Internet: health care and impact of, 333–50, 373–85; historical evolution of, 334–36, 344–46, 346; illness narratives on, 11, 375–76, 386–98; lack of checks and balances on, 5; medical information on, 1, 11; patient-physician relationships and, 11, 347–50, 373–85; typewriters as precursor to, 341–43. *See also* computers

Intimate Matters: A History of Sexuality in America (book), 285

Intuitive Surgical, Inc., 354, 356–57, 371n.2

Invisible Invaders (film), 299

mathematical modeling, robotics in surgery and, 359–64
Mathiasen, Helle, 152, 161, 165
Maurin, Charles, 203
May, William F., 382
Maya software, 369
Mayo Clinic, 353, 360
Mazzi, Christian P., 380
McAleer, John, 239
McCarthy, Anna, 73, 82
McCormick, J., 212
McDonald, Audra, 191
McEntyre, Marilyn Chandler, 9–10
McIntyre, John T., 238–39
MCI WorldCom, 386
McKnight, Fred, 241
McLaughlin, Greg, 56, 66
McLaughlin, James, 220–21, 244
McLellan, Faith, 11, 373–85
McLemee, Scott, 391–92
McMullen, Ken, 392
M.D. Health Plan, billboard advertising by, 123–24
Means, Richard K., 314n.2
media: categories of, 8; coverage of medicine in, 1–11; early portrayal of television in, 73–74; impact on surgery of, 351, 365–71, 372n.4; social activism coverage in, 38–40; zealotry portrayed by, 36–37
Medic (television show), 210–11, 216–18, 229–30
Medicaid funding, surgical technology and, 366
Medical Center (television show), 220
medical education: historical evolution of, 333–34; history of, 198–214; in hospitals, 166–67; influence of Internet on, 383–84; television's influence on, 211–13, 216–18
medical ethics. See bioethics
medical experts, lack of reliance on, in mental illness coverage, 64–69
"medical gaze," Foucault's concept of, 30–34, 131–33, 200–201, 319–30

Medical Journal of Australia, 376
medical journals: Internet access to, 375–85; pharmaceutical advertisements in, 17, 19–23; prepublication press conferences by, 2–3; television advertisements in, 77–81; x ray development recounted in, 336–37. See also specific journals
medical procedures, broadcasting of, 5
medical quackery, medical advertising policies and, 95–97
medical research: dissemination of, 5; film images of, 172–74, 180–94; historical evolution of, 334–36; in hospitals, 166–67; Internet's impact on, 374–85; media awareness of, 2–3; visual images of, 202–14
Medical Story (television show), 224, 231
Medicare: AMA hostility toward, 230–31; health care advertising and, 111; impact on physicians of, 98
medications, lack of images of, 22–23
medicine: cinematic images of, 129–32; communications technology and changes in, 339–41; content analysis of ER's and Chicago Hope's portrayals of, 244–60; fictional depictions of, 5; information technology and changes in, 338–39, 341–43; Internet's role in, 346–50, 373–98; number-manipulating technologies and, 343–46; prestige of, changes in, 202–14, 217–18, 304–8, 367–71; surgical technology and, 351–71; technology's influence on, 333–50; television's influence on, 73–92, 216–33; visual history of, 197–214. See also health care
Medicine of "ER," The (book), 246
MEDLINEplus database, 375
Meltzer, Newton E., 298n.7

O'Connor, M. M., 259
Oedipus complex, scopophilia theory and, 15–18
Office International d'Hygiène Publique (OIHP), 301
Of Two Minds: The Growing Disorder in American Psychiatry (book), 29
Olin, Margaret, 21
Operating Room (television show), 226
Operation, The (painting), 203–5
Oppenheimer, Peter, 361
Oregon, assisted-suicide laws in, 41–42, 44, 46
Oregon Health Plan, 366
Osborn, Barbara B., 61
Ostbye, T., 259
Ostherr, Kirsten, 10
Over My Dead Body (novel), 239

Page, Stewart, 57–58, 62
Pamelor, advertisements for, 27–29, 35n.7
Pan American Sanitary Organization, 301
Panofsky, Erwin, 118–19
Parade Magazine survey, 58
Paramount Studios, 288
Parkinson's disease, in film, 170–71
Pasley, Robert S., 237
Pastorelli, Robert, 236
patent medicine men paradigm: images of physicians and, 200; managed care organizations' use of, 116–25; medical advertising policy and, 94–97, 99
Patient Bill of Rights, 109
patient care: arts vs. science of, 217–18; documentary images of, 318–30; film images of, 149–65, 174–94; historical images of, 197–214; in pharmaceutical advertising, 25–29; role of television in, 78–92; surgical robotics and, 359–64; surgical technology and, 366–71; television surveillance systems, 82–92
patient informatics, 375

patient-physician relationships: content analysis of *ER*'s and *Chicago Hope*'s portrayals of, 252–60; cultural changes in, 109–10; in documentary films, 325–30; film images of, 168–94; Internet's impact on, 11, 347–50, 373–85; in managed care billboards, 114–25; in psychiatry, 24–29; visual images of, 197–214; x ray development and changes in, 338–39. *See also* physicians
Patinkin, Mandy, 155
patriarchal power, images of, in medical advertising, 16–34
Patsos, Mary, 377
Payer, Lynn, 185
Pediatrics magazine, 380
Peer, Limor, 10
peer review, Internet as source for, 375–76
Pemberton, Patrick J., 376
Pender, Stephen, 132
"people-first language" policy, in mental illness coverage, 66
Pergament, Deborah, 373
Périssat, J., 352
Perkins, Elizabeth, 163, 179
Perlman, Ray, 274
personality issues: dominance of, in Kervorkian coverage, 46–54; in euthanasia coverage, 43–46
perspective, in pharmaceutical print advertising, 19–25, 27–29, 34n.3
persuasion, scopophilia as tool for, 16–34
Pescosolido, Bernice, 60
Petroshius, Susan, 17
Petroski, Henry, 341
PHANTOM system, 354, 356, 371n.1
pharmaceutical advertisements: influence in psychiatry, 18–19; scopophilia theory and, 15–34
Phelan, Jo, 59
Philco television advertisements, 79
Phillips, D. P., et al., 3
Phillips, Julie, 56
Philo, Greg, 56, 66

Library of Congress Cataloging-in-Publication Data

Cultural sutures : medicine and media / edited by

Lester D. Friedman.

p. ; cm.

Includes bibliographical references and index.

ISBN 0-8223-3256-6 (cloth : alk. paper)

ISBN 0-8223-3294-9 (pbk. : alk. paper)

1. Health in mass media. 2. Social medicine.

3. Television in health education. 4. Journalism,

Medical. 5. Mass media.

[DNLM: 1. Attitude to Health. 2. Mass Media. 3. Ethics,

Medical. 4. Journalism, Medical. 5. Public Opinion.

6. Technology, Medical. W 85 C9685 2004] I. Friedman,

Lester D.

RA440.5.C835 2004

306.4'61 — dc22   2003024988